Child Care and Inequality

Child Care and Inequality
Rethinking Carework for Children and Youth

Edited by

Francesca M. Cancian
Demie Kurz
Andrew S. London
Rebecca Reviere
Mary C. Tuominen

ROUTLEDGE
New York and London

Published in 2002 by
Routledge
29 West 35th Street
New York, NY 10001
www.routledge-ny.com

Published in Great Britain by
Routledge
11 New Fetter Lane
London EC4P 4EE

10 9 8 7 6 5 4 3 2 1

Library of Congress Cataloging-in-Publication Data
Child care and inequality : re-thinking carework for children and youth / edited by Francesca M. Cancian ... [et al.]
        p. cm.
    Includes bibliographical references and index.
    ISBN 0-415-93350-1 — ISBN 0-415-93351-X (pbk.)
        1. Child care—United States. 2. Children with social disabilities—Care—United States. 3. Youth with social disabilities—Care—United States. 4. Child welfare—United States. 5. Equality—United States. I. Cancian, Francesca M.

HQ778.63 .C52 2002
362.71'2'0973

2002021963

Contents

III: Carework in the Marketplace and Community

Introduction

$\mathcal{A}$re children and youth in the United States receiving the care they need? Many scholars, policymakers, and citizens would answer "No." Too many children face unsafe environments, inadequate schools, and insufficient health care. Those of us who edited this volume, as well as the authors of many of the chapters, believe there is a "care gap" between the needs for care and the resources available to provide and support care. The chapters in this volume analyze the nature of this care gap and its causes and consequences, and propose policies that would improve care for children and youth in the United States.

Inequalities in Carework for Children and Youth

This volume confronts two myths that prevent the United States from closing the care gap for children and youth. The first myth is that the work of caring for children and youth is and should be done solely by families, particularly mothers. The authors of the chapters challenge this myth and demonstrate that there is a broad range of people and institutions that can and do contribute to providing care for children and youth. The second myth is that parents and other caregivers for children and youth have equal access to plentiful resources. Despite a growing awareness of diversity in U.S. families—by economic status, race/ethnicity, and sexual orientation—scholars and citizens continue to talk about "the family" or "family values" as if all families had the same resources with which to raise their children. In this volume, we challenge both myths. We also propose directions for "rethinking carework."

The chapters in this volume confront the myth that mothers and family caregivers are and should be the sole providers of care by considering some of the many kinds of people and institutions that provide care for children and youth, including schools, community organizations, and government-sponsored programs. The interdependence of parental care and support from outside organizations is especially clear in families with teenagers, whose lives increasingly focus on school and peers outside the home. Demie Kurz's chapter shows that mothers of teenagers rely on neighborhood networks and schools to keep their children safe, a primary goal of carework for all parents but one that is especially difficult to achieve for parents of teenagers living in dangerous neighborhoods. However, even mothers (or other primary caregivers) of newborns depend on others to help with infant care, social support, and the money they need if they are to be healthy, responsive caregivers (see the chapter by Christa Kelleher and Bonnie Fox). Adherence to the myth of the mother or nuclear family as the sole caregiver is one of the primary reasons that the United States lags behind other developed countries in providing the necessary supports for caring for children and youth, such as paid parental leaves, subsidized day care, universal health care, and subsidized housing.

Second, the authors of the chapters in this volume demonstrate the impact of inequality on children and youth and on their care providers. In contrast to the myth that families are fairly homogeneous and have equal opportunities to provide good care, chapter authors examine how families differ profoundly in the resources they have to provide care. For example, one of the main goals of carework for virtually all parents is to make sure that their children can achieve a good job or career and a decent standard of living, and almost all parents realize that a good education is central to this goal. Yet parents' success in providing good schooling for their children is heavily dependent on their income or wealth. Affluent families can afford to live in neighborhoods that provide high-quality public schools, or they can pay for private schools, while low-income families must typically send their children to inferior schools.

Inequalities based on gender, racial and ethnic identities, and sexual orientation also impact carework for children and youth, as several chapters in the volume show. Moreover, the effect of inequalities among families on the quality of care that children receive increases as welfare, subsidized housing, and other government supports shrink. Increasingly, child care and other types of carework are being privatized and controlled by the norms and practices of the marketplace. Those with little money cannot buy adequate care for their children (or themselves) and must do without, and those most in need of care are more likely to have little money, as Paula England and Nancy Folbre discuss.

Dominant beliefs and discourses about care reinforce inequality. They encourage low-income parents to believe that they should be able to provide good child care with limited resources and no external support. They teach parents that the proper standard for child care is to model affluent parents, even though this standard does not fit the life situations and values of most nonelite families (see the chapters by Francesca M. Cancian, Demie Kurz, and Barbara Bennett Woodhouse).

Not only does inequality affect care, but the organization of carework also reflects and creates inequality based on class, race and ethnicity, and gender. Beliefs about mothers, not fathers, being the "natural" caregivers for young children, and the public policies and labor-market practices that result, pull women out of the labor force or out of high-paying jobs, and disadvantage women by reducing their incomes (see, for example, the chapter by Karen Christopher). Low wages for child care providers and the sexual and racial ethnic organization of this work reinforce inequality along gender, racial ethnic, and class lines (but are increasingly challenged by community activists and union organizers, as demonstrated in the chapter by Mary C. Tuominen).

Inequalities based on age or generation also shape carework. For example, there is an implicit inequality built into carework for children and youth. Children and youth are cared for primarily by adults. Children are in most cases less powerful and more dependent and in need of care than the adults who care for them. These asymmetrical relationships between careworkers and children and youth are differentially located in social hierarchies that influence needs for care and resources to provide care. The chapters in this volume challenge us to think about how inequalities in dyadic relationships, communities, organizations, welfare states, and labor markets shape the carework for children and youth that is done by mothers at home as well as by paid workers or volunteers in formal settings.

Besides differences in resources and power, differences in the needs of children and youth also impact carework, as several chapters in this volume show. Infants and teenagers, healthy children and those with chronic illnesses, require different care from hands-on caregivers, and different supports from the community and the state (as evidenced in the chapter by Andrew S. London, Ellen K. Scott, and Vicki Hunter). Children with a stigmatized status, such as gay, lesbian, bisexual, and transgendered youth, require yet other types of care, and again, tensions exist between the forms of care needed and the resources available to meet those needs, as documented in the chapter by Eric R. Wright and Robert E. Connoley.

Rethinking Carework for Children and Youth

We have titled our volume *Rethinking Carework for Children and Youth* because we believe that current conceptions of carework must be expanded beyond "mothering" and "child care" as a face-to-face, dyadic interaction. The chapters in this volume suggest that this conceptualization of carework needs to be broadened in at least two ways. First, we should include in our understanding of carework the wide range of individuals and groups who are involved in care: family and community members, care professionals, professional organizations, support groups, and community activists. Second, we want to expand the kinds of activities included within the framework of carework to include political and community organizing on behalf of children and youth, careworkers, and their communities. For example, JoAnn DeFiore's analysis of carework in rural Paraguay shows us the importance of social networks in caring for children and youth. She describes how mothers and "fictive kin" (godmothers and othermothers) create a "community of caregiving" and thereby buffer some of the worst consequences of extreme poverty for children. Nancy A. Naples's analysis of community workers extends our thinking about carework in other ways, by challenging us to include advocacy on behalf of others' children—activist mothering—in our conceptualizations of mothering.

Mark Chesler's chapter on organizations of parents of children with cancer demonstrates the value of including "caring organizations" within our conceptions of carework. These organizations assist parents and children by providing information about medical centers and staff, financial help, support groups, summer camps for children, and lobbying medical professionals for more child-friendly treatments. We believe these kinds of activities should be included in our conceptions of "carework." Considering these kinds of carework and care organizations raises new issues of inequality and hierarchy within and between organizations. For example, as Chesler demonstrates, in caring for children with cancer, medical experts have much more formal power and social legitimacy than organizations of parents.

Developing an expanded framework for viewing care also raises new questions. Is a program director who works tirelessly to create and maintain an organization to provide services to gay and lesbian youth, but who rarely directly serves those youth him- or herself, doing carework? What about a social worker who spent 15 years on the front lines of child abuse and neglect, but then becomes a manager and rarely sees clients? She (sometimes he) is still subject to the relatively low pay that is associated with carework and is doing work that supports face-to-face carework. And finally, what about a couple that decides to have one partner be the primary caretaker and the other the primary breadwinner? Is the breadwinner a careworker?

On the one hand, these people and groups are critical to the care of children and youth and deserve recognition. Further, as just noted, most of those who are part of the delivery of carework suffer from the same invisibility and low social prestige as those who do hands-on carework. On the other hand, we are aware that there is a danger in making the concept of carework too broad. It is those who do face-to-face carework with children and youth who experience the greatest difficulties caused by the low status and low pay for carework. Therefore, although we advocate broadening the concept of carework, we believe that researchers and policy-makers should give the highest priority to those who do face-to-face carework.

A final issue that needs rethinking is terminology, specifically, the relative merits of the term *carework*, in contrast to *caring*, *caregiving*, or *care*. Increasingly, scholars from numerous disciplines have chosen to conceptualize "care" and "caregiving" as "carework" to emphasize the hard, skilled labor that good care requires. This reconceptualization also serves to challenge the persistent undervaluing of carework in the home and the labor force that results from the association of care with women and the construction of caring as part of women's nature. Moreover, it challenges the persistence of the ideology of separate, gendered spheres, one focused on feminine care and the other on masculine work.

However, the term "carework" is not perfect. It may direct too much attention to the hard physical work of caring, and too little to the emotional and empathic dimensions of care. Like the authors of these chapters, we chose to use the term *carework* in the title to this volume, even though there is a tension here that we recognize. By using the term *carework*, we are striving for a revaluation of care and a recognition of the labor that is involved in caring, whether it is done by mothers for their own children in their own homes or by paid workers in public settings and institutions.

Finally, we want to point to some issues that are important in understanding carework for children and youth but are not sufficiently addressed in this volume. Carework in other countries and comparative studies need much more attention than we were able to give. The perspective of children and youth—the care recipients—also needs much more attention. Activities of school systems and state policies to support child care also need careful consideration. Hopefully, this volume will inspire others to integrate these areas more fully into the emerging field of carework.

Overview of the Volume

The sections of the book, which incorporate the themes just described, begin with carework in the family and expand to include the intersections of carework and state policy. A third section focuses on carework in the marketplace and the community.

Section I, "Rethinking Family Carework," examines the impact of unequal income and social resources on family members' care for children. After an analysis of the history of women's care for sick and disabled children since the mid-19th century, chapters examine carework for teenagers, community care in rural Paraguay, and infant care by mothers. The final chapter shows how child care experts create standards of care that reinforce inequality. Section II, "Family Intersections With the State," considers state policies that enhance or constrain the resources available to careworkers in different settings. The first chapter considers the impact of recent changes in child welfare laws and foster-care policy. Two chapters follow, one that analyzes how changes in the welfare system affect the carework of mothers with chronically ill children, and another that compares the treatment of mothers in welfare systems in different countries. The third section, "Carework in the Marketplace and Community," opens with an analysis of the limits of the market in organizing care, and continues with a chapter comparing child care in different settings. The next two chapters analyze caring organizations: a community center in which professionals care for gay, lesbian, and bisexual youth, and organizations of parents of children with cancer. We conclude the volume with two chapters that describe activism by mothers and by child care providers to better the conditions under which carework takes place.

Concluding Comment

It has been a great pleasure for us as coeditors to work on this volume together. The volume was equally conceptualized and edited by all five coeditors. We share a commitment to bringing more research on carework to wider audiences and to increasing awareness of the need for supporting both those who need and those who provide care. We hope that someday the provision of affordable, quality, and well-compensated care will be one of the highest priorities of social policy in the United States.

Those interested in research and policy on carework can join the Carework Network, a group of researchers interested in increasing the visibility of carework in the academy and in public policy arenas. The Carework Network originated at the 1999 annual meeting of the American Sociological Association, when Francesca Cancian and Demie Kurz hosted an informal meeting open to all who had interests in carework. In the course of the discussion, a steering committee was elected to organize a carework network and a conference for the following year.

The first carework conference was held at Howard University in Washington, DC, in August 2000. The chapters in this volume were given as papers at that conference (supplemented by a few additional papers solicited specifically for the volume). A second conference was held in August 2001 at the University of California at Irvine, and future conferences are being planned. We thank these institutions and the Alice Paul Center for the Study of Women and Gender at the University of Pennsylvania for support of the Carework Network and for helping to make this volume possible.

To find out more about the Carework Network, consult the web site at www.sas.upenn.edu/carework. The web site also gives instructions for joining the Carework Network listserv. We encourage you to join us in our research and advocacy of both carework and care workers.

I: Rethinking Family Carework

Rethinking Family Carework

$\mathcal{A}$ mother caring for her child in her home—this has been the dominant image of child care in the United States since the 19th century, when the economy shifted from family farms to wage labor, and the pattern of breadwinner husband and homemaker wife developed. In recent decades, child care has moved out of the family into child care centers and other institutional settings, as mothers increasingly joined the paid labor force. Research on child care echoed this image and pattern. Until recently, it focused mostly on mothers caring for children in the home. Now more research is focused on the organization, financing, and quality of carework in institutional and community settings.

Despite these shifts, women in families continue to do most of the carework for children, which restricts their employment opportunities, leisure, and lifetime income. Moreover, many Americans still believe that child care should be provided by women without much assistance from men or social services. Partly because of this belief, the United States ranks behind almost all other developed countries in providing subsidized child care and other governmental benefits that support family care. The limited and inadequate support our government provides for family carework intensifies inequality across families.

The chapters in this section examine the impact of unequal income and social resources on how parents care for their children. The chapters also illustrate how dominant beliefs and discourses about motherhood and individualism obscure the ways that constrained public resources influence the organization and provision of family care. Most Americans, including many of the mothers and fathers discussed in this section, believe that caring for children is the responsibility of families, especially mothers, not the community or the government. When their children have problems, parents tend to blame themselves and are blamed by others. Ideologies of individual responsibility overshadow the roles that structural conditions and constrained resources for care play in the lives of parents and children.

The section opens with Emily K. Abel's analysis of the history of women's care for sick and disabled children since the mid-19th century. Then (and now), caregiving was primarily women's work, and the interests of different groups of women were in conflict. Poor women, slaves, and servants helped care for the children of affluent families, but received little care themselves or support for the care of their own children and families. Thus, the children of affluent parents received better care, which helped to reproduce the inequality of families across generations.

Next, Demie Kurz focuses on carework for teenagers and how such carework is affected by unequal access to resources. Like their more affluent counterparts, poor parents of teenagers struggle to keep their children safe from harm and try to support their children's success in school. However, they must organize and provide care with far fewer economic resources, and the demands of their low-wage job (or jobs) often leave them with less time at home. Moreover, their teenagers face more dangerous neighborhoods, more violent peer groups, and poorer schools. As a result of these structural disadvantages, the teenage children of poor mothers, especially children of color, are at greater risk of school failure, injury from neighborhood violence, and diminished life chances.

Some communities and societies place less emphasis on mothers and nuclear families doing all the carework themselves, as JoAnn DeFiore's analysis of comothering in a rural Paraguayan neighborhood shows. "Godmothers" and "othermothers" are part of a "community of caregiving" in this impoverished neighborhood. Their collective approach to child care serves to shield their children against some of the most extreme social inequalities in their society. However, at the same time, it reinforces gender inequality and the belief that women, but not men, are natural caregivers.

The construction of gender inequality in the care of infants in their first month of life is explored in the next chapter, written by Christa Kelleher and Bonnie Fox. The 70 mothers they interviewed, most of whom were from the middle and upper classes, worked hard to ensure the health and well-being of their babies and their husbands or male partners. Often, they did so at the expense of their own needs for sleep, recovery, washing their hair, or even going to the bathroom. They expected their husbands to be involved only if the carework was pleasant and easy, and if it did not interfere with their husbands' roles as breadwinners. Despite the toll it takes on them physically and emotionally, these mothers see the unequal division of carework as natural and do not envision alternative infant care arrangements.

The final chapter demonstrates how child care experts create standards of care that reinforce inequality by class and race/ethnicity. Researchers in child development have defined good parenting as following the child's lead and using indirect control, instead of telling the child what to do. These parenting styles are favored by middle-class, White Euro-Americans. Alternative parenting styles, which are favored by working-class people and people of color, are labeled as authoritarian and inferior.

Together, the chapters in this section suggest some directions for positive change. Carework should be more equally distributed, the authors agree. Moreover, the material resources that make it possible to provide good care need to be increased and more equally distributed. Mothers, fathers, paid care workers, and communities need to receive sufficient public support, including financial resources, to enable the provision of quality care for children from infancy through young adulthood. Mobilizing families to support the political changes necessary to provide living wages, affordable housing, safe neighborhoods, and good schools will require a change in the dominant discourse of care. Current ideologies focus on the individual responsibility of families for the care of children, with recent policy changes tending to reinforce the privatization of carework. Rethinking carework for children and youth will require a renewed focus on our collective responsibility for the well-being of all families, children, careworkers, and communities.

American Women Tending Sick and Disabled Children, 1850–1940

Emily K. Abel

*T*he debate about the appropriate policy response to caregiving today often involves different understandings of the past. Clinging to a romantic vision of a vanished world, some policymakers argue for a return to the patterns of the 19th century, when families delivered virtually all care. A common feminist response is that caregiving traditionally has been women's work, that it has imposed overwhelming burdens on their lives, and that they suffer disproportionately as policies increasingly reimpose obligations on the home. Feminists less frequently note that history also highlights the theme of inequality among caregivers. Although some 19th- and early 20th-century women crossed class and race divides to nurse each other, caregiving frequently accentuated social cleavages. Among the many advantages privileged women enjoyed was the ability to hire other women to assume the most difficult caregiving tasks; many employers felt little responsibility for servants who fell ill or whose own family members required care. Moreover, a central concern of some White middle-class mothers of disabled children was to differentiate those children from the offspring of socially marginalized groups.

This chapter incorporates material from my recent book, *Hearts of Wisdom: American Women Caring for Kin, 1850–1940* (Abel 2000), which explores how caregiving changed over a 90-year period and what that activity meant to different groups of women. I arrange the material in a new way to illuminate the divisions as well as the commonalities among women caregivers. As usual, the nature of the sources limits generalizability. I draw heavily on women's personal writings. Because female diarists and letter writers during the 19th and early 20th centuries tended to be overwhelmingly White, Eastern, affluent, and relatively leisured, I try to oversample the writings of less privileged women. To elucidate the caregiving responsibilities of enslaved women, I rely on published slave narratives, as well as the extensive secondary literature on slavery. I base my examination of poor women, immigrant women, and women of color between 1890 and 1940 primarily on the reports of charity workers, public health nurses, and government officials. Although those reports provide glimpses of the experiences of women too frequently ignored, they remain the "texts of the dominant" and thus must be read with caution.

The chapter emphasizes women caring for sick and disabled children. Because infectious diseases were rampant throughout the 19th century, children frequently required nursing care. With the control of epidemic diseases and the decline of childhood mortality after the turn of the 20th century, caregiving increasingly focused on older people suffering from chronic ailments. Nevertheless, sick and disabled children continued to demand enormous attention. The chapter first discusses the period between 1850 and 1890 and then examines the changes that occurred between 1890 and 1940.

Gender Inequality

The gendered allocation of caregiving has a long history. When illness struck 19th-century households, fathers were responsible for summoning doctors. This was a difficult task without telephones and automobiles, especially when inclement weather made travel arduous. Anne Ellis later described the journey of a man who volunteered to "fetch" the doctor when one of her family members was dying in a Colorado mining camp: "It is seventeen miles over Ute Pass—the snow in dreadful drifts, but he makes it, sometime riding, other times leading his horse and breaking trail. He is all night" (Ellis 1929:166–67).

Mothers, however, had the primary obligation for spooning soup and broth into the mouths of sick offspring, wiping their fevered brows, and making and administering medications. Moreover, women routinely cared for an extensive network of kin, friends, and neighbors. Sickness among members of this broad community pulled women away from home, often for days or even weeks. Mary Wilder Foote wrote that when her baby was very ill, "My kind friend, Mrs. Pierson, sat with me four days, leaving all her family cares. Nobody ever tended a child so exquisitely, and in her lap I could place my darling, and feel at ease" (Tileston 1918:92–93). When Martha Shaw's infant fell ill in 1890, Martha initially relied on her mother- and sister-in-law. As the baby worsened, Martha marshaled a broader network of support. On June 26 she reported, "Eva Herman and Mrs. Wm Baker helped me all day." The following day she commented, "Mrs. Pettit and Mrs. Ed Johnston were with me when baby died" (Farnsworth 1890). During epidemics, women moved continually from house to house in the community, sometimes nursing neighbors' children through the same diseases that had struck their own offspring.

Increasing numbers of single women went out to work during the 19th century, but female workers at all levels of the occupational hierarchy quit their jobs when family members fell ill. Velma Leadbetter had learned dressmaking in hopes of achieving economic independence. Her work separated her from her family in Nanticoke Valley in New York, but she was recalled periodically to assist during sickness. Her daughter later wrote, "The maiden woman in a country family belongs to everybody in case of illness" (quoted in Osterud 1991:126). The history of 19th-century women teachers is filled with stories of women who left their posts to nurse family members. Lettie Teeple had just begun her first teaching job in Michigan in 1848 when she "was hurried away from school by [family] sickness" (Yzenbaard and Hoffman 1974:272).

Caregiving obligations not only brought teachers back home but also followed them to work. On May 12, 1886, Sarah Gillespie, an Iowa teacher, described the various misfortunes that had befallen three of her students: "Rena Allen went to town this forenoon and had Dr. Trim cut out a tumor which was as large as hazelnut above her eye. She came this afternoon. Alice Traver has a poisoned foot—She hobbles around on the other—I had her home with me to stay till Amos McNeil came past with the milk. Charley Mead had the sick-head-ache so I have been Homeopathic today" (Huftalen 1886).

Few formal services relieved women of caregiving responsibilities. According to Charles E. Rosenberg (1987:18), "Most Americans in 1800 had probably heard that such things as hospitals existed, but only a minority would have ever had occasion to see one." The situation had not changed greatly 70 years later. When the first government survey was conducted in 1873, the nation had only 120 hospitals (Vogel 1980:1). Middle-class patients rarely entered hospitals. Although low-income people had fewer options, most families were reluctant to entrust sick relatives to such facilities (Abel 2000).

Caregivers also received little help from professionals. Many families could not afford the fees physicians charged. Few had access to doctors during emergencies. Emily Gillespie, an Iowa farm woman, noted in her diary that when her son Henry hit his thumb with an axe and "cut it nearly off" in May 1884, "He held it on while I done it up. I hope it will grow on again without leaving too bad a scar" (Gillespie 1884). Transportation difficulties not only delayed doctors' arrivals but also prevented them from providing continuing care. Emma Reid sent a messenger 11 miles to summon a doctor when her baby was "terribly burned" in Idaho in 1879. "The doctor came and dressed the burns once," Emma wrote to her father a few weeks later. "Since then I have taken care of them myself" (Reid 1923:69–70).

Skepticism about physicians further deterred many women from relying on them. According to Nannie T. Alderson, a Montana woman, "Some of those who practiced out west in the early days spent much of their time in the clutches of the demon rum, having come here because they couldn't keep a practice back east" (Alderson and Smith.1942:196–97). Moreover, children's illnesses frequently revealed the limits of doctors' knowledge. Many 19th-century doctors did not bother to learn about children's health, assuming that mothers were competent to treat their own offspring. Dr. J. Marion Sims, a famous surgeon, wrote that when he was summoned to visit a sick baby shortly after graduating from Jefferson Medical College in Philadelphia in 1837, he "examined the child minutely from head to foot . . . But, when it came to making up a prescription, I had no more idea of what ailed the child, or what to do for it, than if I had never studied medicine. I was at a perfect loss what to do" (Sims 1968:139). In 1840 Rachel Simmons, an Ohio woman, wrote to her mother, "We are all well but my little babe. It has been sick for two weeks and last Wednesday she was taken with hard fits . . . We sent for Dr. Thompson. He came and gave her calomel. In a day or two he came back. Did not think he could do much for a child so young." Rachel beseeched her mother to come and help (Heiser 1941:135). In another case, Maria D. Brown resolved to avoid physicians whenever possible after her daughter died of diphtheria in Iowa in 1862. She later told her daughter-in-law:

With any fair treatment, she would have pulled through. But old Dr. Farnsworth gave her terrible doses of quinine and cayenne pepper . . . [A]fter she was gone, I said to myself: "Never again! When the next trouble comes, it will be between me and my God. I won't have any doctor.". . . I had a pretty hard test. Three of my children, Charlie, Lizzie, and Gus, came down at the same time with scarlet fever. All but Will were ill, and I was expecting another baby. Nevertheless, I nursed them through without the help of doctor or nurse. (Brown 1929:152–53)

Still another reason caregiving consumed women's attention is that the reigning ideology assigned that endeavor to women alone. The domestic manuals, religious tracts, etiquette guides, and women's magazines flooding the market in the mid-19th century expounded a new doctrine exalting women's sphere. At the heart of the domestic code lay the belief that women were calmer, purer, more loving, and more sensitive than men. The traits that are considered essential to caregiving—responsiveness to the needs of others, patience, and an ability to adapt to change—became part of the cultural definition of womanhood. In addition, prescriptive literature exhorted women to strive to please others and subordinate their own needs (Ryan. 1981).

Inequality among Caregivers

If caregiving was primarily women's work, it also opposed the interests of different groups of women. White, middle-class women typically ignored the needs of the very women who fulfilled their own. Although 19th-century domestic servants often helped their employers nurse sick family members, servants were expected to work long and unpredictable hours, subordinating their own caregiving responsibilities. Servants who fell ill tended to receive little sympathy. When Ellen Birdseye Wheaton's servant Eliza became critically ill on August 8, 1853, Ellen twice summoned the doctor. On August 10, however, she wrote, "Eliza moved to her sisters . . . They are poor, and it will come hard on them, but there was no other way. I could not think it my duty to keep her" (Gordon 1923:171). A major function of 19th-century hospitals was to shelter servants exiled by employers and bereft of family support.

Poor women faced special difficulties rendering care, even when they were not doing the work of more privileged women. Household labor for most 19th-century women was extremely arduous. The making of textiles, soap, and candles had moved from the home to the factory by the early years of the century, but indoor plumbing did not reach most households until 1900 or later. Laundry alone was a day-long ordeal, demanding that women carry and heat gallons of water, lug pails of wet clothes, and scrub and rinse each item and hang it on the line, exposing their hands to lye and other caustic soaps (Strasser 1982). Some of the tasks women performed when family members fell ill were indistinguishable from their routine household labor. Sickness, however, also imposed extra burdens, such as cooking special food, washing sheets and bedclothes more frequently, and preparing medicine. After Sarah Gillespie's brother Henry suffered a serious accident in 1884, Sarah helped her mother nurse Henry each night. On October 19 she described her household responsibilities: "I can't tell how many washings and ironings I have done. But a doz. pillow slips had to be changed each day besides sheets and clothes and I [remember] washing and ironing 23 slips one day when I came home and then baking a doz. Pumpkin pies and making cake and washing all the dishes making the beds and to see every thing else." She also complained about the toll caring took on her own health: "I wrenched my back lifting and turning Henry and now my left wrist is 'gun' out. He can not turn over or get on or off the bed without lifting" (Huftalen 1884). Women who had the most arduous domestic chores and the least access to household help were most likely to experience caregiving as taxing.

Enslaved women in the antebellum South had by far the greatest difficulties rendering care. A host of illnesses, including dysentery, typhus, diarrhea, rheumatic fever, diphtheria, and whooping cough, ravaged slave communities. Quarters were overcrowded and lacked proper sanitation and ventilation; hard physical labor, combined with inadequate rest, diet, and clothing, heightened vulnerability to disease (Jones 1985; Savitt 1978). It was even more likely in slave communities than among Whites that caregiving focused on children. More than half of the slave population between 1830 and 1860 was under 20 (Jones 1987:100). The health status of enslaved infants and children was extremely poor. Almost 50% of slave infants died within the first year of life, almost twice the rate among whites (Steckel 1996:249).

The conditions of slave quarters, which abetted the spread of disease, also made caregiving a herculean endeavor. A cabin consisted of one room with a dirt floor, no window, cracks in the walls, and a chimney made of clay and twigs. Two or more families frequently shared such cabins, which measured between 10 and 21 feet square. The great majority of slaves lacked privies and any sanitary means of garbage disposal (Mintz and Kellogg 1988). And many women could eke out time to care for their families only when they returned at night, exhausted from work in the fields or big house. Fannie Moore, a former slave, told interviewers that when her younger brother was dying, "Granny, she doctored him as best she could, every time she got way from the white folks' kitchen. My mammy never got chance to see him, except when she got home in the evening." When the mother learned one night that her son had died, she knelt "by the bed and cried her heart out." Shortly afterward, the boy's uncle buried him. The mother "just plow and watch them put George in the ground" (Rawick 1979:130–31).

The Changing Context of Care, 1890–1940

The mass production of consumer goods and services and the development of the formal health-care system between 1890 and 1940 dramatically transformed the content and meaning of care. These changes affected different groups of caregivers in different ways. Caregiving remained especially grueling for women who could not afford new domestic technologies. Poor women still were lugging pails of water inside to bathe sick family members and wash their bedding long after more affluent women had indoor plumbing (Kessler-Harris 1982:119–21). Poor women also had the least access to services. Private-duty nurses, for example, rarely were an option. Their average annual salary was $950 by the early 20th century and $1,300 by the late 1920s. As Susan Reverby wrote, "Such an expense was beyond the grasp of the average white earner" (Reverby 1987:98).

The job of mediating between family members and the health care services that were available also was especially difficult for low-income women. Few hospitals and clinics were located in poor neighborhoods. Nurses at a Cleveland dispensary in 1907 described a mother who walked 4 miles each way to bring her ailing baby for regular check-ups (Report of the Nurses 1908:40). According to a 1938 report, mothers in some areas of New York City were "travelling long distances" to take babies to municipal health stations, "in many instances paying two bus fares" (Committee on Neighborhood Health 1938). Travel was even more arduous in rural areas, where facilities were often farther apart and public transportation nonexistent. Once they reached the clinics or dispensaries, poor people waited hours to be seen (Davis 1921:329, 335).

The rising cost of health care during the early 20th century also affected different groups unevenly. The poor alone benefited from free or low-cost clinics and hospital care. Many poor people, however, lacked access to such care. Those who did occasionally shunned free services, which they considered inferior. In a letter to Eleanor Roosevelt in 1940, a California mother described herself as "almost worried to death" about her 3-year-old son, who had both a rupture and an undescended testicle. She had tried to save money to pay for a private doctor, but her income was too meager. "Perhaps you will ask 'Why don't I take him to the County Hospital?'" she wrote. "I will answer honestly. I haven't any confidence in them. I have had him out there before. Please try to under stand. He is my boy and I love him. I want him under a good doctor" (Z.M. 1940).

In the absence of either public or private health insurance programs, most people paid for care out of pocket. But by the 1930s, the incomes of working-class people were insufficient to cover the cost (Technical Committee on Medical Care 1938:21–29). A Louisiana woman with a "sick boy" implored Eleanor Roosevelt for assistance. "He has Mastoid," the mother explained. "There are a month that he hasn't been treated for I haven't any money to take him to the Hospital he was suppose to see the doctor every week. My husband is working on the W.P.A. and he only get $29.92 a month . . . Now Mrs. Roosevelt if I use this little salary to take care of the sick child, What will the rest do. I have to support 3 boys going to school what will I give them to eat?" (J.L. 1939).

Race and ethnicity as well as income level shaped caregivers' interactions with formal health care services. Access to the medical care that lightened caregiving responsibilities was almost completely blocked for people of color. One prominent African American physician estimated in 1927 that "each white citizen of the United States has fourteen times as good a chance at proper hospital care as has the Negro" (quoted in Hine 1989:56). Throughout the South, hospital care typically was available only in segregated wards, located in the basements of city hospitals (Stevens 1989:137–38). In 1940, the city health officer of Asheville, North Carolina, explained her inability to satisfy one mother's request for surgery for her son: "Our hospital facilities in Asheville for colored people are very limited, there being only fifteen beds available for them. During the winter months these beds are filled with sick patients and it is only during warm weather that we can use them for a tonsillectomy" (Lord 1940).

The Merriam Report, written at the request of the Secretary of the Interior in 1928, reported that many hospitals and sanatoria serving Native Americans had too little equipment to provide even rudimentary treatment, and many Native Americans had access to no facility (Brookings Institution 1928). Public health nurses employed on reservations during the 1930s frequently complained about parental opposition to institutional placement of children. But many nurses convinced families to enroll offspring in institutions only to discover that vacancies did not exist (Abel and Reifel 1996). "No room at the inn," wrote Anna A. Perry, a Wisconsin nurse. "I wish I had a good stable somehwere for T.B. children of pre-school age" (Perry 1933). When African Americans and Native Americans fell ill, they were more likely than Whites to remain at home, receiving care from family members.

Work and Care

Poor women and women of color also were especially likely to work for pay. The cost of health care was an important factor propelling such women into the labor force. Mrs. H., a South Bend, Indiana, woman, told interviewers that she worked in an underwear factory because her husband's salary was inadequate to pay the "thousands" of dollars of medical bills accrued for her son's operations (Women's Bureau n.d.). During the late 1920s and early 1930s, the mother of a diabetic boy frequently complained to his doctor about her difficulty paying for insulin and office visits. When her husband died suddenly, she asked, "Do you happen to have a woman patient who would like to live in the country by chance? I am desperate and must find a way to make a little money to help keep Arnold going as I should . . . I would not bother to ask you if it were not that I must do something and am trying every way I can think of" (quoted in Feudtner 1995:78).

Women with paid jobs faced the problem of fulfilling competing demands during working hours. Unlike healthy children, seriously ill patients could not easily be left with neighbors. Day nurseries refused to accept sick children. A New York mother who described herself as "a poor woman working for the W.P.A." wrote to President Roosevelt in 1938, requesting assistance in finding an institutional placement for her daughter; all day nurseries had rejected the girl because of her heart ailment (S.S. 1938). Children who enrolled in nurseries had to stay home whenever they fell ill.

Taking sick and disabled children to work rarely was an option. A New York City charity worker reported in 1900 that a widow, the mother of an 11-year-old girl with "some mental difficulty," tried to bring the girl when she did "day's work." This was "a great hindrance" to the mother, who "many times had no carfare and [was] obliged to work and drag the child with her." Partly as a result, the charity worker wrote, "the woman became overtaxed and she had to be removed to the hospital" (Community Service Society 1900). Ten years later another charity worker wrote that an employer had fired a live-in servant: "Work was very satisfactory but as her child was not well she had to devote too much time to it and for this reason had to give up the work" (Community Service Society 1910).

Some working mothers left sick children unattended. In 1907, a dressmaker asked a physician to send her two young tubercular sons to a sanatorium where they previously had resided. Although the boys "were well for some time after coming home," she now found them "as bad as ever." "Having no mother during the day," they ran "wild" and returned each night with wet feet (Eulis 1907). A physician employed in the New York City Department of Health noted in 1915 that a few working mothers locked children with whooping cough in the home (Dickson 1916).

Other low-income women found remunerative work they could do at home, taking in boarders, laundry, and piecework. But home work consumed time and energy needed for care. The mother of a severely disabled 7-year-old boy complained in a letter to Eleanor Roosevelt in 1938 that when she added sewing for pay to her normal housework, she lacked "time to give him the attention & care that he should have." She feared that she would "have to leave the sewing alone," although "every little bit helps" (C.R.S. 1938). In addition, labor performed at home paid very poorly. The Women's Bureau concluded in 1937 that 80% of homemakers earned less than 20 cents an hour (Pidgeon 1937:67–68). Testimony at a hearing conducted by the National Recovery Administration in 1934 cited the example of an Italian woman who had taken in piecework to help support her bedridden son. Her earnings for 96 hours of work were 15 cents less than the amount needed to pay for medicine prescribed for the boy (National Recovery Administration 1934). And some women undermined rather than promoted family health when they brought work home. Investigators in the early 20th century attributed the high rate of lung infections among homemakers' children to the chemical fumes and fabric particles they inhaled (Cohen 1992:105). Accidents resulted from sewing machines, hot irons, and boiling water (Boris 1992; Boris and Daniels. 1989). Work that involved children's participation deprived them of time for play and sleep (Community Service Society 1888–1918).

It was especially difficult for domestic servants to reconcile work and care. Between the mid-19th century and 1930, more women entered domestic service than any other occupation (Glenn 1986:99). Excluded from many forms of paid employment, African American, Mexican American, and Japanese American women were especially likely to work as servants (Glenn 1992). As Phyllis Palmer noted, "Domestics were envisioned as single women, young or old, cut off from any attachments except those to the employer's family" (Palmer 1989:87). Servants who lived in had virtually no opportunity to provide care. An African American Southern woman stated, "I see my children only when they happen to see me on the street when I am out with the [employer's] children or when my children come to the 'yard' to see me" (quoted in Hunter 1997:106). Day laborers, too, complained bitterly about their long hours. One wrote to the National Association for the Protection of Colored People in 1931, "I leave home quarter of 7 every morning. I finish 9:30 P.M. When I get home it is 10 o'clock . . . The people treat me as one of their family and I suppose I should not kick. But—I certainly would like to know more about Domestic rules and laws if there be any" (quoted in Palmer 1989:74).

Caregiving not only pushed women into the workforce but also drew them back home. Some women took days off without pay or relinquished their jobs to nurse family members. Other women needed paid jobs but were kept home by caregiving obligations. In 1939, a separated New York woman whose husband was too ill to work justified her request for financial assistance this way: "In the past I have supported my family with out help and I was happy in doing so. Now my child is to [sic] sick for me to leave. His diet has to be watched he can't go out in all weather" (F.F. 1939). The same year, a Louisiana widow explained her inability to work: "I have a little afflicted baby. She is 3 years old and can't talk and I have to tend her like a little baby" (G.C. 1939).

In short, low-income women faced stark choices when illness visited their households. They could work, earn little, and leave sick family members alone, or they could decline work to provide care and suffer extreme poverty.

Preserving Privilege

The theme of inequality in caregiving emerges not only in the struggles of poor women, but also in the efforts of White, middle-class mothers to sustain their children's privileges. One reason many early-20th-century mothers of deaf children embraced the doctrine of "oralism," which emphasized lipreading rather than sign language, was that it helped to separate offspring from the stigmatized deaf community (see Cohen 1994:118; Padden and Humphries 1988:51–52). Affluent mothers of "feebleminded" children similarly sought to preserve the family's social status. In his study of "feebleminded" people in the early 20th century, James W. Trent wrote, "To have a defective in the family was to be associated with vice, immorality, failure, bad blood, and stupidity. To place that defective in a public facility was to be associated with the lower classes" (Trent 1994:187). Mothers of such children often sought to distance themselves from the taint of heredity by blaming their children's problems on injuries or on diseases like encephalitis or spinal meningitis, which had no genetic component. Some also stressed that other children in the family were healthy and "normal," developing satisfactorily and doing well in school (see Abel 2000).

In addition, mothers sought to avoid the stigma of state institutions. Private facilities proliferated during the early 20th century. When the Great Depression put them beyond the reach of many families, some mothers wrote to the federal government, pleading for help obtaining tuitions. "I am from one of the oldest families in Hillsboro," wrote an Illinois woman, the mother of a 15-year-old "feebleminded" boy, in 1935. "We lost our money during the depression . . . We have tried to find some backward school for Peter, but the ones we can send him to are private schools and they cost too much." One reason she cited for refusing to consider the state institution at Lincoln was that the boy "has been brought up in a good religious home" (N.H. 1935).

Special-education classes were equally abhorrent to some middle-class women. A Pennsylvania woman explained why she recoiled from the suggestion that her son enroll in the class she visited near her home: "[The] special class was a disgrace to a township as rich as Montgomery Co. A dismal room with colored boys and girls, 3 feeble minded from 1 family, a place to send a child in order to be relieved from their care" (S.M.B. 1930).

The Legacy of the Past

One advantage of a historical perspective is that it highlights current patterns we often overlook. Because our society continues to be riven by divisions of class, race, and ethnicity, it is perhaps unsurprising that many of the patterns I have described remain intact. Although caregiving today, as in the past, is predominantly women's work, it continues to oppose the interests of different groups of women. Evelyn Nakano Glenn demonstrated that poor women and women of color, who previously might have worked as domestic servants, today increasingly enter low-level service occupations such as home health care (Glenn 1992). Because most people pay privately for home care services, caregivers benefit when agencies save money by keeping the wages of home health aides low. A study conducted in New York City found that 99% of such workers are women, 70% are African American, 26% are Latina, and 46% are immigrants. A high proportion are single mothers with three or four children. Eighty percent cannot afford adequate housing, and 35% often cannot buy enough food for their families (Donovan 1989). The Los Angeles Times described the plight of Amanda Figueroa, a home care aide who "out of kindness provides more hours of care to an 88-year-old-diabetic patient than she is paid for." Figueroa and her husband support a family of five on $14,000 a year; neither receives health insurance. When their daughter contracted pneumonia, the mother refused to take her to the emergency room, terrified of receiving a bill that would greatly exceed the family's resources. "[Our clients] have somebody to care for them," Figueroa stated. "But nobody cares for us" (Ellingwood 2000:A269).

Some caregivers in affluent families turn for assistance to the large pool of marginal workers who cannot secure better employment. Companions and attendants hired through ad hoc, informal arrangements typically receive very little pay, and most lack benefits, whether Social Security, workers' compensation, unemployment, or health insurance. Many family caregivers feel unable to pay more. But a fee that seems high to caregivers often does not constitute a living wage for the workers they hire.

Caregiving remains especially onerous for poor women, even when they are not working as aides or attendants. The low-status jobs they can obtain tend to have little or no flexibility in hours or days worked. Caregivers thus suffer greater penalties if they phone sick and disabled relatives from work or take time off to help them during working hours. Some lack access to health insurance. And poor women typically cannot purchase medical equipment or supplies, retrofit their homes to accommodate a sickroom or wheelchair, or "buy out" of their obligations by hiring other women (see Heymann 2000).

Finally, part of the caregiving work of White middle-class mothers continues to involve sustaining their children's social privileges. Just as high-status mothers of "feebleminded" children in the early 20th century struggled to differentiate their offspring from students in state institutions and local special education classes, so privileged parents of children who perform poorly in school today try to have such children defined as "learning disabled" rather than "slow" or "mentally retarded." A "learning disabled" label entitles the children to receive special resources in regular classrooms rather than being shunted into stigmatized special education programs (see Kelman and Lester 1997).

Although the patterns delineated in this chapter have lasted more than 150 years, they are neither inevitable nor immutable. Tracing the long history of inequality in caregiving reminds us of the necessity of framing a very broad agenda for change. We should spread the work more equitably throughout all sectors of society rather than imposing it on the most socially marginalized groups. And we should adopt policies that address the needs of all caregivers, not just those with the greatest privilege and political clout.

Poor Mothers and the Care of Teenage Children

Demie Kurz

*M*other blaming" in public discourse and social research has created stereotypes of poor mothers that obscure many aspects of their lives (Garey and Arendell 2001; Hays 1996). In popular thinking, poor families, especially single-mother families and families of color, are typically found deficient and blamed for the failures of their children (Baca Zinn and Dill 1994; Roberts 1995). They are said to lack the proper style of discipline or to fail to monitor their children's social activities or schoolwork. In social science research, it has also been difficult to gain an understanding of the work that poor mothers do on behalf of their children and the obstacles they face. According to Garey and Arendell (2001), many researchers attribute children's problems to the failed parenting of their mothers.

In order to get beyond these stereotypes, in this chapter I examine the challenges poor mothers face as they raise their teenage children. I focus on two of the things mothers are most concerned about during their children's teenage years—keeping their children safe, and helping them succeed in school. I describe the work they do and the strategies they use to manage their teenage children.

Mothers view raising teenage children as difficult. As their children become more independent, parents lose a lot of control over where their teenage children go and with whom, whereas peers and activities outside the home in the neighborhood exert a strong influence on teenage lives. Thus, at this stage of parenting, the quality of neighborhoods, including how safe they are and what kinds of resources they have, is critical to the lives of children and the work of parenting. The common view of the family as a self-contained private unit where parents control what goes on inside the four walls of the house and protect children from the dangers of the outside world does not hold for families with teenage children, especially poor families. As I describe, mothers are constantly trying to guide and control their teenage children, but their teenagers are very often out of the house, with friends.

My second goal in this chapter is to locate the work poor mothers do for their teenage children and the obstacles they face within larger systems of racial and class privilege. Until recently, mothers have typically been viewed as sharing a uniform, unchanging status (Glenn 1994). This view has obscured the fact that mothers do the work of parenting under very different conditions. Systems of racial and class privilege grant more resources to White, higher-income women; poorer women and non-White women face harsher conditions and have fewer social supports. In this chapter, in addition to describing the work poor mothers do, I identify these mechanisms of privilege.

Unfortunately, the way that privilege structures mothers' lives and the consequences this has for poor women and children have often been invisible. Until recently, researchers who study youth and families have tended to focus on the quality of parent–child relationships and on what happens inside households, rather than on the broader conditions under which parents do their work. Much of this research has been dominated by a social psychological perspective that explores the relationship between characteristics of mothers and the problems of their children (Phoenix, Woollett, and Lloyd 1991). Since crime rates and indicators of school failure are higher among children of the poor than other children, it has been assumed that bad parenting is the cause of children's problems (Cancian, this volume; Garey and Arendell 2001). A major problem with this work is that it has neglected the community context within which parenting takes place (Simons et al. 1997).

Recently, some researchers have begun to turn their attention to rebuilding an older tradition of research on neighborhoods and resources that has been neglected for some time (Anderson 1999; Brooks-Gunn et al. 1997; Furstenberg et al. 1999; National Research Council 1996; Simons et al. 1997; Wilson 1991). These researchers have focused on the connection between neighborhood characteristics, parent characteristics, and outcome measures for children and youth. This research produces some interesting findings, but except in unusual cases, such as the work of Furstenberg et al. (1999), it does not focus on mothers' experiences or the actual work they do for their children under conditions of hardship.

Scholars in one group, including scholars of color, have challenged dominant, universalized conceptions of motherhood and have highlighted the role of race and class, as well as gender inequality, in shaping the work of mothers (Baca Zinn and Dill 1994; Collins 1991; Glenn 1994; Segura 1994). They argue that the experiences of minority families are different from other families. The root of this difference, they claim, is not cultural, but is due to differences in resources, with minority families being much less likely to have adequate resources to raise their families. These scholars view White women's experiences and the experiences of women of color as relational—connected in interlocking systems of inequality that provide greater access to resources for some, and less for others.

Understanding the context of power and inequality within which mothers do their parenting is critical not only for research, but also to inform social policy, which, like a lot of research, frequently ignores the environments in which parents must raise children and often blames and even punishes them when their children get into trouble. For example, laws in some jurisdictions hold parents criminally liable for the truancy or delinquency of their teenage children. Certain jurisdictions have statutes that mandate that parents be imprisoned if their children are repeatedly truant (Cahn 1996).

In this chapter, after describing the sample on which my conclusions are based, I examine the work poor mothers do and the strategies they use to try to keep their children safe and ensure that they do well in school. I then describe the time constraints poor mothers face as they do this work, which are greater than those of other mothers. In describing mothers' work, I demonstrate how systems of privilege disadvantage these poor mothers, while they advantage higher-income women. I also show how race further disadvantages the African-American mothers in my sample.

Sample and Data

The data and conclusions on which this chapter is based are from an interview study of parents, primarily mothers, and teenage children. In this chapter I focus on mothers, who do the majority of the work of parenting and of constructing and maintaining families, including families with teenagers (Larson and Richards 1994). I have interviewed mothers from four samples, three of them random samples. Two are from the city of Philadelphia, one of parents of high school students, one of parents of 22-year olds. A third random sample is from a suburban White middle-class community and includes interviews with parents of junior high and high school students. The fourth is from a snowball sample of upper-middle class mothers who are professionals, from different urban and suburban neighborhoods. Although these samples are not representative of the state they are in or of the nation as a whole, they do provide data on families with a range of income, race, and urban–suburban differences.[1]

To date, I have interviewed 81 mothers and 17 fathers, 65% White, 30% Black, and 5% other. Sixty percent are from the city of Philadelphia and 40% are from middle- and upper middle-class suburbs of Philadelphia. The sample includes single mothers, lesbian mothers, and mothers of children with disabilities. I have also interviewed 25 teenagers, analyzed data from 50 more teenagers, and done focus groups with three groups of high school students and two groups of college students.

Safety

All mothers want to protect their children from harm and keep them physically safe. In my sample, all mothers fear for their children's safety. Recent highly publicized incidents of school violence have made mothers particularly fearful. Statistics indicate the dangers adolescents face. Over half of today's youth between the ages of 10 and 17 have experienced two or more risk behaviors, including drug or alcohol abuse, school failure, delinquency, and crime, as well as unsafe sex and intercourse leading to teenage pregnancy (Lerner, Entwisle, and Hauser 1994; Zill and Nord 1994), and 10% of these youth engage in all of these behaviors (Dryfoos 1990). Tragically, the mortality rates among adolescents have been increasing, with particularly high rates of injury and death occurring in poor communities (Carnegie Corporation 1995).

Although mothers in my sample believe their children need more freedom as they get older, they worry greatly about their teens as they circulate more widely in the world among peers. They worry about the harm that could come to their children from others on the streets, in school, and when they are driving or in cars with other teenagers. They also worry that their own teenage children could engage in unsafe or illegal activities or get involved with what they believe is the wrong group of peers. Mothers worry about their teenagers' friendships with other teens if those teens look like "bad kids." They also don't want their teens spending time in empty houses where they might use alcohol or drugs or have sex. There are specific gender components to parents' concerns. Mothers have greater fear for their girls than their boys over issues of sexuality and worry that their daughters could be taken advantage of, raped, or become pregnant. Parents of boys worry more about accidents and physical violence.

Parents adopt many strategies to monitor their children's social life. For example, they try to keep their teenagers close to home. They make rules about when their children can go out and where. They try to persuade their children not to associate with certain peers and they monitor their teenagers for signs of trouble—for example, by watching carefully for signs of alcohol and drugs. Some parents buy cell phones and pagers for their children in order to communicate with them frequently. To keep their children close to home, some remodel their basements and tell their teenagers to invite their friends to come over and "hang out" there. Many mothers try to get their children involved in school and church groups to keep them out of trouble. For girls, they make special rules about when they can date, the age of the boys they can see, and where they can go on dates.

Not only do parents use many similar strategies to keep their children safe, but according to recent data, parents across different income groups are equally competent in their use of these strategies. Furstenberg et al. (1999), in their study of working-class and poor neighborhoods with a wide range of income levels, indicate that there are no significant differences across these neighborhood groups in mothers' competencies at parenting. These data run counter to stereotypes in popular and academic thinking that find poor parents, particularly poor mothers, deficient in their parenting.

Although all parents are fearful for their children's safety and work hard to protect their children, parents in unsafe neighborhoods face greater dangers, and poor mothers have to do more work to keep their children safe. Poor mothers' accounts feature many more examples of violence, crime, school truancy, and dropping out of school than do those of other mothers. They live in neighborhoods with high crime rates where the dangers mothers fear, such as gangs, are right outside their front doors on the street and in the neighborhood (Anderson 1999).

How do poor mothers cope with danger? Furstenberg et al. (1999) and Litt (1999) argue that poorer mothers become more restrictive of their children's activities. Although it is possible to restrict the movements and activities of younger children, however, it is more difficult to restrict the activities of older children. They want and need to go out. Some mothers do manage to monitor their teenage children's actions very carefully. Others try to teach their children about danger, a task that can be difficult because teenage children don't necessarily see things the same way as their parents and may not feel they are in danger. This grandmother, who is raising her 15 year-old grandson, says:

R (Respondent): My grandson doesn't think there's a soul out there gonna bother him. I don't know why but I be so afraid when he's out and my phone ring my heart goes, dear Lord Jesus, don't let it be bad news. That's how afraid I am for him. Now just last year in, ah, November. My cousin, my cousin's son got killed, 17 years old, over there in (name of neighborhood) around the corner from the house.

　　She always tell him, stay away from that corner, stay away from that corner. When somebody had an argument with somebody. The person said—I be back. And the person came back, both of them got shot.

　　Her son, both of her sons. The youngest got shot and died. The other one got shot in the shoulder here somewhere. The guy that they were shooting at didn't even get a scratch. Now see this is what I tell my son. I say, they don't have to be at you.

I (Interviewer): And what does he say?

R: "Oh, grandmom, ain't nobody gonna bother me. You, you always think something be happening to people. You shouldn't think like that." He just don't believe me. He just do not believe that he can get in harm's way out there. But I prays all the time when he's out in that street. When my son's out in that street, I, I pray.

All mothers try to educate their children about danger but as this quotation illustrates, for poor mothers in high-crime neighborhoods there is an immediate urgency about this task.

Mothers in poor neighborhoods have to have particularly well-developed monitoring strategies for handling issues of safety, for example, reading the signs of potential danger on the street.

I: Is living in a neighborhood like this, does that have an impact on raising children?

R: Um, yes, because you have to be more aware of what's going on. Um, you know, you have to know what to um, protect them against. What to tell them. You know, give them different signs to look out for. So, yeah, it does have an impact.

I: What do you tell them? What kinds of things do they have to look out for?

R: OK, for instance, my son takes a bus to go to school. He's in high school now. And that corner is bad, the corner on the left of us. So he can't walk down by that direction. He has to catch . . . You know, he has to go the other way, the opposite way really, a block out of his way to catch the bus to go to school and also to come home. And when they want to go outside it's just, you know, it's just seem like it's crowded or like something that's going . . . You know, sometimes you can just feel it. They just . . . Because something's going on. You know, they have to come in. They have to stay in the house.

　　Or if they outside, they have to come in. Um, they wouldn't go to the store. And if you see like groups of, you know, boys out there and stuff like that, you know, my husband or myself will go. It's safer for one of us to go as opposed to my son.

I: Okay. How big is a dangerous group?

R: Oh, wow, it can be from three on up. But a lot times if it's a group even three if they want to start trouble, you know, three against one that's all.

Another mother spoke of how she and her husband would instruct their children in what to do when they heard the shots of drug dealers. Two mothers who live in the inner city memorize the color of their children's clothing before they leave the house. That way, if they hear of an accident or shooting involving teenage children on the radio or television, they may be able to identify their children.

Many African-American mothers do not feel they can turn to the police to help them if their children are in trouble. They don't trust the police and feel their children would be treated much more harshly by them than White children would be. This is in contrast to some of the White middle-class mothers in my sample who, if their children are engaging in risky or illegal behavior (using drugs, stealing things), are sometimes happy when their children have a police encounter. They feel this will "knock some sense" into their children.

As previously noted, part of keeping children safe, parents believe, is keeping them associated with the right kind of peers. This is harder to do for mothers in poor neighborhoods where there are more antisocial gangs. Anderson (1999), in an ethnographic study in a low-income African-American neighborhood, demonstrated the pressures on many young men to join gangs and on girls to become pregnant. Mothers in my sample fear "losing" their children to groups of peers, or "bad kids." One African-American mother expressed her fears about raising a Black male in our society. When I asked one woman, "What do you worry about most with your kids?" she answered:

> I worry about school, them finishing school, and that they're ok. And with a Black male in this society . . . They want to prove themselves. They want to be a man. I'm constantly telling my son, "You are your own person. You don't have to prove yourself. You don't have to do what the group wants. Walk away."

Another thing that mothers in more dangerous neighborhoods do is try to maintain good relations with young people in the neighborhood. One mother, who was very careful to keep a good relationship with neighborhood teenagers, held them accountable when they were doing something they shouldn't be doing, but also welcomed them into her house and treated them with a respectful attitude. This mother served as an "other mother" for neighborhood children, checking in on them and supporting them because she cared about them (Collins 1991; see also DeFiore, this volume). She was also watching out for these children so they would not give her trouble. According to her, one of her neighbors simply got angry at neighborhood youths for disorderly behavior and they then harassed her. Another family in a poor neighborhood was being harassed in their neighborhood by teenagers who were destroying property. These parents challenged the teenagers, who then threatened to firebomb their house. This family then moved to a working-class suburb.

Another strategy mothers use to keep children out of danger is to get teenagers involved in activities in the neighborhood and in their schools. Poor schools and neighborhoods have few organized activities or community centers, however. Many mothers try to keep their teenage children involved in church activities, but as they get older, many teenagers do not want to attend church. Other mothers encourage their children to get paying jobs to keep them away from what they perceive as bad influences. Some urban teenagers do find jobs at fast-food restaurants, but there is a lot of competition for these jobs from older low-skilled workers who can't find other jobs (Newman 1999).

Keeping teenage children safe involves a lot of work that our typical conceptions of mothers as nurturers do not capture. Mothers must persuade, reason with, lecture at, and negotiate with their teenage children, who have strong opinions of their own. Many parents and teenagers have arguments about where their teenage children can go, the hours they keep, and curfews. Teenage children can and do conceal information from their parents. Parenting at this stage involves careful knowledge of the neighborhood in order to be alert for signs of danger; bargaining skills; and a willingness to change as teenagers become older and gain more autonomy.

Ultimately, the most important strategy for creating safety and opportunities for children is moving to neighborhoods that provide these things. More privileged parents can use their incomes to move to neighborhoods where there are good schools, community activities, and police protection, even to "gated communities." If poorer parents move, however, it can be costly. The family mentioned earlier that did manage to move to a fairly safe working-class suburb to escape the harassment of neighborhood teenagers is now experiencing much greater financial difficulty than it did in the city. The family's mortgage in the new neighborhood is almost four times what it was in the city, and the family is having a difficult time covering basic expenses.

Poorer people, of course, usually don't have the ability to move. Housing policies in the United States create shortages of low- and moderate-income housing. Private markets provide housing for middle- and upper-income citizens, who then support zoning laws that exclude moderate- and low-income housing from their neighborhoods. The federal government fails to provide adequate financial support for moderate- and low-income housing as low-income people in poor neighborhoods struggle to keep their houses from deteriorating (Massey and Denton 1993). Further, there is a history of excluding racial and ethnic minorities from white neighborhoods.

Work in Support of Children's Schooling

The other key concern of mothers is that their children do well in school. All mothers in my sample believe that getting a high school diploma and college education, or a higher degree, is critical for their children's future success and express a strong interest in having their children succeed in school. Higher income parents send their children to high-quality public schools or pay for private school. They have the time to become involved in schools, and a sense of entitlement about their right to do so. If their children need extra help, they can pay for tutoring and for coaching in test taking.

Poorer parents, however, face obstacles to helping their children do well in school, and the schools their children attend are often of low quality. Because education in the United States is financed primarily through local property taxes, poorer school districts have less money to pay their teachers than suburban districts and receive less money for equipment. Parents of children in city schools speak of poor facilities, overcrowded classrooms, and teachers who are too burdened to care.

They need computers. And there aren't enough computers in their school.My best friend, she's white, she told me that in the better neighborhoods they have a room with computers and the children can go to that room and everyone has one. That makes me angry. That's not fair. Our schools are overcrowded and we don't have enough computers.

Parents also complain of not getting notified if their children skip school or have some other problem. Some mothers don't think their children are getting adequate college counseling.

I: So do you think ____ is a good school?
R: It is good, but it is understaffed. The counselors have too many students. I went to talk to one of the counselors of my child who is a senior. I said to him, "Do you know who my son is?" He said, "Well, he has to come and talk to me." I couldn't believe it. My son is a senior and he doesn't know him! He doesn't have a clue. I don't think the counselor is filling out the right papers for my son for his college applications.

McDonough's (1997) study of counseling programs in the high schools of children from a broad range of socioeconomic backgrounds demonstrates that college counseling is of much higher quality at schools in higher income neighborhoods.

Because poorer schools have inadequate resources and don't teach children as much, many poorer mothers try to make up for these deficiencies. Some work with their children at home—trying to motivate them to work harder in school, getting them to do homework, monitoring their television time, working with them to learn things, and keeping them from other distractions. One mother left her full-time job both to take care of a sick relative and to have the time to go over school lessons with her daughter, a high school student who had been getting poor marks in school. Every night, while the mother made dinner, she would have her daughter read parts of her English and social studies assignments and then have her repeat the material in her own words. This child began to do much better in school. Some mothers try to get their children into summer programs.

Due to the lower quality of schooling and the disaffection of some students, absentee rates in poorer urban schools are high (Neild 1999). Parents whose children refuse to go to school for periods of time spend a great deal of energy trying to get their children to school, sometimes being late for work and jeopardizing their jobs. One mother, who was worried about how teachers viewed her daughter, visited her daughter's school and talked to all her teachers to counter a possible perception that her daughter didn't care about school. This mother, who was African-American, said that she was sure that her daughter was trying to act "cool" in school, which meant acting as if she didn't care, to please her peers. But this mother said that her daughter did care, and she wanted the teachers, who were White and who she felt might not understand her daughter's behavior, to know that. Some mothers, who said they had taught their children how to be assertive, also coached their children in how to remain respectful to authority in school.

Another thing that mothers do to keep their daughters in school is try to keep them from getting pregnant. It is beyond the scope of this chapter to describe how they do this, but mothers expend considerable time and energy teaching their daughters to avoid pregnancy.

Besides helping their children individually, many poor mothers go to great lengths to find better schools or programs for their children. Some school districts do have school choice programs that allow families to choose a school other than their neighborhood school. According to some researchers, however, poorer parents have a more difficult time researching all the options and complying with the requirements of applying to other schools (Moore and Davenport 1990). Neild (1999), in a study of the Philadelphia School District, demonstrated that factors outside of parents' control also influence the outcome of the school choice process. For example, schools themselves play a role in school choice, with personnel in wealthier schools encouraging their students to apply for the better schools and advocating for them in the admissions process. Further, there is a limited number of high quality schools to choose from in the district, so only half of students who opt for school choice are accepted to any one of the schools to which they apply. White students are advantaged in this process because the larger district is trying to keep them. Their acceptance rates at the higher ranked schools are higher than those of equally qualified minority students.

The alternative for some lower income people in the city is Catholic school or private Christian school, options that a number of mothers in my sample had considered. Furstenberg et al. (1999) demonstrated that the children of city parents who send their children to Catholic and other private schools do better in school. These options cost money, however. Some parents in my sample had to take their children out of Catholic school because they could not afford the cost. They believe that this had a negative impact on their children.

> R: It (Catholic school) was good and the smaller, you know, classrooms and stuff like that because I know how it is once you get out of . . . once my son got out of the Catholic school and he had all his independence, he's wasn't learning. He felt he could do whatever he wanted.
> I: He got out of the Catholic school after?
> R: Fifth grade.
> I: Okay. How come he left the Catholic school?
> R: Because at the time I was unable to keep, you know, the tuition up.

One mother, whose husband was a veteran of the Armed Forces, found a veteran's boarding school that she thought would be good for her children. She hated to send her children away to boarding school and missed them terribly, but her children could attend for free, and when they began to do much better in school, she felt she had made the right decision. A few parents try to get their children into a public school in another district. Few can afford to pay the fees for schools in other districts, however, so they have to pretend that their children live in another district. This requires considerable paperwork, as well as the cooperation of a person in that district who will allow the student to use an address illegally. Mostly only a close relative or friend would provide the false address, so this course of action is not open to many poor parents, who are less likely to have friends or relatives in more affluent neighborhoods. Many poor parents seriously consider moving, to get into a better school district, but most have to resign themselves to not being able to afford to move. This mother tries to make herself feel better about not being able to move by rationalizing that all neighborhoods are similar:

> All I can do is have an imagination. Now if I was this and I was that . . . you know . . . would have gone to better schools . . . or live in a better neighborhood . . . but nowadays all the neighborhoods are about the same. You have ups and downs in all of them. So you raise 'em the best way you know how . . . wherever you at. And give 'em the best education you can afford to give . . . you know . . . and hope they do the best they can with it.

Actions that parents take on behalf of their children's schooling can be critical. Although I do not have a specific numerical count of parents' actions, many poorer parents in my sample were doing the kinds of things I have discussed. In my interviews, mothers described how, when trouble occurs, they take action—talk to their children's teachers, try to get more homework for their children, coach their children, and if these things don't work, they try to get their children into a different program or school, although, as I have described, this is difficult to do. Furstenberg et al. (1999), in their study of urban families, found that poorer mothers were helping their children with homework at the same rate as other mothers.

Unfortunately, school personnel are not typically aware of all the extra, invisible work that parents do to make up for a deficient system that deprives lower income people of decent schooling for their children. Researchers have studied how teachers are much more likely to respond to the requests of middle-class parents than to those of working-class and poor parents because middle-class parents have more cultural capital, or more legitimacy and influence, based on their education and their membership in higher status social networks (Lareau 1989). School personnel also tend to be more responsive to White parents than to African-American parents (Lareau and Horvat 1999). To create more fairness and equity in schooling, educational policies would have to ensure that resources were much more fairly distributed across social class and ethnic groups. Sadly, at this time, the inequality between school systems in the United States is large and growing, and children from poorer families are not getting the educational opportunities that better off families can provide.

Time to Parent

Not only do unsafe neighborhoods and poor schools create extra work and disadvantage for poor mothers, but these mothers have less time to do parenting work. In public discourse, there is much attention to work–family debates. In these debates, however, writers typically do not distinguish between workers at different income levels or focus on the diversity of experiences among women and the hardships faced by poorer women; often professional women are taken as the norm (Kurz 2000). However, poor mothers' paid labor gives them less time than other women to do the tasks of parenting. In my sample, many working mothers experience stress as they attempt to combine paid work and family life, but more higher income women work at part-time jobs or jobs with flexible hours or hours that accommodate their children's schedules (such as school teaching). Poorer women in my sample have more hours of work, less flexibility in their hours, more night jobs, more oppressive job conditions, and no money to purchase household help. This can lead to less time with children, as well as more physical exhaustion, more health problems, and little vacation time (Kurz 2000; Litt 1999).

Single mothers can have particular difficulty getting time to parent. Although being a single mother can be less stressful than living in a bad marriage, when fathers participate in childrearing, they can make a difference in helping relieve burdens of mothers. Fathers can help whether or not they are married to mothers, but fathers living with mothers undoubtedly help more. Single mothers also typically have less income than other mothers (Kurz 1995). In my sample, single mothers often had to work two jobs to make ends meet. They were unhappy about this because it meant they had less time with their children and sometimes had to leave them unsupervised. For some poor mothers, the lack of time is an even greater hardship because poorer mothers are more likely to have children who are sick or who have disabilities and therefore need extra care (Polit, London, and Martinez 2001; see also London et al., this volume).

One woman in my sample, after being widowed, had to work at two jobs for three years. She worked for 16 hours a day and said it was exhausting and she had to rely on family members and neighbors to check in on her children, who were alone a lot. Another woman had to work three jobs to meet her expenses when her marriage ended. She ended up having a stroke. She and her two sons live in her father's house. Her father has been ill and the house badly needs repairs, but this woman's disability payments are too low to cover expenses for house repairs. Another single mother finds that her low-status job as a nurse's aid is particularly stressful.

> My job is very stressful. Sometimes when I come home I go to my room. I say to my kids, don't bother me for an hour. I can't talk to anyone for an hour. I have to have that. My kids have all these questions. I have to take time. It helps me keep my sanity.
>
> The RN's have more education. They give more of the work to you. If you don't do it their way, you get written up. We're the grunts. I agree, I'm not a brain surgeon, but we do important work.
>
> Nursing homes are run by corporations now. What's happening is a sin. People are locked up. I'm supposed to handle the medication for 30 people. That's scary. The medications for many of them are complicated. They don't take the proper precautions. The supplies are not well stocked, like the diapers.
>
> Sometimes I get low. Sometimes my family gets away with murder. Last night I just didn't feel like cooking. We got pizza. I dug in my purse. I don't have the money, but . . .

Other nurse's aids also talk about very stressful work conditions. On the other hand, I interviewed some registered nurses whose higher status jobs enabled them to negotiate for flexible hours and in some cases part-time jobs, which those who had partners could afford to take.

Glenn (1992) argued that poor mothers are supporting the reproductive labor of White women and paying a price. As she and others have pointed out, racial ethnic women don't have the money to hire help in their home the way White professional women do. Indeed, they are the ones who often provide that help. Racial ethnic women also provide more of the lower level reproductive labor in the public sphere that mothers depend on, including day care and care of the elderly (Glenn 1992). Such work, which pays poorly, enables women who can afford it to work at higher level jobs that pay more money and to buy more services in their own homes, whereas poorer mothers have to take on additional paid work to make ends meet.

The Fate of Children

Although the majority of teenagers do not get into serious trouble, as the statistics presented earlier indicate, some do. In my sample, poor mothers report more serious problems with their children than other mothers, although mothers of all class backgrounds report problems. Middle-class and professional mothers reported drug use and driving accidents, with several reporting a death of a teenager of relatives or neighbors due to drug overdoses. Although some of these mothers reported that their children had had contact with the police, few had been arrested or prosecuted. Poor mothers whose children had problems reported children dropping out of school, getting arrested, or going to prison, as well as deaths. These mothers speak of "losing" their children to peer groups. Minority youth are at greater risk for punishment than White teenagers. In recent years, the criminal justice system has tightened its surveillance of youth and meted out harsher penalties to them, including trying some youth as adults. Minority youth are held under more suspicion by the criminal justice system and are arrested and convicted at higher rates than white youth (Dohrn 2000). The woman quoted next, who is African-American, tried to understand how one of her sons managed to finish high school and successfully complete training as an auto mechanic, while the other went to prison.

> R: After my husband's death, one son kept it all in and one didn't. One strayed away and one didn't . . . so. It's just the way life is. You all keep on going you know.
> I: So what happened to him?
> R: He just got with the wrong crowd and got in trouble. Got to stay in jail for it that's all. He only was two credits away from graduating high school. He was only two credits . . . He was the best . . . he was the brains. Yeah he was the brains. But he was the one that had all the knowledge and didn't use it right . . . that's all. But he had two points . . . that's all he had . . . and all he had to do was finish school . . . but he didn't do that.
> I: So what did he get in trouble for?

R: Cars . . . stealing . . . sellin' . . . he was in with all the crowds. And he took the rap for 'em . . . so. And I mean he didn't do it . . . but he took the rap on himself. So he had to pay the price then. He didn't want to give them up and he had to do it . . . so that's what he did. . . he learned the hard way . . . that's all. He had to learn the hard way.

I: Right. So whenever he gets out . . . you think he'll be able to . . . stay away from that crowd?

R: We hope so. Most of them are grown up and a lot of them are married and moved on with their life . . . so . . . there ain't too many of them out here now. Most all of them is growed up. While he was in there serving time they was growin' up. Stuff that they did . . . but he's the one that got caught with most of the stuff. So . . . he'll come around . . . I guess.

I: Right. So. . . and that took a lot of your time and . . .

R: It took all our time. Family . . . friends . . . and all.

One mother reported that her child is failing in school because he won't attend classes or do his homework, and that he has just had his first encounter with the police after he was involved in a fight in the neighborhood. Another woman, whose child is in prison for 5 years for theft, was feeling hopeful that her son will get on the right path when he is released because he completed a high school equivalency course in prison. A woman whose son died of AIDS, which was brought on by his drug use, reflected on the periods of homelessness the family endured while her son was growing up and their impact on her son's turning to drug use.

Unfortunately, recent data indicate that teenage children of very poor mothers who were enrolled in the welfare-to-work programs that were the precursors of welfare reform have experienced more problems than children of mothers who were on welfare but not in work programs (Lewin 2001). These data seem to indicate that the invisible work mothers do keeping their children safe and helping them in school is very important. Because welfare reform requires mothers to spend more hours in the workplace, they do not have as much time to monitor the activities of their teenage children and guide them along paths that lead to successful outcomes (Scott et al. 2002).

Conclusion

The evidence presented here demonstrates the difficulties poor mothers face at this stage of their parenting career, when teenagers are out in the world with their peers—difficulties in keeping their children safe and in getting them through school while living in environments with few resources. Poor mothers are forced to do extra work to make up for the deficits in their neighborhoods and schools, and they have less time to parent than other mothers. Poor mothers work hard, constantly and creatively strategizing the best ways to keep their children safe and productive. Undoubtedly their efforts make a great difference in the lives of their children. Although their work is difficult and they face greater uncertainty about whether their children will make their way safely in the world, their actions remain unrecognized and they continue to be stigmatized.

These data indicate that current frameworks in scholarship that focus on mothers as responsible for what happens to their children are inadequate and misleading. They envision the family as a self-contained unit where parents control what goes on inside the four walls of the house. We must expand these frameworks to include the conditions and environments within which mothers work, environments that are shaped by race and class hierarchies. These hierarchies are structured in such a way that poor women, who work at low wages, often at service jobs and jobs caring for others, are supporting the reproductive labor of wealthier women, who have more time to raise their children. Wealthier mothers benefit from policies that favor the private sector and keep taxes low, whereas poor mothers must sometimes take on extra jobs to make ends meet. As Glenn and others have stated, the positions of poor and nonpoor mothers are relationally constructed- their experiences are not just different, but connected in systematic ways (Baca Zinn and Dill 1994; Glenn 1992). Research on the parenting of poor mothers must locate the experiences of nonpoor mothers within these relations.

In addition, political leaders and policymakers must think more broadly about "family policy," which should include a consideration of neighborhoods, zoning laws, and school financing. It is essential that government policies make up for failures in the market and equalize conditions for mothers and families and provide funding for safer neighborhoods, better schools, and work—family policies that enable mothers to participate in school life. We also need policies that encourage fathers to do more of the work of raising children, including giving them flexible schedules that enable them to participate more at home.

Finally, a host of measures must be taken to raise the incomes of poorer mothers, who desperately need more money to move to better neighborhoods, get better schooling, and have more time to raise their children. The trend toward regressive tax policies must be halted in favor of progressive ones, the minimum wage must be increased, and policies ensuring a living wage must be enacted. Such a change in priorities requires transforming ideologies of individualism and privatization, as well as racial privilege.

Notes

The author acknowledges the support of the Philadelphia Education Longitudinal Study and the MacArthur Family Study, Department of Sociology, University of Pennsylvania, for the research on which this chapter is based. The author also thanks Francesca Cancian and Andrew London for helpful comments.

1. These samples were drawn from school records. The suburban sample was drawn from one school district. One of the urban ones was drawn from the entire school district of Philadelphia, including neighborhood schools, schools that require some admission, and highly selective magnet schools. The other was drawn from four neighborhoods selected to represent working-class and low-income neighborhoods, both White and African-American. The city samples were randomly drawn from a larger survey sample, which had also been drawn randomly.

Las Madres en el Barrio

*Godmothers, Othermothers, and Women's Power
in a Community of Caregiving*

JoAnn DeFiore

*I*n 1998, I spent 6 months living in barrio Santa Teresa in Yvytu,[1] a small rural pueblo in Paraguay, studying how women mother. Using participant observation, I observed that the mothers in my neighborhood, *las madres*, used *ritual* and *fictive kinship* to create a "community of caregiving." The community of caregiving these women created included the specific mothering practices of collective childrearing, the exchange of goods and services, folk healing (*curanderismo*), and gossip. In this chapter, I describe in detail the ritual and fictive kinship systems these women developed, and provide an in-depth case study of a community of caregiving at a specific historical moment and in a specific geographical location. I argue that the community of caregiving that these women created through a network of godmothers and othermothers provided a structure that allowed them to fulfill their roles as mothers within a larger context of overwhelming poverty, inequality, and oppression.

What is a community of caregiving and how does it serve its members? A community is a framework of shared beliefs, interests, and commitments that unites a set of varied groups and activities. A community is bounded by a common fate, a personal identity, a sense of belonging, and a supportive structure of activities and relationships, but not necessarily a particular size of territory (Etzioni 1996; Selznick 1992). Others contend that "community" usually refers to a local, geographical place where there is a sense of membership, belonging, and commitment (Cancian and Oliker 2000).

Caregiving refers to skilled labor, which is voluntary and unpaid, that involves caring for others' physical, emotional, and economic needs (Cancian and Oliker 2000; Graham 1991). Fisher and Tronto (1990) define caregiving as "the concrete (sometimes called hands-on) work of maintaining and repairing our world," which requires continuous, dense time commitments and detailed knowledge including everyday understandings (Fisher and Tronto, 1990:43). Thus, a caregiving community involves a network of individuals with shared interests and beliefs who are laboring for others' needs.

Communities of caregiving are valuable in that they can be communal and informal, while at the same time being a source of local knowledge and support.

They can be innovative, and serve as an "in-between" support system to institutional and organizational forms (Cancian and Oliker 2000). Dushka (1996) further argued that caregiving communities can lead to a politics of resistance and transformation that celebrates women and affirms their worth.

One drawback of communities of caregiving is that they can bolster gender inequality by reinforcing assumptions that women are natural caregivers (Cancian and Oliker 2000). As a result, women are not able to invest time and energy into activities that would bring them status and wealth (see England and Folbre, this volume). Community caregiving can also be humiliating or coercive; for example, participation can be controlled through the use of gossip. These communities can discriminate by creating a "we" feeling amongst those accepted into the community, which necessarily results in the construction of outsiders. Such boundary construction and maintenance have the potential to reinforce gender, racial/ethnic, social class, and other inequalities.

In this chapter, I first discuss background information on Paraguay in general and the neighborhood I studied specifically. Following that is a discussion of the methodology I employed and my role in the community. I then turn to the benefits and drawbacks of a community of caregiving, including a discussion of motherhood, ritualized kinship, and fictive kin: godmothers or *comadres* and othermothers. Comadres are godmothers, chosen through a religious ritual, who take on the rights and obligations of kin. Othermothers are fictive kin who assist birth mothers by sharing mothering responsibilities. I use these two concepts to examine the specific mothering practices of collective childrearing, the exchange of goods and services, folk healing, and the role of gossip. In the final section, I explore how women in their roles as mothers, godmothers, and othermothers resist oppression, while caring for their children, families, and neighbors within a context of poverty and gender inequality.

Paraguay and the Mothers of Barrio Santa Teresa

Background on Paraguay

Paraguay has an overall population of 4.8 million, most of whom live in the eastern part of the country within 100 miles of the capital, Asuncíon. About half of the inhabitants live in the *campo* or rural areas; however, due to urbanization, this number is decreasing. Ethnically, culturally, and socially, Paraguay has one of the most homogeneous populations in South America: 95% of the population is mestizo, of mixed Spanish and Guaraní Indian descent, and over 95% are Catholic (Hay 1993; Potthast-Jutkeit 1997; Service and Service 1954).

Paraguayan culture is influenced greatly by its bilingual character. Both Spanish and Guaraní, an indigenous language, are the spoken and official languages (Patrinos, Psacharopoulos, and Velez 1995). Most Paraguayans speak both Guaraní and Spanish, whereas less than 5% speaks only Spanish (Hay 1993; Potthast-Jutkeit 1997). In the *campo*, Guaraní is used exclusively as the vernacular, but Spanish is used in the media and government.

The average family size is 6.4 children per woman in rural areas and 3.2 children in Asuncíon (Monteith et al. 1988). The mean age at first marriage is 21.5

years of age for the total population. Education is compulsory until 13 years old, but about 57% of Paraguayans drop out of school before the sixth grade (Patrinos, Psacharopoulos, and Velez 1995). Children attend school for only a half-day because, particularly in the *campo* and *pueblos*, they are needed at home for chores.

Gender Inequality in Paraguay

The mothers of barrio Santa Teresa create a community of caregiving that is shaped by the larger systems of inequality that exist in Paraguay. Fisher (1993) noted that "machismo combines with poverty to deprive peasant women of the most basic human needs. Even by Latin American standards, the status of Paraguayan peasant women is low" (p. 78). The situation in Paraguay has many complexities that require a theory that addresses multiple levels of analysis. Therefore, I look to Patricia Hill Collins's (2000) *Black Feminist Thought* as a theory suitable for explaining the manifold levels of oppression in Paraguay. Collins discussed four domains of oppression and empowerment. I use three to analyze Paraguay in this chapter: the structural domain, which emphasizes large-scale institutions; the hegemonic domain, which deals with ideology, culture, and consciousness; and the interpersonal domain, the routinized day-to-day practices among people.

At the structural level (Collins 2000), Paraguay is highly stratified by class and gender, wherein the male elites dominate government, education, and business, as well as control most of the wealth in the country. The educational system has been successful in providing schooling to both boys and girls at the primary level, but after that point, female participation drops off sharply (Psacharopoulos, Velez, and Patrinos 1994). Moreover, women earn substantially less than men, almost half, regardless of education level (Psacharopoulos et al. 1994:324).

At the hegemonic level (Collins 2000), Paraguayan culture is *machista*, characterized by media images that blatantly denigrate women; high rates of violence against women; a basic belief that men are superior to women; day-to-day practices such as jokes and gestures that objectify women; and the accepted social practice of married men having several girlfriends (Potthast-Jukeit 1997). The other side of *machismo* is *marianismo*, wherein women are viewed as modest, restrained, virtuous, and nurturing. Derived from Catholicism, the chief directives of *marianismo* are self-sacrifice, passivity, and submission to male authority (Gil and Vasquez 1996); suffering is considered an ideal that leads to eventual sainthood (Stevens 1973).

At the interpersonal level (Collins 2000), in the home, peasant women are openly called "my servant," the Guaraní word used to mean wife, by their husbands. Legally, wives are considered the property of their husbands and must obtain their consent to work outside the home (Fisher 1993). Additionally, rural peasant women lack mobility; they cannot go anywhere outside of their neighborhoods without the accompaniment of their husband or children.

A gendered division of labor exists in the household, supported by the segregation of men's and women's lives in general. In the *campo*, men spend most of their time in the center of town or away at work, and women spend most of their time in the barrio. Cross-gender friendships are discouraged.

At the same time, Paraguay has been known historically as "the land of strong women," due to the almost total decimation of the male population after the Triple Alliance War, which lasted from 1864 to 1870 (Potthast-Jutkeit 1991). Women were left to rebuild the country. The myth is that after the war, the preponderance of females led to competition among women for available males, leaving women happy to work to keep a man. Women were said to have taken over production and reproduction, while rural men grew out of the habit of working. This stereotype continues today. However, in practice, rural men and women both endeavor to work to support their families despite high rates of unemployment for men (Potthast-Jutkeit 1991).

Barrio Santa Teresa

Within this larger context of inequality sits the town of Yvytu, a setting that necessitates a community of caregiving. Yvytu, population 2000, is located in the southern part of Paraguay, 3 hours by bus from the capital Asuncíon, and consists of families that range from middle class to extreme poverty. For example, some families on the north side of town had TVs, cars, and indoor plumbing, whereas families on the south side of town did not have running water, indoor plumbing, cars, or access to regular health care. Barrio Santa Teresa is one of the poorest neighborhoods on the southern edge of town. The block I lived on consisted of nine homes and a schoolhouse. The mothers of my study were living in extreme poverty. For example, most used well water, did not have refrigerators, cooked over coals, washed laundry by hand, and often went weeks without any income.

Of the eight families on my block, most came from farming families who recently were forced to moved into the *pueblo* from the *campo*, due to the growth of agribusiness and complex global economic factors. Thus, the women in these families shifted recently from rural life to pueblo life, a change fraught with difficulty and new challenges. The lack of usable, fertile land removed the mothers from their previous way of life and resources. They moved away from a situation where the family had been the economic unit, and where they had worked in the fields and reared their children in the presence of husbands and extended family. In the pueblo, they found themselves isolated by the separate public and private spheres for men and women (Cancian and Oliker 2000; Hooyman and Gonyea 1995). Moreover, leaving the land meant also leaving a familiar set of routines whereby women could provide for their families without having to wait for their husbands to give them money to buy food. New to the pueblo, these women were establishing new identities and new ways of sustaining their families in a cash economy.

Methodology and My Role in Barrio Santa Teresa

I had visited Paraguay a year before my 6-month stay, and stayed in Barrio Santa Teresa for 3 weeks. The women were therefore familiar with me and knew my husband, a Peace Corps volunteer, who had lived with them for 1½ years prior to my arrival in 1998. I was in Yvytu both to live with my husband for 6 months and to conduct research on women's friendships, mothering, and gender inequality. When I arrived I spoke some Spanish, but almost no Guaraní. Over time, my ability to use both languages developed, although I became much more proficient in Spanish. I communicated with the women in my neighborhood mostly through Spanish, which was a second language for all of us, because they grew up speaking Guaraní at home.

As a White woman investigator from the north, I knew that in order to conduct this research, I had to deal with my status and privilege from the outset. White middle-class women historically have not had to confront their own privilege through an understanding of the culture and history of oppressed groups. Based on Third World women's critiques of Western White feminism (Mohanty, Russo, and Torres 1991) and the growing body of literature on whiteness and White privilege (Frankenberg 1993), I hoped to be as vigilant as possible in confronting my privilege while assessing cultural practices of mothering in rural Paraguay. As an aid, I followed two principles of cross-cultural feminist research that emphasize the importance of cultural specificity and the necessity of intensive study (Reinharz 1992). Thus, I kept my sample small in a specific cultural and geographic location comprised of a homogeneous group of women. Second, I used the ethnographic process of immersion as my methodology to allow for intensive study.

As an ethnographer, I steeped myself in the world of the mothers of Barrio Santa Teresa to grasp what they experience as meaningful and important and to see how they carried out their roles as mothers in their community. I adopted the stance that "ethnographic immersion precludes conducting field research as a detached, passive observer; the field researcher can only get close to the lives of those studied by actively participating in their day-to-day activities" (Emerson, Fretz, and Shaw 1995:2). Therefore, I began to emulate the women in my neighborhood. I watched them to learn how to dress, how to cook, how to wash my clothing by hand, what to eat, and what activities were appropriate for certain periods of the day. I spent most of my days in the barrio doing household chores such as cooking and cleaning. The children of the neighborhood spent countless hours on my front porch, playing, singing, talking, and coloring. At the time, I did not have children of my own (although I do now). Nevertheless, the mothers still accepted me as an othermother in the community because, in rural Paraguay, girls are trained to be mothers from a young age. Thus, it was assumed that I had received similar training in my youth.

The children also helped me with my chores in the same way that they helped their own mothers, godmothers, and othermothers. Often, truly speaking, the younger girls showed me how to do the chores better than I was doing them. Young girls aged seven and eight were showing me how to hand wash clothes properly, how to use the machete in the garden, and how to chop onions more quickly. Their mothers were more discreet in their criticism, although occasionally they would wonder aloud why I had done something a certain way, rather than the "normal" way.

As we developed relationships, the mothers or their children taught me how to be a "good Paraguayan woman," which consists of working hard, mothering, nurturing, being modest and subservient, and staying near home. Many times, this

was difficult for me because being a good Paraguayan woman often meant enduring what a White Western feminist would term gender discrimination. For example, I was not free to move outside the confines of the neighborhood by myself.
If I wanted to go out further into the countryside or into the center of town, I
needed to either go with my husband or take a child or two with me. This was a
lesson I learned the hard way after being harassed on a solo walk in the countryside. I returned to the barrio expecting female solidarity on the issues of harassment and lack of mobility. Instead, I was chastised for being so foolish. Later, the
mothers offered their own children as accompaniment if I needed to go into town
or wanted to take a walk.

On the one hand, I wanted them to "be like them" and be as responsible as they
were in the household. They would then compliment me on the laundry I was
doing or my work in the garden, saying I was hard-working, a big compliment in
rural Paraguay. On the other hand, I felt oppressed by my role and insisted that
my husband contribute significantly to the household division of labor, unlike the
other men in the neighborhood. Even with the personal contradictions, as soon as
I stepped into the web of interdependence among the mothers, I felt simultaneously the weight of the responsibility and the support of this community of caregiving.

Motherhood and Ritual Kinship in Rural Paraguay

Las Madres del Barrio

Ña is short for Doña and is equivalent to Mrs. in English and Señora in Spanish.
All of the women were referred to as Ña followed by their *first* name, unlike in
English where Mrs. is followed by one's last name. The women in the study were
in their late thirties to late forties, and most had not completed primary school.

Ña Teresa has eight children and one grandchild.[2] Her husband is a bricklayer
who works when weather permits. She sometimes takes in other women's wash
for pay. Ña Perla has four children and is widowed. She works as a maid during
the day. Ña Rita has four children and one grandchild that live with her. Her husband is a teacher and she works as a maid during the day. Ña Maria gave birth to
11 children, one of whom died in childbirth. Five of her children are under the
age of 8; her husband works seasonally. Ña Angelina has three children and one
grandchild. Her husband lives and works in another city. She watches Ña
Mariana's 3-year-old daughter and 9-month-old son. Ña Carmen has five children
and several grandchildren. Her husband is a logger and handyman. Ña Mariana
has three children. She works in the cotton factory 3 km outside of town. Her
husband works as a hair cutter in Asuncíon, where he lives. Ña Rubina has six
children and her husband is a truck driver who is often away.

The Ideology of Motherhood in Paraguay

In Paraguay, *motherhood* as an ideology is infused with both honor and sub-
servience. Women as mothers are respected in Paraguay, as they are in many
Latino cultures (Trujillo 1987). The ideology of motherhood is associated with
marianismo. The Virgin Mary is revered throughout Paraguay, particularly *La Virgen*

de Caacupe, who is said to have appeared to a Guaraní Indian. On her feast day, December 8, many thousands of Paraguayans will travel miles and miles, often on foot, to visit the site where the Virgin appeared. As the icon for marianismo and motherhood, the Virgin represents the idealized mother who cares for and nurtures an oppressed people; she is pure and serves to make Latina women docile and enduring (Anzaldua 1987).

In the context of extreme poverty, "mother" is the primary positive identity available to women because there are no other acceptable alternatives. As a result, mothers are not able to abandon this identity and the roles that go with it, whereas men can abandon fatherhood because they have other activities available to them, such as work, sexual activity and soccer (Neuhouser 1998).

Becoming a mother signals "womanhood" in rural Paraguay. For young girls, pregnancy is a coveted status and often occurs at a young age during the teenage years. Pregnant girls might get their own bed for the first time and some special treatment, such as release from certain household chores (Neuhouser 1993; Trujillo 1987). Paraguayans view the mother as the center of the family, and both sons and daughters are exceedingly loyal to her.

Ritualized Kinship and Fictive Kin: Godmothers and Othermothers

Ritualized fictive kin bonds are prominent in tribal and peasant communities that are bound social units, such as villages or barrios (Messerschmidt 1982; Vaughan 1983). *Compadrazgo* is associated with choosing godparents and is an extension of the kinship system where the *compadres*[3] take on the rights and obligations of relatives and are included as members of the extended kin network (Hay 1993; Keefe, Padilla, and Carlos 1979; Lopez 1999; Mintz and Wolf 1950; Service and Service 1954; Vidal 1988). Parents select a godmother (*madrina*) and godfather (*padrina*) for a child's ritual ceremony, such as baptism, confirmation, or marriage, who become *comadre* and *compadre* to the parents. Parents can choose the same set of godparents for each child or choose different ones. Rural Paraguayans consider it a great honor to be chosen as a godparent, and their duty is to accept the invitation.

Compadrazgo is practiced for several reasons: economic assistance, experience from older *compadres*, help during times of crisis, and socialization for parents and children. In the cities and among upper classes, "the relationship is primarily an observation of Catholic ritual" (Service and Service 1954:174). However, among the rural and lower class groups, *compadres* provide an opportunity for giving mutual aid. The baptism *padrinos* are quite literally expected to raise and educate a child in case of the death of the parents.

In rural Paraguay, compadres are obligated to aid each other and treat each other very respectfully (Hay 1993; Service and Service 1954). The relationship connotes tremendous admiration between *compadres*, and also between godparents and godchildren. According to Service and Service (1954:176), "The bond is not broken by the death of the child or even by a quarrel between the *compadres*."

Compadrazgo strengthens social ties in two ways. When used with nonkin, it extends the family circle of support and aid. When used with family members, it strengthens kin ties (Salgado de Snyder and Padilla 1987). The ritual kinship title can even supersede the original kin delineation. For instance, Ña Rubina consistently referred to her only sibling Juancito as *"compadre"* instead of as "brother" or by his name.

The ritualized godmother relationship can also cross class lines, particularly in cases of poverty. Parents often pick a wealthier relative, neighbor, or *patron*. For example, Ña Teresa chose a wealthier *comadre* Señora Laura who was a teacher at the local school and whose husband was also a teacher. Among other things, Señora Laura would provide a large Christmas meal and invite Ña Teresa's family of 10.

Godmothers assist each other economically, socially, and psychologically. One of Ña Rubina's wealthier *comadres* Señora Lordes had just given birth. Right after the birth, Lordes discovered her husband was having an affair. So, Ña Rubina sent her teenage daughters over to help their *madrina* take care of the new baby now that she was alone. In return, Lordes spent many hours at Ña Rubina's house discussing the affair and receiving emotional support.

Alongside the godmother roles, women in Barrio Santa Teresa are also othermothers. Collins (2000) defined *othermothers* as women who assist bloodmothers by sharing mothering responsibilities resulting in an organized, resilient, women-centered network. She found that among African-American women, these relationships can exist between kin and fictive kin, and also between neighbors and friends caring for one another's children and exchanging goods and services. Carol Stack (1975) also defined fictive kin in a black urban poor community as clusters of kin and nonkin who live near one another and carry out domestic functions. The women of Barrio Santa Teresa function in a similar fashion.

The main difference between godmothers and othermothers is that one relationship is formed through a formal ritual, whereas the other is not. However, the dividing line between the two types of fictive kin is not as distinct. Lopez (1999) found that women in her sample extend the practice of *compadrazgo* beyond those formally invited as godmothers to include friends who participated in mothering activities. Similarly, in Santa Teresa, not all the women shared the title of *comadre*, but as neighbors and othermothers, they created a community of caregiving where they engaged in the tradition and practices of mothering each other's children.

Mothering Practices in a Community of Caregiving

Collective Child Care

One of the benefits of the community of caregiving in Barrio Santa Teresa is collective childrearing, one of the most communal aspects of mothering in rural Paraguay. The mothers allowed their children to go into most of the other homes in the neighborhood and assumed that the other women were keeping an eye on their children. Additionally, it was an unspoken rule that all children in the neighborhood got fed, albeit often in small amounts, if they were at your home during mealtime. Thus, a woman who was low on money one week could be assured that her children would be fed at a neighbor's house.

Because Paraguayan women's work is so labor-intensive (Fisher 1993) and because they have many children, it is imperative that women know that they can count on each other to watch out for their children while in the neighborhood. Moreover, when children are very small and need constant care, women might trade childcare for goods, services, or pay. As an othermother, Ña Angelina watched Ña Mariana's infant and 3-year-old because Ña Mariana had a factory job outside of town and her husband worked and lived in the capital. Regardless of the shift, Ña Angelina and her daughters cared for the two children in exchange for pay, an arrangement that also benefited her because her husband was also working in another city and he rarely came to Yvytu. Thus, she went for long stretches of time without any money.

Later on, Ña Angelina was unable to continue to watch the children. Ña Mariana was able to switch to the day shift and one of Ña Rubina's teenage daughters Lupe began to do the child care. The mothers applauded this arrangement as great training for Lupe's future role as a mother. This example reveals the fluidity of the barrio in action; when one person needs a change, another mother fills the gaps.

Exchanging Goods and Services

Another benefit of the community of caregiving is that the mothers exchanged goods and services on a daily basis, where the mothers drew upon their local knowledge and skills to aid each other. Each day, the mothers or their children would go among and between the houses in a somewhat regular pattern to exchange goods. All the mothers knew where the resources were embedded in their community, so their everyday actions involved the maintenance of relationships with the people who had what they needed or might need in the future.

One very typical example of the exchange of goods is the constant flow of food among households. Children were used to transfer the food from house to house and reciprocity was expected. In Paraguay, in order to save face, if someone gave you an entire meal, you would send a small portion of whatever you had in your kitchen (even if you only had mandioca[4]) to exchange.

The mothers also pooled their resources. Ña Teresa owned the pressure cooker needed to cook the mandioca. Each day, Ña Rubina sent her daughter to Ña Teresa's house to borrow the pressure cooker; thus, two households shared one kitchen item. Ña Teresa also owned one of two refrigerators in the neighborhood, so several families, mine included, would keep a few items there.

In another situation involving a godmother relationship, Ña Rubina wanted to move out of her one-room house, where she had been living with her six children, her husband, and often her brother. However, she needed more money to afford the higher rent of the larger house. One of her much wealthier *comadres* lived about two blocks away, so she temporarily employed Ña Rubina's two eldest daughters as maids. Similarly, Ña Perla, who was recently widowed, had two young daughters who worked at the small store of their *madrina*. These *comadres* did not necessarily need the help of 8- and 10-year-old girls, but rather considered it their service and duty to the community to employ them.

Not only were goods exchanged, but services were as well. For example, among the women in Barrio Santa Teresa, education level varied, but most did not finish elementary school. Thus, Spanish proficiency varied among them. Most of the mothers spoke what the majority of Paraguayans speak: *jopara* (which means "mix" in Guaraní), a minimum way of speaking that uses elements from both major languages (Corvalan 1977). However, because Guaraní and thus *jopara* are considered the language of the lower class, Spanish is used for any official business: government, school, or church. As rural peasant women, they would have been belittled for speaking Guaraní in such situations. The mothers relied, therefore, on those women or their daughters who were in school and could speak Spanish fluently for situations when they needed to interact with public officials or conduct business outside the barrio. For example, any of the women needing to make a phone call would bring Ña Carmen's daughter Lordes with them because she spoke the best Spanish.

Curanderismo: *Folk Healing*

Although the work of the mothers was often invisible, it became readily apparent whenever a child became sick in the neighborhood. The mothers and their daughters had extensive knowledge of herbal and folk remedies (Keefe et al. 1979), commonly called *yuyos*. Because these families lacked the resources to go to the doctor for anything except emergencies, they had to determine the diagnosis on their own. Many times during my stay, I witnessed the following:

Word spreads rapidly around the neighborhood that someone is sick, usually someone's child. All the mothers gather around the sickbed discussing what they think is wrong. They talk quickly and forcefully in Guaraní. Eventually, a consensus is reached concerning the diagnosis. Although secretly some women disagree, they do not say so publicly then, but rather wait until later to see the outcome. Then each woman goes home and returns a little while later with her recommendation of a remedy. Each woman brings over what she thinks is best for the patient, and we all wait to see which one works. All the mothers participate in this process, knowing their *comadres* and othermothers will reciprocate when their child is sick.

Gossip

One of the drawbacks of a community of caregiving is that it can be coercive and humiliating, particularly through the use of gossip as a way of controlling behavior and participation in the group. The women gossiped about each other's mothering abilities and by doing so defined and judged the status of women in the neighborhood. A woman was considered a "good woman" and given higher status if she was viewed as a good mother (i.e., if her children were fed and clothed properly). When a woman was considered a questionable mother, children were told to avoid her house.

A woman's status could change at any moment, depending on what the gossip was for that week. For example, Ña Maria was simultaneously pitied and derided. She was the newest to the neighborhood. She came following an emergency cesarean section, which resulted in the death of her 11th child. Her family was now destitute, because they were in debt to the hospital. Her health was extremely poor and she experienced a great deal of pain. She had five children under the age of 8. Physically, she could not do the labor needed to feed and clothe her children. Other children were told by their mothers not to frequent her house. The mothers may have also known that Ña Maria was not in the position to fulfill her othermother obligations at this point, so the children may have also been kept away so as not to be an extra burden.

Ña Maria's children would not suffer due to their economic hardship because the community would care for them. Yet some of the other mothers found this relationship to be confining due to its obligatory nature. They confided to me that at times they did not want to feed these kids; sometimes, they barely had enough food for their own families. They knew, however, that it was their duty to feed them. Although there was a hierarchy among the women, the children themselves were not allowed to suffer the consequences.

Similarly, Ña Carmen had been out of favor with many of the mothers for a few months because they thought she treated her teenage daughter poorly. After speaking with her, several of the mothers decided to make amends with her, and she was brought back into the group.

Inequality Is Reinforced

As noted previously, community caregiving is supported by an ideology that reinforces gender inequality because it is shaped by beliefs that women's caregiving is natural (Cancian and Oliker 2000). Moreover, economic inequality is associated with carework. Because women's time that is used for caregiving cannot be invested in activities that bring them wealth, power, and prestige, and market-based carework is not valued as the skilled labor that it is (Cancian and Oliker 2000; England and Folbre, this volume; Graham 1991), women are economically disadvantaged.

Communities of caregiving can also reinforce racial/ethnic and social class inequality by creating a sense of "we"-ness for those within the community versus those outside the community. Most families in Yvytu were mestizo, of both Spanish and Indian descent. However, just outside barrio Santa Teresa lived a family of "Indios" or Guaraní Indians, who were extremely poor compared to the mothers in this study. The children of this family attended the neighborhood school. Although this community of caregiving proved to be supportive for the women within its domain, this mother and her family were considered outsiders—physically, in that their house was located outside of town, and in terms of race/ethnicity. Thus, this woman and her family drew none of the benefits of the community.

Women's Power and Resistance in a
Community of Caregiving

The institutional value of the mothers' caregiving is worth very little; it is a job that is often not rewarded and always unpaid. However, within the context of the family, the neighborhood, and the community, its social value is enormous. Thus, women's social position in Latin America is ambiguous due to their ability to command some power at the interpersonal level by creating informal social groups with economic, social, and psychological benefits (Jelin 1990; Saffilios-Rothschild 1982). For Latin American women, oppression is not just about a lack of rights, but also includes other rights and identities not shared by men, particularly the capability of forming these networks of supportive relationships in the private sphere. As Jelin (1990:187) noted, "In this sphere lies the strength of the woman/mother, it is her specialty and it is here that the ambiguity of her oppression becomes apparent."

In Barrio Santa Teresa, mothers, godmothers, and othermothers developed networks of solidarity and mutual help through the workings of their daily life in the neighborhood. These mothers developed a community of caregiving to help protect themselves and their children from their oppressive environment. The community these women created provided resources and a location for the exchange of care, particularly child care, and became a possible site for women's political work.

In the domains of the family and community, we need to uncover women's hidden resistance practices against poverty and oppression. According to Jelin (1990:201), "In numerous insignificant daily and domestic chores, women developed a practice—often not accompanied by a concurrent reflection on the matter—of resistance and change." Thus, we need to study the daily life of peasant women in order to examine how the apparently trivial events are aspects of poor women's survival strategies and efforts to make things better for themselves and their children.

One prominent example of women's resistance derived from seemingly inconsequential events stands out. Earlier in this chapter, I mentioned an incident where I took a walk in the countryside alone and was later reprimanded by the mothers in my neighborhood. The mothers, their daughters, and I continued to discuss walking in the *campo*. Even though many of the women expressed their desire for walking, they felt it was not a luxury that their schedule could afford, nor did they think their husbands would approve of them leaving the neighborhood at all. Eventually, though, some of them began to suggest we walk together, accompanied by many children. I noticed on our first trip that the other mothers began collecting a particular plant that they used to make brooms. Each time we went, they gathered more broom material even though they did not need it. Under the guise of collecting broom materials, the mothers actively resisted their oppression and lack of mobility. Over time, we took these walks regularly, and more mothers and daughters went.

The mothers also employed cultural resistance through rituals (Jelin 1990). Unlike men, in rural Paraguay women rarely gather in groups; they are working in their homes most of the day and are not permitted to simply congregate in their free time, unless for religious activities. Many of the women of Barrio Santa Teresa did meet for the daily ritual of praying the rosary. This was one time during the day that they could say to their husbands, "I need to go out" and they would not interfere. Women are considered spiritually superior in cultures where *marianismo* dominates (Stevens 1973), so it is expected that women will engage in rituals that would enable them to fulfill their role as the spiritual head of the family.

The mothers also assemble when the statue of the Virgin Mary comes to town and is passed nightly from house to house. This special occasion is one of the few times that significant numbers of women convene in one location. It was shocking to me to see so many women gathered in one place. I wondered at first if someone had died, the only other time considerable numbers of women congregate. During the time when the statue of the Virgin is in town, women use this opportunity to cease their work and have ample justification to do so. Both men and women feel it is the woman's role to participate in these religious events. Some of the mothers in my neighborhood even left their homes completely to travel to *Caacupe* on the feast day of *La Virgen de Caacupe*. For some, this is the only time of the year that they leave the neighborhood at all, let alone unattended by their husbands. Women actively utilized their connection to spirituality and religious events in order to gather freely on these specific occasions.

Finally, the mothers educated their daughters, a bolder form of resistance. Although most of the mothers themselves had not completed primary education, they made sure that their daughters attended high school, even over sending some of their sons. Patrinos et al. (1995) found that a "specialization" of sorts occurs in families: Some of the children work for pay so that others can go to school and finish high school. Mothers orchestrate the school attendance of their children to ensure the education of their daughters where possible. Most of the mothers who had high school age daughters made sacrifices to send them to school. Ña Perla sent her oldest daughter to high school and was planning on sending her on to become a pharmacist. Ña Rubina moved into the pueblo for the express purpose of sending her daughters to high school. Ña Teresa often did not have the money to send her daughter Lucia to school, but borrowed from her *comadres* to ensure Lucia's continued attendance.

The mothers who were able to send their daughters to high school talked openly about their desire for their daughters to be educated. They were proud that their daughters were receiving an education and were not becoming mothers at a very young age. The mothers who were unable to send their daughters to high school were silent on this issue. Both Ña Rita and Ña Carmen had teenage daughters who became pregnant and needed to quit school in order to work to support their children. Ña Maria needed her teenage daughter to work in order to help with her 10 children. As noted earlier, teen pregnancy is often the symbol of womanhood in rural Paraguay, an area rife with poverty and lacking opportunities for women. For Ña Rita and Ña Carmen's daughters, the cultural tradition of becoming a woman through motherhood exerted more pressure than the need for education.

Conclusion

In sum, even with their complexities, othermothering and godmothering practices enable women to create communities of caregiving in their neighborhoods, which act as a shield against larger social inequalities. Within the neighborhood, this shield allows women to self-define status, regardless of the machismo of the larger culture. It gives women access to a wide range of resources, such as child care, health care, and food for their children in the face of poverty. Although gender inequality denigrates and alienates women, mothering in a community of caregiving empowers women by giving them economic, social, and psychological resources, and social status within their neighborhood.

The lives of these eight mothers in Paraguay tell a story that no statistics concerning poverty or oppression can tell. This story sharpens our focus on gender inequality, and reinforces Patricia Hill Collins's (2000) notion that power is not just about domination over others; it can be about creativity, resistance, and community. The othermothers and godmothers in this community of caregiving in rural Paraguay demonstrate just that.

The practices of godmothering and othermothering within a community of caregiving enable the mothers of Santa Teresa to fulfill their roles as mothers. Paraguayan women have found that communal childrearing makes an impossible job possible, or a dire situation bearable. The strength of women can be seen in the strength of their collective commitment to their children. No child in my neighborhood would go unfed, or remain improperly clothed. Because of the mothering practices described in this chapter, no children are left out; they are always tied into something bigger than they are, bigger than their family, and always slightly bigger than the constant lack that seemed to exist at every turn. In fact, that is the point: There is no individual family in the barrio, only the web of extended families spun by the mothers.

Notes

I would like to thank the following persons for their invaluable help in preparing this manuscript: Leslie Ashbaugh, Erik Foley, Betsy Fomon, Diane Gillespie, Becky Reed, Andrew London, Rebecca Reviere and the editors for their insightful comments and helpful critiques.

1. The name of the town has been changed.

2. All of the names of the women have been changed to protect their anonymity.

3. In Spanish, the masculine form of a plural noun can refer to both genders, or to men only. The feminine form of a plural noun refers to groups of women only. Thus, *compadres* refers to both men and women who serve as godparents, while *comadres* refers only to godmothers.

4. Mandioca root is a tuber similar to potato (it is also known as yucca). Mandioca root is a staple in the diets of poor Paraguyans.

Nurturing Babies, Protecting Men

The Unequal Dynamics of Women's Postpartum Caregiving Practices

Christa Kelleher and Bonnie Fox

*A*lthough caregiving takes a variety of forms in our society,[1] the responsibility for people's welfare still rests primarily with families. The privatization of basic caregiving—the fact that it is a private, family responsibility rather than a social, community responsibility—is a product of the adjustments people made to the development of a capitalist economy in the 19th century (Glenn 2000). As market production left the household, and the roles and responsibilities of the private and public spheres separated, women came to assume responsibility for childrearing (Coontz 1988; Davidoff and Hall 1987; Ryan 1981). In the 20th century, some aspects of caregiving moved to the market sector, but the continuing privatization of motherhood ensures that most essential forms of caregiving remain in the home under the purview of women. In turn, motherhood is at the heart of gender inequality in the labor market and in the home. It is surprising, given its importance, that relatively little research attention has been given to the process by which couples initially negotiate the gendered division of child care. This chapter focuses on the patterns that develop shortly after the birth of a child, to shed some light on the gendered division of caring work done in the household.

The failure of men in dual-earner couples to share household responsibilities and work is an ongoing concern for feminists (Hochschild 1989; Luxton 2001). Although much of the sociological research on this lopsided division of household work has either focused solely on housework or conflated housework and child care, some researchers empirically distinguish housework and child care. Research indicates that men are more likely to take on additional child care than housework when women take on paid work (Goldscheider and Waite 1991). Nevertheless, despite media images of involved fathers, there is a growing concern that most fathers continue to be much less involved with their babies than are mothers (LaRossa 1998; McMahon 1999). The common pattern of fathers' involvement is still that they "help" their partners with baby care and act as playmates to their babies (Cowan and Cowan 1992; Walzer 1998), while they focus primarily on breadwinning (Fox 1997).

This gendered division of parenting is important. Some research has indicated that early months of parenthood is particularly significant to the development of a gendered division of household labor (MacDermid, Huston, and McHale 1990; Perkins and DeMeis 1996; Rexroat and Shehan 1987). Because of the immediacy of babies' needs in the early postpartum period, patterns of care are negotiated very quickly. It is especially important, then, that the dynamics of the early post-partum period be carefully examined; they should help us identify how gendered patterns of parenting develop and promote gender inequalities in families.

Our interviews with women in the early postpartum period reveal that they were working to ensure not only the health and well-being of their babies but also the health and comfort of their partners—at the expense of their own needs. The pattern of women caring for men is surprising given the nature of the postpartum period. Most of the women we interviewed experienced the stresses typically associated with mothering a new baby. Many experienced "baby blues"[2] and anxiety; most seemed overwhelmed—as is common (Entwisle and Doering 1981; Taylor 1996).

Our description of this pattern of women caring for men follows a brief discussion of our methods. We consider the themes that emerged from women's discussions of their caregiving practices and their partners' involvement in newborn care. Their acceptance of men's limited and conditional participation and the sacrifice of their own needs are the two major themes. We conclude by suggesting some reasons underlying these gendered dynamics.

Data and Methods

This study is based on data from two independent but intersecting research projects: Bonnie Fox's study of first-time parents and Christa Kelleher's examination of postpartum care provided to women and newborns. Based on a combined total of 70 semistructured interviews with mothers living in greater Toronto, we rely on grounded theory in order to analyze women's thoughts and experiences. Most women in the study experienced vaginal birth in a hospital, and were at home on maternity leave serving as the primary caretaker of the infant at the time of the interview; in most cases, the women's partners returned to full-time employment shortly after the birth. Although the majority of women were Anglo-Canadian, middle class, married, and breastfeeding exclusively, the socioeconomic and ethnic/racial backgrounds of respondents varied to some extent.

Fox's study involved a series of in-depth interviews with first-time mothers and fathers, spanning the period from late in the pregnancy to the end of the first year of parenthood. Only the postpartum interviews with the women—occurring 2 to 4 weeks after the birth—were used in this chapter. Ten of these interviews took place in 1991 and 1992 in a pilot project, and 30 interviews were conducted in 1995 and 1996 in a larger project involving the same sets of questions. People were recruited for participation in the study through childbirth classes—some given by hospitals for a sizeable fee, some Lamaze classes that also were paid for, and others sponsored by the city's public health department that were free of charge. All of the women gave birth in the hospital; six of the women experienced cesarean births.

Nine of the 40 couples were working class (as defined by education and income); five of these working-class couples were living on very low incomes, as were four other couples in the study. Aside from social class, other differences were minimal because fluency in English was essential for participation in the study. Only two couples were immigrants from non-English-speaking countries. Most of the group was White; two of the women and one of the men were African Canadians—all with White partners. Finally, four couples were unmarried when first interviewed, and one of them remained unmarried a year after the baby's birth.

Kelleher's study included 30 respondents recruited primarily from a hospital postpartum unit, and took place in 2000. Semistructured interviews were conducted in the mother's home approximately 1 month after birth. Except for two women who gave birth at home, all other women gave birth vaginally in a Toronto hospital. All women were married or coupled. Twenty-two women were primiparae and eight were multiparae. Twenty women were Canadian or Anglo-Canadian, and 10 women were recent immigrants[3] to Canada. Twenty-two women spoke English as their first language and for eight women English was not their primary language. Six women may be considered working class based on their education and income and 24 were middle to upper class. Pseudonyms have been given to all respondents referred to in the following analysis.

Although we cannot claim that our sample is representative of women living in the greater Toronto area, the individuals who participated in our studies did not seem to be particularly unusual in terms of their birth experiences, relationships with their partners and families, or patterns of caregiving. The women's reactions to their birthing experiences ranged from very positive to very negative (in that they were angry, upset or both). A few had very easy births and others experienced very long, painful labors and deliveries, whereas most had experiences in between these extremes. All of the women were in need of recovery from a range of problems (from lack of sleep and physical exhaustion to damage due to surgery). Being home with a new baby was difficult, even stressful, for most of these women. As is typical in North America, despite their own need to recover, and despite the difficulties involved in learning to meet the needs of babies, these women usually were home alone for much of the day within 2 weeks of leaving the hospital (Rosenberg 1987; Taylor 1996). Further, most of the women in Fox's study (and several in Kelleher's study) experienced "baby blues," although these were less common among the relatively few who had substantial help and support (Fox and Worts 1999). Most important for the purposes of the analysis presented in this chapter, the gendered division of work and responsibility that typically emerges in the lives of heterosexual couples when they become parents developed for most of these couples (Cowan and Cowan 1992; Walzer 1998). There were exceptional couples too, however—and we discuss them as well.

Findings

Our main finding is that in spite of the heavy demands of early motherhood, and in spite of their own needs for recovery and help with their babies, most of these mothers worked to care for, and even protect, their partners. Further, women's protective behavior entailed the acceptance of men's limited and conditional participation in baby care. As a consequence, these women often sacrificed their own physical needs, particularly their need for rest, in order to safeguard men's well-being.

Protecting Dad

These women most commonly demonstrated their commitment to ensuring men's well-being by safeguarding men's ability to sleep. The majority of women we interviewed felt that it was inappropriate for their partners to be burdened with the baby's needs at night—and to lose sleep—when they had to go to work the next day. Therefore, most women expressed approval of nighttime arrangements that left them with full responsibility for the baby. For example, Stephanie's perspective invoked concepts of fairness and realistic expectations:

> In an ideal world your husband would get up in the night and sit and talk with you but that's not realistic. Because he has to get up. He's gone for long periods during the day so that's not fair. But of course it would be nice in the wee hours of the morning to have somebody get up and get you a drink . . . But I would never expect that of anybody.

Often women connected their protection of men's sleep to breastfeeding. Breastfeeding meant that women simply had to wake up at night: There was no alternative for feeding the baby unless pumped breast milk was available. Most women explained that it was impractical to have two people get up to address the baby's needs. For example, Eleanor asserted: "I don't see the point of both of us being up. No point in both of us being dog tired." In general, women accepted it as their duty to stay up with a crying baby or to address any other nighttime needs that arose; this meant that women were often in charge of diapering, burping, and settling the baby at night.

Further, most women were not at all critical of these nighttime arrangements. Many women explained that they had rejected men's offers of assistance, in order to ensure sufficient rest for the men. Pat said that her partner "was getting up in the night, but I kind of stopped that a little 'cause I don't want to go back to sleep, so what's the point of both of us being up and being tired? So I've been letting him sleep." Leah referred to her husband's participation as a kind of privilege. What seems to be at issue here, in fact, is Leah's weaker position relative to the privileged position of her breadwinner partner (Luxton 1980). This father routinely got up with his older children at night and was as helpful as he could be with the baby. Leah stated that her baby "doesn't often stay up, you know, crying for no reason [but when that does happen] he'll take her. That's the thing. I sort of feel he's the one who doesn't get a chance to nap the next day. But I don't like to abuse that privilege." Some women approached the issue of men's help with babies' nighttime needs in terms of a rational, cost-benefit analysis, implicitly acknowledging the importance of men's breadwinning. Rachel described the pros and cons of waking up her husband as follows:

> I can't have him not sleeping when he has to go to work—that's number one . . . Even though I think he should do with a little less sleep . . . I'd much

rather have him be stable and healthy so that he can help me when I really need it . . . Before I wake him up, I weigh the pros and cons. It's funny how strategic I have to be.

The possibility of taking naps during the day was another reason why women protected men's sleep. Most of these women were absolutely exhausted, and sleep deprived, most of the time. How much sleep they could get was a major issue with them all. Of course, most women agreed that the only appropriate time to nap was when the baby was sleeping, so their own naps depended on the baby's sleeping practices. Yet very few women napped during the day. In general, they seemed too pressured by other responsibilities to allow themselves to nap. Most women cooked and cleaned while their babies napped. Leah's remark indicated that household responsibilities competed with her need to nap, as they did for other women. She said: "But now if I get a nap, which is like top priority on my list, lots doesn't get done in the day." In response to the interviewer's interjection, "And that's okay with you?," Leah replied, "I'm trying to make it be okay with me."

The underlying assumption for most women was that being home with the baby entailed doing housework (Fox 1997). In Eileen's words: "I see it as that's what part of me being at home is about. Taking care of the baby but also taking care of the house." Other women's comments indicated the need they felt to do housework rather than rest. Alternatively, some women suggested that naps wasted valuable time that could be better spent on other activities that didn't involve household chores, such as taking a walk or reading.

Even though most women said that they felt it was important to care for the house as well as the baby, many women spoke about conscious efforts to recognize that they could not do everything on their own and without some help. When asked what advice they could offer women about the initial period at home with a newborn, women nearly consistently replied that there was no need to try to be "superwoman."

Yet the leniency women tried to grant themselves when it came to doing housework and other non-baby-related activities seemed to present a serious challenge for women who felt pressure to get it all done anyway. Our data demonstrated that there was a dissonance about trying to focus solely on baby care while household chores simultaneously demanded women's attention. Although most women argued that it was important to limit one's activities and chores and rest whenever possible, they found it extremely difficult to accomplish this objective. Arguing that mothers should take whatever help they are offered, Joan advised:

> Because a lot of mothers sort of feel that they want to do it themselves. Here I am giving advice and I don't even take my own advice but I didn't rest and I should of . . . I felt very weak and as I told you, I ran a fever. I thought I was going to collapse. It was my own fault. I was up and down the stairs. I was up and down the stairs like fifteen, twenty times a day. Too many times.

Joan's outlook on handling the demands of the early postpartum period was shared by many women in the study. The tension that women faced—the pressure to address both home and baby needs while simultaneously trying to accept letting some of it go—is a consequence of the combination of privatized mother-work (and housework) and pervasive ideologies of "intensive mothering" (Hays 1996). The privatization of carework and dominant ideologies heighten expectations about the proper care of children, and put tremendous demands on mothers. The isolation associated with privatized caregiving compounds the pressure: It leaves women home alone all day to provide child care with very limited support. It also carries the message that all household work is women's responsibility.

The reality (and the contradiction), however, is that there is a limit to what any woman can do. Nevertheless, in this culture, assistance seems like a dream. Also, taking naps often seemed like a dream for many women. Alex described how "my mother will come over sometimes and take [my two year old] for a walk and [the baby] will be sleeping and I can take a nap and that's like a dream. I love that." The fact that new mothers accept all the responsibilities that they do and sacrifice their own needs in the attempt to fulfill them—in spite of the fact that they cannot fulfill them—is another indication of the privilege men have as breadwinners.

In lieu of substantial help, women more commonly worked on trying to make their nighttime experiences better. For example, one woman breastfed at night, but would not burp the baby or change the diaper (unless it was soiled). More commonly, women breastfed in bed, which allowed them to sleep as needed.

In contrast were the couples who had a clear sense that night duties should be shared by both parents. In the interests of promoting men's participation at night, these couples frequently employed a routine in which women were in charge of feeding and men were in charge of changing or burping. Some couples explicitly addressed each other's sleeping needs. One woman reported that she and her husband took turns sleeping on the side of the bed closest to the baby's bassinette so that the person who was less tired would be the one to get up to address the baby's needs.

Some men in the study did not feel "excused" from helping with the baby at night because of their daytime work commitments. Usually these were the men who were generally more likely to do housework and child care. Often this more egalitarian pattern was a product of women consistently pushing their partners to be involved. Sometimes, men were very involved in baby care because they felt that their partners had been through a lot (e.g., a difficult birth experience with lasting physical problems). For a few couples with lower incomes the baby was the primary focus of the couple's lives—and seemed to reflect a sense of achievement. In these cases, men were more likely to be involved in baby care.

Accepting Dad's Limits

Although women perceived their relationship to their baby to be founded on the baby's complete dependence, they referred to men's participation in the baby's life in much different terms. When the mothers we interviewed discussed how men interacted with their babies, they frequently alluded to the boundaries and contingencies of their partners' participation. In fact, generally, men were involved in baby care only in limited and conditional ways when they were home.

Several mothers remarked that their partners were not completely involved or comfortable with certain baby care tasks, such as diapering and soothing. As Claire explained: "He will prepare the bottle. He doesn't like the diapers."

In explaining men's circumscribed involvement, there was a common invocation of the physical attributes of babies and of men: The fragility of babies and the "rough" or "large" hands of men seemed to conjure up feelings of fear and anxiety in men. Anna stated: "He says 'uh I'm so rough I don't want to hurt them' and this and that. So he's a little nervous at this stage." Another physical condition identified as a factor in men's limited involvement was simply that men did not have breasts. A mother of two, Antoinette, explained how she thought "most men feel helpless because they don't have breasts. So they're just like 'here, here's the baby. Go to your mom. I don't have the equipment you need so.'"

Aside from references to physical characteristics, women at times mentioned that their partners didn't like to change diapers or didn't diaper properly. For example, Mary said that "he knows how to change the diapers but not too good. So he will wake me up to change his diaper. He won't change poo yet, but he is getting there." That men's dislike of changing diapers could excuse them from the work demonstrates the option of choice afforded men in the context of early parenting. However, only a few women indicated that men didn't diaper properly or needed improvement.

There were other ways in which men's involvement in baby care was limited, often conditional, and thus fragmented. Sarah Anne claimed that although her husband would hold the baby, he often did so for only five to ten minutes, before offering the baby back to her for feeding. She stated: "He'll hold him 5 to 10 minutes and he'll think he's hungry. [And I will say] I don't think he is. I just fed him." Sarah Anne's experience was shared by other women.

Another example of men's segmented caregiving was offered by a woman who expressed disappointment with her husband's lack of interest in and commitment to the baby. Joan's story highlights how different her husband's assumptions were than hers about what needed to be done when feeding the baby a bottle or giving the baby a bath. She contended that his expectation of bottle feeding did not include cleaning and preparing the bottle. Similarly, she explained that he didn't recognize all of the work associated with bathing: He assumed that the water, soap, and other bath necessities would be ready for him when he bathed the baby. This kind of compartmentalized approach to caring for a newborn may be distinguished from the approach most women took—which involved full responsibility for meeting the infant's needs. The different notions of responsibility for the baby underlie the gender inequalities that characterized early parenting patterns in our study.

Despite these gender inequities, women typically expressed satisfaction with their partner's level of involvement with the baby. This satisfaction may be a product of the fact that women defined men's "bonding" with the baby as a priority, or at least more important than men's caregiving. This conceptualization of father involvement had the effect of reducing women's expectations of men's participation in baby *care*. In short, the father–baby relationship became understood in terms of interaction rather than caregiving. The logic seemed to be that although the baby's physical needs could be served by anyone (except for breast-feeding), the father–child bond required dad.

Not only did the father–child relationship take priority over dad's caregiving, but many of these new mothers went to some lengths to create opportunities for their partners to bond with their baby. Some women seemed to be actively engaged in "constructing" the father–child relationship. Moreover, the language employed by women on the topic of men's participation in infant care reflected a common belief that women should approach the baby–father relationship carefully. Thus, several women went out of their way to create a comfortable atmosphere for their partner in order to facilitate the bonding process. For instance, some women made sure the baby was fed, changed, and settled before handing the baby to dad. Women also spoke about the importance of fostering men's involvement in ways that were comfortable for men. Sue applied the notion of a "comfort zone" to the relationship between the baby and her husband. She explained that she wanted her husband to participate to the extent that he wanted:

> There was no pressure there at all. I just wanted him to get involved if he sort of felt comfortable. As I said he had never been around babies at all. He's just so good with her . . . I try really hard to not be one of those mothers that always has the right answer. He sort of found his comfort zone. He will spend time with her when I need time to myself.

There is another possible explanation of these new mothers' acceptance of their partners' limited involvement in baby care. Many women indicated the belief that the limits to men's caregiving were temporary, that their partners would become more involved in the future. Annie summed up the expectations of many of the women interviewed: "I know he will graduate to dressing her and to changing her diaper. I'm sure."

Because the dominant belief among women was that they were to serve as primary caretakers of their babies and that men were secondary caregivers, it seemed acceptable for women to confer on men the ability to accept or reject baby care tasks. As a consequence, men were able to compartmentalize their caregiving. In simple terms, men chose how extensively to be involved in meeting their baby's needs.

As is common, fathers were seen as helpers to women, who expected to both request and delegate types of assistance (Cowan and Cowan 1992; Walzer 1998). Because many of the men did not take initiative in assisting with the baby, but helped when asked, it was women who shouldered the burden of requesting men's help. Further, women often seemed calculating in their decisions about when to ask for men's assistance—and did so only when it seemed necessary. Women identified specific circumstances that caused them to solicit men's help, such as extensive periods of newborn crying or fussiness. Additionally, women who had other children besides their newborn were more likely to ask for men's help. In the end, these new mothers seemed to consider men's willingness to help to be the sign of their commitment to shared infant caregiving.

Even though many women spoke of the limitations associated with their partners' involvement with the newborn, a number of women characterized their partners as "sharers." These men took part in all baby-related tasks except for breastfeeding, were more likely to take initiative than the other dads, and often expressed a desire to be involved. Joanna said her husband "completely took care of the baby for the first three days pretty much and was amazing at it. Now that we're home we share everything that way too. He probably changes as many diapers as I do." As was true of the men who participated in nighttime care, the men who acted as sharers often were also more engaged in housework than were other men.

Although the reasons why some men are more active in baby care are complex and varied, time availability seemed to have a clear impact on men's levels of involvement. Men who were not working at all, were only working part-time, or were working from home were somewhat more likely to take an active part in caregiving. Additionally, the physical incapacity of several women served as the impetus for some men to share parenting. Finally, some women's active encouragement of their partner's involvement mattered.

In addition to the term *sharer*, some women referred to men's role as reliever or soother for the baby. Although providing relief did not necessarily mean a more equitable division of caregiving, dealing with the baby in this particular way is significant. Diane explained that her husband was the "big reliever" whose voice and presence seemed to soothe the baby.

Overall, although some couples invoked the notion of shared parenting, the majority of fathers engaged in baby care in limited and conditional ways. This kind of approach to parenting in the early postpartum period left many women unable to address their own physical needs. Even the most fundamental body maintenance routines were often neglected in the weeks following birth.

Women's Physical Needs: Secondary at Best

In their accounts of the postpartum period, women often highlighted the fact that their bodies were still recovering from the birth and adjusting to the demands of breastfeeding, the strains of reduced rest, and the physical labor associated with newborn care. Most women were experiencing problems that caused a range of feelings, from discomfort to significant pain. Nipple problems due to breastfeeding, perineum injury usually due to episiotomies, and uterine pain associated with breastfeeding were some of the key problems. The limited nature of men's carework must be considered in light of women's needs to recover and adjust to new responsibilities. The physical condition of mothers is one of the reasons why their practice of protecting and serving male partners necessitates critical analysis.

One first-time mother, Tanya, described her condition as follows: "I feel quite overwhelmed. I'm in so much pain. I didn't realize it would take this long to recover. I'm so overwhelmed with the physical aspects of getting through a day." When Ruth reflected on her condition in the days after leaving the hospital, she concluded:

I'm amazed at what I did—when I came home from the hospital, how I functioned. I was such an idiot. I should have demanded so much more of him and I think he was an idiot not to realize; I mean I have stitches in my perineum and my body was a total aching thing, and my breasts were broken and scabbed.

Not every woman had physical problems in the early postpartum period. Some women mentioned that they did not experience much postpartum discomfort at all. Common to all of these new mothers, however, was physical fatigue, and a sense that having a newborn involved heavy physical demands. Additionally, at least the first-time mothers were almost all overwhelmed by the sense of heavy responsibility.

Given the extent to which women put their babies' and partners' needs before their own, it might be expected that women were unable to take care of their most basic needs—especially their capacity to rest—in the first month after birth. Women frequently expressed concern and frustration about the difficulty in getting enough sleep in those weeks following childbirth. They made repeated references to sleep deprivation and lack of sufficient rest. When asked what it felt like to be a mother, Antoinette said: "Tired. Mostly tired. To describe a new mother is tired." Melanie referred to her "downtime—when I started to feel stressed about the fact that I'm so tired. Lack of sleep that started to build up." For women who had to care for a young child or children in addition to their newborn, sleep deprivation had a heightened impact. In general, women discussed their forfeiture of sleep as a part of the newborn caregiving experience that was expected and accepted. Still, several women commented that they hadn't realized—until they lived it—the degree to which they would suffer from a lack of rest after birth.

Although sleep deprivation represented the most common way in which women ignored their own physical needs, other bodily needs were also neglected during the early postpartum period because women believed that the baby required their full attention. Eating well, taking showers, and otherwise using the washroom were other activities that became difficult to do with the new baby. Eileen confirmed this common sentiment: "All I know is that I barely have a spare moment. If you can have a shower, it's a good day. If you get your hair washed, it's a good day." Women explained that food preparation became hard and that having a shower or a moment alone in the washroom was a luxury. As a result, women's basic needs were often attended to only when there was someone else available to look after the baby or when the baby was asleep.

Women spoke of reconciling the challenges they faced in meeting their own body's needs in two specific ways. The first involved recognizing the need to address personal needs before taking care of the baby. Mary Jo explained: "We just haven't been eating very well and I was really feeling it. That's when I made a commitment. I'm not going to sit down to nurse unless I'm prepared. Not doing things like nursing when I really have to pee first." Other women made similar decisions, usually on realizing the extent to which meeting their own needs was connected with meeting their babies' needs. Nevertheless, just as sacrifice of their needs was a product of privatized mothering, so too this coping strategy involved women relying solely on themselves to solve the problem.

Second, there was a strong sense that even though women were unable to satisfy some of their body's needs during the day, there would be relief provided by their partners once they returned home from work (and additional relief on the weekends). This strategy underlines again the significance of men's limited involvement in baby care.

Discussion

In the early postpartum period, mothers seem to engage in a continuum of practices to protect and accommodate their male partners. That is, women varied in the extent to which they subordinated their needs in order to protect their partners. Representing one extreme, Jane summed up her entire first year of motherhood as follows: "I spent the whole year trying to make [her husband's] life easy." Most women did something less extreme in the early postpartum period: They tried to protect their husbands' lives from disruption, and to preclude the need for them to make sacrifices. Related to women's protection of men seemed to be a belief that family life should not only be undisturbed by parenthood, but also that it should be even more rewarding and pleasant than it had been before the baby's birth.

Why did women feel compelled to engage in caregiving practices that prioritized men's needs as well as babies'? Although there are many reasons, the fact that the responsibility for babies is privatized in North America—that is, held by the parents alone, with very minimal support from the larger community—is key here, we think, and seems to have two main effects. First, the situation impresses on mothers the fact that they are responsible for the well-being of a helpless and totally dependent human being. Additionally, standards of infant caregiving idealize individualized care arrangements based on intensive, and somewhat exclusive, mother–baby relationships. A common reaction among these women seemed to involve proving to themselves that they could "do it all." Although women spoke about their partner's assistance with the baby, they consistently focused on the importance of their own ability to handle and care for their baby, especially after the short period of time their partners were on leave from work. Of course, women's limited access to postpartum support and resources required that women address their babies' needs, to a large extent, on their own.

Second, in a society where the responsibility for children is privately held, in order to properly meet the demands of "intensive mothering," mothers are dependent on having a partner who provides for the household financially. Thus, caregivers become dependents. The fact that women felt that the man's welfare was important to the financial security of the household—even women who were on leave from their paid jobs—was clear in many of the interviews. Accommodation to and protection of men's well-being seemed integral to ensuring financial security in the home.

Additionally, at the level of interpersonal dynamics, many women seemed to be actively constructing the father role for their partners, and sacrificing their own needs in the process. Women's active construction of the father role was motivated by several factors: Men are critical in their breadwinning capacity, central to the creation of "family," and they still have a certain level of choice about the extent of their involvement in child care.

Women's discussions of newborn care revolved around the notion that it was important for them to be in charge, ready and able to care for their baby, because the baby was completely dependent on them. In terms of how women should act toward their babies, Deva explained: "Every minute, every second just look after them. Don't leave them and say I'm tired and walk away." In turn, a mother of two, Anna, summarized her position: "I knew it was going to be rough. You knew what you were getting into. One step at a time. I got myself into this position. I need to do this on my own." Men provided relief, a rest, an opportunity to take a break, or a helping hand, but generally baby care was considered to be the woman's burden. Several women were clear that it should be just this way. Some (like Anna) insisted that the baby was a woman's own responsibility, a responsibility that came from making a decision to have a child.

At the same time, most women felt that the father should take an active role in baby care, and some thought their partners did too little. Other women felt that the responsibilities of parenthood should be fully shared. Some men were very involved in newborn care. Most of these men had a pattern of significant involvement in household work before the birth. For some couples, a nearly egalitarian pattern was a product of a commitment to feminist ideals, and conscious struggle toward an equitable arrangement. For these and some other couples, women often systematically pushed their partners to take on more work and responsibility. In other cases, circumstances surrounding the birth pushed men to assume responsibility for the baby (and sometimes the home). For instance, women in most need of recovery following childbirth were more likely to have partners who were very actively involved with the baby (Fox and Worts 1999).

More usually, assuming baby care was largely their responsibility, women acted in ways that conserved the limited resources to which they had access after birth. Their comments indicated that they tended to utilize resources only under particular conditions rather than routinely. This strategy indicates again that women sought a level of independence from their partners, as well as from outside the family unit. However, it also underscores the extent to which women felt that the additional care resources available to them were constrained, and needed to be rationed and conserved because they would not be replenished.

Compounding the effect of women's financial dependence was the common assumption that mothers needed their partners. In Fox's sample, virtually every woman expressed the belief early on that they "could never make it" through the first few months of motherhood without their partner. These women were convinced that they needed their partner for much more than financial support. This conviction may seem contradictory to the previously mentioned ideal of independence to which women adhered. However, the help men gave was experienced as essential to these women. Women's needs from their partners ranged from concrete forms of assistance like help with baby care in the evening to something as immaterial as acknowledgment of the hard work motherhood entailed, and recognition of how well they were doing as mothers. That most women were alone for much of the day, with all the responsibility that motherhood entails, ironically underlined the need for their partner's tangible and material support.

In short, the privatization of motherhood enhanced women's dependence on men. Given that there is so little support for mothers in this society, and women are home alone most of the day, women feel they need to learn to handle things on their own. At the same time, this privatized responsibility forces women to be dependent on men and therefore accommodating to their interests, because the reality of the situation leaves women scarcely any other choice.

Furthermore, in light of men's *choice* about the extent of their involvement with their baby, and women's need for various kinds of support from their partners, many women seemed to feel it necessary to draw the man into active involvement with the baby. In a sense, they "constructed" the man's role as father (Fox 1998, Walzer 1998). These efforts occurred at considerable cost to the women engaging in them, and protecting the man was one of those costs—because it meant they sacrificed their own needs in the process.

Drawing the man into active involvement with the baby involved two strategies. One was to directly create times for the man to be with the baby—times that were likely to be pleasant. These women seemed to assume the fragility of the process by which fathers "bond" with their babies, and they were leaving nothing to chance. Some women set aside certain activities for the father; others consciously chose to encourage the father's play with his baby, rather than pressing him to do housework.

The other strategy for creating the man's involvement with his baby was indirect. It involved the women's efforts to create a pleasant "family life," a project that takes shape more clearly in the months after the baby is born. In short, many women were beginning to take time to set the scene for pleasant family interaction. Some women did the housework during the week to free the weekends for "family time." Others concentrated their daily homemaking efforts on preparing a good meal—feeding the baby beforehand—so that everyone would be able to relax and enjoy it. In addition, women planned visits to relatives, and other social events that they saw as family-creating occasions. These efforts by women to create "family" are significant for several reasons. Most obviously, they involve extra work for the woman, and loss of potential help by the man (e.g., with housework), and thus enhance gender inequality in these relationships. Moreover, the conscious efforts to create family evidence both a concern about drawing the man into responsibilities that (with a baby) seem to have fairly few rewards and a desire to create some of those rewards—in the form of a happy family life.

In conclusion, the picture of parenting that emerged from our interviews is one in which mom does most of the work while dad has the opportunity to play with baby on returning from work and spend quality time with the family on the weekend. Although men often engaged in fragmented baby care, women hardly ever had an opportunity to think about the baby in this way. This was the case especially at night when breastfeeding was so often tied to other needs such as diapering, burping, and soothing. So although men faced no obstacles to providing segmented care, women accepted responsibility for most nighttime needs, thereby connecting breastfeeding to other activities. This gendered pattern of care inextricably linked baby's needs to men's needs because making the home environment comfortable and enticing for men (and creating family) entailed accepting the limitations of men's involvement. Thus, women were disadvantaged by making themselves responsible for ensuring the health and well-being of all family members except for themselves. Additionally, women felt that it was important to protect their partners, whose breadwinning was important during this time of transition. The prioritization of the breadwinner in this way reflected a clear hierarchy of work done by women and work done by their partners. As other researchers have documented, breadwinners' needs tend to take priority in families (Luxton 1980), and unpaid caregiving work is considerably devalued, both ideologically and materially (Glenn 2000; see also England and Folbre, this volume). Thus, women's postpartum practices aimed to protect the person perceived as the legitimate and essential worker in the family.

In short, women's accordance of secondary status to their own essential needs is a practice that exists within a structural framework of limited postpartum resources, as well as societal expectations about mothers. Although it is striking that women were accepting of men's limited and conditional involvement in caregiving activities, it is not surprising given the social conditions that women face after childbirth. The process of gendered parenting that develops following childbirth and the implications for women's personal well-being call for a radical reconceptualization of the valuation and expectations of infant caregiving as well as a transformation of societal resources for those engaged in infant care.

Notes

Fox's study was made possible by a grant from the Social Sciences and Humanities Research Council, and several General Research Grants from the University of Toronto. She thanks Diana Worts and Sherry Bartram for excellent research assistance, and Rebecca Fulton, Ann Bernardo, and Elizabeth Walker for careful transcribing. She also owes heartfelt thanks to the 40 couples and one single mother who spent so much of their time telling her about their changing lives. Kelleher's project was supported by grant R03 HS10790 from the Agency for Healthcare Research and Quality. She is grateful to all of the women who shared their experiences and insights. She thanks Katrin Križ for helpful comments on earlier drafts of this chapter.

1. We are referring to North America, with a focus on Canada.

2. By "baby blues" we mean the short-lived emotional volatility common to North American mothers several days after they deliver their baby.

3. Recent immigrants are defined as individuals entering Canada no more than a few years prior to the time of the interview.

Defining "Good" Child Care

Hegemonic and Democratic Standards

Francesca M. Cancian

A 3-year-old girl starts to take away the doll that a 2-year-old girl is holding, and the younger child starts to cry. What should the mother or care-worker do? Tell the older child to stop? Distract her? Move away and let the children resolve the conflict?

According to the dominant or hegemonic standard of child care in the United States today, the careworker should use indirect methods of control, like distraction. Direct methods of control such as telling the child to stop or restraining her would be labeled as "authoritarian" by most experts in child development; such methods would undermine the child's autonomy and independence, they would assert.

"Good" child care, according to the hegemonic standard, means providing children with authoritative control (as opposed to authoritarian or permissive control) and giving them responsive nurturance (warmth that responds to the child's cues). This standard is part of the dominant values and ideals about families and relationship that have been documented by many scholars (Bellah et. al. 1985; Cancian 1987; Skolnick 1991). As Karen Pyke stated, in contrast "to the traditional family systems of many cultures, contemporary American family ideals stress democratic rather than authoritarian relations, individual autonomy, psychological well-being, and emotional expressiveness" (Pyke 2000:241).

A major problem with the hegemonic standard of care is that it reinforces inequality. White, affluent Euro-Americans tend to accept the hegemonic standard, because it fits their values and social situations. Nonelite groups are more likely to "deviate" from the standard and emphasize obedience and duty, as I show in this chapter. Thus, according to the hegemonic standard, White, middle-class Euro-Americans are judged to be better parents than working-class people or people of color. Carework researchers have avoided developing explicit standards of good care, largely because hegemonic standards of care typically reinforce inequality. However, explicit standards of care are essential to carework research and advocacy, I argue.

In this chapter, I first discuss why standards of care are necessary. Then I consider why standards tend to be oppressive, and suggest some remedies. I critically evaluate the current hegemonic standard of care for children and the research in child development that legitimates this standard. Finally, I present guidelines for moving toward less oppressive standards of care. My analysis focuses on care for young, preschool children, and includes both unpaid family care and paid care.

The Dilemma of Standards of Care

Hegemonic standards of child care, like most aspects of the dominant culture, tend to reinforce existing hierarchies of class, race/ethnicity, gender, nationality, and sexual orientation. So why should carework researchers and advocates develop standards of good care, because most of us are committed to reducing inequality and validating the perspectives of diverse groups and cultures, especially those that are less privileged?

Why We Need Standards

Explicit standards of care are necessary because most carework researchers conceptualize care giving as a skilled practice requiring knowledge and training, not as a natural emanation of femininity (Abel and Nelson 1990; Cancian and Oliker 2000; Carrington 1999; Meyer 2000). We emphasize skill in order to raise the social value of caring. Because caring is skilled work, we argue, it deserves respect and appropriate pay (Cancian and Oliker 2000; England 1992; Foner 1994). Skill assumes explicit criteria for discriminating between better and worse care. If caring is skilled work, then there must be standards of care.

Another reason for developing standards of care is that researchers and advocates need to be explicit and self-critical about their own standards of care. We need to correct the tendency to covertly impose our own deeply felt beliefs on others. People like myself and most carework researchers—highly educated, articulate professional women, often with positive experiences of psychological therapy—tend to value verbal responsiveness and empathic talk about feelings more than people from other backgrounds. It is easy to simply assume that everyone is like us and to evaluate the care practices that we study according to our particular perspective (see for example Noddings 1984). For example, research on hospital care often criticizes the medical model of care for ignoring patients' feelings and individual needs and overemphasizing medical procedures, but many patients support the medical model as the best standard of care (Larson and Dodd 1991). Researchers and advocates need to explicitly address this conflict and examine the validity of their own standards.

Finally, shared standards of care are necessary for setting public policies designed to help children and families. The participation of carework researchers and advocates in public debates about care giving is needed to promote attention to issues of social justice and diversity. Public discourse on carework and families is dominated by conservative politicians, and by doctors and experts in child development who promote the current hegemonic standard of child care (Pyke 2000). The involvement of carework researchers and advocates in setting standards of care would contribute to challenging and replacing the hegemonic standard.

Why Carework Researchers Avoid Standards

Despite the need for developing standards of care, carework researchers typically avoid this issue. The main reason, I believe, is that standards have historically been used to oppress the relatively powerless (Abramovitz 1988; Ahn 1994). For centuries, poor and immigrant families and families of color have been punished, scrutinized, and demeaned in the name of promoting "good" child care. They have had their children taken away, because they support alternative standards, because of racist assumptions that their family patterns are inferior, and because they lack the resources to meet their own standards of good care.

The history of child protection and child welfare in the United States documents how dominant standards of good care translate into oppression of poor and non-Euro-American people. Linda Gordon's study of child protection in Boston from 1880 to 1960 showed how "child protection" meant that poor Italian and Irish immigrant families were much more likely than native-born families to have their children taken away. Caseworkers "saw cruelty to children as a vice of inferior classes and cultures which needed correction and 'raising up' to an 'American'standard" (Gordon 1988:28).

Contemporary child welfare shows a similar bias against the poor and people of color, along with the provision of protection and assistance. The great majority of children in foster care and in the child welfare system are from poor and minority families (Barth et al. 1994; Courtney 1994). Forty percent of the children in out-of-home care in the United States were African-American in the early 1990s, while African-American children were only about 15% of the national total (Brown and Bailey-Etta 1997). Some of the children in the welfare system are physically or sexually abused and need protection. However, neglect, not abuse, is the usual grounds for removing children from their families. A large random-sample study of all children in foster care in California found that two-thirds of the children were removed from their homes because of neglect or caretaker absence or incapacity; 27% were removed because of abuse (Courtney 1994).

Neglect is strongly linked to poverty. A national incidence study of child abuse and neglect in the 1990s found that the rate of child neglect for families with incomes below $15,000 was 9 times higher than average, and the rate of abuse was 4.5 times higher (Sherman 1994). The child welfare system must decide whether the child is the victim of intentional neglect or of poverty. "Judging that situation can unleash the forces of racial and middle-class prejudice," observed Renny Golden (1997). "Too often it is not the actual family that is being 'saved' but the ideal of the white middle-class nuclear family" (Golden 1997:18). Criteria for neglect charges and the loss of one's children include failure to get immunizations for children, and poor hygiene, nutrition, or clothing; these are conditions that most families would probably avoid if they could afford to. Denise Plunkett, a social worker in charge of infants who are wards of the state in Chicago, said, "The finding *neglect* on a mother's part is just another word for impoverished. Amongst the other terrors a poor family faces, the state could take your kid" (quoted in Golden 1997:47). Racial bias also makes parents of color more vulnerable to judgments of child abuse than middle-class White parents. For example, hospitals tend to over report African-Americans and Hispanics and underreport Caucasians (Ahn 1994; Hampton and Newberger 1985). In sum, child protection in the past and present offers many examples of how standards of care can be used to reinforce inequality.

Carework researchers avoid the issue of standards, not only because standards tend to oppress poor people and people of color, but also because they tend to oppress women.   Many feminists have examined the sexist implications of hegemonic standards of good mothering (Ehrenreich and England 1978; Hays 1996; Margolis 1984; Silva 1996; Stacey 1998). Standards of child care have played a large role in maintaining the gendered division of labor for carework, which is a cornerstone of gender inequality. Parenting standards typically place very high demands on women's time, energy and skills. The demands placed on fathers for hands-on care are much lighter. As a result, women have less opportunity than men to pursue well-paid jobs, leisure, or other individual goals. Women are also burdened with more guilt and anxiety about being inadequate caregivers. For example, research on children's needs for attachment with their mothers fueled the belief that mothers of young children needed to be home full-time, a dominant belief in the United States until the 1960s (Cancian 1987; Skolnick 1991).

In sum, standards of good child care typically reinforce sexism, and contribute to the oppression of poor people, immigrants, and people of color. Yet standards are necessary. This leads us to the question: How can the oppressive nature of standards of care be avoided or mitigated?

Causes of Oppressive Standards and Possible Remedies

Structural or neo-Marxist theories clarify the causes of oppressive standards. Structural theories assume that the dominant culture tends to reflect and reinforce economic and political inequalities. In Marx's words, "the ideas of the ruling class are in every epoch the ruling ideas" (1972:136). According to this perspective (in simplified form), dominant cultural beliefs and practices are shaped by those who own and control economic enterprises and those who shape the policies of the state, in conjunction with managers and professionals who produce knowledge and culture. These elite groups have the resources to disseminate their beliefs much more successfully than others. They direct the mass media and train the experts. The beliefs of other groups are either ignored or are defined as peculiar, deficient or even disgusting. Elites maintain and justify their power and privilege by portraying dominated groups as less deserving, less capable, or less human. This logic justifies the status quo, which gives the elite more money and privilege.

The Marxist image of a monolithic, hegemonic culture that reflects the perspective of a unified ruling class does not fit contemporary social reality. Social movements challenge dominant beliefs and subgroups within the elite disagree. The socialist and egalitarian ideals of many carework researchers and other social scientists exemplify the divisions within the elite. Nonetheless, the dominant standard of child care continues to justify the elite and stigmatize others.

Scientific expertise is an important part of cultural domination in setting standards of care. Experts often make recommendations that are not strongly supported by evidence but reflect their own elite status. Researchers themselves typically come from elite backgrounds, and academic and professional institutions have long been dominated by affluent white Euro-Americans. So it is not surprising that most research on child care has favored the values and perspective of the elite, as I document in the next section of this chapter, even though some scientific research challenges the elite.

Another important part of cultural domination in setting standards of child care is ignoring the negative impacts of economic and political inequality on children's well-being, and focusing only on the impact of parents or other child-care providers (McLoyd 1990; Ogbu 1981). Ignoring the effects of poverty is especially pernicious in the United States, where the level of child poverty is the highest of all developed countries, because of the low level of government-funded programs (Gauthier 1996). Poverty has strong, negative effects on childhood, ranging from low weight at birth, and lower achievement in school and in tests of cognitive ability, to poor physical and mental health in adolescence and higher rates of illegal activities (Burton et al. 1998; Miller and Korenman 1994; National Academy of Sciences, 1993; Smith, Brooks-Gunn, and Clebanov 1997).

Child care studies typically ignore poverty and other "macro" or structural variables such as poor employment prospects, poor schools, dangerous neighborhoods, and rebellious peer cultures. Researchers measure children's performance and parent's childrearing, and fail to measure structural factors. Therefore, when they find differences in children's performance, they conclude that nonelite children have problems because of the inadequate childrearing methods of their parents; they blame the victim (Ogbu 1981). Social programs to assist children also focus on "at-risk" parents, typically low-income women of color, and teach them "the right way" to care (Olds et al. 1997). The impact of the wider environment usually is given little attention. These programs cover up the harmful effects of poverty, and reinforce the demeaning assumption that nonelite caregivers need to be taught how to care by the elite.

How can we remedy these powerful forces leading to oppressive standards of child care? Respecting the childrearing standards of diverse communities is one necessary step toward creating more democratic standards. Child-care researchers need to begin their projects with an attitude of respect for existing standards within the community they are studying. This attitude is common among ethnographers in anthropology and sociology. An ethnographer typically assumes that what people are doing makes sense to them, and is adaptive to local conditions in some ways; the ethnographer's task is to realize that she or he doesn't yet understand what is going on, and to observe and learn, not judge (Lofland and Lofland 1995). The ethnographic attitude is especially important for researchers who are "studying down," or investigating groups with less power and prestige than the group with which researchers are identified. In nonresearch settings, like child-care centers, respecting the standards of others means including diverse groups in setting standards. Parents and careworkers from different social backgrounds would need to join experts and administrators in setting policies about how to treat children. Including the perspective of low-income communities would help to highlight the impact of poverty on children and families. At the end of this chapter, I give more detail on how the ethnographic attitude and the inclusion of diverse groups can be accomplished.

In the next section of the chapter, I describe the current hegemonic standard for child care, which was developed by child psychologists and focuses on the interactions between caregiver and child, ignoring the wider environment. Then I propose guidelines for developing less oppressive, more democratic standards.

The Current Hegemonic Standard of Child Care

The current hegemonic standard is that children need parents or caregivers that are authoritative (as opposed to authoritarian or permissive) and responsively nurturant (warm in a way that responds to the child's words or actions, or follows the child's lead). This standard dominates most academic research, popular books, and social services aimed at improving child care.

Authoritative Care

Authoritative parenting (or child care) has been a focus of research in child psychology since the 1960s (Maccoby and Martin 1983). The concept was developed by Diana Baumrind and other child psychologists in a series of studies that was synthesized in an influential review of research in child psychology by Eleanor Maccoby and John Martin (Baumrind 1967; Maccoby and Martin 1983). Baumrind defined *authoritative* parenting as including "clear standard setting . . . ; firm enforcement of rules and standards, encouragement of the child's independence and individuality," and "open communication between parents and children, with parents listening to children's point of view, as well as expressing their own" (Maccoby and Martin, 1983:46). In contrast, *authoritarian* parenting includes attempting to control children "in accordance with an absolute set of standards, valuing obedience, respect for authority, work, tradition," and "discouraging verbal give-and-take between parent and child" (Maccoby and Martin 1983:40). *Permissive* parents, the third type, "take a tolerant, accepting attitude toward the child's impulses, including sexual and aggressive impulses . . . , use little punishment," and avoid "asserting authority or imposing controls" (Maccoby and Martin 1983:44). Authoritative parenting is the best for children, according to Maccoby and Martin. Compared to the other two types of parenting, authoritative child care resulted in children being more independent, "socially responsible, able to control aggression, self-confident and high in self-esteem" (Maccoby and Martin 1983:48).

The concept "authoritative parenting" originally focused on discipline, but also included verbal interaction and responsiveness. Later researchers further expanded this broad concept to include warmth and consistency, and treated "authoritative parenting" as virtually synonymous with good care (Gray and Steinberg 1999; Steinberg et al. 1992). For example, a recent article defined authoritative parenting as consisting of "parental acceptance, inductive discipline [explaining reasons for discipline], nonpunitive punishment practices, and consistency" (Gray and Steinberg 1999). The article states that authoritative parenting produces virtually everything a parent could want for their child: "children raised in authoritative homes score higher than their peers raised in authoritarian, indulgent, or neglectful homes on measures of competence, social development, self-perceptions, and mental health" (Gray and Steinberg 1999:574). Another recent article, on fathers' impact on their children, defined authoritative parenting as including support (responsiveness, encouragement, assistance) and control (rule formulation, monitoring, and discipline) (Amato and Gilbreth 1999). Children's well-being, the article stated, depends not on the presence of fathers, "but the extent to which fathers engage in authoritative parenting" (1999:559). Studies like these indicate that authoritative parenting is the best way to care for all children.

Responsive Nurturance

The second component of hegemonic standards of care is responsive nurturance. Responsive nurturance (or sensitive responsiveness) refers to a combination of warmth or affection, and following the child's lead, or responding to the child's cues and listening to him or her. It can be contrasted with forms of warmth and affection that are more physical, less verbal, and do not necessarily follow the child's lead, which I label "holding nurturance." An example of holding nurturance would be an adult who approaches a child, picks the child up, and then holds and rocks the child.

Responsive nurturance, or sensitive responsiveness, was defined in a recent review article as "attention to the infant's signals, accurate interpretation of their meaning, and appropriate and prompt response" (Thompson 1997:49). The key component is being child centered, or following the child's lead.

A large body of research on mother–child attachment emphasizes the importance of responsive nurturance (or sensitive responsiveness) to children's development. John Bowlby's early work on the stunted development of institutionalized infants laid the foundations for attachment theory (Bowlby 1969). Forming a secure attachment is a prerequisite to healthy psychological, social, and cognitive development, according to most attachment theorists (Thompson 1997; Wendland-Carro, Piccinini, and Miller 1999). Secure attachment between infant and mother leads a child to independent exploration and a positive self-concept, and forms the basis for successful interpersonal relationships. The development of a technique for measuring the security of a child's attachment, by assessing a child's response to a laboratory situation in which the mother leaves the child with a stranger and then returns, led to an enormous body of research on responsive nurturance and mother–child attachment. Intervention programs to teach "at-risk" (usually low-income) mothers how to become more responsive have developed as the result of this research (van den Boom 1994).

The concept of responsive nurturance has had a very large impact on the standard of care reflected in academic theories, social programs, and the popular culture. Essays on caring by philosophers and feminists often view responsive nurturance as "the essence of good care" (Noddings 1984). The influential book *Maternal Thinking*, by Sara Ruddick, argued that attentive, responsive love is a core component of good mothering. Attentive, responsive love means learning to ask "what are you going through and to wait to hear the answer rather than giving it . . . A mother [with attentive love] really looks at her child, tries to see him accurately rather than herself in him" (1995:121). Good child care means following the child's lead rather than the adult's.

The leading contemporary advice books on childrearing are emphatic about

the importance of responsive nurturance, as Sharon Hays's analysis of child rearing manuals documents (1996). In the manuals by Benjamin Spock, Penelope
Leach, and T. Berry Brazelton, love and affection that responds to the child's cues
"is considered the absolutely essential foundation for the proper rearing of a child"
(1996: 57). For example, Brazelton stated that every baby knows what is needed"
and will show "a sensitive parent" just what to do (Hays 1996:57). These manuals
also endorse authoritative parenting, or setting firm limits, and explaining the
reasons for rules to children old enough to talk (Hays 1996:61).

In contrast to responsive nurturance, holding nurturance refers to expressions
of warmth or affection that need not follow the child's lead. The concept focuses
on the provision of warm, relaxed physical comfort and acceptance, and a sense
of protection and security, not on responsiveness. For infants, "holding" or providing enfolding and protective physical contact is the "prototype of all infant
care," according to the child psychoanalyst D. W. Winnnicott (1987:37; see also
Scheper-Hughes 1992:359; Winnicott 1964). For older children, a caregiver
might provide holding nurturance to a child by moving or talking in a warm,
relaxed way, or simply by sitting next to him or her and watching TV.

An ethnographic example of holding nurturance is provided in Valerie
Suransky's (1982) description of a child care center for preschoolers in a low-
income African-American neighborhood in Chicago. The staff was mostly
African-American and included three grandmothers who were volunteers. The
grandmothers, Suransky writes, "were indulgent, yet extremely authoritarian
toward the children." For example, one morning at the center, "Grandma Jones
noticed that Tan was sitting alone at the breakfast table with an unfinished bowl
of cereal. She went to the child, commenting 'Don't like seeing a little one sitting
there all alone,' and sat down, put the child on her lap, and proceeded to feed her"
(pp. 146–47). The grandmother shows a nonresponsive type of nurturance in
which the caregiver is guided by her own perception of what the child needs, not
by the child's cues. In contrast, a responsively nurturant careworker might
approach the child, sit near him or her, and wait to see what kind of interaction
the child would initiate.

Most research on child care examines only responsive nurturance and ignores
other types of nurturance. Holding nurturance is occasionally noted by people
who have observed families in other cultures. For example, T. Berry Brazelton
commented:

> In the highlands of Mexico where I have done research, mothers rarely, if ever,
> interact with a baby face to face. But they carry the baby in a serape all day long.
> They breast-feed the baby up to 70–90 times a day. That's being "there" for the
> baby! (Brazelton and Greenspan 2000:12–13).

However, this comment is buried in a long discussion of nurturance that
emphasizes children's need for face-to-face interaction that is cued to the child's
emotions, and suggests that without such responsive nurturance, a child's cognitive and emotional development will be retarded. Most researchers, experts, and
popular writers agree: The only good way to care for children is to be authorita-

tive and responsively nurturant. However, they probably are wrong, as I now demonstrate.

The Hegemonic Standard Does Not Predict Positive Outcomes for Children

If a particular type of child care is best, then it should lead to significantly better outcomes for some valued aspects of children's attitudes or behavior. Yet there is little strong evidence that authoritative, responsively nurturant child care produces better outcomes for children than other types of care. In studies that do find positive outcomes, the strength of the relationship is usually weak. In their 1983 review of research, Maccoby and Martin qualified their endorsement of authoritative parenting by noting that in every study the three types of parenting (authoritative, authoritarian, and permissive) accounted for very little variance in child behavior (p. 48). More recently, Parke and Buriel (1998) and others have argued that the three types of care should be rejected as models of good care because they are not strong predictors of positive child outcomes (Harris, 1995).

The most damaging evidence refuting the hegemonic standard of care comes from studies showing that authoritarian child care has better child outcomes than authoritative care, among nonelite or non-Euro-American groups. Baumrind's study of a small group of African-American girls found that "if the black families were viewed by white norms they appeared authoritarian, but . . . unlike their white counterparts, the most authoritarian of these families produced the most self-assertive and independent girls" (1972:261). Research on Chinese families also reports that children raised by authoritarian parents perform better in school (Chao 1994). Authoritarian care also seems to have better outcomes for children raised in working-class neighborhoods (Furstenberg 1993). In contrast, for elite children, following the standard tends to have a weak but positive effect.

These studies suggest that children have better outcomes if their care givers follow the childrearing standards of their local community. This pattern fits with John Ogbu's theory (1981) that all stable cultures or communities develop child-care practices that train children in the competencies that are required to survive and succeed in their immediate environment. The requirements of the larger environment determine what behavior leads to success, and child-care patterns in stable communities encourage those behaviors.

Ogbu's position seems too radically relativistic, because it legitimates all child-care practices in all stable communities. Oppression, poverty, and other deprivations can have negative consequences on the standards of both the oppressors and the oppressed (McLoyd 1990; Scheper-Hughes 1992). Moreover, the child-care practices of some groups that are not obviously oppressed seem abusive or bad for children, such as severe corporal punishment. The best approach to these practices, I believe, is neither indiscriminate acceptance, nor rejection and imposition of the dominant standards of care. Instead, some compromise solution has to be negotiated among involved groups. The challenge of developing standards of care (like the challenge of defining human rights) cannot be short cut by total relativism. A more moderate and useful version of Ogbu's position is that child-care practices in a stable community are likely to have some positive consequences. Therefore, researchers should carefully consider the possible positive consequences of particular child care practices, instead of quickly judging them as deficient.

In sum, research does not support the claim that authoritative and responsively nurturant care is best for all children. In contrast, there is strong evidence that the hegemonic standard is biased.

Evidence on Class, Racial/Ethnic, and Cultural Bias in the Hegemonic Standard

The ideal of authoritative and responsive child care fits the values and practices of White, upper-middle-class Euro-Americans much better than it fits other groups, according to numerous studies. Because of these studies, child psychologists are increasingly rejecting the hegemonic standard. As Margaret Beale Spencer stated in the introduction to a special issue of the leading journal on child development devoted to minority children, until recently "'normative' development had been defined according to Eurocentric standards, forcing from the realm of 'normal' all but the most assimilated minorities" (1990:267). Ruth Chao concluded her comparison of Chinese and U.S. childrearing by rejecting the authoritative–permissive–authoritarian styles as "ethnocentric and misleading" (Chao 1994:1111). Chinese parents are labeled as "authoritarian," according to the three styles, because they do not value individualism and autonomy as much as Americans.

A recent review of research in the *Handbook of Child Psychology* concludes that the superiority of authoritative child care cannot be generalized across different social classes or ethnic/cultural groups.

> In lower-SES families, parents are more likely to use an authoritarian as opposed to an authoritative style, but this style is often an adaptation to the ecological conditions such as increased danger and that may characterize the lives of poor families. Moreover, . . . the use of authoritarian strategies under these circumstances may be linked with more positive outcomes for children. (Parke and Buriel 1998:473)

Studies of social class differences in child rearing in the United States and other countries consistently find that compared to more affluent parents, working-class and poor parents are more likely to demand strict obedience from their children, to value conformity to external authority, and to use physical punishment. They also are less likely to be very verbal with children and to give detailed explanations for their decisions (Bronfenbrenner 1958;Kohn and Schooler 1983; McLoyd 1990; Parke and Buriel 1998).

Comparisons by race and ethnicity report a similar pattern. Latino child care places more emphasis on being obedient and respectful to parents, and identified with the family, and less emphasis on individual autonomy and following the child's lead, compared to Euro-Americans (Dornbusch et al. 1987; Parke and Buriel 1998). African-American parents and child-care providers tend to be more adult-centered than Euro-Americans, and more concerned with obedience (Ahn 1994; Lubeck 1985; Parke and Buriel 1998).

Asian-American parents also appear deficient if they are judged according to the hegemonic standard of care. Compared to Euro-Americans, they tend to be more "authoritarian," less verbal, and less responsively nurturant (Ahn 1994; Parke and Buriel 1998; Pyke 2000). Children of immigrant Asian-American families, however, often accept the hegemonic standard of care and criticize their parents, according to a recent study of college students (Pyke 2000). One 18-year-old Korean-American student said, "In Asian families you don't have conversations. You are told to do something and you do it" (Pyke 2000: 246). Paul, another Korean-American student said: "My father is very strict . . . (and) very much falls into that typical Asian father standard." He wished that his father were more like Mike Brady in "The Brady Bunch" TV show because Mike Brady "was always so supportive." These immigrant children follow the wider culture in judging the hegemonic standard as the one right way to care.

In sum, the hegemonic standard of care is biased in favor of elite values and practices, and it stands on very weak scientific evidence. There is little evidence that authoritative and responsively nurturant child care substantially improves children's development. There is strong evidence that the hegemonic standard discriminates against people who are not upper middle class, White Euro-Americans.

How to Develop Less Oppressive Standards

To develop less oppressive standards of care, researchers need to respect the child-drearing patterns of diverse groups and develop an "ethnographic attitude," as I have discussed. They also need to recognize the limits of scientific knowledge, and investigate the impact of poverty and other environmental factors on the quality of care. A growing number of sociologists and psychologists have supported these goals in recent decades, but much more work remains to be done.

The preliminary guidelines I have constructed for child-care researchers are summarized in the four steps presented below. The first step in doing research that contributes to less oppressive standards is to develop an ethnographic attitude that includes the perspective of the people being studied in the research. Possible methods are doing interviews or observations in the community, including community members in the research team, and reading ethnographic descriptions of the community. Participatory research methods, in which representatives of the community have considerable involvement in and control over the research, are another option (Cancian and Armstead 2000). The goal is for the researcher to develop an attitude of genuine respect for the knowledge of the people being studied, as opposed to an attitude of superiority or domination. Without a respectful attitude, any method can be used to reinforce oppression.

The next step is to identify the standards of care in a particular community, clarify how they differ from dominant standards, and develop a respectful understanding of community standards. Part of respecting local practices would be to consider the adaptive potential of existing practices within the local environment and belief system. The process of understanding local standards will probably require researchers to question their own standards, and the standards endorsed by the elite. The third step to developing less oppressive standards is to recognize the impact of poverty and political and social inequality on child care. Research designs would shift away from focusing exclusively on parents, families, and care-givers and pay more attention to poverty, neighborhoods, and the wider social and cultural environment. The field of child development as a whole would make this shift, even though some studies would continue to focus on interactions between children and their caregivers.

The final step in doing research that contributes to less oppressive standards of care is to follow the norms of good science by stating findings in modest, precise, and nonjudgmental language. This is especially important for findings about what types of care produce positive and negative outcomes for children, because such findings are used to justify laws and social programs, and to judge the moral worth of racial/ethnic, social class, and cultural groups. The use of judgmental, emotionally laden concepts like "authoritative" versus "authoritarian" is a clear violation of scientific norms. "Authoritative" parenting was originally defined in opposition to the "authoritarian" parenting that supposedly produced Nazis and the Holocaust, according to studies conducted after World War II.

A recent article comparing child care by middle-class Puerto Rican and Euro-American (or Anglo) mothers provides a positive example of research that con-tributes to less oppressive standards of care. Robin Harwood and her colleagues observed and interviewed 18 Puerto Rican and 22 Anglo mothers of 12- to 15-month-old children, focusing on cultural differences and variability in maternal behavior over situations, such as, feeding versus playing (Harwood et al. 1999). The overall differences between the two groups fit the typical pattern. In the lan-guage of the hegemonic standard, the Puerto Rican mothers were more authori-tarian and less responsively nurturant than Anglo mothers. But the researchers use an alternative, less judgmental language to describe these differences, so that the practices of both cultural groups seem equally good. The researchers also relate the differences to broader patterns of Anglo and Puerto Rican culture. Puerto Rican values and perspectives are included in the research, although the paper does not describe the methods used to obtain this information.

The paper reports that the Puerto Rican mothers gave more commands and directions to their infants, whereas the Anglos tended to give suggestions, not commands. The Puerto Rican mothers were more likely to feed their child and engaged in more touching, whereas the Anglo mothers encouraged their children to feed themselves. The researchers interpreted these differences in terms of the emphasis in Puerto Rican culture on "interdependence" or "seeing oneself as part of an encompassing social relationship and recognizing that one's behavior is determined . . . [by] the thoughts, feelings, and actions of *others* in the relation-ship" (Markus and Kitayama, quoted in Harwood et al. 1999:1005). In contrast, the researchers observed, Anglo culture emphasizes individualism, and sees a person as an "independent, self-contained, autonomous entity who (a) comprises a unique configuration of internal attributes . . . and (b) behaves primarily as a consequence of those internal attributes (Marcus and Kitayama, quoted in Harwood, 1999). Thus Anglo mothers avoid direct commands and cultivate autonomy and personal choice in their infant, whereas Puerto Rican mothers directly guide their child, "thus highlighting the child's sense of interpersonal obligation" (Harwood et al. 1999:1013).

The article states findings in modest and precise language. Significant differences are carefully presented, with no implicit judgment of which group is better overall. For example, in presenting some of the results on maternal verbal behaviors, the authors stated: "Puerto Rican mothers were more likely to . . . offer affection during teaching, [and] issue directives in the form of commands." Anglo mother "were more likely to praise their infants' efforts . . . and issue directives in the form of suggestions" (Harwood et al. 1999:1011). The article also uses nonjudgmental language. For instance, the most characteristic interview responses of Puerto Rican mothers are labeled "Decency and Proper Demeanor," whereas the Anglo mothers' responses emphasized "Self-Maximization and Self-Control."

The article reports the same pattern of empirical differences between groups as countless other studies: more direct control and physical contact in non-Anglo groups. But it avoids treating Anglos as superior by showing how child-care practices fit into each group's social context, using nonjudgmental language, and avoiding overstating findings. This study illustrates the possibilities of doing research that contributes to developing more democratic, less oppressive standards of care.

Guidelines for Child-Care Programs

Developing standards of child care in public programs such as child-care centers, training programs for child-care workers, or child-abuse laws and regulations, entails similar problems as doing research on child care. Similar guidelines for democratizing standards would be useful, such as including the perspectives of diverse groups, and acknowledging the impact of poverty and the wider social environment. There is a major difference, however, in the appropriate power of scientific experts. In research, scientists are rightfully in charge, even though they need to learn from the people they are studying if they want to contribute to developing nonoppressive standards of care. In negotiating standards for public programs, scientists need to be much less powerful.

Limiting the power of scientific experts is a major challenge to developing more democratic standards in public programs. The existing evidence on child care is too weak and contradictory to justify broad standards of care on scientific grounds, as I have shown. On some specific issues there may be strong evidence, such as the age at which a child can understand complex instructions. However, on complex, value-laden issues such as the benefits of authoritative versus authoritarian child care, scientific evidence will probably never be decisive, so experts should not have a decisive role in setting standards for these issues. Restricting the domination of experts is crucial to a democratic process of negotiation, because of the strong tendency of high-status, well-educated experts to take over and silence less educated people. On the other hand, the contribution of scientific researchers needs to be respected, as one voice among others. Systematic evidence, although imperfect and biased, is needed to design effective as well as democratic standards for child care.

The first step toward developing democratic standards of child care in a public program would be to set up a process of negotiation and discussion that included the major groups involved, such as parents from diverse social backgrounds, careworkers, administrators, and experts. Input from experts would be limited to issues on which there is strong scientific evidence. Such a process of negotiation among the major groups involved in a child-care center would result in standards of care that were more democratic than the current standards, even though the elite participants in the discussion probably would have more influence than other people.

In conclusion, standards of care need not be as oppressive as the current hegemonic standard. By including the perspective of diverse groups, attending to the impact of the wider environment, and limiting the claims of scientists, researchers can contribute to constructing less oppressive standards. Recent research in child development, like the Harwood study of Puerto Rican and Anglo mothering, illustrates how this can be done. Similar guidelines can be used to develop more democratic standards of care for child-care centers and other public institutions.

Historically, standards of care have served to reinforce the supposed superiority of elites and the inferiority of others. Yet standards of care are necessary. They are part of redefining carework as a skilled practice that deserves respect and rewards. They are essential for guiding carework in public institutions and shaping government policies about care. The preliminary guidelines presented in this chapter suggest some ways that researchers and advocates can continue their work of understanding and improving care, without also strengthening inequality.

Note

I thank Charles Kalish for helpful advice in navigating the child development literature, and Frank Cancian for thoughtful comments on an earlier draft of this chapter.

II: Family Intersections with the State

Introduction to Section II
Family Intersections with the State

The state plays an overarching role in organizing, regulating, and subsidizing family-, market-, and community-based care for children and youth. Through its legislative, judicial, regulatory, and redistributive functions, the state directly and indirectly influences the care of children and youth. Some government policies provide direct regulation of public institutions that serve children, such as day-care centers, children's hospitals, and schools. Other policies, such as tax and social welfare policies and housing and health care policies, affect child- and youth-related carework within the "private" domain by influencing the resources that families have available to meet their needs.

State policies can either enhance or constrain the resources available to careworkers in different settings. The chapters in this section demonstrate that across a variety of contexts, recent state policy changes have diminished public resources and support for some types of care, while increasing support for the privatization of carework for children and youth. As these chapters indicate, the impact of these policies of privatization falls most heavily on women, who do the majority of work for children and youth, whether in the home, in the community, or in the marketplace. The decline of public resources and increasing privatization also disproportionately impact poor individuals and communities. Although more affluent families typically have access to resources to meet their child care commitments without state subsidies or interventions, poor families must draw on public resources to augment their "private" capacities to care adequately for their children. They are therefore more exposed to the surveillance, mandates, and regulations of the state.

In the first chapter in this section, Barbara Bennett Woodhouse examines how changes in child welfare laws and reduced resources for protective interventions have shifted the emphasis from foster care and family preservation to rapid family dissolution and reconstitution through adoption. Under the Adoption and Safe Families Act of 1997, long-term state-managed fostering is discouraged through time limits on the length of time children can remain in foster care before parental rights are terminated and the child is made available for adoption. Woodhouse argues that this policy change can be seen as a form of "privatizing" child welfare, redefining the role of mother, and changing the public–private partnership aimed at protecting vulnerable children and families.

In the second chapter, Andrew S. London, Ellen K. Scott, and Vicki Hunter examine how welfare-reliant women who have long-term care commitments to children with chronic health problems and disabilities are faring under welfare reform. In the past, women caring for children with serious health problems used AFDC (Aid for Families with Dependent Children) and related programs to support their long-term, child health-related carework. Under the new law, exemptions from welfare reform's work requirements and time limits are only granted under limited circumstances. As a result, welfare-reliant women have increasingly turned to their networks either to support their full-time carework or to make it possible for them to go to work. In addition to drawing on network support, some women have also turned to the market and have become the paid home-care providers for their own children. The longitudinal, qualitative case studies presented in this chapter illustrate another way in which state policy changes are contributing to the increasing privatization of carework for children and youth.

The final chapter in this section, by Karen Christopher, provides a cross-national comparison of the extent to which welfare states are "friendly" to mothers and single mothers relative to other citizens. She documents that there is substantial variability in the resources that welfare states make available to mothers and single mothers. Some welfare states provide benefits that allow mothers and single mothers choice and relative autonomy, whereas others, like the United States, relegate mothers and single mothers to a sort of second-class citizenship, poverty, and social disadvantage.

The chapters in this section make it clear that researchers, policymakers, and the public must pay more attention to the ways that public policy changes affect the provision of carework for children and youth, including how much care is available, who provides that care, and who ultimately pays the social and economic costs of caring. Because women provide the majority of care and the poor have fewer resources to manage the responsibilities of child care and breadwinning, retrenchment in public commitments to care serve to further disadvantage women and the poor, two overlapping groups who already bear disproportionate carework burdens.

Making Poor Mothers Fungible

The Privatization of Foster Care

Barbara Bennett Woodhouse

*O*ne of the most ancient and traditional forms of carework is the fostering of minor children. Foster parents are temporary caregivers, paid by the child's parents or by the state, who take over when biological parents are unable or unwilling to care for their own children. This chapter explores the history of publicly funded fostering in America as a response to family disruption. It examines the impact of new federal legislation that radically shifts the emphasis away from the preservation of biological families through fostering, to a policy favoring dissolution of disrupted families and the creation of new families through adoption. It analyzes the positives and negatives of this new policy and concludes that, although the objective of assuring that all children have safe and permanent homes is a worthy one, the new reforms run a severe risk of treating women engaged in mothering—especially poor women and women of color—as if they were fungible commodities that can be interchanged without cost to child, parent, or society. It also denigrates paid mothering as a deviant form of carework and entrenches a tendency to demand that "real" mothering go uncompensated in order to command social respect and moral recognition. It poses a real danger of devaluing both biological mothers who work for free and their sisters who work as paid foster mothers.

Fostering and the Trend toward the Fungible Mother

Traditionally, motherhood has been treated as a unique legal bond that could be dissolved only by a voluntary consent to adoption. A mother who was temporarily unable to care for her child could place the child in foster care (a state-funded child welfare system) and could regain custody when her circumstances improved. In the most extreme circumstances of unfitness or abandonment, the state could dissolve the relationship against the mother's wishes, through a court-ordered "involuntary termination of parental rights" (TPR). The past decade has seen a development in U.S. child welfare policy that has sweeping implications for the status of mothers and substitute careworkers. Congress has amended the laws governing subsidies for protective interventions in the family, diminishing the emphasis on family preservation and promoting speedier termination of the biological family relationship. The new laws accelerate termination of parental rights to free children for adoption, and shift government subsidies away from foster care and efforts at family preservation, favoring instead the options of adoption or permanent guardianship. Adoptive parents are eligible for permanent subsidies and state-funded medical insurance if they adopt a child with special needs. A policy shifting resources into promoting adoption as opposed to state-managed foster care was initiated by Congress with the Adoption and Safe Families Act of 1997 (ASFA). ASFA, which can be viewed as a form of "privatizing" child welfare, took effect in 1998, and during that year its policies were extended nationwide by legislation enacted at the state level.

ASFA and its state law counterparts clearly signal a seismic event in our national policies with respect to the paid and unpaid careworkers (primarily female) who are raising America's children. Explicitly aimed at providing "safe and stable homes" for children at risk, ASFA also represents a critical moment in the process of defining and redefining the meaning and role of "mother" as a basic unit for care of children. ASFA reflects a merging of two contemporary trends evident in the United States. First is the trend, in culture and in law, away from defining parenthood as an immutable relationship, built around the "biological" parent and "nuclear family" (married heterosexual parents who bear and beget children), and toward supporting and recognizing the more mutable and subjective notion of the "de facto parent" and the "functional family" (those who are actually engaged in or are willing and able to do the work of parenting) (Cahn 1997; Czapanskiy 1999; Woodhouse 1996). Biological family members are linked by ties of blood and marriage, whereas functional family members may be linked by looser kinship bonds or by no blood or legal ties at all. The second trend is the political trend toward privatization of many functions assumed by government in the New Deal and Great Society eras, including the function of providing a safety net to preserve the poor family. Just as public utilities and prisons have been privatized in recent years, so too has the public safety net for at-risk children been privatized, with increasing emphasis not only on the provision of services to children by private agencies but on adoption by private actors as the ultimate solution for removing children from the public welfare rolls.

In a democratic society, the family has traditionally been the unit entrusted with nurturing and acculturating each new generation of citizens (*Prince v. Massachusetts* 1944). Assigning this role to families rather than the state preserves diversity and autonomy as key values of social life. Family, however, can have many meanings. Each society determines how to balance the mix of blood relationship, legal formality, religious meaning, social investment, community continuity, and nurturing care that constitutes what we consider the defining attributes of "the family." Each society also allocates between public and private spheres the responsibility for supporting family functions—public education, school lunches, public health care, and mothers' allowances are examples of this public/private partnership in the "carework" of childrearing.

In comparative law terms, a distinguishing feature of U.S. family policy is our delegation of the work of childrearing to the private sphere of family life, where it is performed as unpaid labor primarily by women (Fineman 1995; Glendon 1989; Woodhouse 1992). Welfare—the practice of using taxpayer dollars to help poor mothers care for their children—has been stigmatized in the United States as a "handout" and not viewed or structured as an entitlement. Carework provided in a family setting, in sum, does not give rise to claims for compensation from the community, even though it makes possible the continued existence of the community (Schultz 2000). Fostering of children has long been an exception to this rule. Children who have been removed from their biological mother or voluntarily placed in state care are cared for *in a substitute family by a substitute (foster) mother* at the public expense. Increasingly, the lines in child welfare between public and private have blurred. Kinfolk and extended family have been recruited to serve as paid foster mothers, and by 1998 at least half of the states' placements of children was with relatives (U.S. Department of Health and Human Services 1998). Although this shift has elicited comment and criticism from critics who see it as undercutting the principle that women should care for family members out of love and duty and without compensation, children's needs for stability in relationships have outweighed this concern. Abused, neglected, and abandoned children, and those who care for them, seem to have escaped the stigma of shiftlessness and dysfunction attached to poor mothers, allowing a major commitment of government resources to the daily care of children in professional or kinship foster placements without serious protest from the right.

Viewed in this context, ASFA represents a radical turn away from subsidizing the care of poor children and toward privatization of these child welfare services. It reduces the role of "public" fostering of children while incentivizing formation of "private" adoptive families to take on the parenting role, supplanting the original parents. Under ASFA, long-term state-managed fostering is discouraged, and ASFA promotes permanency primarily in terms of getting children out of "the system" and off the child welfare rolls through adoption, whether with kin, with foster families willing to adopt, or with strangers. This most recent drive toward privatization of welfare first emerged in "welfare" reform. In the context of "welfare," in 1996 Congress enacted a program called Temporary Assistance to Needy Families (TANF), which limits time on welfare and emphasizes programs intended to move unemployed mothers into the workforce. This "reform" shifted responsibility for providing income to poor mothers to the private sector, where mothers who do not have a breadwinner mate must "earn" enough to support themselves and their children through employment or rely on private charity. Although rarely discussed, it was assumed that the children of mothers who failed to make the transition to work within the allotted time would end up in foster care—the safety net of "child welfare." Recent reforms of "child welfare," exemplified by ASFA, reject the notion of long-term substitute care at government expense and enlist the private sector (potential adoptive parents) to reduce the involvement of government in providing care for dependent children.

The idea that the "private" sphere of family operates independently of the "public" sphere is, of course, an illusion. Government and family always have been partners in child rearing, to the extent that government invisibly subsidizes middle class families through tax breaks, social insurance, and public services. One unique aspect of ASFA is its emphasis on subsidizing adoption of "special needs children" by families too poor or too fearful to take on the full costs of adopting these children. The notion of subsidized "special needs" adoptions opens a new chapter in the history of how the private sphere of "family" and the public sphere of "government" interact in raising children. Before TANF, government provided meager subsidies called Aid for Families with Dependent Children (AFDC) to poor mothers to enable them to stay at home to care for their children. Abused and neglected children were removed from their homes, and their care was paid for by government and contracted out to professional foster parents who received payments far in excess of those available through AFDC. TANF placed a limit on the time mothers might receive benefits and, after 2 years, sent the welfare mother off the rolls and into the marketplace. In the post-ASFA scheme of child welfare laws and policies, the time a child may spend in foster care (like mothers' time on TANF) is strictly limited. After 15 out of 22 months in care, the state must move to terminate the mother's rights. If a TPR is granted, the biological parent is to be replaced by the adoptive parent or a permanent guardian, who becomes a legal custodian with full legal rights and responsibilities.

These two trends—redefinition of parenthood and the family and privatization of child welfare—intertwine in ASFA. In a society where widespread divorce and geographic mobility make family relationships highly fluid, families seem endlessly malleable, even fungible. Families are made and unmade not by God and Nature, but by personal choice. Thus, reunification services and professional foster care to preserve "failed" birth families are seen as endangering children and wasting money for no good reason. These supports are seen merely to contribute to a "lifestyle" of dependency, with no gains for the children whose formal birth family is preserved but who continue to lack the functional caretaking relationship that Americans increasingly describe as a "real" family. Taxpayers' money, so the argument goes, should be used not to support failed families but to incentivize the creation of new and presumptively "functional"[1] adoptive families, bound together by demonstrated commitment and ability to provide the time consuming and emotionally taxing work of chil rearing.

Riding this sociological shift in how we conceptualize the family, government can "get out of the business" of fostering displaced children. By redefining what counts as "family," government can redistribute resources to private entities that can accomplish the work of "family" within the private sphere. The family remains the basic unit for childrearing, but the legally autonomous family has been recreated out of the ashes of the dysfunctional biological family, through adoption.

In theory, the replacing of dysfunctional with "functional" families makes eminent good sense. Surely, children must be reared in homes that meet their basic needs for love and nurture. However, stories abound of children needlessly removed from poor mothers. Sometimes they are removed because the homes are dirty or disorganized, judged by middle-class standards, but not dangerous or truly dysfunctional. Sometimes the children's mothers place them "voluntarily" in foster care, during a family crisis. Race and class play a large role in these cases. Studies have shown that, given two hypothetical cases, one involving a White caretaker and the other a Black caretaker, judges and lawyers will judge the mother of color far more harshly (Williams 1997). When race and poverty combine, families are at heightened risk of inappropriate interventions. Every parent advocate has seen cases in which poor mothers lost their children because of circumstances beyond their control, such as being burned out of their homes or driven out by domestic violence (Bailie 1998). Will the post-ASFA child welfare system adequately protect poor mothers and families of color, or will it further hasten the decline of families already placed at heightened risk by socioeconomic factors? Does it risk the downgrading of carework provided by the professional foster mother, by pressing her to take on the role as an unpaid volunteer? The following sections describe the enactment of ASFA, placing it in historical context, allowing us to better explore these larger questions.

The Adoption and Safe Families Act of 1997

How ASFA Changed Existing Federal and State Laws

In 1997, Congress passed the Adoption and Safe Families Act (ASFA), which amended the federal Adoption Assistance and Child Welfare Act (AACWA) (Pagano 1999). AACWA had been passed in 1980 in response to concerns that state agencies were removing children unnecessarily from their homes and then leaving them to drift in foster care. In AACWA, Congress had created strong incentives for states to pass child welfare laws that would emphasize family preservation and reunification.[2] In the scheme envisioned by the authors of AACWA, children were not to be separated from their families unnecessarily. AACWA offered federal funds to the states for foster care and other services, but only if the state enacted laws guaranteeing that "in each case, reasonable efforts will be made (A) prior to placement of a child in foster care to prevent or eliminate the need for removal of the child from his home and, (B) to make it possible for the child to return to his home."[3] Under laws enacted by states to conform with AACWA, agency social workers and families, together with their lawyers, would participate in drawing up a Family Service Plan (commonly referred to as the "FSP") identifying a goal for the child and outlining programs and services the state must provide to the family. It was hoped that periodic court reviews of these FSPs would speed reunification. Only if a family showed no progress over an extended period of time, despite the state's best efforts, would it be appropriate to terminate the parent–child relationship to free the child for adoption by a new family.

In practice, the initial goal for almost every child under AACWA was "reunification." The issue of "permanency"—whether or not the parents could realistically care for the child in the foreseeable future and, if not, who would care for him or her on a permanent basis—was supposed to be addressed 18 months after placement, but often was delayed well beyond this time. A goal change to "adoption" at 18, 24, or 48 months did not provide permanency, but merely shifted the focus from reunification to the long and arduous process of terminating parental rights and searching for an adoptive home.[4]

After 15 years of AACWA, calls for reform were universal. Between 1985 and 1995 the population of children removed from home and placed in "substitute" care had almost doubled, from 276,000 to 494,000, and continued to increase (Berrick 1998:72; Silver 1999). Of the more than three million children reported abused and neglected each year, approximately 250,000 were being taken into protective custody, under the control of county or state agencies with names like Administration for Children's Services, Department of Human Services, or Department of Youth and Family Services (Besharov 1998:120). Although the parents retained vestigial rights, for all intents and purposes the state had become responsible for rearing the child. State and county agencies, either directly or through contracts with private nonprofit organizations, employed social workers to manage the children's cases and to supervise their placement with paid licensed foster families. A new class of children was now being raised by the state and not their families. How did these half a million children enter "state care"? Some were surrendered voluntarily by parents who could not cope, due to mental or physical illness, addiction, family dissolution, or other disruptive circumstances. Others were involuntarily removed by court order under state child protective laws empowering police and child protective workers to intervene in cases of abuse and neglect, often because of drug involvement of the parent. Sometimes a "voluntary" placement was made under threat of coercive court intervention, making it difficult for policy analysts to determine how many children were removed under duress.

By 1997, critics from both right and left believed the child welfare system was failing in its most important purposes. More children were streaming into the system, entering younger and remaining longer, and still the national rates of child abuse and fatality were rising. As popular sentiment turned against big government and social welfare programs and in favor of privatization and personal responsibility, the child welfare pendulum swung away from family preservation and reunification, and toward more aggressive child protection and a greater emphasis on moving children out of the child welfare system into permanent adoptive homes where they would no longer be wards of the state. Some believed that AACWA was being misinterpreted and employed in ways that institutionalized foster care as a "way of life" for both parents and children.[5] They charged that the laws valued parents' rights and preservation of the biological parent–child relationship more than the welfare and safety of children. Critics pointed out that the average child who entered foster care would have to wait 3 years before any decision was made about his or her future and twenty-one states were failing so badly in managing their child welfare systems that they had been forced to enter into consent decrees (143 Cong. Rec. S12211). An overemphasis on "reasonable efforts" was preventing children who would never realistically be reunited with their parents from moving on to find safe, permanent families through adoption (Gelles 1996; 143 Cong. Rec. S12198). AACWA, its critics contended, encouraged authorities to return children prematurely to unsafe families and prevented their timely removal from dangerous situations.

Advocates for parents countered that far too many children were being removed in the first place (Guggenheim 1999). These children were being removed not because of gross abuses but because of more nebulous concerns about "neglect." Child protective workers who were fearful of making a fatal mistake, or who viewed the world through White middle-class spectacles, saw danger where no real danger existed. Moreover, critics charged that funding policies set at the national level skewed state policies. Congress was willing to reimburse foster care outlays but was slow to fund basic income support or in-home services, with the result that many children were removed because of their parents' poverty and lack of education, when appropriate income transfers and social supports might have prevented removal (Roberts 1999).

Congress decided to amend AACWA and enacted ASFA as its response to the child welfare crisis. Under ASFA, any state that wished to share in federal funds earmarked for foster care and child protective services must pass laws embodying a new set of priorities. As described by Senator Rockefeller of West Virginia, "The major objective of this bill is to move abused and neglected kids into adoption or other permanent homes and to do it more quickly and more safely than ever before" (Cong. Rec. S12199).

The Basic Provisions of ASFA

In this section I summarize ASFA's basic goals and the provisions intended to accomplish them.

1. *Making Children's Safety and Health the Paramount Concern.* Critics of AACWA had focused on the "reasonable efforts" language, arguing that it encouraged courts and agencies to initiate efforts at reunification or preservation in circumstances which placed children at unacceptable risk. Under ASFA, the state scheme is eligible only if it provides that "in making such reasonable efforts [at reunification], the child's health and safety shall be the paramount concern" (42 U.S.C. §671 (15)). This language shifts the emphasis from balancing of various values such as family autonomy and child safety to a priority of child safety over competing values such as family preservation or parental rights.

2. *Moving Children More Rapidly out of Foster Care and into Permanent Homes.* A second major goal of ASFA was to shorten children's stays in foster care. After a child has been in care for 15 out of 22 months, ASFA shifts the burden to the state to show why a TPR petition should *not* be filed. Thus parents have only 15 months to "get their act together" before they must face a petition to end the child–parent relationship.

To speed permanent placement, ASFA introduces two new concepts: (1) a duty upon the state to make reasonable efforts at *permanency planning,* once adoption or permanent guardianship becomes the goal, and (2) the concept of "concurrent planning"—the practice of planning simultaneously for two mutually exclusive alternative goals such as adoption and reunification (42 U.S.C. §675(E)). Thus social workers, whose primary objective was once reunification, must now plan two parallel tracks, one of which assumes that the parent's efforts at rehabilitation will fail. As soon as a goal change is approved by the court, the pressure is on the social worker to terminate the child's prior relationships to make way for a new adoptive parent or guardian.

3. *Facilitating Adoption.* A third goal of ASFA was to remove barriers to adoption, including racial and economic barriers. Racial barriers had already been addressed in laws that Congress enacted pursuant to its Fourteenth Amendment powers. The ASFA language tracks these recently enacted civil rights laws, which prohibited the delay or denial of placement, based on racial matching polices. The most

significant policy shift of ASFA is contained in the provisions reducing economic barriers to adoption. The federal government has been subsidizing private adoption of children in foster care since at least the mid-1980s. However, ASFA significantly increases funding of adoption assistance agreements guaranteeing cash subsidies and other benefits to adoptive families, to encourage and support adoption of "special needs" children. The term "children with special needs" may sound like a small subset, but in practice it covers the great majority of children in foster care. "Children with special needs" is child welfare jargon for children who are hard to place.[6] It acknowledges the barriers to adoption faced by children with neurological, physical, and emotional disabilities, children over the age of 5, children from minority racial groups, children in sibling groups—in brief, the typical child at risk of drifting indefinitely in foster care. ASFA addresses these barriers not only by encouraging and funding cash subsidies to adoptive parents to defray some of the extra costs of rearing these children, but also by insuring that children will remain eligible for government-funded health care and mental health services after they are adopted. Ordinarily, families must be extremely poor to qualify for government-paid health care. After ASFA, a middle class adoptive family need not fear bankrupting itself to care for a disabled child nor be financially ruined if the child needs residential care.

To break down bureaucratic inertia and give the states a fiscal stake in encouraging adoptions, ASFA creates a system of "adoption incentive payments" for the states. Once a state exceeds a certain baseline quota of adoptions, the state is eligible to receive a $4,000 bounty for each additional adoption. Finally, ASFA requires that states make funding for family support and preservation programs available to families who adopt children to support their postadoption needs. In essence, ASFA shifts money and services from biological families and foster families to adoptive families

4. *Fast-Tracking Severe or Repeat Abusers.* One major concern with AACWA was the presumption favoring reunification or preservation of a child with his or her family even though the parents had already severely harmed a child in their care. ASFA provides that in cases involving a parent who has murdered the child's sibling, or committed a felony resulting in serious bodily injury to the child or sibling, the case must be listed for a permanency hearing within 30 days. ASFA leaves to each state to decide what additional "aggravated circumstances" will trigger assignment to the fast track, but the statute provides examples such as torture and abandonment. In this subset of cases, ASFA provides that the state need not expend any time or resources attempting to preserve or reunify a family (42 U.S.C. §671 (D) to (E)). Overall, the bill reflects a growing conviction on the part of policymakers that many families simply cannot be fixed and therefore courts must terminate parental rights early in the process, while children are still young enough to be adopted by new families. The fear is that "[i]f the window of opportunity is missed the child leaves the system as a legal orphan" (Cong. Rec. §12211). Many parents' advocates protest that ASFA goes too far. Most controversial is the idea that one involuntary termination, no matter how long ago or for whatever reason, would mandate fast-tracking without any reunification efforts in any subsequent case involving that parent.

In the period after ASFA's passage, the states rushed to conform their laws to federal requirements. The results have been spotty and often poorly integrated into existing child welfare laws. The chaotic process of "law reform" at the state level that follows a major bill attaching conditions to federal funding raises constitutional concerns as well as policy concerns. State legislatures that depend heavily on federal subsidies to operate their child welfare systems have no realistic choice but to amend them, and often do so without confronting or taking responsibility for the underlying policy implications of what they are doing. The spending clause, if overused, can create distortions in the constitutional balance of federal and state authority and contributes to sloppy and illogical state laws.

The Brave New World of ASFA: Positives and Negatives

ASFA's Positive Aspects

There is much in ASFA's vision of a "Brave New World" for children that advocates for children and their caretakers find appealing. Feminists generally support a focus on family functions as opposed to forms because this approach recognizes the daily reality of the lives of caregivers and children. A focus on the functional parent role empowers those who do the carework of nurturing. What does it matter that a caretaker, whether she provides childrearing for free or for the slender wages paid by the foster care system, is not biologically related to the child? Shouldn't the family be defined by caretaking, not by biology?

Another positive aspect of ASFA is its support of those adoptive parents (both kinship and unrelated) who are willing to take on the work of child rearing but cannot afford the high costs of raising a child, especially one whose history of abuse and neglect or medical needs may call for costly therapy. Subsidies for special needs adoptions help to resolve this dilemma for some foster parents. They allow a foster parent to take on the role of permanent legal parent without sacrificing state support. Advocates for women and children should welcome the notion of government subsidies for special needs children, as a recognition that all children and their caretakers are "our" responsibility. By creating a public–private partnership in rearing dependent children, the subsidy model departs from the tradition of privatizing the social costs of dependency within "the family."

A third positive aspect of ASFA is its funding of research into risk assessment. Despite the money poured into the system, the child welfare system has failed miserably in its goal of insuring children's safety. Shockingly, 48% of child-abuse deaths in 1995 involved children previously known to the authorities (Besharov 1998, citing National Committee to Prevent Child Abuse 1996:3). Sometimes it is a story of underintervention—of a child left in his or her home after reported abuse only to be beaten to death. Sometimes it is a story of overintervention—of a child removed from home only to be abused by the new foster parent. As the National Commission on Children reported, "If the nation had deliberately designed a system that would frustrate the professionals who staff it, anger the public who finance it, and abandon the children who depend on it, it could not have done a better job than the present child welfare system" (1991:293).

The core failing of our child welfare system has been its poor track record of sorting out those children truly at risk of harm from the masses of children whose families, although not perfect, are capable of meeting their basic needs for safety. Risk assessment in too many systems is still a matter of the social worker's "gut reaction" to the sights and smells of poverty. The development of risk assessment tools that reduce arbitrary judgments and can be reviewed for reliability is a crucial step in the right direction.

Finally, as an advocate for children, I applaud the emphasis on child safety. Feminists who fought the battle to treat wife battering as a serious crime requiring state intervention should understand that battering of children requires an equally unambiguous response. The cost to children and society of preserving the privacy of the family by ignoring domestic abuse is simply too high. Children, like mothers, have a right to be safe and secure in their own homes.

ASFA's Negative Aspects

ASFA responds to children's needs to have a functional caretaker, by deemphasizing the biological tie and allowing the role of mother to pass from one to another person with far greater ease and efficiency. New mothers take over from old mothers with a minimum of fuss and legal impediment. However, to observers concerned with family stability and with the dignity of carework, the notion of the fungible mother can be profoundly unsettling. It is in tension not only with pluralist democracy but also with a just system of labor that respects the nurturing work of women and with a child-centered policy that respects the attachments created between caretaker and child. Once children form primary attachments to their mothers, they are not fungible. Separation brings acute pain and trauma to both child and mother. Even a relationship with an imperfect mother (which includes all of us) provides crucial emotional stability to the child. ASFA projects, to some extent, the image of mother as a fungible commodity—to be speedily replaced if she should falter in her role.

A second aspect of ASFA of concern to those interested in the status of careworkers is its tendency toward "de-professionalization" of fostering. The profession of "foster mother," although poorly paid, has been recognized as a distinct form of carework. ASFA, for good or evil, places "term limits" on fostering—at least for a particular child. Long-term foster care is no longer an option. After 15 months, a foster mother who wishes to maintain a relationship with a foster child will be pressed to choose whether to assume the role of adoptive parent (with or without subsidy) or permanent guardian. To complicate matters, a permanent guardian loses her foster-care payments but is generally not eligible for adoption subsidy. The system is constructed to pressure all foster parents including family members—the aunts and grandmothers whose carework costs have been partially defrayed by foster care payments—to choose between terminating the biological mother's rights or taking on the burdens of unpaid carework. The only other alternative is to allow the child one has nurtured to be displaced into a new and strange environment, to then struggle to form new attachments and new bonds of trust. To the extent the statute focuses on adoption as the one true form of permanency, professional fostering, already a low-status occupation, has suffered additional loss of status.

Even foster-care subsidies have their negatives. Subsidies segregate from the general population those children who have been removed from their homes of origin and provide special assistance to this group alone. One might argue that all children (and their families), not just those whom the state seeks to shift off its child welfare rolls, should be eligible for needed medical care and support services. The work of all mothers and family caregivers, not just those recruited to adopt children with special needs, ought to be given appropriate public support.

Perhaps the most profoundly troubling aspect of ASFA is its impact on poor women and women of color already struggling with the impact of recent "welfare reform." Let me return to the interconnection between these two recent reforms. Although rates of poverty and rates of child abuse and neglect are intimately connected, lawmakers often act as if "welfare" policy and "child welfare" policy were entirely unrelated (Dohrn 2000; Roberts 1999). Yet it seems self-evident that a decrease in subsidies to poor mothers is highly likely to lead to more family disruption, higher stress, and an increase in rates of abuse and neglect. As noted earlier, a year before enactment of ASFA, Congress replaced the primary "welfare" program, AFDC, with a new program called Temporary Assistance to Needy Families (TANF). In both the welfare and child welfare contexts, the recent reforms effectively limit the time during which families that lack monetary or parenting resources may be maintained at taxpayers' expense. As women unable to find employment are forced out of the welfare system, their children will be at increased risk of entering the child welfare system.

Politicians from both parties have embraced the idea of "ending welfare as we know it." The American public has enthusiastically jumped on the bandwagon of "personal responsibility." Yet the connection between TANF and ASFA, with the first aiming to end welfare subsidies for poor mothers and the second aiming to end child welfare subsidies for poor foster children, has escaped public notice. Although the image of the "welfare queen" captured the public's imagination, no such image of dependency had ever attached to the child welfare debate—in fact, people hardly know that foster care exists. As one observer has remarked, "foster care is one of those social institutions that never seem to hold public attention for long . . . Foster care might as well take place in another country" (Traub 2001:24).

Why is fostering so invisible to economists and politicians? The mothers who lose their children to the system, the children who grow up in foster care, and the women who work as foster mothers, at least in our larger cities, "are almost entirely poor and black or Hispanic, and their suffering poses no threat to the white middle class" (Traub 2001:24). In times of stress and family disruption, middle-class families can rely on paid careworkers from the private sector or on economically secure extended families. There is an excellent system of "foster care" for the affluent—it is called sleep-away camp and boarding school (Rimer 2001). On the other hand, poor mothers and their kin must rely on public resources to survive disruptions such as homelessness, unplanned pregnancy, divorce, domestic violence, physical or mental illness, and loss of employment. ASFA's laudable goal of saving abused and neglected children, often from poor minority communities, from growing up in foster care poses a real threat to poor mothers of color who suffer temporary interruptions in their capacity to meet their children's needs without some external assistance. In a society committed to equal rights, ASFA's disparate impact on poor women of color should be grave cause for concern.

Mindful of this disparate impact, many critics argue that ASFA's time frames are so short that it will destroy poor families that should be preserved. Many parent advocates worry that a year is not sufficient to rehabilitate a drug-involved parent, even when that parent is committed to changing. Parent advocates are sure to legally challenge the new state laws based on constitutional claims that they infringe on parental rights. The federal Constitution places important limitations on state and local authorities. The Constitution has been interpreted by the Supreme Court as requiring that the state show a compelling reason for infringing on rights of family privacy and for overriding parental autonomy, because these are fundamental liberties protected by the Fourteenth Amendment guarantees of due process.[7] The Supreme Court has also held that, under the due process clause of the Fourteenth Amendment, courts may not terminate a parent's rights without "clear and convincing evidence" (*Santosky v. Kramer* 1982). As long as state and local authorities do not unlawfully burden those rights protected by the Constitution, they are theoretically free to formulate their own child protection and child welfare policies. Parents' advocates, however, can argue that ASFA encourages terminations without setting a sufficiently strict substantive standard. Is clear and convincing evidence that a parent is *temporarily* unable to care for a child or has had his or her rights terminated to a *different* child, a sufficient basis for entering a TPR?

Children's advocates also may have reason to challenge ASFA as applied in various settings. ASFA's statutory timelines encourage a one-size-fits-all approach. A child-centered policy would reflect a child's changing sense of time. For an infant who desperately needs to form a stable parenting relationship, a year is arguably too long to wait for an addicted or mentally ill parent. For a child of 10, who knows and loves an addicted or mentally ill parent, a year is not long enough.

Critics are also concerned that courts and legislatures may read ASFA's provisions without fully understanding them. Advocates for children argue that the tendency to oversimplify—seeing only binary choices where choices are far more complex—is the fatal flaw of all child welfare reform (Lowery 1998:123). They fear that caseworkers and courts will not apply culturally and ethnically sensitive methods to measuring whether a family is so dysfunctional that it cannot meet the needs of its child. ASFA's short time frames and fast-tracking will reduce drift, but they will also make it harder for parents' advocates to combat unjust interventions. ASFA poses a serious danger that the value to children of attachments to kin and foster parents who cannot or prefer not to adopt will be ignored in the rush to promote adoptions. ASFA encourages explorations of kinship placements, foster family adoption, and open adoption, but it does not fund long-term guardianship with a family member or foster parent. This is a serious flaw that new proposals seek to address. It is becoming clear that the model of the infant who needs to be freed quickly in order to find a safe and permanent home—the image of permanency that clearly drove the drafters of ASFA—may not fit the older child who has already formed attachments with family and substitute care-givers. For such a child, stability and permanency may mean preserving the status quo (Courtney 1998). For such a child, the professional foster mother is the ideal, not the compromise solution.

Perhaps the biggest unanswered question, and one that raises frightening specters of a generation of displaced persons, is the question of what will happen to children after a TPR is entered (Gordon 1999). How many of these "state orphans" will realize the goal of finding adoptive homes? How many will con-tinue to drift in foster care limbo until they "age out"? How many will be adopted into unsafe and impermanent homes, with kin or with strangers, only to arrive back in the child welfare system as cases of abuse or disrupted adoptive place-ment?

Conclusion

ASFA is a sweeping reform yet to be fully implemented. Was reform of the child welfare system necessary? The consensus view, which I share, holds that child welfare reform was imperative. The system's critics—on all sides—were right. Too many children not truly at risk were being removed, especially within the African-American community. However, those left in their homes or reunified with abusive parents were too often the very children most at risk of harm. Clearly, the toughest challenge for child welfare was, and remains, the difficulty of measuring the level of risk presented in each individual case. Until we can master that art, we will continue to fail the children we seek to protect.

Was ASFA the right path to reform? To the extent that ASFA funds research on risk assessment, it is surely a step in the right direction. To the extent it frees chil-dren whose families are irretrievably broken to find new safe and permanent fam-ilies, it serves the needs of children for real homes and gets the state out of mismanaging their lives. To the extent it forces bureaucrats to respond to chil-dren's needs in a timely manner, employing both sticks and carrots, it offers some hope of breaking the log jam of inertia that has plagued child welfare systems for so long. To the extent that subsidized adoption provides a revitalized model of public–private partnership with children's caregivers, ASFA contributes to rethinking family policy.

But ASFA also poses great risks. Over the decades, we have seen periodic shifts in the philosophy behind child welfare and child protective services. In the golden age of orphanages, the late 19th century, children were to be protected from their mothers, whose poverty made them dangerous and shiftless by defini-tion, and from the toxic environment of the slums. In the age of AACWA, the late 20th century, children were to be protected from the harm caused by drifting in the care of foster mothers and must be reunified with their "real mothers" even when reunification posed risks to the child. In the new age of ASFA, the 21st cen-tury, mother is considered not so much dangerous as fungible—or perhaps infi-nitely renewable. The New Age foster mother is urged to become a "real" (unpaid) mother, replacing the original mother and trading her paid professional status as foster mother for the unpaid status of family careworker. Through these swings of the policy pendulum, only one factor remains constant—the social devaluation of mothering, especially when done by working-class women and women of color.

It has been easy for those in power to separate "us" from "them." We are presented with sharply contrasting images of motherhood and carework, both of which rely heavily on myth as opposed to fact: On one hand, we have the image of the middle-class White mother, who can afford to donate her carework because her wage-earning husband supports her. On the other hand, we have the image of the poor Black or Brown welfare mother who must beg for handouts because she has neither a spouse nor a job in the wage economy. The first appears secure in her role as "mother," whereas the second is fungible and constantly at risk of state intervention. Yet there is a devaluation of carework inherent in both these images that poses a threat to all women, and should not go unchallenged. In a world that values carework, all mothers would be recognized for their work, all would be fairly compensated, and no child would be at risk of separation from his or her mother for lack of social and economic supports.

Notes

David H. Levin Professor of Family Law and Director of the Center on Children and the Law at Fredric G. Levin College of Law, University of Florida.

1. I use quotes around terms intentionally. Many concepts such as "functional" are strongly contextual and depend on cultural assumptions.

2. In addition to AACWA, the Family Preservation and Support Act granted funds to states for family preservation and support.

3. This passage from the Adoption Assistance and Child Welfare Act of 1980 was subsequently singled out for criticism by Congress (see 143 Cong. Rec. S.12198).

4. The Supreme Court held in *Santosky v. Kramer* (1982) that states must have "clear and convincing evidence" that the parents would be unable to care for the child before terminating parental rights. Any lesser standard would violate the parent's constitutional rights to due process under the Fourteenth Amendment. Under *Stanley v. Illinois* (1972), unmarried fathers as well as mothers were entitled to notice and could claim constitutional rights to raise their offspring.

5. The comments of senators in the Congressional Record illustrate their belief that past measures had failed and new policies were required (143 Cong. Rec. S12210 et. seq.). Adopting the rhetoric of recent "welfare reform" aimed at weaning adults from the dole, Senator Grassley of Iowa stated, "Set up to serve as a temporary emergency situation for children, the foster care system is now a lifestyle for many kids" (143 Cong. Rec. S12211).

6. 42 U.S.C. §673 defines eligibility for "special needs" subsidies, requiring in part that "(1) the State has determined that the child cannot or should not be returned to the home of his parents; and (2) the State had first determined (A) that there exists with respect to the child a specific factor or condition (such as his ethnic background, age, or membership in a minority or sibling group, or the presence of factors such as medical conditions or physical, mental, or emotional handicaps) because of which it is reasonable to conclude that such child cannot be placed with adoptive parents without providing adoption assistance under this section or medical assistance under Title XIX."

7. Although the term "family" is nowhere mentioned in the U.S. Constitution, the U.S. Supreme Court has interpreted the scope of the "liberty" protected by the Fourteenth Amendment as reaching the rights to marry and form a family, rights of family privacy, and the rights of parents to custody and control of their children. In addition, the court has applied other provisions of the Constitution in contexts relevant to child welfare laws. See *Meyer v. Nebraska* (1923) (vindicating parents' substantive due process rights to control the upbringing of their children), *Stanley v. Illinois* (1972) (recognizing unmarried biological father's rights to raise his children), and *Wisconsin v. Yoder* (1972) (protecting parents' First Amendment right to keep children out of school in order to inculcate them with their own religion). See also Barbara Bennett Woodhouse, "The Constitutionalization of Children's Rights: Incorporating Emerging Human Rights into Constitutional Doctrine." For a persuasive argument that in America these rights are rooted in the history of the Civil War Amendments, which repudiated slavery as an assault on basic human rights of family integrity, see Davis (1997).

7

Children and Chronic Health Conditions

Welfare Reform and Health-Related Carework

Andrew S. London, Ellen K. Scott, and Vicki Hunter

*C*ash assistance and associated programs are a safety net for poor women caring for children with chronic health problems and disabilities (Aron, Loprest, and Steuerle 1996). Recognizing this, several authors have recently called for more information about how welfare reform is affecting poor women who are caring for children with such problems (Chavkin 1999; Heymann and Earle 1999; Rosman and Knitzer 2001). This is an important subgroup of the welfare caseload on which to focus attention because the prevalence of children with such needs for care is disproportionately high among welfare-reliant women (Loprest and Acs 1996; Meyers, Lukemeyer, and Smeeding 1996; Polit, London, and Martinez 2001), the demands of care for children with chronic health problems are substantial (Jacobs and McDermott 1989; Leonard, Brust, and Sapienza 1992; Litt, Fletcher, and Winter 2001), and having a child with special needs often constrains labor force participation (Breslau, Salkever, and Staruch 1982; Lukemeyer, Meyers, and Smeeding 2000; Salkever 1982; 1990).

In this chapter, we respond to this call for more information by examining data from longitudinal, ethnographic interviews with welfare-reliant women who have children with chronic health problems that constrain their ability to work in the paid labor force. Our data indicate that these mothers often say that they would like to enter the paid labor force if they can arrange adequate care for their children. However, the demands for care these women face are often overwhelming and unpredictable, making it difficult for them to either enter or maintain employment even when they make arrangements for alternative care. Several believe that they will be eligible for an exemption from welfare's time limits and work requirements, even in the face of direct statements from caseworkers to the contrary.

Based on these women's stories and other published research, we argue that the demands of child health-related carework will make it extremely difficult for many welfare-reliant women to meet the work requirements and time limits associated with welfare reform, or to earn enough to support their families if they leave welfare (Danziger et al. 2000; Lukemeyer et al. 2000; Polit et al. 2001). Although exemptions, if and when they are granted, will allow some women to maintain their long-term commitments to their children's care, and private sources of care or support are sometimes available, we conclude that current welfare reforms will further disadvantage an already disadvantaged group of women and children if additional public programs and supports for child health-related carework are not made available.

Welfare Reform and Carework for Children with Chronic Health Problems

Demands for child health-related carework are high among welfare-reliant women. Chronic diseases and disabilities disproportionately affect the poor, African-Americans, and Hispanics (Williams and Collins 1995), who are also overrepresented in the welfare caseload. Moreover, children from poor and low-income families have disproportionately high rates of accidents, injuries, activity limitations, disabilities, and chronic health problems (McLeod and Shanahan 1996; Miller 2000; Montgomery, Kiely, and Pappas 1996; Newacheck 1994). Although women do more carework than men generally (Abel and Nelson 1990; Cancian and Oliker 2000; Neysmith 2000), they also do more carework for both children and adults with chronic illnesses and disabilities, particularly in impoverished and racial/ethnic minority communities that lack the workplace- and community-based resources to which many more-affluent women have access (Heymann, Earle, and Egleston 1996).

Carework generally is both gendered and devalued labor, whether it occurs in the home or in the marketplace (Cancian and Oliker 2000; England and Folbre, this volume). Because unpaid health-related carework often precludes full- or even part-time labor-force participation, many poor women with limited economic or social resources initially go on, and often stay on, welfare in order to obtain health insurance and minimally support their carework (Oliker 2000; Polit et al. 2001; Seccombe 1999). The unpaid carework for children (and others) with chronic health problems that welfare-reliant women do in their own homes could in theory be conceptualized and valued socially as the vital public care resource that it is. In its absence, substantially publicly funded care would have to be provided for many of these women's children. However, like women's domestic carework for children generally, welfare-reliant women's carework for their children with chronic health problems has not been valued as work or as a public care resource. Rather, it has been underrecognized, undervalued, and undersubsidized.

We are further reminded of this historic undervaluing of carework in the current context of welfare reform, with its goal of "ending welfare as we know it." Prior to the passage of the Personal Responsibility and Work Opportunity Reconciliation Act (PRWORA), women who were taking care of a household member who was ill or incapacitated were not required to participate in welfare-to-work programs. This is no longer the case. Like all other welfare-reliant women, except those granted "good cause" exemptions or extensions, women who are providing health-related care to a child or family member are now required to meet the work requirements specified in their state or county TANF program. Even though commitments to care are often not time-limited or contingent, welfare receipt now is. As Madonna Harrington Meyer stated recently, "No welfare retrenchment has proved more telling, or more chilling" (2000:164).

Removing this support for poor women's carework makes it clear that such work is not adequately valued. If one has the private means with which to choose to perform family carework, then one has the right to do this labor. Without such means, there is no such right (Harrington Meyer, Herd, and Michel 2000). For many poor women, under current welfare laws, such carework in fact becomes extraordinarily difficult.

Removing these public resources will have social consequences. As a society, we depend on the private labor of families to raise children, as well as to care for the sick and the disabled (Abel, this volume). If we remove one of the primary means by which poor women can perform this labor, then we must shift this responsibility from the private sphere to the public sphere (Harrington, Meyer, and Storbakken 2000; Stone 2000). Yet it is not clear that public resources are adequate to fill the gap that will be left when these mothers enter the labor force. In a time when there is a deficit of care (Ungerson 2000), removing a critical resource that sustains maternal carework is short-sighted and will further disadvantage an already disadvantaged group of women and children.

In the remainder of this chapter, we examine how welfare-reliant women who are caring for children with chronic health problems are responding to and experiencing the mandates of welfare reform. After briefly describing the design of the Project on Devolution and Urban Change, we present a series of case studies that illustrate how the "proximate contexts" (Oliker 1995a; 1995b; 2000) of women's lives constrain and enable decisions about work and care. We describe some of the diverse strategies these women develop as they try to make ends meet, respond to welfare reform, and care for their children and families. We conclude with a discussion of the intersections of welfare reform and care, and the choices welfare-reliant women and policymakers face.

Data and Methods

The data in this chapter were drawn for Manpower Demonstration Research Corporation's Project on Devolution and Urban Change, which was designed to examine how welfare reform affects urban neighborhoods of concentrated poverty and high welfare receipt (for additional details about the study, see Quint et al. 1999). For this chapter, we rely on data drawn from longitudinal, ethnographic interviews with welfare-reliant women from neighborhoods of concentrated poverty in Cleveland and Philadelphia who were providing care to children with severe health problems.

In these two sites, 75 women were recruited for participation in the study from six census tract clusters (three in each city), where at least 30% of families were living in poverty in 1990 and at least 20% of families were receiving welfare. In each city, we selected two predominantly African-American neighborhoods and one predominantly White neighborhood. Approximately 12–15 women were recruited from each neighborhood. All of the women were reliant on welfare at the time they joined the study.

Data for this chapter were drawn mainly from the first- and second-year main interviews conducted with women who had a child with substantial health problems. When possible, we also drew on data from the third-year main interviews, field notes, and interim follow-up interviews. All interviews involved open-ended questions about a broad range of women's life experiences. These lengthy, 4- to 10-hour interviews closely document women's experiences as they face time limits and negotiate the transition from welfare to work. The main interviews were conducted annually between 1997 and 2000. All interviews were tape-recorded with permission and transcribed verbatim for analysis. All names used in this chapter are pseudonyms.

Caring for Children with Chronic Health Problems

For most of the women in our sample who had children with serious health problems, their commitment to caring for their children was the lens through which they focused their decisions about welfare and work. This carework for chronically ill children occurred in the context of ongoing responsibilities for their other children and relatives, limited social and financial resources, and few community- or market-based alternative sources of care. Race, class, and gender inequalities, as well as the geographies of these women's lives, constrained their access to supportive resources (see Kurz, this volume).

Most of the women who were caring for children with chronic health problems did very little paid work, if they did any at all, despite the fact that they professed a willingness and desire to work (see also London, Scott, Edin, and Hunter 2000; Scott, Edin, London, and Mazelis 2001; Scott, Edin, London, and Kissane 2001; Scott, London, and Edin 2000). Sometimes they did not work because they believed that they would eventually be exempted from work requirements and time limits, or that they could be if they needed to be. However, more commonly, women experienced problems finding child care. As is the case with welfare-reliant women generally, difficulty in finding adequate, reliable, safe child care was often seen by these women as the main obstacle to their employment.

Market-based child-care options for children with chronic health problems are extremely limited. Thus, with one notable exception, which we discuss at length at the end of the chapter, all of the women in our sample who were caring for children with chronic health problems either provided care themselves, or relied on privatized, family- and network-based solutions. Sometimes when they provided care themselves they relied on cash assistance from welfare to support this carework; at other times, they relied on private financial support from husbands or absent fathers of children. Always, they continued to live at or very near the poverty line.

In this section, we provide several case studies to illustrate the crisis of child care for families with a chronically ill child, and the types of family- and network-based strategies women used to make ends meet and provide care. In the next section, we discuss the case of one woman who had relied on welfare so she could provide care for her daughter for the first 18 years of her daughter's life, but who ultimately became an agency-based, paid caregiver for her own daughter as a means to solve her child-care dilemma. These cases all illustrate the demands of care and the extent to which caring for a child with a chronic health problem is skilled labor. Moreover, although each of these case studies illustrates the particularities of one woman's circumstances, taken together the set documents some of the challenges welfare reform poses to poor women who are struggling to maintain their carework commitments and support their families.

Private Support: Family- and Network-Based Strategies

Privatized, family- and network-based support took two different forms in our sample. Some women received child-care assistance from family and network members (husbands, former husbands, fathers of children, parents, older children), whereas other women relied on financial transfers from family and network members to subsidize their own carework. We begin by discussing several stories of women who had child care provided directly by family and network members. We then discuss two instances where women relied on financial support from family and network members to maintain their child health-related carework commitments while they neither worked nor received welfare.

Direct Care by Family and Network Members

Several women relied on direct family- or network-based support to help them with child care when they went to work or if they had a personal crisis. Sometimes, that care was adequate; at other times, it clearly was not.

Debbie, an African-American woman from Cleveland, was married and had three young children at home: one school-aged, one infant, and a 4-year old who was severely brain-damaged due to lack of oxygen at birth. When we first spoke with her, Debbie was 26 years old and had recently completed an associate's degree in medical assistance. She was not working and said that her 4-year-old daughter required a lot of extra care; she was unable to feed herself and was "basically on a two to three month level." Debbie and her husband received SSI benefits for this child.

Shortly after the first interview, Debbie found a telemarketing job selling home security systems. For a brief period, she worked a second job as a part-time medical assistant earning $6.50 per hour. Neither job had medical benefits, and she ultimately left both to take a full-time position doing medical billing for the Bureau of Workman's Compensation. Debbie felt she could not afford to purchase medical benefits at this job, and was still receiving transitional Medicaid at the time of the second main interview.

When asked if caring for her daughter made it difficult for her to work, Debbie responded that it did. However, she also described how she and her husband managed the demands of dual-earner employment and caregiving. Debbie worked first shift and took care of the kids at night; her husband worked second shift and was home during the day to get their daughter on and off the bus that transported her to and from the school she attended for 4 hours per day.

During our second main interview with her, Debbie reported that she thought she could receive welfare and be exempted from work requirements and time limits if she needed to stay home with her daughter. She said: "I was just told, but I'm not for sure. But, say I needed to stay home, take care of the baby, with my daughter...I would then receive the ADC benefits, you know, beyond the basic months for however long that I, that she needs me home...because of her disability." Debbie never pursued the possibility of getting an exemption because she preferred to work and thought her children would be better off as a consequence of the choices she and her husband were making.[1]

Since shortly after she began participating in the study, Debbie has not received cash benefits. She is one of the few women in our sample who made the transition from welfare to stable work over the course of the first year of the study (see Scott et al. 2001), and she is the only woman with health-related caregiving responsibilities to have done so. The presence of her husband and his contributions to the care of their disabled daughter, their other children, and the household in part made it possible for Debbie to seek and maintain full-time work outside of the home. Her relatively high educational attainment, her pro-work attitudes, and the absence of other substantial barriers to employment besides her carework responsibilities also contributed to Debbie's relatively positive employment and carework outcomes. Although it was difficult, Debbie and her husband seemed to be doing what they felt they needed to do to care for their family. Their choices were, by and large, consistent with the ideologies of welfare reform.

Like Debbie, Melissa, a White, 32-year-old mother of four from Philadelphia, was also married. However, unlike Debbie, Melissa did not transition from welfare to work in the first year of the study. Even when she worked for pay, she remained on welfare and took advantage of the more generous earned income disregards associated with welfare reform. Melissa had not graduated from high school and was not working when we first interviewed her. When she talked about going to work, she said: "The only problem I have is findin' somebody that could handle my son. Be[ing] with his asthma and . . . he's very hyper." She thought her parents would "normally do it [watch her son]," but also felt that "they can't handle my son." As a result of not perceiving other alternatives, Melissa talked about ways that she could stay close to home. In response to a question about the kinds of jobs she was looking for, Melissa said: "Well, I want to do computer [sighs]. But . . . I'm looking for a school around here, that's close. Cause of my son being with asthma. I don't want to leave him and go real far."

Ultimately, in the first year of the study, Melissa took a job at a dollar store for about 4 months. Although she had previously expressed concern that her parents were ill equipped to handle her son because of his asthma and hyperactivity, they ended up watching her son and her other children until her husband came home from work.

The potential inadequacies of family- and network-based care for children with severe health problems are suggested in Melissa's story. When she took a job, she ended up leaving her son with family members who she felt couldn't care for him adequately. However, the extent to which some direct, family- and network-based care for children with substantial health problems may be inadequate is more dramatically illustrated in the case of Wendy, a 33-year-old White mother of two from Cleveland. Wendy had multiple barriers to work; caring for her son, who had substantial mental health problems, was only one of them. With this case study, we show how caregiving and other problems interact to influence both employment- and care-related choices and outcomes. Wendy's story also illustrates how some kinds of network support can appear helpful, but may ultimately be harmful to women and children.

Wendy had a high school diploma and had completed three semesters of a medical assistance program. She had a substantial amount of work experience, but it was intermittent. She had been on and off welfare for about 10 years, at least partly because of her substantial caregiving responsibilities, and also because of her own significant health problems (asthma, anxiety disorders, a back injury, and a foot injury that became significantly worse over the course of the study). Wendy's two children were both fathered by her former husband, to whom she had been married and divorced twice. Her former husband abused alcohol and drugs, had lost jobs due to his substance abuse, and was abusive to Wendy and both children. Despite this history of abuse and her distrust of him, she still relied on him for a substantial amount of assistance with the children, especially when she was experiencing a health crisis herself. She also felt she had to rely on him because, in her opinion, no one else could or would take care of their son.

Before the age of 10, Wendy's son was diagnosed with attention deficit disorder, bipolar disorder, schizophrenia, and posttraumatic stress disorder. He was very hard to care for. Wendy told the interviewer that he had threatened to kill both her and her husband, he played with fire, he harmed himself by banging his head against walls and doors, he talked of killing himself, and he ran away repeatedly. When asked how long her son's problems had been evident to her, Wendy responded: "I had been seeking help for him since kindergarten. He physically attacked a principal in kindergarten, kicking her, biting her, scratching her, you know, stuff like that. And the destruction of his toys at home. I wanted to get him help earlier, but no one would listen. Until the point where they had to."

Wendy indicated that the care for her son made it very difficult for her to take or keep a job. She did not trust others to care for him, and she did not believe that she could find someone willing to do so: "When I start working, I don't know, because it is hard. Even the county providers do not take children like [him]. They will not be responsible for his medication. And he's on such powerful drugs . . . so, no I can't trust just anybody with them."

During the second main interview, Wendy disclosed a history of extensive physical and sexual abuse at the hands of her ex-husband. She also described how he was abusive to their children. Despite her ex-husband's behavior, Wendy relied on him to help her with caring for their children, especially their son. For example, Wendy's ex-husband housed the family (including Wendy) for 1 month when they became homeless; he did a lot of routine transporting of the children and the family's laundry (which Wendy got him to do in exchange for not reporting his whereabouts to child support enforcement); and when Wendy could not manage the children due to her own health crises, the children would go and stay with their father. Wendy felt she had no one else to turn to.

Overall, Wendy wanted to go to work, but was unable to do so because of her need to find adequate care for her son and her own health problems. Even if she was physically well enough to work, it is likely that lack of child care for her son would have prevented or disrupted her labor-force participation, as it had in the past. As Wendy thought about trying to meet the requirements of work (in the future) and caregiving, her ex-husband and the abusive father of her children figured prominently. With few community-based or formal care resources available for a child with such severe mental health problems, what choice did she have but to care for him herself or rely on his father for help? Although reliance on family and network support is consistent with the ideology of welfare reform, Wendy's story clearly illustrates that not all family and network support is the same, nor are pro-work attitudes necessarily enough to overcome severe personal and structural barriers to work.

Family- and Network-Based Financial Support for Carework

In our data, private support for child health-related carework was not always provided in the form of direct care. Sometimes women provided the care themselves with financial assistance from family and network members. We illustrate this with two case studies. In one case, the woman was supported financially by her husband (from whom she had been separated); in the other case, she supported herself through informal child support from the fathers of her children. In both cases, these women were dealing with emergent health crises in their children's lives that required a considerable amount of their time and energy.

Like most of the women with whom we talked, Andrea, a 27-year-old African-American mother of three children from Philadelphia, said she wanted to work. For the first year of the study she was combining welfare and work, but she was laid off in July 1999, shortly after the second year main interview was completed. She expected to collect unemployment benefits amounting to half of her salary for 9 months. Although she was no longer receiving cash benefits at this time, she did receive Food Stamps, Medicaid, and a Section 8 housing subsidy, which reduced her rent to zero.

Shortly after Andrea was laid off, her daughter began having major health problems that required significant medical care for diagnosis and treatment. Andrea reported that she had stopped looking for work because of her daughter's illness. In November 1999, the doctors told Andrea that they thought her daughter had rheumatoid arthritis; in December, they said they thought that her daughter might need surgery on her hip. When we interviewed Andrea in the spring of 2000, we found out that she was still not working even though her unemployment benefits had run out. Her daughter had spent time in the hospital in January and February because of her hip. About a week after she was released from the hospital, she was readmitted and diagnosed with diabetes. In March 2000, Andrea told the interviewer: "I am still unable to work, but it's not because . . . I can't find a job. It's because of my daughter being sick right now, and for the last three months. Hopefully, in the next three months, I'll be able to look for another job."

After her daughter was diagnosed with diabetes, Andrea spent a lot of time and energy learning how to provide good care. She learned how to prepare food, to test blood sugar, to give insulin shots, and to monitor her daughter's attempts to manage these things for herself. Andrea said she did not want to go back to work until she was sure her daughter's diabetes was under control. In this period of crisis, she and her husband, from whom she had been separated since we first met her, got back together. Andrea said that he had always been involved, and now, with what was happening with their daughter, he wanted to be closer. The money her husband was earning was enough to sustain the family minimally. She repeatedly told the interviewer that she would eventually go back to work, not to wel-fare. However, she told the interviewer: "If she's not at a stable condition where I feel comfortable, then I'll prolong [full-time carework]. But, eventually, I'm gonna have to get out of here [to re-enter the labor force]." During this period Andrea was trying to learn about SSI and put in an application for her daughter. She was having some difficulty getting accurate information about benefits and proce-dures, at least in part because she was hearing different things from neighbors. She was also having difficulty ensuring Medicaid coverage for her daughter and coordinating the management of her case across different public agencies. Andrea said that welfare was "a headache. For a little bit, they threaten you over anything. Uh, for instance, um, that I filed for social security for my oldest daughter, they sent me a paper, a form to be filled out by the doctor and me, to say why I can't work, why is she disabled and stuff like that. And they said if I don't bring, um, return the form [to the welfare office also], her medical will be cut off, but she'll still get stamps . . . That's what it's like . . . This is the caseworker. If you don't cooperate, she's gonna be taken off the medical, knowing she needs her insulin and the things that goes with it. The sugar testing, they don't care. What good is the stamps if she can't have medical?" Making sure that her daughter had access to the public resources for which she was eligible took a lot of time and energy (see also Litt et al. 2001).

By December 2001, Andrea's daughter was receiving SSI and was undergoing physical therapy to help her walk and stand up straight. Andrea was regularly pro-viding child care in her home to three children to help make ends meet. She felt confident enough about her daughter's health to do some paid work, but also felt that working at home provided her the flexibility she needed to be available to her daughter during her rehabilitation.

Barbara, a 31-year-old White, divorced woman from Cleveland, also faced an emergent health crisis with her daughter. In contrast to Debbie, who had family support that facilitated her stable attachment to the paid labor force, and Melissa and Wendy, who relied on family and network support in their attempts to move into the paid labor force, Barbara (like Andrea) had family and network support that allowed her to remain out of the work force (and off welfare too). She received $860 in direct, unreported child support payments from the fathers of her three children and Food Stamps. This income, in conjunction with some assis-tance from her mother who lived nearby, allowed Barbara to have the flexibility required to manage her daughter's serious kidney problems and dangerously high cholesterol. Barbara knew that a job would not allow her to do the necessary care-work: "I run my daughter back and forth all the time to the doctor . . . I was gonna do it [apply for a job] this year, but then all the medical problems she's been having and going in and out of, you know, doctors, hospitals, and stuff . . . I couldn't expect to leave and have a job. I'm not going to get paid for that! So, lemme get things situated and straightened out before I go and [apply for a job]."

These case studies illustrate different ways that family and network support can influence the employment- and care-related choices of welfare-reliant women who have children with substantial health problems. Sometimes private support takes the form of direct care. Other times it takes the form of financial support

that enables women to remain out of the paid labor force, and sometimes off welfare as well. The extent to which these family- and network-based strategies, in
these instances maintained in the context of families and communities with limited resources, can or will be maintained over the long term is uncertain.

The Transition to Market-Based Care

Although family- and network-based strategies and welfare were the most
common means by which women supported and cared for children with health
problems, one other strategy warrants discussion. In this example, one woman
shifts from using welfare to subsidize her unpaid carework to being an agency-
based paid caregiver for her own daughter. Although this market-based solution
to the dilemma of caring and making ends meet holds some promise, we must not
overly romanticize what is in essence a transition from welfare to low-wage,
undervalued, market-based child carework that offers little hope of upward mobility or a living wage. Ultimately, this example underscores how poverty, isolation,
deprivation, and minimal access to public resources shape women's health-related
carework.

When we first met her, Tasha was a 45-year-old, unmarried African-American
woman living in Cleveland with her two children. Tasha was one of the best-edu-
cated women in our sample; she had completed 3 years at Ohio University, but
dropped out to help care for her father and to work in the family restaurant when
he got cancer. Subsequently, she became the primary caregiver for her daughter,
who had a severe seizure disorder that developed in the first year of her life. She
provided this care for 18 years without knowledge or use of community-based
and publicly funded resources that might have assisted her (see Aron et al. 1996
for a comprehensive discussion of the various programs that serve children with
disabilities). Until recently, Tasha had been disconnected from the fragmented
home and respite-care resources that support community-based, long-term caregivers, although she did utilize welfare, Food Stamps, Medicaid, SSI for her
daughter, and school-based special education. No public agency or official with
whom she was connected assisted her to access these other support resources
until she sought them out herself after learning about them during a random
encounter on a bus with a stranger who asked her why she looked so tired.

When her infant daughter developed a severe seizure disorder, Tasha quit the
job she had taken at the Federal Reserve bank and got on public assistance in
order to care for her: "So, that's why I had to get on public assistance. I told [the
caseworker] that I wouldn't be down here, you know, getting welfare, if it weren't
for her being so sick. And she told me about SSI. I thought that was only for
adults . . . So, she was put on SSI." Tasha had been on public assistance since this
time; her daughter still received SSI at the time Tasha entered the study.

Tasha did no paid work, reported or otherwise, during the first year of the
study, and she seemed to have little family or network support that could assist
her with her daughter's care. Tasha's elderly mother helped a little, but was too
frail to manage the physical labor involved in caring for Tasha's adolescent daughter. Tasha believed that she would be exempted from work requirements despite
direct messages from her caseworker that this would not be the case. Her com-

mitment to taking care of her daughter and her belief that she would get an exemption were the predominant influences on her decision to remain on welfare. Managing her daughter's care was in itself a full-time job. Tasha not only provided direct care, she also functioned as an informal case manager, coordinating and advocating for various services (see Litt et al. 2001).

In the second year main interview, Tasha made it clear to our interviewer that her caseworker was pushing her to get off welfare even though she was caregiving. Tasha still thought she would qualify for an exemption, but she said that she was willing to work if she could trust those giving care to her daughter. She sought a way to balance the demands of paid work and carework, and meet the mandates of welfare reform, so began training to become a home health aide.

By the third main interview, Tasha had resolved the conflict between the requirement that she work and her commitment to caring for her daughter. Tasha was hired by an agency and assigned to care for her own daughter. She was paid for 30 hours of carework per week. She found out about this opportunity from her daughter's case manager (not her welfare "Self-Sufficiency Coach"). At the time we interviewed her, Tasha had been doing this for almost a year. She had been off of welfare for most of that time; her cash assistance check, which she was still eligible for because of the earned income disregard, would have been reduced to $73. Her caseworker advised her to stop it and save the time she had remaining on her welfare clock. As a result, Tasha believed that she had "banked" 9 months of cash benefits "in case something happens, maybe I get sick again (she had an emergency hysterectomy the year before) and I can't work, and I need to get back on that cash assistance." Tasha said that this solution to her dilemma "was like a weight was lifted off of my shoulders."

For this paid work, Tasha earned low wages and received no medical benefits. She still relied on Medicaid. However, when asked how she was feeling about herself now that she was working, Tasha responded: "I feel good, good, you know because like I said, I feel fortunate that I could still do things at home. I went to look at some living room furniture the other day and the guy said: 'Are you employed?' And I said: 'Yes, I'm employed.' You know my social security number, you know, you check it out. So, that kinda thing, it makes you, it makes you feel good, it makes you feel good, it really does. You know, you're in a different status [when] you're not considered unemployed."

Rather than hire someone else to care for her daughter while she worked elsewhere, probably in someone else's home or a facility doing health-related carework, Tasha managed to enter the labor market and find a privatized way to become the paid careworker for her own daughter. Thus, the boundaries between the public and private spheres of carework blurred. The shift in the state investment from a cash welfare grant for Tasha to a cash grant for the agency providing care for her daughter probably had relatively small fiscal consequences for the state. However, it had large consequences for the meaning of this work. Tasha, welfare administrators, and the state all seemed to agree that Tasha's care for her daughter, conducted as paid work for a home health agency, had legitimacy that the same work performed with the support of cash welfare benefits did not. Moreover, with her employment, Tasha obtained the personal benefits of enhanced self-esteem, somewhat increased income, and enhanced social status because others valued her work.

Although her situation was in these ways improved, Tasha was at risk for losing health insurance, and her prospects for raising her income by doing undervalued, underpaid carework were minimal. She had ongoing concerns about her own health and that of her elderly, increasingly frail mother, and her need to secure a long-term care arrangement for her daughter. Her situation remained somewhat precarious. Nevertheless, at the last main interview we have done thus far with Tasha, she seemed to be doing relatively well and was optimistic about her future.

Discussion

Welfare-reliant women caring for children with serious, chronic health conditions, behavior problems, and disabilities face specific and unique challenges to meeting the mandates of welfare reform. Although caring for chronically ill children with limited resources has always been challenging, the passage of the PWRORA fundamentally changed the circumstances of welfare-reliant women who provide child health-related care. Until 1996, poor families could count on welfare to enable them to provide care for ill children. With welfare reform, the economic safety net became time-limited and contingent, despite the fact that health-related carework commitments are not necessarily so. Madonna Harrington Meyer (2000:166) recently noted that "the welfare state has the ability to shape care work, either easing or increasing the burdens placed primarily on women." The case studies presented in this chapter illustrate some of the choices welfare-reliant women who are caring for chronically ill children now face, and some of the issues for which policymakers must find solutions.

First, despite the mandates of welfare reform, not all women will be able to work. They will face sanctions, run out their time clocks, and perhaps attempt to obtain exemptions or extensions. It remains unclear how much need there will be for extensions and exemptions in different locales, or whether the need for them will exceed the allowable 20% of the average monthly caseload (Polit et al. 2001). However, it is clear that obtaining exemptions and extensions will not be a viable strategy for any or all women with health-related carework commitments if clear and specific guidelines regarding the circumstances under which such extensions or exemptions will be granted are not formulated and communicated. It is critically important that TANF program managers develop and communicate clearly to welfare-reliant women the set of factors that will qualify them for extensions and exemptions, or the options available to help them cope with the particular circumstances they and their families face. This will necessitate the development and implementation of effective screening mechanisms for identifying women who qualify for such extensions and exemptions without unduly infringing on their privacy or burdening them.

Second, many women will find some means to combine paid labor with unpaid health-related carework. As illustrated in many of these stories, some women will draw on husbands, boyfriends, and other members of their social networks to help them care for and supervise their children while they work. Alternatively, some women may draw on formal child-care slots if they are available, affordable, and the providers can assure adequate and reliable care for chronically ill children. It is noteworthy that none of the women in our sample used such formal child-care resources, with the exception of Tasha, who became the paid child-care provider for her own daughter. The extent to which Tasha's "solution" is viable for other women, or can be coordinated and supported by TANF programs, needs further exploration by policymakers and researchers (see Ungerson 2000).

Third, as illustrated in the cases of Andrea and Barbara, some women will find private means of support for themselves and their children through marriage, cohabitation, reliance on members of their family of origin, or access to child support resources from absent fathers of children. The extent to which this will be a viable, long-term strategy for a substantial number of welfare-reliant women who are caring for chronically ill children in unknown. Moreover, one potential, unintended consequence of policies that encourage increased reliance on social networks is that some women may end up increasing their reliance on fathers of children or other network members who have in the past been or currently are violent or abusive toward them. This possibility was illustrated in Wendy's case (see also Scott, London, and Myers 2002).

We need more information on the consequences of welfare reform for welfare-reliant women who are providing care to chronically ill children and children with disabilities. As the case studies in this chapter illustrate, health-related child carework occurs at the intersection of the family, community, market, and welfare state. The appropriate roles for each of these sectors in carework are contested in the policy arena. Nevertheless, it is critical that policymakers recognize that welfare-reliant women who are caring for chronically ill children (and other relatives) are providing essential but undervalued and undersubsidized labor that benefits their families and society. As such, policymakers and Americans more generally must broaden their definition of what counts as work and develop and implement flexible public assistance policies that allow women (and men) to fulfill their health-related carework commitments to their children without risking poverty and loss of health insurance. Policymakers must, at the same time, expand available child care and home care services for chronically ill children and develop other programs to support work for low-income women who have children with special needs but who want to do work other than unpaid health-related carework. Although these kinds of targeted programs won't solve the overarching and more general health insurance, long-term care, and child-care crises that exist in the United States, they are necessary to ensure that low-income women who are providing health-related care for their children have a minimal, long-term, and publicly funded safety net available to them. In the absence of such policies and programs, welfare reform will further disadvantage a substantial number of already disadvantaged women and vulnerable children.

Notes

Data used in this chapter were collected under the auspices of MDRC's Project on Devolution and Urban Change. Analyses were supported in part by MDRC's Next Generation Project. We thank Gordon Berlin, Barbara Goldman, Robert

Granger, Virginia Knox, and our national collaborators for their support. We are particularly grateful to Kathryn Edin for making data from the Philadelphia site of the Urban Change project available to us for analysis. We also thank Averil Clarke, Susan Clampet-Lundquist, Lorna Dilley, Ralonda Ellis-Hill, Karen Fierer, Rebecca Joyce Kissane, Samieka Mitchell, Keesha Moore, Kagendo Mutua, Laura Nichols, and Sarah Spain who helped recruit the samples and complete the interviews. Additionally, we thank the women (and a few men) who shared their stories with us; each in her (his) own way contributed to making this chapter possible. Finally, we thank Demie Kurz, Jacquelyn Litt, Elisa Rosman, and Mary Tuominen for their helpful comments on earlier drafts of this chapter.

1. Given the way that the TANF program has been designed and implemented in Cuyahoga County (Cleveland), it is unlikely that Debbie would have in fact received such an exemption or extension if she had pursued it at that point. With the implementation of the time limit in October 2000, such exemptions or extensions have become possible; however, very few have in fact been granted.

Caregiving, Welfare States, and Mothers' Poverty

Karen Christopher

*D*uring the past few decades, across Western nations women's economic and social status changed rapidly: Their labor force participation increased, cohabitation increased, and single parenthood grew more prevalent. In light of these changes, some cite an increasing "care deficit" that occurs because most women are no longer caregivers at home on a full-time basis (Glenn 2000; Hochshild 1995). Hochshild (1995) discussed several different strategies to address the "care deficit." Some nations prefer the "traditional" solution, in which women provide care privately for their own children and are often full-time caregivers. In other nations, welfare states can subsidize women's care—in "warmer" ways that combine personal and institutional care, or in "colder" ways that rely heavily on institutional care. Here I focus on the "traditional" strategy and examine how social policies in nations that rely heavily on this strategy affect caregivers' economic outcomes. These policies often assume a "male breadwinner" family—a married couple in which women are the primary caretakers of children, the elderly, and household affairs, and men are the primary breadwinners.

The contribution of this chapter lies in its analysis of how different welfare states affect the economic status of primary caregivers—mothers and single mothers—compared to other citizens.[1] Although existing research examines the gendered assumptions underlying social policies (Lewis 1992; O'Connor, Orloff, and Shaver 1999; Sainsbury 1994; 1996), little research examines the economic effects of living in "male breadwinner" welfare states. Past research rarely focuses explicitly on mothers and single mothers, even though these women are typically the most economically disadvantaged citizens in nations (Casper, McLanahan, and Garfinkel 1994; Christopher et al. 2001; McFate, Smeeding, and Rainwater 1995). Thus, I focus on the economic penalties or advantages that mothers incur when they live in welfare states that privilege women's unpaid carework over women's paid work.

I begin with a review of the literature that considers the gendered assumptions upon which many welfare states base their social policies. Next I present my research questions, discuss data and methods, and present analyses of how welfare states affect the poverty rates of mothers, single mothers, and other citizens in nine Western nations (Australia, Canada, Finland, France, Germany, the Netherlands, Sweden, United Kingdom, and the United States). The analyses show the extent to which social assistance programs reduce mothers' and single mothers' poverty rates—in an absolute sense, and also how welfare states reduce their poverty rates relative to the poverty rates of other groups (such as female nonmothers or nonsingle mothers). I find that the welfare states most representative of the "male breadwinner" model (Germany and the Netherlands) are problematic not only with their gendered assumptions about women's carework; compared to other countries, they also do less to reduce mothers' poverty rates relative to those of female nonmothers and men. In other words, in Germany and the Netherlands, many social policies assume that mothers are primary caregivers, but their social assistance programs fail to lower mothers' poverty rates relative to those of other citizens. I conclude with the implications of these findings for mothers' economic dependence on male partners. First, I present a brief discussion of the theoretical literature on the gendered nature of welfare states.

Gendering Welfare States

The literature on gender and welfare state regimes in large part consists of reactions to Esping-Andersen's (1990) influential classification of welfare state regimes.[2] His classification of welfare regimes overlooks how welfare states are gendered in their assumptions and outcomes. Orloff's (1993) renowned critique points out that Esping-Andersen's concept of independence from labor markets— "de-commodification"—is not inclusive of women; especially in past decades, many women were not reliant on the labor market but on male partners for their economic survival. In addition to independence from labor markets, feminist scholars stress women's independence from family relationships, or "defamilialization" (Knijn and Ungerson 1997; Lister 1995). Orloff (1999) stressed that women should be able to create and maintain autonomous households, and this "require[s] an absence of coercion, including the kind imposed for years on women to marry because of their own dismal economic prospects" (p. 12). Given persistent gender inequalities in the family—in which women have been disproportionately responsible for caregiving—and in the labor market, many women continue to be economically dependent on their partners. And in many welfare states, social policies bolster women's economic dependence on men. These issues are not considered in Esping-Andersen's classification of welfare state regimes.[3]

Other feminist scholars are more upfront about how welfare states embody gendered assumptions and affect gender inequality. Sainsbury (1994; 1996) created a typology based on two ideal types of welfare regimes—the "male breadwinner" and "individual" models. The "male breadwinner" model includes policies that uphold a strict division of labor within couples, receipt of benefits by the male breadwinner, entitlement based on the male breadwinner family form, and private, unpaid care labor.[4] In contrast, the individual model includes policies that encourage: a shared division of labor, an individual (rather than familial) basis for entitlement to and receipt of benefits, and state-subsidized, paid care labor (Sainsbury 1996). In short, the "male breadwinner" welfare states leave caregiving responsibilities to mothers. In contrast, the "individual" model states take steps to externalize the responsibility of caregiving to the state (and to men in the most progressive welfare states). In welfare states based on the latter model, women are more able to engage in paid work and thereby to be less economically dependent on male partners.

Sainsbury (1996) discusses the marked differences between countries in their adoption of "male breadwinner" or "individual" policies. With her analysis of the United Kingdom, the United States, the Netherlands, and Sweden, she found that although all four countries show some vestiges of the "male breadwinner" model, the Netherlands most closely resembles the "male breadwinner" model while Sweden corresponds to the "individual" model.[5] An in-depth discussion of the extent to which different welfare states adhere to these different models is beyond the scope of this chapter; see Christopher (forthcoming) for a detailed discussion of how social policies across different nations resemble the "male breadwinner" and "individual" models. Of the nations considered here, Netherlands and Germany adhere to the "male breadwinner" model, while Sweden, Finland, and France adhere to the "individual" model. Generally, social policies in the English-speaking countries reflect both of these models.

Social scientists have also categorized welfare states by the social policies available to single mothers. As Sainsbury (1994; 1996) and Hobson (1994) suggested, the social and economic status of single mothers is often quite distinct from that of married mothers. In caring for their children on their own, single mothers often face a severe lack of money and time.[6]

Regarding single mothers, Lewis and Hobson (1997) formulated a typology of welfare states based on two ideal types: the Caregiving model and the Parent/Worker model. The former model describes policies such as social transfers or tax credits that allow or encourage women to stay home and care for young children rather then enter paid work. The latter includes employment supports like paid leave and subsidized child care that allow mothers to enter and stay attached to the labor force; in the Parent/Worker model, women are expected to enter paid work at equal rates with men. Of the sample nations discussed, the Netherlands, Germany, and the United Kingdom are more representative of the Caregiving model, while Sweden, Finland, and France are the most representative of the Parent/Worker model. Social policies in the English-speaking countries represent both of these models.[7]

Although the literature on gender and welfare states has thoroughly examined the gendered assumptions underlying different social policies, research rarely examines how women, mothers and single mothers fare economically in the different models of welfare states described above. I turn to these issues in the analyses below.

Research Questions

There is an abundant literature on how welfare states affect the economic outcomes of families. [For recent cross-national analyses of the effects of social transfers and tax systems on economic outcomes, see Behnrendt (1999), Kenworthy (1999), and McFate et al. (1995).] Yet this literature rarely considers two things: the economic consequences of living in more- or less-gendered welfare states, and how welfare states affect the economic outcomes of mothers and single mothers compared to other citizens.[8] Both Sainsbury (1996) and Lewis and Hobson

(1997) suggested that the "male breadwinner" model and Caregiving models of social policy may not have adverse economic effects, particularly in nations like the Netherlands where social transfers are relatively generous. To assess these claims, I consider several research questions: First, what are the poverty rates of mothers and single mothers across several Western nations, and how do they compare to those of other citizens? Second, to what extent do social assistance programs pull the families of mothers and single mothers out of poverty? Third, I examine how welfare states treat mothers and single mothers vis-à-vis other groups: Given that nations reserve a limited amount of social transfer and tax relief for citizens, to what extent do they target mothers and single mothers? With these questions I aim to examine how the different models of welfare states discussed affect mothers' and single mothers' poverty outcomes.

Data and Methods

To address these issues I use the Luxembourg Income Study (LIS).[9] I use poverty as an economic indicator. With this measure I assume that money income is the central resource used to obtain goods and services, and hence many kinds of social participation. Of course there are important resources that money cannot buy, such as living in safe neighborhoods, large social networks, or social capital. But because money is so liquid, it is a very important determinant of a person's life chances. Moreover, equal participation in society is perhaps more important for women, who historically have not been granted equal citizenship with men (see O'Connor 1993); thus poverty is an especially important indicator with respect to women's economic outcomes. In the following, I use poverty status as a litmus test of social policies: Welfare states that reduce poverty rates by significant amounts are "friendlier" than those that do not.

The conceptualization of poverty I use here concerns whether families have adequate material resources relative to others in one's nation. In this analysis, poverty is measured by having a disposable income (after government transfers and taxes)[10] of less than 50% of the median income of one's country. This is a relative measure of poverty rather than an absolute measure (such as the U.S. poverty line); people are compared to others within their own country rather than compared to the same income level across all countries.[11] Like almost all measures of poverty, I use an equivalence scale to adjust family income for family size.[12]

The methods that follow include the following analyses: mothers' and single mothers' poverty rates and poverty ratios and the extent to which social transfers and taxes reduce mothers' and single mothers' poverty rates and poverty ratios. (In these analyses tax payments are considered social transfers, because in many countries the tax system redistributes money through tax credits.)

I first provide poverty rates and poverty ratios for mothers and single mothers. Poverty rates indicate the percentage of people whose disposable family incomes (adjusted for family size) fall below the poverty line. For example, as seen in Table 1, about 18% of U.S. mothers live in poverty. Poverty ratios divide the poverty rates of one group by those of another group; they indicate the extent to which the poverty rates of one group are higher or lower than those of another

TABLE 1

Mothers' and Single Mothers' Poverty Rates and Poverty Ratios

	Poverty Rates		Poverty Ratios[a]			
	Mothers	Single Mothers	Moms/ NM	Moms/ Men	SM/ N-SM[1]	SM/ SFNP[2]
Australia 94	12.2	37.8	1.23	1.31	4.02	2.10
Canada 94	12.3	38.3	1.32	1.43	4.51	1.90
Finland 95	2.7	5.1	1.00	0.73	1.96	0.80
France 94	6.5	12.9	1.12	1.18	2.53	1.40
Germany 94	13.7	40.9	1.51	1.44	4.35	2.69
Holland 94	7.6	20.4	1.21	1.27	3.24	2.24
Sweden 92	1.8	4.4	0.72	0.49	2.32	1.05
U.K. 95	14.2	31.6	2.33	1.54	4.00	3.62
U.S. 94	18.2	45.4	1.69	1.70	4.20	2.18

[a] Poverty ratios refer to the poverty rate of one group divided by the poverty rate of another group.

[1] Poverty rates of single mothers divided by the poverty rates of nonsingle mothers, or all other women.

[2] Poverty rates of single mothers divided by the poverty rates of single female nonparents.

group. The poverty ratio of 1.69 for U.S. mothers is computed by dividing the poverty rate of mothers (18.2%) by that of female nonmothers (10.8%) and indicates that mothers' poverty rate is 69% higher than that of female nonmothers. The mother poverty ratios compare the poverty rates of mothers to those of two groups: female nonmothers and men. The single mother poverty ratios compare the poverty rates of single mothers to those of four groups: female nonsingle mothers, single female nonparents, married mothers, and men. These poverty ratios are useful because they show mothers' and single mothers' poverty rates *relative to those of other groups.*

I go on to show by how much countries' tax and transfer systems reduce the poverty rates of mothers, single mothers, and their comparison groups. I then ask which government transfers and tax systems most effectively reduce the mother and single mother poverty ratios—or mothers' and single mothers' poverty rates relative to those of their comparison groups. In order to examine the role of social transfers and taxes in reducing poverty ratios, I examine the poverty ratios that result after any social transfer or tax payments a household receives are deducted from disposable income. If these pretransfer, pretax ratios are higher (indicating that mothers are worse off) than the posttransfer, posttax ratios, then the social transfer/tax system brings more mothers out of poverty than their comparison group. In this scenario mothers fare better (relative to their comparison group) when transfers and taxes are included in household income, and they fare relatively worse when transfers and taxes are deducted from income. These comparisons using mother poverty ratios give us a sense of on which family types governments focus their anti-poverty social transfer and tax policies.

Results

The analyses that follow focus on mothers, single mothers, and other citizens. I first provide descriptive analyses of the extent of poverty among them; then assess the extent to which social transfers and tax credits reduce poverty among them; and then examine the extent to which social transfers and tax credits reduce the poverty of mothers and single mothers more or less than that of other citizens. Altogether, these analyses show which welfare states are most instrumental in allowing mothers and single mothers to form autonomous, solvent households independent of male partners.

Poverty Rates and Ratios

First I present the poverty rates of mothers and single mothers. As seen in the first two columns of Table 1, U.S. mothers and single mothers have the highest poverty rates. Australian, Canadian, German, and U.K. mothers have poverty rates around 12% to 14%, all lower than the U.S. mothers' poverty rate (18%). Dutch, French, Finnish, and Swedish mothers have the lowest rates at 8%, 7%, 3%, and 2%, respectively. With single mothers' poverty rates we see a similar ordering of countries, although poverty rates are higher across the board. In the English-speaking nations and Germany more than 30% of single mothers live in poverty, whereas in Finland and Sweden, fewer than 5% of single mothers live in poverty.

As seen in column 3 in Table 1, the mother poverty ratios indicate that in all but two countries—Finland and Sweden—mothers are more likely to be poor than female nonmothers. These ratios indicate, for example, that U.S. mothers have a poverty rate 69% higher than U.S. (female) nonmothers, while in the United Kingdom, mothers' poverty rate is 133% higher than that of female nonmothers. This comparison essentially measures how the presence of children affects poverty differences among women; in most nations, children make women poorer.

I also compare the poverty rates of mothers to those of men. In all countries except Finland and Sweden, mothers are more likely to live in poverty than men. This effect is most pronounced in the United States, where mothers' poverty rate is 70% higher than that of men. In other countries, especially France and the Netherlands, the disparity in poverty is much smaller.

The last two columns in Table 1 show single mothers' poverty rates compared to two groups—other women who are not single mothers, and single female nonparents. We see that in all countries, the poverty rates of single-mother families are typically much higher than those of other family types. Single mothers are the most disadvantaged vis-à-vis other women in Australia, Canada, Germany, the United Kingdom, and the United States, where their poverty rate is over three times as high as that of other women. When comparing single mothers to single female nonmothers, the former have lower poverty rates than the latter in Finland, and the disparity is low in Sweden. In all other countries except France, single mothers are much more likely to live in poverty than single female nonmothers. In other words, in most countries, among single women the presence of children substantially increases poverty rates.

Thus, in absolute terms, mothers' and single mothers' poverty rates are the lowest in Sweden, Finland, the Netherlands, and France. Mothers' and single mothers' poverty ratios are the lowest in Sweden and Finland, the nations most representative of the "individual" or Parent/Worker model. In these nations, it appears that women are most able to form autonomous, nonpoor households independent of men. In contrast, mothers' and single mothers' poverty rates and poverty ratios are the highest in the English-speaking countries and in Germany.

The Effect of Social Transfers/Taxes on Poverty Rates

To examine the role of welfare states in reducing poverty, I compare poverty rates based on disposable income (posttax and posttransfer income) to poverty rates based on pretax and pretransfer income. Table 2 shows the percentage reduction in the pretax/pretransfer poverty rates that occurs after I include social transfers and any tax credits in measures of family income.

The most striking contrast in Table 2 is that the U.S. social transfer and tax system is by far the least effective, reducing the poverty rates of U.S. mothers and single mothers by only 13–14%. The German, Canadian, and Australian welfare states reduce mothers' and single mothers' poverty rates by about 28–44%. The U.K., Dutch, and French welfare states reduce mothers' and single mothers' poverty rates more substantially (by about 50–73%). The Finnish and Swedish

TABLE 2
The Percent Reduction in Poverty Rates
Due to Each Country's Tax/Transfer System

	AS	CN	FI	FR	GE	NL	SW	UK	US
Mothers	43.3	38.5	79.2	69.2	28.6	53.4	89.8	49.3	13.3
Single Mothers	44.2	31.4	86.3	63.7	28.0	73.2	89.1	56.9	14.0
Female Nonmothers	47.1	41.1	79.4	77.1	47.7	68.3	84.8	60.6	16.3
Men	40.0	39.9	74.7	70.6	34.5	58.3	78.2	48.6	10.8
Single Female Nonmothers	32.1	28.6	74.3	63.6	36.4	70.4	85.7	65.3	6.3
Nonsingle mothers	45.0	42.6	77.2	75.9	40.5	59.6	86.7	51.2	15.0

welfare states are the most generous to mothers and single mothers, reducing their pretax, pretransfer poverty rates by 79–90%. In general, this ranking of countries holds up for the other groups listed in Table 2. One exception is that the German welfare state reduces poverty more effectively among groups other than mothers and single mothers. Overall, we see that the "individual" and Parent/Worker welfare states most effectively reduce mothers' and single mothers' absolute poverty rates.

Yet in order to ascertain the generosity of welfare states toward mothers and single mothers, we need to examine how welfare states reduce their poverty rates relative to the poverty rates of other groups. In other words, from the standpoint of reductions in poverty rates, who benefits the most from the welfare state? To assess the role of social transfer and tax systems in reducing mothers' and single mothers' poverty relative to other groups, Tables 3 and 4 show the mother and single mother poverty ratios, measured by disposable (or posttax and posttransfer) income and by pretax and pretransfer income. For all of the comparisons, if the social transfer and tax system pulls more mothers out of poverty than their comparison group, we expect a lower mother poverty ratio in the first row where social transfer/tax payments are included and a higher mother poverty ratio in the second row where social transfer/tax payments are excluded. In this scenario, mothers fare better (relative to their comparison group) when social transfers and

TABLE 3

Mother Poverty Ratios[a] with Poverty Rates Based on Disposable (Posttax/Posttransfer) Income and Pretax/Pretransfer Income

	AS	CN	FI	FR	GE	NL	SW	UK	US
Mothers/Nonmoms									
Disposable (Posttax/ Posttransfer) Income	1.23	1.32	1.00	1.12	1.51	1.21	0.72	2.33	1.69
Pretax/Pretransfer Income	1.15	1.27	.99	0.83	1.10	0.82	1.08	1.81	1.63
	-	-	-	-	-	-	+	-	-
Mothers/Men									
Disposable (Posttax/ Posttransfer) Income	1.31	1.43	0.73	1.18	1.44	1.27	0.49	1.54	1.70
Pretax/Pretransfer Income	1.39	1.40	0.89	1.13	1.32	1.13	1.04	1.56	1.75
	+	-	+	-	-	-	+	+	+

[a]Mother poverty ratios consist of the ratios that result when dividing mothers' poverty rates by the poverty rates of two comparison groups: female non-mothers and men. They indicate the extent to which mothers' poverty rates are higher or lower than those of their comparison groups; for example, a ratio of 1.23 means that mothers' poverty rates are 23% higher than those of their comparison group.

taxes are included in their incomes. (In the tables, a plus sign under the two ratios indicates this scenario.) These two tables show the extent to which welfare states reduce the poverty rates of mothers and single mothers relative to the poverty

TABLE 4

Single-Mother Poverty Ratios[a] with Poverty Rates
Based on Disposable (Posttax/Posttransfer) Income and
Pretax/Pretransfer Income

	AS	CN	FI	FR	GE	NL	SW	UK	US
Single Mothers/ Other Women									
Disposable (Posttax/ Posttransfer) Income	4.02	4.51	1.96	2.53	4.35	3.24	2.32	4.00	4.20
Pretax/Pretransfer Income	3.96	3.77	3.26	1.67	3.59	4.88	2.83	4.53	4.16
	-	-	+	-	-	+	+	+	-
Single Mothers/ SF Nonmoms									
Disposable (Posttax/ Posttransfer) Income	2.10	1.90	0.80	1.40	2.69	2.24	1.05	3.62	2.18
Pretax/Pretransfer Income	2.55	1.97	1.49	1.40	2.38	2.48	1.37	2.71	2.38
	+	+	+		-	+	+	-	+
Single Mothers/ Men									
Disposable (Posttax/ Posttransfer) Income	4.07	4.45	1.38	2.35	4.31	3.40	1.19	3.44	4.24
Pretax/Pretransfer Income	4.37	3.90	2.55	1.90	3.92	5.28	2.38	4.10	4.40
	+	-	+	-	-	+	+	+	+
Single Mothers/ Married Mothers									
Disposable (Posttax/ Posttransfer) Income	4.25	4.97	2.22	2.93	4.17	3.24	4.00	3.19	4.20
Pretax/Pretransfer Income	4.40	4.10	4.13	2.13	4.09	7.53	3.54	4.34	4.26
	+	-	+	-	-	+	-	+	+

[a]Single mother-poverty ratios consist of the ratios that result when dividing single mothers' poverty rates by the poverty rates of four comparison groups: all other women, single female non-mothers, men, and married mothers. They indicate the extent to which single mothers' poverty rates are higher or lower than those of their comparison groups; for example, a ratio of 4.02 means that single mothers' poverty rates are .02% higher than those of their comparison group.

rates of other citizens. In nations where welfare states are more instrumental in reducing mothers' poverty rates relative to those of other citizens, mothers are more likely to be able to form autonomous households that escape poverty.

The Effect of Social Transfers/Taxes on Poverty Ratios

Table 3 shows us the mother poverty ratios measured by posttax and posttransfer (or disposable) income and by pretax and pretransfer income. The ratios compare mothers' poverty rates to those of female nonmothers and to those of men. Again, when the latter ratio is larger than the former—or if after transfer and tax payments are excluded from the measure of poverty rates, the relative poverty of mothers increases—these welfare states are more generous to mothers.[13] By this measure, only Sweden is "mother-friendly" when comparing mothers to female nonmothers. In all other countries, the poverty ratios comparing mothers to nonmothers actually increase when transfers and taxes are included in income measures. These countries do not bring more mothers than female nonmothers out of poverty with their social transfer and tax systems. One possible explanation is that some countries have many benefits tied to labor force participation, and female nonmothers often have higher employment rates than mothers. In addition, because nonmothers include those who may have children that no longer live in the household or are older, some female nonmothers may be receiving social retirement benefits.[14]

Comparing mothers to men, we see that the social transfer/tax systems in all countries except France, Canada, Germany, and the Netherlands pull more mothers out of poverty than men. In the latter three countries, there are many social assistance benefits tied to labor-force participation, and mothers have lower employment rates than men. The French case is surprising, given that its welfare state is known for targeting families with children.

Thus, with its highly developed universal policies like family allowances and paid leave, only the Swedish welfare state reduces the poverty of mothers more than other comparison groups. Finland is also friendlier to mothers than other welfare states. This suggests that the social assistance programs in the "individual" or Parent/Worker model are the most instrumental in reducing caregivers' poverty rates vis-à-vis the poverty rates of other citizens. In contrast, the social assistance programs in the "male breadwinner" or Caregiver model welfare states—namely, Germany and the Netherlands—reduce the poverty rates of other citizens to a greater extent than those of mothers; this does not bode well for mothers' ability to form nonpoor households without male partners.

With respect to single mothers, Table 4 shows the poverty rates of single mothers divided by those of four comparison groups: female nonsingle mothers (or all other women), single female nonmothers, men, and married mothers. (These poverty measures are analogous to those in Table 3, so I use the same indicators to assess how welfare states treat single mothers relative to other groups.) With the first single-mother poverty ratios in Table 4, we see that four welfare states—Finland, the Netherlands, Sweden, and the United Kingdom—reduce the poverty rates of single mothers more than those of other women. It is surprising that the other five countries do not target single mother's poverty with their tax/transfer systems, given that single mothers have higher poverty rates than other groups across all nations. This may be because single mothers have low employment rates in some nations, so are less likely to qualify for social transfers and tax credits based on employment.

When compared to single female nonmothers, more single mothers are pulled out of poverty in several countries: Australia, Canada, Finland, the Netherlands, Sweden, and the United States. The first two countries have means-tested benefits for single mothers but often few (if any) policies for single nonmothers. Finland and Sweden have many policies geared toward families with children and some supplements for single mothers. The Dutch welfare state is known for its relatively generous social transfers for single mothers.

The tax and transfer systems of all countries except Canada, Germany, and France bring more single mothers out of poverty than men. The former two countries have many social policies that are geared toward workers, which may disadvantage single mothers. In France, most benefits are available to all families with children, and there are very few targeted programs for which only single mothers qualify (Bergmann 1996).

Lastly, I examine single mothers compared to married mothers and find outcomes similar to the previous comparison, except that in this case Sweden does not reduce single mothers' poverty relative to that of married mothers. Thus Canada, France, Germany, and Sweden bring more married mothers than single mothers out of poverty with their tax/transfer systems. Germany is likely to privilege married mothers due to social transfers and taxes that reward the male breadwinner family, as discussed earlier. And as seen in Table 2, although Sweden does reduce the poverty rate of single mothers substantially, it does not reduce their poverty rates more than those of married mothers. One surprise here is France. With its comprehensive welfare state aimed at keeping children out of poverty, one would think that single mothers would receive more generous social transfers than other groups. But France does not target the poverty of single mothers with its welfare state. One explanation for this is that France offers much more generous benefits to larger families than to smaller families (Bergmann 1996), and single mothers often have smaller families. And, as stated earlier, in France there are few social assistance benefits for which only single mothers are eligible (Bergmann 1996).

Overall, only the Finnish and Dutch welfare states target the poverty of single mothers across all comparisons—their social transfer and tax systems consistently reduce the poverty of single mothers more than other groups in society. Sweden reduces the poverty rates of single mothers more than those of other groups in most comparisons. Thus, with the exception of France, the Parent/Worker welfare states are generally "friendlier" to single mothers than other welfare states; these welfare states facilitate mothers' ability to live on their own and escape poverty. In contrast, neither France nor Germany reduces single mothers' poverty ratios across any comparison.

Summary of Findings

The social transfer and tax systems in English-speaking countries (except the

United States) moderately reduce the poverty rates of mothers and single mothers (Table 2). The English-speaking welfare states reduce mothers' and single mothers' poverty ratios in some, although certainly not all, of the preceding analyses. With respect to reducing mother and single-mother poverty ratios, Canada is the least effective English-speaking welfare state (Tables 3 and 4). Overall, U.S. mothers and single mothers fare quite badly: they have the highest poverty rates, high poverty ratios, and their social transfer and tax system is the least effective in reducing poverty rates (Tables 1 and 2).

In Finland and Sweden, mothers and single mothers have the lowest poverty rates and ratios (Table 1), and the Finnish and Swedish welfare states generally most effectively reduce mothers' and single mothers' poverty rates and poverty ratios (Tables 2, 3, and 4). Both of these regimes represent the "individual" model of social policy, or for single mothers, the Parent/Worker model. The other "individual" or Parent/Worker nation, France, substantially lowers poverty rates with its welfare state (Table 2). Yet France does not reduce any of the poverty ratios of mothers or single mothers (Tables 3 and 4).

Dutch mothers and single mothers have moderate poverty rates, whereas those in Germany have high poverty rates (Table 1). The social transfer and tax systems in these countries moderately reduce mothers' and single mothers' poverty rates (Table 2). Germany and the Netherlands are quite unfriendly to mothers (relative to others) with their social transfer and tax systems, and the social transfer and tax system in Germany decreases the poverty ratios of neither mothers nor single mothers (Tables 3 and 4). However, the Dutch system quite effectively reduces the poverty ratios of single mothers (Tables 3 and 4).

Conclusion

The "male breadwinner" model or Caregiving regime is problematic not only with its assumptions about the primacy of mothers' caregiving; "male breadwinner" social transfer/tax systems also fail to reduce mother's poverty rates vis-à-vis those of other groups. In this sense, the welfare state in Germany and the Netherlands devalues the work of caregivers—allowing them (and perhaps expecting them) to stay at home with children, but failing to lower their poverty rates relative to those of other citizens. In the absence of social transfers to keep their poverty rates low, many German caregivers work outside the home—which may give them some degree of economic independence from men. But when German caregivers work part-time, or are not employed, they are likely to have high levels of economic dependence on their male partners when in relationships, or high poverty rates when not in relationships. Although the Dutch welfare state is relatively friendly to single mothers, Dutch mothers and single mothers have low employment rates, which can also lead to economic dependence on men. Economic dependence on male partners has many troubling implications for women; for one, battered women may face the difficult choice of staying with an abusive partner, or leaving—which could push them and their children into poverty.

In contrast, in Finland and Sweden welfare-state services support labor-force participation among mothers and single mothers, and tax and transfer systems help keep their poverty rates low. In these countries, the welfare state makes economic dependence on a male partner less common—and "defamilialization" more likely. Although Scandinavian nations have high rates of part-time work among women and sex-segregated workplaces, caregivers nonetheless fare quite well with respect to poverty outcomes.

Thus, if the Dutch and German welfare states continue to respond to the "care deficit" by reinforcing caregiving as women's private responsibility in the home, it seems that many caregivers in these nations will be economically dependent on male partners. An alternative would be to follow the "individual" or Parent/Worker model and increase state subsidized childcare and paid leave services, allowing more women to be employed for longer hours. An ideal solution for caregivers would combine these policies with those that encourage more flexible work schedules for all parents and men's greater involvement in caregiving. For example, Norwegian and Swedish "daddy leaves" have "use or lose" clauses in which the family loses a portion of the paid leave if the father does not take it (Leira 1998). These "daddy leaves" are some of the few social policies in existence that actively encourage men's caregiving in the home. These aforementioned policies are more representative of the "warm-modern" approach to caregiving (Hochshild 1995), in which women and men engage in personal caregiving, and also use institutional supports for caregiving. Certainly the English-speaking countries—typically stingy with state-subsidized care services—could treat caregivers more fairly with these "warm-modern" approaches as well.

Yet, particularly in the English-speaking nations, the adoption of more "warm-modern" social policies may be difficult. For one, the political philosophy of liberalism, particularly popular in the United States and Canada, emphasizes market provision of income and social services and supports only very limited state provision of these resources. In these nations, it may be difficult to garner public support for "warm-modern" policies. Second, the "individual" or Parent/Worker welfare states are those in which left political parties have had the longest incumbency and strongest electoral support, and these parties typically support woman-friendly social policies such as subsidized child care (Korpi 2000). In addition, Swedish and Finnish women are among the most likely to hold political office, particularly at the national level. Thus, left or social democratic political parties and governments with more female politicians should support "warm-modern" policies more than conservative political parties and male-dominated governments (Hernes 1987); countries that lack the influences of left parties and female politicians should have a harder time passing "warm-modern" social policies.

Of course, women differ substantially in their degree of support for social policies surrounding caregiving. But policies based on the "warm-modern" approach could bridge the divide between feminists who see employment as a necessary condition of women's citizenship and those who see the valorization of caregiving as integral to a new conception of citizenship. Nations with more "warm-modern" social policies would allow all parents more flexibility in caring for their children when they are young, and would provide institutional supports (like subsidized child care) to facilitate parents' labor force participation once their children are older. Thus, ideally, "warm-modern" social policies allow women to choose how they divide carework and paid work, encouraging a form of social citizenship that values both kinds of work.

Welfare states that encourage women's caregiving—in their current form—often do not allow women's economic independence from men; thus, the "male breadwinner" or Caregiving welfare states are currently inadequate in their provision of women's social citizenship. With their generous welfare states that keep mothers' poverty rates low, the Parent/Worker welfare states are more likely to promote women's social citizenship; yet, in these welfare states, women's employment is often necessary to ensure their low poverty rates. Thus, women in these welfare states could also benefit from more "warm-modern" policies that promote and subsidize caregiving among fathers and mothers of young children.

In sum, the contribution of this research lies in its analysis of how different welfare states treat caregivers relative to other citizens. Further research should continue to focus on primary caregivers, paying closer attention to how their increased employment rates affect their economic and social well-being, and that of their families. As the preceding analyses focus on social transfers and tax credits, we need further research on how employment supports like subsidized child care and other policies that encourage either parental or institutional caregiving—or a combination of the two—affect caregivers and their families. While there are strong reasons to believe that "warm-modern" policies will be advantageous for caregivers and their families, we need future research to assess the extent to which these policies bolster caregivers' attainment of social citizenship.

Notes

Karen Christopher is assistant professor of sociology at University of Pittsburgh and also serves on the Women's Studies teaching faculty. The author gives particular thanks to Demie Kurz and Mary Tuominen for their helpful comments on earlier drafts. Paula England also provided useful input on earlier versions of this chapter. An earlier version of this chapter was presented at the Carework Conference in Washington, DC, August 2000.

1. While in recent decades men have increased their participation in caregiving, women remain the primary caregivers of children, even in nations where social policies encourage men's participation in caregiving (Cancian and Oliker 2000).

2. Esping-Andersen (1990) outlines three types of welfare state regimes, based on their provision of social rights, their contribution to social stratification, and their nexus of state-market-family relations. In his scheme, the ideal welfare state is characterized by "de-commodification," under which the welfare state allows workers to enjoy a decent standard of living independent of labor force participation.

3. In his recent work, Esping-Andersen (1999) more fully integrates gender into his classification of welfare state regimes. He equates "defamilialization" with "policies that lessen individuals' reliance on the family; that maximize individuals' command of economic resources independently of familial or conjugal responsibilities" (45). He examines the existence of "defamilializing" policies across his different regime types with measures such as public spending on family services,

the percentage of children under age 3 in daycare, and the average hours of women's unpaid work. Yet Esping-Andersen (1999) does not speak to the dimension of "defamilialization" that concerns many feminists— the extent to which welfare states (or markets) allow women to form autonomous household without male partners.

4. "Male breadwinner" welfare states also emphasize joint taxation of spouses and employment policies that benefit men. In contrast, "individual" welfare states emphasize separate taxation and employment policies that benefit women and men.

5. Dutch benefits are often paid to the (typically male) head of household, and male breadwinners are privileged in tax, wage, and pension legislation. For example, in the early 1990s wives could not receive their own pension or unemployment insurance if their husband was currently working outside of the home. In contrast, Swedish women receive benefits as mothers and caregivers (regardless of marital status), individual benefits under social insurance, and supports for paid work such as state subsidized childcare and paid parental leave (Gustafsson 1995; Sainsbury 1994, 1996).

6. By "single" I am referring to never married, divorced, or widowed women. Some "single" women may have ex-husbands, male boyfriends or relatives that help them raise their children, so these women may not care for their children on their own. But given the low percentage of divorced women who receive alimony and child support payments in full, many single mothers are raising children largely with their own resources.

7. For in-depth discussions of social policies available to single mothers in these countries, see Christopher (forthcoming) or Gornick, Meyers, and Ross (1998).

8. A notable exception is Gornick, Meyers, and Ross (1998), who provide a compelling analysis of how family policy packages—income transfers and employment support services—affect women's and mothers' economic outcomes. They examine differences in economic outcomes according to parental status, but they do not include single mothers in their analysis.

9. The LIS is a cross-national consortium of surveys from 25 industrialized countries, with comprehensive information on household income sources. All data sets include nationally representative samples of the population in each country. My sample includes: Australia (1994), Canada (1994), Finland (1995), France (1994), Germany (1994), the Netherlands (1994), Sweden (1995), UK (1995) and US (1994). In order to exclude most women and men who are students or retirees, my sample includes people age 25–60. Motherhood status applies to those who have children age 18 or under living in their household; if women have children above age 18 or who no longer live at home, these women are not considered "mothers" here. In the analyses below, "single" includes those who are unmarried, divorced, or widowed. Cohabiting couples are considered as "married," as it seems likely that cohabiting couples share resources in ways similar to married couples.

10. Disposable income in the LIS includes all social transfers and near cash transfers (such as food stamps and cash-based housing allowances), net of income and payroll taxes. Disposable income does not include non-cash benefits like

childcare, health care, and education. The benefit of using disposable income to measure poverty is that it reflects the spending money available to families, because it is after-tax income that includes social transfers.

11. I use a relative measure of poverty for two primary reasons. First, nations vary considerably in the social services (such as health care, child care and employment programs) they offer their citizens, and using an absolute measure of poverty would ignore these important cross-national differences. In contrast, a relative poverty measure compares citizens to others within his/her nation—who face the same set of social/economic services. Second, individuals are more likely to compare their economic situation to those within their own country rather than to some absolute, international standard.

12. I use a common equivalence scale in cross-national research, in which family income is divided by the square root of household size. See Christopher et al. (forthcoming) for an in-depth discussion of equivalence scales.

13. I should clarify that these welfare states are more generous in the sense of bringing more mothers above the poverty line. This does not always mean that their tax and transfers systems give higher payments to mothers. This is because all of these measures are relative to the poverty line. The comparison groups (like men) may have higher incomes so are above the poverty line or very close to the poverty line with their pretax/pretransfer income. Given this, men are more likely to be lifted above the poverty line with taxes and transfers because they typically start off closer to it.

14. This applies to a relatively small number of women, because the cutoff age for my sample is 60. Descriptive statistics show that few of these women receive social insurance (or pension) payments.

III: Carework in the Marketplace and Community

Introduction to Section III
Carework in the Marketplace and Community

*W*ith scarce public resources and changing patterns of family life, the care of children and youth is increasingly a commodity to be bought and sold. When child care becomes a function of the private market, families with enough wealth can buy good care, or they can forego income and provide care directly to their children. The great majority of American families, however, struggle with limited resources to provide or purchase quality care for their children. The chapters in this section examine the results of an approach to care that is largely uncoordinated, often confusing, and fragmented between the family, the state, and the market.

A lack of organized support for carework leads to a concurrent lack of support for careworkers as well, as evidenced by the low wages, low status, and marginalization of those who provide care. Thus, inequalities in care for children and youth manifest themselves among children (in the quality of care they receive), among families (in their ability or inability to provide direct care or to purchase quality care), and among care workers (through the economic, social, and political vulnerability that result from engaging in carework).

In the absence of substantial government support, the care of children and youth is left largely to families (as discussed in sections I and II of this volume) or to the market. But leaving carework solely to the market does not work (as is evidenced by the chapters in this section). As Paula England and Nancy Folbre argue, a market that provides care is a contradictory notion. Markets are designed for profit. However, caring for children and youth is not an immediately profitable endeavor. The practice of care reveals another market-based dilemma, as well: We often need care when we are most vulnerable and least able to pay for it. England and Folbre discuss the inequality careworkers experience as a result of our reliance on these contradictory market ideologies and forces and the subsequent low wage penalty that careworkers experience.

The stresses resulting from this gap between what is preached regarding the value of care and what is practiced has implications for the delivery of care. As Heather Fitz Gibbon demonstrates, motivations and conditions of carework, as well as limited opportunities and gendered ideologies that make women responsible for both paid and unpaid carework, shape the perceptions these workers have of themselves and of their work. Working in an atmosphere of disrespect, careworkers find it hard to appreciate fully their own worth and to demand that it be valued.

Children and youth with special needs pose a particular problem in a social system that leaves a gap between needs and resources—despite a stated commitment by policymakers to the well-being of all children and youth. Mark Chesler focuses on the interorganizational struggles that can occur when groups compete for scarce resources. He discusses the negotiations that families of and grass-roots organizations for children with cancer sometimes face when dealing with the medical community and with large formal organizations to find the best care for children. Eric R. Wright and Robert E. Connoley discuss an organization for gay, lesbian, and bisexual youth and the roles that professionals play in providing a support system for these youth. Theirs is a success story, but one that is too rarely replicated and one that even here reveals the tension between what forms of care and support these youth need in a hostile society and what resources are available to meet those needs.

The final chapters reveal the challenges and rewards of working for positive change through organizing and activism. Mary Tuominen documents a successful labor organizing campaign among paid child care workers—a campaign complicated by the relational qualities of carework, differing commitments to antiracism work, and the challenge of two activist organizations seeking to work in coalition. Nancy A. Naples demonstrates how community workers challenge conventional definitions of mothering, such that community carework becomes "activist mothering" to secure economic and social justice for community members. The workers in these two chapters provide a model for those who fight against poverty, racism, and class oppression, and who fight for both care and careworkers.

All these chapters end with a call for creating a just society—a society that values both carework and careworkers. Despite the knowledge that today's social and economic investment in our children and youth is an investment in a healthy and productive citizenry, we fail to adequately fund that investment. We are challenged to examine our present approaches to providing care and to demand policies that offer wages, benefits, and prestige appropriate to those who care for our children and youth.

Care, Inequality, and Policy

Paula England and Nancy Folbre

$\mathcal{E}$galitarians have at least three reasons to be concerned with work that involves providing care to others, work such as caring for children, teaching, providing medical care, or providing physical or psychological therapy. In this chpater we explore the reasons for the link between care and these three distinct aspects of inequality.

First, there is considerable inequality in people's access to care when they need it. People who are disadvantaged on dimensions of race, class, nation, national origin, (dis)ability, age, or gender are likely to have lower income, and therefore less ability to purchase the care they need. Those with lower income may have rich informal networks of kin and near-kin willing to help them, but their networks are likely to contain others with similarly low resources.

Second, providing care often has the effect of lowering income.[1] Much care by family members is offered without pay, mostly by mothers and female kin (Meyer 2000). These caregivers may have periods with no earnings, leading not only to economic dependency but also to future disadvantages in earnings-based access to private pensions and social security. Empirical research shows that motherhood also reduces the wages of employed women, even if women do not reduce their hours of work. Lower access to earnings puts caregivers at a disadvantage in bargaining with their intimate partners (England and Kilbourne 1990; Lundberg and Pollak 1996). Providing care for pay is also associated with low income, because caring occupations pay less than other jobs, relative to experience, human capital, and the skill demands of the work.

Third, many caregivers come from groups that have traditionally been disadvantaged and vulnerable to discrimination in the labor market. Caregivers are disproportionately female. Further, women of color are overrepresented in many of the most poorly paid caring jobs, such as child care, elder care, and health care performed within clients' homes. Both pay and working conditions in these domestic services perpetuate inequalities based on gender, race, and ethnicity.

None of these dimensions of inequality flow simply from reliance on the market as the primary means of providing care and distributing rewards from care. Other factors come into play, such as the preexisting distribution of resources, the special characteristics of carework, and economic and cultural processes that reproduce group differences. However, market processes do little to reduce these dimensions of inequality, and often they exacerbate them. We define market processes in conformity with textbook economic theories of both the neoclassical and Marxian persuasion: forces of supply and demand in markets that reflect the narrowly self-interested decisions of individuals and the profit-maximizing decisions of firms.[2]

The role of markets in perpetuating and sometimes intensifying inequalities related to care provision helps explain the need for collective action to implement progressive public policy. Many feminists have grappled with the questions of how best to serve people's needs for care and careworkers' needs for support (see, for example, Meyer 2000; O'Connor, Orloff, and Shaver 1999). We believe that consideration of the causes of care-related inequalities can help inform such policy discussions.

Inequality in Access to Care

What explains inequalities in people's access to care? In the proximate sense, the answer is simple. Those with more income can purchase more and higher quality care services in the marketplace, just like they can purchase more of any other commodity.[3] As hours of paid employment increase, the supply of available unpaid family care declines, and care services become increasingly commodified. With enough money, one can pay for a higher quality and quantity of child care, medical care, nursing home care, and so forth. If care services are not available from a family member or friend and are not provided by the state, then those needing care must purchase it or rely on someone else to purchase it for them. The more important these purchases become, the more salient are the inequalities in people's ability to pay for them.

Such inequalities can be exacerbated by public policy. For instance, changes in welfare laws made in 1996 imposed paid work requirements and time limits on mothers receiving public assistance, thus reducing their ability to spend time caring for their own children (Oliker 2000).

Despite significant increases in public support for child care since that time, the number of subsidized child care slots has never covered more than about 15% of all eligible children (U.S. Department of Health and Human Services 1999). The overall quality of subsidized child care is low, because it was designed to increase welfare mothers' employment rather than benefit their children. Furthermore, the costs of paying for child care reduce the disposable earnings of many single mothers, concealing the extent to which their standards of living may decline when they move from partnered homemaking or welfare to paid work.

Scholarly debate focuses on the extent to which poor families receive help with care (or money to buy care) from their friends, neighbors, and kin. At issue are questions concerning the level of assistance both in absolute terms and relative to affluent families, and possible declines in reciprocal aid and informal networks over time (for different positions, see McAdoo 1986; Rochelle 1997; Stack 1974; and see an excellent review in Oliker 2000). Either way, it is important to recognize that the poor have disproportionately poor kin as a result of family transmission of poverty and advantage. The poor also have disproportionately poor neighbors (Jargowsky 1996). Race is an axis of privilege that generates income differences among those with similar class backgrounds. Thus, due to racial segregation of neighborhoods (Massey and Denton 1993) as well as past and present discrimination and other disadvantages in labor markets, African Americans and some other people of color have kin and informal networks largely made up of coethnics, many of whom are themselves relatively poor. This is another mechanism contributing to low network access to resources among those who have little money to purchase care themselves.

Income is related to care in another way. Needing care badly tends to make you poor—just when you most need the income to buy care! This is an important sense in which care differs from most goods and services. With most commodities, how much we need or want is not related to our income (although our ability to buy the good may be). But our need for care is greatest when we are most dependent. We need care the most when we are young children, when we are old and dying, and when we are physically, mentally, or emotionally ill. When we were babies, we could hardly work to earn the money needed for our child care! Neither can the seriously ill person, nor can many elders earn money for their health care. Many adults can purchase insurance to protect against these risks, but the costs are high and some risks inevitably remain.

Thus, the need for care is often indicative of an inability to garner the resources to get it. Some of this dependency is inherent in the human life cycle. We are all dependent on others when we are very young. Most of us will be dependent on others for care at some point in our old age. And many of us will have an unwelcome illness or injury that creates dependency. At such times, we must rely on the altruism of others unless we have savings or sufficient insurance; we cannot work to buy our care. Sometimes our inability to purchase care for our children or ourselves is because of our poverty, which may result from having been an unpaid caregiver. For example, a single mother may have low earnings because she has been at home taking care of her children.

When we need care but do not have sufficient resources to purchase it, we must rely on the family, the state, or other redistributive institutions (such as religious organizations or nonprofit organizations) for the direct provision of care or financial assistance to purchase care. In each of these cases, we rely on individuals or institutions that allocate resources or care on some principle other than narrow self-interest. This principle may be unconditional love, a norm of reciprocity (as between spouses), or a norm of obligation (e.g., that people *should* take care of their own children or parents, or members of their religion or community or race or nation or the broader human community). But precisely because we have little ability to produce or give when we are most in need of care, many who need care will not get it unless some principle other than narrow self-interest is operative in familial, community, or societal systems of distribution.

The analytic point is not merely that *markets* will not produce care for those who cannot pay for it and have no one willing to purchase it for them. The point is a deeper one. If the most caricatured version of rational choice theory were true, such that actors were all narrowly self-interested, dependents would not be able to obtain care through informal family or community networks either. Even the informal system will fail to produce needed care if everyone is selfish. This is because dependencies that make us need care not only render us unable to produce in the market to earn money, but also make it more difficult to find people willing to treat us with the love and obligation we associate with "family" if we don't already have them. If a person becomes seriously mentally or physically ill and cannot hold a job because of this, a faithful spouse or significant other may stick with him or her, holding down the job that provides health insurance for treatment, and providing financial and emotional support. But the single person who is beset with this same illness is unlikely to be chosen as a partner (even by one who, had the partnership already started, would remain faithful). Our social norms permit and even encourage more selfishness in our choice of partners than in our behavior toward a partner once we have made a commitment. Thus, the relationship between income and need for care is similar to the relationship between being in a relationship of obligation and the need for care. When one most needs a partner obligated to provide care or pay for its provision, one is least able to attract a partner to take on this obligation. This is certainly true for babies. If parents have a seriously disabled child, most parents, particularly mothers, have sufficient love, altruism, and sense of duty that they will stick with and raise the child (Heimer and Staffen 1998), but few people seeking to adopt a child will adopt a disabled child.

The general point is that some principle of distribution other than narrow self-interest is necessary to obtain care because the very conditions that lead us to need the care make it hard for us to either make money or attract others into the bonds of obligation or altruism that could provide this care. A specific corollary is that if you don't already have bonds of family or life-partnership connection that imply some altruism and commitment when an extreme need for care occurs, you are unlikely to find such care. Neither markets nor any informal system with narrowly self-interested actors will provide care to those who are too poor to pay for it.

Inequality Resulting from the Characteristics of Care

Caregiving seldom makes people rich, and sometimes makes them poor. This is because carework tends to be paid less than other forms of work, all else equal (England et al. 2002). Pay differences cannot be attributed simply to the economic and demographic characteristics of care providers, because the "care penalty" persists even after controlling for these. In this section, we review this literature, starting with evidence of the effect of mother's unpaid care of children on their earnings, then considering the compensation offered in the labor market for carework.

The Motherhood Penalty

Mothers often reduce their employment to provide care to their children, and fathers occasionally do the same. Such reductions lower parents' lifetime earnings, most directly through creating a period when they have no earnings. But several recent studies find that mothers earn less than other women in the United States and elsewhere even when they are employed (Budig and England 2001; Harkness and Waldfogel 1999; Joshi and Newell 1989; Lundberg and Rose 2000; Neumark and Korenman 1994; Waldfogel 1997; 1998a; 1998). The penalty occurs for married and single women, but is larger for the married (Budig and England 2001).

Men suffer no such penalty; indeed, their earnings are either unaffected (Loh 1996:580) or go up after having a child (Lundberg and Rose 2000).

Several explanations have been offered for this motherhood penalty. One explanation is that some mothers take months or years out of employment for childrearing, and earn lower wages as a result of their lower experience or seniority. A recent study estimated that this explains about one third of the penalty (Budig and England 2001). Other explanations are more speculative. Some suggest that mothers are less productive than other workers because the demands of mothering at home make them more exhausted or distracted and hence less productive on the job (Becker 1991). Still others suggest that the penalty may result from mothers trading off high wages for "mother-friendly" jobs. For instance, Budig and England (2001) found that being in part-time work had a significant effect. The penalty may also come from the demand side of the labor market: if employers discriminate against mothers in making pay and promotion decisions.

The motherhood penalty probably reflects a combination of several of these mechanisms. But whatever the mechanism, this penalty lowers the earnings of those who do unpaid caring labor. Where mothers are single, this is especially likely to lead to poverty.

The Wage Penalty for Paid Caring Labor

Several studies have tried to isolate the net effect on pay of working in a job involving caring labor, compared to doing other kinds of work. These studies generally control for other individual and job-level determinants of pay such as education, experience, cognitive and physical skill demands of the jobs, unionization, whether the job is in the public sector, the sex composition of the occupation, and so forth. England (1992, Chapter 3) created a dummy variable for what she called "nurturant work," by making a judgment from each detailed Census occupational title as to whether a primary task in the job is giving a face-to-face service to clients or customers of the organization for which one works. The study found that both men and women earned less if they worked in a "nurturant" occupation in 1980 (England 1992, Chapter 3), and a replication on 1990 Census data showed that this is true for 1990 as well (England, Thompson, and Aman 2001). Kilbourne et al. (1994) developed a scale to measure nurturant skill from the dummy variable developed by England (1992) described earlier, plus other measures from the *Dictionary of Occupational Titles* involving dealing with people, and demands for talking and hearing. Other things equal, working in an occupation scoring higher on this scale reduced earnings for both men and women. One limitation of these studies is that the measure used included face-to-face service work, such as receptionist or retail sales, that we would usually not include in care work. However, using a narrower definition of care work also produces the conclusion that care work pays less than other kinds of work (net of other factors). For example, England et al. (1994) found a wage penalty for working in a caring occupation using a measure constructed from a survey of undergraduates asking them to rank jobs according to "how much they involve helping people, encouraging the development of people, or taking care of people." In an analysis of the New York State civil service jobs, Steinberg et al. (1986) found that a number of scales that tapped caring social skills had negative returns. These included communication with the public and group facilitation (Steinberg et al. 1986:152). England, Budig, and Folbre (2002) defined caring labor to include child care, teaching, giving medical services, and social work, but excluded service work such as receptionist and retail sales. They also found a negative effect of caring labor on individuals' wages, net of human capital, skill demands of the occupations, and other controls.

We argue that several intrinsic characteristics of care work help explain the low level of remuneration for it (England and Folbre 1999a). One important reason is that this labor produces "public goods." As defined by economists and other rational choice theorists, such goods have the property that it is impossible to keep those who don't pay for the good from using it. This is called "nonexcludability." Some jobs pay well because they involve providing a valuable good or service to someone who can afford to pay for it and who will be kept from getting the fruits of the work if s/he doesn't pay. These jobs involve a good or service from which nonpayers are "excludable." Consider, for example, the business services (e.g., accounting or legal services) sold to corporations or affluent individuals. One offering these services for pay can earn a substantial amount because the services will not be provided if the purchaser isn't willing to pay the asking price. Being willing and able to withhold one's services unless the beneficiaries pay for them contributes to high pay within a market system in which actors try to optimize their consumption.

Caring labor deviates from this ideal type of "excludability" in that there is no way for the care provider to collect from many of the beneficiaries via market processes. Care providers contribute to the development of human capabilities that are of value not only to the client, but to all those who interact with him or her. How could the teacher collect from the employer and neighbors who later benefit from her labors? How could a grandmother collect from her grandchildren who are better off as adults because of caring capacities their mother learned from their grandmother? The work of caring is unusual in the extent to which benefits are spread beyond direct recipients of the service. This diffusion makes it easy for others to free ride, enjoying the benefits of care without paying the costs (England et al. 2002; England and Folbre 1999a, 1999b). The "public good" features of care work can contribute to low pay.

Another reason why caring labor pays badly is that, as we discussed earlier, those who need and receive care often can't afford to pay much for it. Thus, unless someone else subsidizes or pays for the caring labor, it will be badly paid or unpaid. When those with few resources need care, sometimes a third party is available who can and will step in and pay for care to be provided by paid workers. These "third parties" are typically family members or the state. Sometimes the pay comes indirectly from charitable contributions from those who are strangers to the recipients of care. Given these sources of funds, the amount available to pay the caring worker depends on how affluent the family members are, or how rich the economy is from which the state draws taxes or the charitable organizations draw their contributions. The level of resources available also depends on the altruism of family members (in the case of family provision), fellow citizens (in the case of state provision), and those who contribute to charity (in the case of nonprofit provision). All these factors affect the wage that is offered to those who do care work for pay.

Inequality Resulting from the Characteristics of Care Workers

The low wages offered to paid care workers also reflect the characteristics of the labor force that supplies care, which is predominantly female. Black women and Latinas are not overrepresented in care jobs in general (England et al. 2002). However, they are particularly likely to take responsibilities for the work of caring for other people in their own homes as nannies or domestic care workers (Hondagneu-Sotelo 2000; 2001). Women of color, including immigrants, are especially vulnerable to discrimination.

Demographic characteristics also affect labor supply. In the United States today, women's educational attainment closely resembles that of men. However, Blacks and Hispanics have lower levels of education than Whites. Immigrants often face additional difficulties related to language and nontransferability of credentials, and cultural adjustment. These aspects of human capital, however, may be less influential than the cultural construction of care as a feminine activity requiring little or no skill or initiative, something that "any loving person" can do.

The gender dimensions are perhaps the most obvious. Care is seen as an extension of the services that women are expected to offer to their family members out of love, reciprocity, and duty. Indeed, paid carework largely involves forms of care for dependents historically performed by women within the family that have now been relocated to state- and market-governed institutions. The way we think about this work is strongly affected by cultural schemas about gender and motherhood. "Devaluation theory" suggests that our culture devalues women relative to men, and in something akin to guilt by association, any activity done largely by women is valued less than that it otherwise would be. This is one of the central claims in research showing that the sex composition of jobs (or occupations) affects their wages, net of a host of controls (England 1992; Kilbourne et al. 1994; Sorensen 1989).

However, this is not the only factor at work, because these studies show a pay penalty for caring labor that exists even when controlling for the sex composition of the occupation or job. This net negative effect may reflect the indirect and perhaps quite subtle effects of the cultural construction of gender, motherhood, race, and ethnicity. Our idea that mothering is "natural" and should be given freely creates resistance to generous remuneration in care work that may be even greater than employers' tendency to devalue other "female" jobs (such as secretarial work) simply because they are done by women. If we deconstruct the gender rhetoric, it seems to imply that commodifying care dries up real love, or worse, makes the sacred profane. The discourse surrounding this sounds as if its motivation is to maintain the respect for the sanctity of care work, even to put care workers on a pedestal of respect, but, ironically, the result is often to deny them decent pay (MacDonald and Merrill forthcoming; England and Folbre 1999a).

Care work is also "racialized" (Romero 1992). Cultural stereotypes of women of color as more emotional, more "loving," and less skilled than Whites help rationalize lower pay. Employers may fantasize that women derive so much pleasure from the process of providing care for dependents of the affluent that they really do not want or need higher wages. These misperceptions may contribute to occupational segregation and low pay. Cultural norms may also affect the supply of caring labor. Joan Tronto (1987) argued that subordination may contribute to a tendency to identify with a dominant group in ways that contribute to subordinate groups having more selfless, "caring" attitudes toward the dominant group.

The influence of these cultural norms based on gender, race, and ethnicity suggests that the larger care penalty cannot simply be attributed to market processes. State socialist societies might provide relatively generous care for those who need it. However, planners who are subject to forms of gender and racial/ethnic bias that culturally devalue care may set pay scales quite low. For instance, studies of the Soviet Union before the fall of the Communist Party showed that physicians in that country, who were predominantly female, were poorly paid relative to other highly educated workers (Lapidus 1978).

On the other hand, market processes do not necessarily weaken such forms of cultural bias. Neoclassical economic theory as developed by Gary Becker (1975) argues that competitive forces tend to erode discrimination when it is based on personal preferences. Even Becker's analysis, however, allows for the possibility that cultural norms can have a more pervasive effect, encouraging employers to coordinate their actions in ways that reinforce bias.

Public Policy and Care

We have considered three dimensions of inequality connected with care. First, inequality of income affects people's access to care, just as it affects access to many other things. Axes such as race, gender, nation, national origin, (dis)ability and so forth affect income. The very dependencies that generate our need for care make it difficult for us to earn the money needed to pay for it, or to attract people into bonds of altruism or obligation with us. Thus, neither markets nor any informal system where actors are entirely self-interested can redress these income-based inequalities in access to care. Families and the state redress these inequalities somewhat, but our society has little commitment to state provision of care or adequate income for all. Some simply do not receive the care they need.

Second, we have examined the possibility that some characteristics of care work contribute to inequalities in income between those who provide care and those who don't. Mothers and other family caregivers make commitments to dependents that lead them to withdraw from paid employment, reducing their future as well as their current earnings. Employed workers who specialize in caring occupations earn less money than their counterparts in other occupations.

Third, we have emphasized the direct and indirect impact of the composition of the work force providing care. Women, especially women of color, tend to have less bargaining power within the labor market. Black women and Latina women have lower levels of education than White women, and are especially vulnerable to discrimination; these factors affect undocumented immigrants even more strongly. These factors that contribute to lower pay are compounded by the cultural construction of care as a feminine responsibility that is seen to come particularly "naturally" to women, especially immigrants and women of color.

Let us now examine the implications of these causal factors for feminist public policy. Most, if not all feminists make a case for greater public provision or subsidy of care services especially in the areas of child care, elder care and health care (for a notable exception by a libertarian feminist, see Burggraf 1997). The social democracies of Western Europe are politically attractive both because they provide a more effective social safety net and because they offer greater equality of opportunity for children to develop their capabilities (Folbre 2001).

In making a case for such policies it may be useful to point out that they are not merely an expression of egalitarian values but also a response to market failure: Narrowly self-interested workers and profit-maximizing firms will not provide care for those who cannot pay. The level such workers and firms offer will be directly related to the level of public support. A good example is the crisis in nursing home care in this country. Most residents of nursing homes are indigent elderly whose costs are paid by federal Medicaid program, which sets reimbursement rates so low that those facilities unwilling to reduce costs by reducing quality are forced out of business. Unpaid family caregivers are often forced to take up the slack (Meyer and Storbakken 2000).

Market provision may actually work better (for the care recipient) in reality than in theory, because workers are not always perfectly self-interested and firms often have goals other than profit maximization. Some private care providers, for instance, choose to charge sliding scale fees to their customers rather than whatever the market will bear. Some workers are willing to take a lower wage to work in a job helping others. But such "pro-care" commitments are costly, and often have the effect of lowering wages for workers and profitability for firms. Lower profits, in turn, make it harder for firms to raise funds in capital markets, since most investors seek to maximize their rate of return. Still, we shouldn't let the private sector off the hook by assuming that they cannot or will not respond to care needs (Nelson 2001). The growth of socially responsible investment funds in recent years suggests that it may be possible to encourage shifts in social norms that could foster greater pro-care values among investors, owners, and managers.

However, given the tendency for market forces to reward profit maximization, we also need to encourage greater public support for many different forms of care provision. The question of which strategies can best mobilize support for such policies is complicated, difficult, and largely beyond our scope here (see Stone 2000b). However, we note that advocates of greater public subsidies for the care of children can invoke both the rhetoric of efficiency as well as the concept of equal opportunity. Children are the raw materials of human capital, and the high rates of poverty currently inflicted on black and Hispanic children, in particular, lead to a waste of human resources (Duncan and Brooks-Gunn, 1997). Emphasis on the fact that poverty and lack of access to high-quality education place some children at a serious disadvantage appeals to widely held principles of fair play. Economic analysis emphasizes the cost-effectiveness of investments in early childhood education (Currie 2001). Such empirical research strengthens the claim that children represent our most important "public goods."

One objection to this rhetorical strategy is that it applies more obviously to children than to the elderly. However, public support for elder care can also be supported on related grounds that social insurance for old age is more efficient and more equitable than private alternatives. Provision of care in families has traditionally been a life-cycle process based on intergenerational reciprocity. It makes sense to think about public provision of care in similar terms (Folbre 2001). It has often been observed that the elderly as a group have been more successful than children in garnering public support, partly for the obvious reason that they have the right to vote, as well as bigger bank accounts than children (Graetz and Mashaw 1999; Preston 1984). All the more reason to develop cross-age coalitions around the larger issue of public care provision.

We have also examined the economic penalties imposed on caregivers both in the home and in the labor market. These suggest the need for policies that provide money to those who provide care. "Maternalist" policies in other nations have provided family allowances or state subsidies of leaves that parents take after children are born. More generous paid vacations also give family members more slack to take care of one another without sacrificing income. In the United States, such benefits are far more limited.

Furthermore, the modest benefits in place tend to increase inequality. The value of tax benefits and credits for children, as well as the income tax deduction for child-care expenses, add up to a more generous package of support for affluent families than for those with incomes under $50,000 a year. The Survivors' Insurance component of Social Security provides support to widowed parents and their children that is far more generous than the income-tested benefits provided to poor families through TANF (England and Folbre 2002). High wage earners are far more likely to enjoy employer-paid family leaves than low wage earners (Canter et al. 2001).

The motherhood penalty may be highest in absolute terms for highly educated career women. But the impact of the motherhood penalty on the welfare of women and children is probably greatest at the bottom of the income distribution. Opposition to recent changes in our welfare system has sparked a number of proposals to provide a basic minimum income for caregivers (Mink 1998; see also www.caregivercredit.org). This suggests the need to build a strong cross-class and cross-race coalition that could focus not only on greater public support for parents, but also on ways of restructuring paid work to make it easier for families to meet their care needs (Williams 2000). One danger, of course, is that making motherhood less costly will encourage women to specialize even more than they already do, by reducing pressures on fathers to participate in direct care. This is a problem that can be addressed by providing incentives for fathers to participate more actively in care provision and creating new cultural norms based on shared responsibility.

Consideration of the care penalty in paid work highlights the fact that state provision or subsidy of care does not remove it entirely from markets or lead to "decommodification." Most forms of state provision rely heavily on labor markets, whether individuals paid to provide care are employed by the state or by private firms who are reimbursed by the state directly or through a voucher system. The poor pay and working conditions of elder-care workers in Medicaid-financed nursing homes—as well as early childhood education teachers in Head Start programs—serve as an example of this problem.

Initiatives for "comparable worth" in the 1980s would have raised pay of some paid care workers as part of the eradication of sex discrimination in wage setting. But courts failed to interpret existing discrimination law to require that employers use consistent principles to set wages in predominantly male and female jobs (England 1992; Nelson and Bridges 1999). And, even this reform was conceived as limited to equitable compensation *within*, not between, organizations (just as all discrimination law involves comparisons between how a single employer treats various workers). Thus, equal pay for jobs of comparable worth would have done nothing about the fact that entire firms and industries that are in the care sector— education, child care, health care—may have lower wages than workers producing goods or services with a higher ratio of private to public benefits.

A number of specific strategies have been suggested as a way of raising wages in the paid care sector of the economy. Efforts to garner more public support for child care and elder care typically emphasize the link between low wages, high turnover, and low quality of care (Whitebook 1999). A recent bill introduced into the Massachusetts state legislature calls for a higher minimum wage, or "living wage," for all state employers in care jobs (Shannon and Barrios 2001). Unionization in the care sector could also play an important positive role (AFSCME 2001). All these strategies deserve more careful and sustained discussion than we can offer here.

We support a pro-care political push that demands both reduced inequality in access to care and more support for care workers. However, it is important to note that a significant trade-off comes into play: Doing either makes the other more expensive; they are multiplicative rather than additive. Thus we should not be surprised when political conflicts of interest emerge between providers and those seeking increased availability or lower costs of care. Coalitions between providers and clients are possible (MacDonald and Merrill forthcoming), but finite resources generate inherent tensions. For instance, for each million dollars the state allocates to child care, the higher the wage offered to child care workers, the fewer children that can be served (holding constant caretaker to child ratio and quality of workers). The more children that are served, the lower is the wage that can be offered for the same total expenditure. We can use politics to make the total portion of the state "pie" available for care bigger, and even increase it through increased taxation. But we can't make this trade-off go away. It is there in private decisions about provision of care as well (for a given dollar amount devoted to child care, if you pay your child-care provider better, you can't buy as many hours of service).

We have analyzed three links between inequality and care: People with low income are often unable to buy the care they need. Workers who provide care tend to pay an economic penalty. Workers who provide care also tend to come from groups with relatively low levels of economic, political, and cultural power. Our analysis of the sources of each of these inequalities led to arguments about the effect of market processes based on narrowly self-interested choices and profit maximization. These processes are unlikely to provide adequate care for those most in need, to offer adequate compensation for carework, or to help traditionally disadvantaged groups move toward greater equality. We believe these arguments can help strengthen the case for greater public provision of care. However, we have also pointed out that greater public provision may be a necessary but not sufficient condition for improvements in "the care economy." The cultural construction of altruism, care, gender, race, and ethnicity also have important independent impacts, and these should urge us to rethink and rewrite the rhetoric of family values.

Notes

1. There is another important issue of inequality related to care that we do not deal with here: income too low to allow one to spend time providing unpaid care. For example, unmarried women, or women living with or married to poor men, may want to care for their children or ill family members at home but be unable to because they do not have access to any source of income other than their own earnings. Holding a job that provides earnings limits ability to provide unpaid care. This is a particularly poignant issue for poor women of color in the United States (Abel 2000; Mink 1998; Romero 1998).

2. We use the term "narrow self-interest" here to denote selfishness, that is, not caring about the well being of others. In technical economic terms, this implies no interdependent preferences. We distinguish selfishness from the broader concept of "self-interest" to call attention to the fact that caring about others' well being is not contrary to self-interest if individuals derive pleasure from others' well-being (England 1993).

3. One exception to the notion that money can buy higher quality care concerns the impact of personal feelings of affection and concern. As the song goes, "money can't buy you love." However, if you have more money, those who love you often do too (because of family transmission of advantage and race and class segregation of neighborhoods and friendship circles), so money may give you access to loving people with more resources to help you. If you are poor, the person who truly loves you may well not be able to afford to care for you. Also, if you need care and have a person who loves you and who would like to stay out of the labor market to care for you, you can support that person while he or she does this, whereas without the money, the person may have to seek employment. So even people's ability to have higher quality care on the dimension of being cared about by the caregiver is affected by income.

Child Care across Sectors

A Comparison of the Work of Child Care in Three Settings

Heather M. Fitz Gibbon

*D*espite an ideology that views caring as a natural activity for women (and thus reasonably unproblematic), caring is a complex activity imbedded in social constructs and structures that are both gendered and hierarchical. The act of caring is multifaceted, involving emotional, cognitive, and physical labor. At times the labor may be mundane, as in the routine changing of a child's diaper. At other times the caring may be quite extraordinary, as in providing comfort to a child during a traumatic event. Care can therefore be defined as simple and unimportant, or as meaningful and invaluable, but how one defines care is closely tied to the status of the caregiver and the location of the provision of care.

When I began this research, I hoped to learn why the turnover rate in child care is so high (currently as many as one third of the personnel leave the field each year; Whitebook 1999:150). After a short time in the field, the answer to the question of turnover became evident: providers are poorly paid—on average, child care workers earn $6.70 per hour, with few receiving any benefits (Whitebook and Phillips 1999; Tuominen, this volume)—and the work is extraordinarily difficult. The more interesting question then was, why do providers enter the field in the first place, and given the economic limitations of the work, why do they stay?

The answer to these questions lies not only in market factors, but in the meaning and value of child-care work for the providers. Although they share membership in a low-paid, poorly valued occupation, providers come to their work from different backgrounds and with divergent visions of the nature of their work.

This chapter explores how child-care providers in three sectors define their work. Through a comparison of family child-care providers, and center-based workers in both for-profit and nonprofit child-care centers, I examine how caregivers' definitions of their work are linked to their motivations for entering the field and to the organizational constraints of their work. I argue that providers adopt one of two models of caring—one based on caring as teaching, and the other emphasizing the relational and nurturing aspects of caring. These models

arise within a broader societal environment that devalues the emotional components of carework and offers limited opportunities for careworkers.

Theorizing the Dimensions of Caring

On the face of it, the meaning of caring is self-evident. We know when we are
cared for: we feel loved and cherished, and our physical and emotional needs
have been met. But beyond the romantic ideology of caring, caring is work, sometimes paid, often not. This work occurs within particular organizational contexts
that shape its definition, value, and meaning. Depending on these contexts and
on the personal constraints facing individual caregivers, each will come to define
the work differently.

The inherent tensions in the work of child care provide the broader foundation
for the conflicting definitions of care. As Uttal and Tuominen (1999) stated, "[a]
tension exists, however, when child care work is simultaneously viewed as commodified service work, implying that it can be compartmentalized into discrete
and clearly defined tasks—and also as relational care that is an equivalent substi-
tution for mothering because it provides authentic emotional relationships
between child and caregiver" (p. 771). Child-care work is liminal—neither public
nor private, not only paid work, but also not simply mothering.

Given these inherent contradictions, there is no singular model for how care
should be defined. Broadly viewed, as we move from a model where caring is
based in the home, to a model of market-based caring, and finally to a model of
bureaucratic caring (Fisher and Tronto 1990), the nature of the care changes.
Care based in the home emphasizes kinship networks and community contexts,
and provides women some power in the caregiving process (Fisher and Tronto
1990:46). Market-based care is located in the public sphere, is punctuated by an
exchange mentality, and is dominated more fully by the needs of the market.
Bureaucratic care, such as that represented in large child-care centers, is often targeted at low-income care recipients and is located within the logic of the welfare
state. Such care is oriented toward efficiency, attention to regulations, and the
dominance of tasks rather than emotional care (Foner 1994).

Beyond the broad societal parameters, the definition of caring is constructed
through the process of work, and within particular organization contexts. Paid
child-care work can occur either in a home or in a public facility.[1] These disparate
organizations each carry their own constraints, expectations, and ideologies.
Workers derive from these organizational settings cues about how they might
best construct definitions of care that are most advantageous to their employment
futures and their commitments to personal ideologies of care.

Just as the quality of care has been found to be related to the location of care
(Galinsky et al. 1994; Helburn 1995; Morris 1999), there is also an elective affinity between locations of care and particular definitions of care (Gerstel 2000).
Thus, a home setting invokes familial ideologies where relationships between
individuals are paramount, and the expressive and relational aspects of caring are
emphasized. This care involves demonstrating or giving love, comforting, or
engaging with the emotions of the individuals for whom one cares. Similarly,
workers located in public facilities such as child-care centers are more likely to

appropriate the model of other bureaucracies such as schools. Within these formal settings, care more resembles teaching, or the imparting of information or skills, the preparation of children for school or for their future, and fragmentation of the day into specific subjects or structured activities.

. But although the home may be more conducive to nurturing care, and the center to teaching, in reality all carework involves at minimum some elements of both models. In additional to the organizational constraints, then, careworkers come to identify themselves more fully with one or the other models depending on their motivations for entering the work, and their educational background and social class. These various definitions of care further serve to recreate status differences among the providers.

Methods

The data for this chapter come from two sources. The first is a study of family child-care providers (individuals who provide child care in their homes for unrelated children), including interviews with 45 providers and a survey of 122 providers. The second source of data is interviews with 31 center-based child care providers. The sample of center-based providers is drawn from three centers: two nonprofit and one for profit. The for-profit center (referred to henceforth as "Kelly's") employs 17 full-time providers, and is an independent center licensed for about 170 children, with about half receiving child care subsidies from the county. Both of the nonprofit centers are licensed for about 70 children and employ 6-7 full-time providers. One of the nonprofit centers ("Community Child Care Center") serves mostly low-income children, and the other ("The Caring Place") serves mostly children from middle-income families.

The background and characteristics of both family child care providers and center-based providers in the sample were very similar. All but two of the providers were women, and all but one White. Most came from working-class backgrounds, were married, and were relatively young. There were, however, some important differences between the two samples that, although not generalizable, are nevertheless suggestive of trends.

Overall, the women working in the centers were younger than those providing care in their homes (32 years old vs. 42). Similarly, family child-care providers were more likely to be married than center-based providers (70% vs. 60%), and more likely to have children of their own (82% vs. 43%). Consistent with national surveys (Fuller and Kagan 2000; Whitebook and Phillips 1990), providers in both samples were slightly better educated than the average population: among the family child-care providers, 43% had completed some college, whereas 37% of center-based providers had attended college. Though the samples are too small to be terribly conclusive, the for-profit center employed slightly fewer college graduates than the nonprofit centers. The average pay for providers in the centers was about is $7 per hour. Kelly's offered health insurance and reduced child-care costs for employees, whereas the two nonprofit centers offered no benefits other than free child care.

As is the case nationally, the turnover rate in both samples was very high. Among the family child-care providers, the number of years the women in this sample had been caring for children ranged from 1 to 26 years, with a mean of 7.9 years and a median of 4 years. This rate is higher than the national average, most likely due to the fact that my sample of providers was drawn more heavily from licensed providers. Among the three child-care centers, turnover was much higher, with providers working at the centers for a mean of 4.3 years and median 1.5 years.

Providers' Motivations for Entering the Field of Child Care

Child-care providers enter the profession for a variety of reasons and bring with them differing backgrounds and expectations. These motivations and the conditions of their work combine to construct alternative definitions of care, some aligned more with nurturing, and others with teaching. Although their motivations differ, however, for both family child-care providers and center-based providers the definitions derive from limited labor market opportunities and ideologies that place the responsibility for care both in the home and outside the home with women.

Family Child Care Providers

Although nearly all workers in all three sectors cited loving children as an important motivator for entering the field, the motivations for family child-care providers were located most clearly in their negotiations of their conflicts between the public and private spheres. For some, many of whom referred to themselves as "babysitters" (Fitz Gibbon 2001), the motivations for the work stemmed mostly from their desire to be home with their own children coupled with the need to provide income to the family. The traditional ideology of intensive mothering persists for these women, but it is broadened to include making financial contributions to the family as well. Others, especially those who saw themselves as "professional providers," although also wanting time with their family, also sought to fashion a career from the home care.

For many "babysitters," family child-care work was accidental. For example, Angie, a mother of two and former bank teller, explained that she quit her job after her second child to be a stay at home mother. She added:

> I didn't really think, "Oh I'll go into day care to supplement my income." It was more just that a neighbor up the road from where I lived had a daughter and she came to a garage sale one time and said, "I have a little boy and I need to find a sitter. Would you ever do it?" That's how it started.

For "babysitters," their perspectives on motherhood were most important. As Angie stated, "It's perfect for what I want, for the way that I felt about motherhood."

For many, however, and especially for "professional providers," the decision to become a home provider arose out of frustration with their prior work outside the home. Of my sample, 79% had worked outside the home at an earlier point, mostly in sex-stereotyped jobs with low mobility. Of those in my sample who had previously worked, 28.6% worked in technical sales or administrative support (primarily as secretaries), 3.5% in service, 35.7% managerial or professional (60% of these worked as teachers, teacher's aids or nurses), and 10.7% were laborers or operatives. Only two of those interviewed had college degrees. These patterns are very similar to those found, for example, by Nelson (1990) in her study of Vermont providers.

To augment their income as providers, similar to other samples (Tuominen 1998), the women often held additional jobs, many also home based. Jean, for example, a full-time home provider for four years, also sold cosmetics and crafts from her home, and worked weekends at a local grocery store as a clerk. Prior to her recent marriage, Jean had been a single mother for 10 years, working as many shifts as she could piece together as a nurse. Five years prior to our interview she married a machinist, giving her the freedom to quit her job (and more importantly giving up the health benefits her job offered) and work out of her home. Although she was always exhausted, Jean saw her present arrangement as a great improvement in her life because she could be home when her child returned from school and she felt she had more control in her life.

Faced with emotionally and monetarily unrewarding jobs, women find the choice to leave the paid workforce outside the home an easy one. The jobs they leave are often alienating, whereas in contrast home child care provides the promise that they will be able to control their daily lives, have some power and responsibility in their work, and spend more time with their children (Tuominen 2000). Child-care workers often experience a sense of powerlessness in their work (Rutmann 1996), but family child-care work does provide more autonomy than many other blue-collar jobs. With perhaps one exception, the women I interviewed were happy to leave their jobs to care for children in their home, and did not plan to return to their former careers. Although a few left jobs involuntarily due to lay-offs or firings, none indicated a feeling of great sacrifice in leaving the formal work force.

Linda, for example, talks about how she began family child care:

I had a house cleaning business, and before that I was a nursery school teacher. That [housecleaning] was a real isolating job. It was rewarding in some sense, in that you could see some productive work, but I guess to go any further, I needed some real challenges. The only way I could go any further was by doing two jobs a day. I was exhausted after the first one. So my youngest was in home day care, and I would go to pick her up, and I was like—there was all these babies, and I would stay there for an hour and help and play with all these babies—and the provider, she says, why don't you do this?

For some, the lack of opportunities outside the home led them to recognize that they had special talents as child care providers. As Sarah, a family child-care provider for 3 years, indicates, the need for income combined with the desire to be home with her children led to her decision to leave her work in a factory and to start a home child care.

Well, I was employed at [xx], and after I had my second child I was struggling. I was not happy with the people that were watching my children. And when I was two years out of high school I worked for the YMCA and I had gotten my feet wet with day care and the summer camp programs. And I thought, you know, I've got what it takes. I've got more than anyone I've run into . . . So I thought, you know—I had to do something to have an income. To have an input. And I knew that my kids would be getting quality care, and I knew that I could provide quality care.

This was not merely a mechanism for earning extra money, but represented a new career direction that she committed herself to fully.

For "professional providers," family child-care work offers a new career direction that allows them to maintain their family obligations while continuing an early commitment to paid work. For "babysitters," it is a temporary state, a stop between their roles as full-time mothers and out-of-home workers. For both types, however, their motivations for entering the field stem mostly from within their roles as mothers and wives. As such, their definitions of care revolve around these domestic roles and models of nurturing and "intensive mothering" (Hays 1996). These models assume that mothers are the natural caregivers of their children, and that the mother–child relationship is of most importance. Many family child-care providers choose their work to maintain that relationship with their own children, and seek to replicate it, if only in the "shadows" (MacDonald 1998), with the children for whom they care.

Center-Based Providers

As with family child-care providers, the center-based providers cited a love of children as their primary motivation for entering the field of child care. Child care is not, however, the only possible occupation involving interaction with young children. In explaining why they chose child-care work over other venues such as school-based teaching, as with family child-care workers the center-based providers referred to their limited labor market options. Based on their responses, center-based providers fell into three general categories: "career girls," "former homemakers" and "teachers in training."

Career Girls. "Career girls" is a term used by one of the older teachers I interviewed in the for-profit center, referring to those young women who attended a 2-year child-care program in the local vocational high school. Almost half of the center-based providers I interviewed fell into this category. These women either had no desire to attend college or lacked the financial means to do so. They often started working at a center right out of high school, and most had considered no other job than child care. The term "career girl" is significant, because although child care work does not offer a career in the sense of a series of jobs of increasing responsibility and remuneration, the women in this category adopt a careerist language and seek to actively construct images of career progression.

A rare long-timer in the field (18 years at Kelly's center), Sonya's background is typical of "career girls":

I've wanted to go to child care ever since fifth grade. When we did reports, I did reports on it. And I've always liked kids, so I—I took two different things [in coursework]. I was either going to take food service or [child care], but at the time I took child care because I thought, well, it would be an easy program, in and out of school, because I did not like school.

As with other career girls, Sonya was envious of the pay, reputation, and working conditions of public school teachers, but she never considered pursuing a career in teaching. She disliked school, and could not imagine herself attending college.

A few career girls did have dreams of being teachers, but had neither the money nor the time to go to college. For many, as with Gina, teaching was a fairly unattainable dream:

I would like to do that [teaching], and probably, maybe, oh eventually I'll get there. I haven't done anything as far as taking any college courses or anything, so I don't know how I will.

Gina was 35, and had worked at Kelly's off and on for three years. She began working at Kelly's immediately after high school, but soon found herself pregnant with the first of four children. She stayed home with all four, until financial pressures led her to find full-time work.

Mona also was pressured by family members to go into teaching. Just 20 years old, she started work at the Community Child Care Center right out of high school. When I asked if she had looking into teaching, she replied:

Not really, my dad's like, be a teacher, be a teacher. You get summers off. I'm like, yeah, but I don't want to go to school for another 4 or 5 years. I said, I couldn't stand high school, let alone going back to college. I may in the future. My dad's always bugging me; well you should go to college so you can be a teacher. And I'm like, well I would, but it's not right now for me.

Although the lack of education explains why these providers did not seek teaching positions, it does not explain why they chose to work at centers rather than out of their homes. Some of the center providers did in fact see themselves as opening family child-care homes down the road. But for most, their marginal lifestyles (poor housing conditions and unstable family lives) limited their ability to work at home. Penny, employed at Kelly's for 10 years and the mother of two children, spoke longingly about working as a family child-care provider:

Yeah, my mom even suggested it. My brother suggested it; everybody in my family thought it was a good idea. The only problem is that I live in a house that's 1917, and it's not really up to code for anybody, so it'd be kind of hard, and we don't have the money to bring it up right away. I'd even gone as far as to draw pictures of my own day care center and how I would like to have it, and make it out, what I would like to do. I've always kind of had that dream, but I don't see it happening. I don't have a whole lot of money; we just live from day to day.

Jennifer took plans to be a home provider even further, but had not yet succeeded:

> I did. I was going on and look to be certified. I live in an apartment, and I live
> upstairs, so yeah it was really hard. And the lady downstairs is 83, and she gets a
> little upset when my girls are running around. So I had thought about it, but it
> really wasn't ideal for where I live. But I just applied for a Habitat house, so if
> everything goes well with that, if I have my own home someday, I'd like to check
> into that. Cause I love to babysit.

For most of the career girls, the lack of education greatly limited their mobility
and provided them with fewer options than available to family child-care
providers.

Although the career girls at times thought about going back to school, none of
them thought that college was necessary for their jobs. Sarah, at the Community
Child Care Center for 10 years, responded to the question of college as a requirement for work as a child-care provider in this way:

> Not if you don't have any common sense. Because I know we have had some
> people in here that have had college education that have no common sense. And
> sometimes I feel you really need the education as far as to know what to do with
> kids, but at the same time you need that common sense more than anything else
> because that's what gets you through the day.

Gina was also very firm in her attitude toward college:

> No. I feel like I know just as much as the college student coming in. And I guess
> that's putting us down saying, if you're not college then you can't teach kids. Well,
> I think I'm just as good as somebody who comes through college and teaches kids.
> I just really totally disagree with that, because I feel like that's why we go through
> the training to get the experience in teaching kids. Being a parent has a lot to do
> with it too.

Career girls find themselves in a precarious position. Given their lack of extensive formal credentials, in order to legitimate their right to hold their jobs they
must turn to their innate abilities as women, and parents reinforce the belief that
the most important qualities needed to be a good child-care provider are love,
patience, and common sense. Nonetheless, their hopes to lay claim to the status
and pay of professional workers requires them to appropriate the language of
care as teaching.

Former Homemakers. Former homemakers make up another important, although
small, portion of the workforce in child-care centers. These are generally older
women seeking to augment their incomes for a limited period of time. The Caring
Place especially sought to hire older women with grown children. As the assistant
director explained, "The best people are the ones that have had their children, raised
them, have a husband who has benefits, they don't really need the income, but they
have this love. Those are the best people 'cause they're not looking out for money."

Five of the women I interviewed fell into this category. They were in their fifties, and had just returned to work after many years home with their children. These women were all married, their husbands had benefits, and they were looking to supplement their family income.

After her children were through elementary school, Norma began looking for ways to bring in extra income. Her children had both attended a local preschool, so she began her search there. Following work at the preschool a few days a week for about 2 years, Norma left and found a job at The Caring Place. Her children were beginning college, and she needed the extra money to support their tuition.

Another former homemaker, Esther, echoed the perspective of care expressed by others. Although she had attended college, she argued that being a mother had given her a far better background for her work in a child-care center:

Q: Should child care providers go to college?

A: No, I think motherhood helped me more. I'm very mixed about that. I'm thinking if I had gone and finished four years of college, and maybe the cost is what I'm thinking of, what you spend on education, and then, this is my job? I'm just thinking, I'm not sure all the classes or money was worth it. Because I think you need an awful lot of hands on experience, working with different children.

When asked what they most wanted to provide the children, these women replied that they hoped to provide them a home away from home. Although they recognized that a good part of their work involved teaching, they believed that the love and security they offered the children was far more important. Their perspectives were quite similar to those of family child-care providers, and as with many at-home workers, they were not expecting to stay in the field for long.

Teachers in Training. The final group of center-based providers are "teachers in training." This group included the only two men in my sample. Teachers in training are for the most part recent college graduates, working in child care centers until they can find full-time teaching jobs in the public schools. Not surprisingly, they don't stay in centers very long. Some find teaching jobs very quickly, and others learn that work in a child-care center is much less structured than that found in a school. Throughout the past year, in an effort to increase the level of education of its staff, the Community Child Care Center hired six education majors right out of college. At the end of the year, only one remained, and he was likely not there for long. In response to my question of how long he saw himself working there, he stated: "Probably until after the summer program. Because I want something more, some related to what I was trained for. But if I can't find anything that suits me, then I'll go back and get my master's."

The center was not able to pay college graduates much more than those without college, and a local shortage of public school teachers made it very difficult to find or keep college graduates. Most had little previous experience working in a child-care center, and were unprepared for the less controlled atmosphere. Even those originally planning a career in child care soon found themselves pulled into the teaching profession. Gretchen, for example, was a recent graduate with a B.A. degree in early childhood education. She chose child care because she preferred

working with younger children, and was presently working with the half-day
kindergartners in the center. Nonetheless, she didn't see herself working at the
center for long:

> I'm realizing how low paid it is! I mean, I knew, but when you're in college you
> don't really know. My parents say, oh, come on, be a teacher, go in the schools,
> you're going to get this, you're going to get that. I knew I wanted this age, but I
> am now going back for schooling, for elementary certification. My husband does
> not have benefits, not what you get in the schools. And having worked with these
> kindergartners, I love them. I kind of think now that's where I'd like to be.

Gretchen found it difficult justifying the money she spent on college given her
present income of $7.25 per hour. Although she had once thought she might
want to be a center director, she soon realized that a promotion would mean that
she would have little chance to teach and interact with children.

The emphasis on teaching carried through to the providers' attitudes toward
their work. Gretchen, for example, explained why she preferred working with
older children:

> They are old enough that they can handle most things, they can focus much more
> on learning and more activities rather than the tying the shoes, carework. I really
> like that. I guess they are just so willing to learn. I like seeing the progress from
> the beginning of the year to the end. I can advance and just do more things with
> them, and getting them ready for kindergarten. And I like that too. I like being
> able to teach them things that they are eventually going to learn, but to give them
> a head start.

Several times in the interview Gretchen made the explicit distinction between
carework and teaching. She complained that it seemed that more and more of her
work was taken up with carework, leaving little time for teaching. The implica-
tion was that "carework" was the less valuable task.

The Organizational Context of Care

As important as providers' motivations for entering work and their background
and training, the context in which they worked helped to structure their definitions of care. The home and the center each supply their own tensions, limitations and opportunities and each provides a template for understanding carework.

The home evokes particular images of nurturing and children's needs.
Correspondingly, Julie's response to my question of what she had to offer children
was typical of family child-care providers:

> Just this [she sweeps her hand across the kitchen]. Safe. Warm. Cookies. Grilled
> cheese sandwiches. A little TV, a little play, a little nap time. This should be the
> place that most kids should grow up. Or spend a couple of years. But this is just a
> nice place to bring up kids. I'll be the first one to tell you I'm not a preschool. I

don't have ABC days; I don't have color days. A lot of moms don't want a lot of structure, they just want somebody that's going to hug the child, hold him while he has a bottle, make sure he's in a warm bed, dry bed, dry pants. That's all I'm trying to do. This is just a transition thing with my kids this age. I wanted them to have a little exposure with other kids.

Consistent with other studies (Galinsky et al. 1994), only 3 of the 45 home providers I interviewed suggested that providing an educational experience for the children was their most important goal. They instead saw their work as family work, involving not only the children but the parents as well. Home providers were frequently asked for advice on parenting, and often saw themselves as friends of their client:

> I kind of look at it more like we're all working together. Or if one kid's had some kind of a problem, they'll go, "Ask so-and-so's mom what she thinks." So they'll meet at the door or whatever. So I just kind of look at it as a whole big parenting thing here, you know. I'm just the one who got elected to stay home. So, um, I really like that, really like that aspect of it a lot, when we can all kind of just share our own ideas and stuff.

By framing their caring work within the logic and language of the home, home providers open the door for others to deemphasize their expertise and devalue their talents as providers—in the words of the provider just quoted, they are no different from other parents. Sarah, a home provider active in a local network, discussed how some parents take advantage of the home environment:

> It amazes me that parents will go to a day care, even though admittedly they would prefer family day care if they could find it, they'll fork over a $30 registration fee, an annual fee to cover insurance, they'll pay whether the child goes or not, whether the child's ill or not, they'll pay extra for tumbling classes, but then when they come to the family day care provider they're late with the fees, and they don't want to pay unless the child comes, and they'll admit as soon as they come in that the child's safer and happier and better taken care of, and yet by the same—they have this shortcoming of wanting to treat you as someone they can take advantage of. Like someone they borrow money from and have no intention of paying back.

As family child-care providers are offering not only their services but also their homes, their carework is defined more within the private sphere. Although the introduction of money into a formerly nonexchange environment does change the nature of the relationship (Nelson 1990; Uttal and Tuominen 1999), nevertheless the carework is seen as more intimate, more individual, and more as an arrangement between friends.

Given the more highly structured atmosphere of a child-care center, it is not surprising that center-based providers were more likely to stress the elements of teaching in their caregiving. Providers in centers are called teachers, and their rooms are referred to as classrooms (even sometimes the infant rooms). Care in centers far more closely approximates a bureaucratic model of caring (Fisher and Tronto 1990), resembling that found in public schools. In order to serve a large number of children, centers rationalize and fragment the process of caring (Ritzer 2000) into discrete tasks. The higher status and better paid tasks are those that most resemble teaching—these individuals are referred to as "head teachers" and their work involves making lesson plans, speaking with parents, and reporting to the center director. Lower level workers (aides) deal more directly with the daily needs of the children. This hierarchy suggests that the work closest to caring is the work that is most devalued.

This deskilling of the process of care is often what parents seek in a child-care relationship. As Hertz suggested (1997), some parents choose center-based child care because they wish to reserve the emotional aspects of caring for themselves. They engage "professionals" to supplement parental teaching, but not to take the place of mothering.

Part of teaching for the center-based providers involved more than ABCs or counting, but learning to be in a structured environment with other kids. Karen talked about what she hoped to offer the children:

> I guess respect. For the teachers and the other kids. I think that nowadays that's one thing that is being lost. I think modeling respect, and making them respect other children, and making them understand how what they say is not respectful or caring. Making sure they have the knowledge of empathy. So that they know, trying to make them understand how this makes other children feel. That they aren't the only child. To make sure they realize that everybody is important. That they aren't the only child here, and when they go to school, they're going to be with all these other kids. That they are respectful to other children, and learn how to play and cooperate and not use mean words to get what they want. That's my goal with them.

As teachers, the providers in centers had a different relationship with the children, but also with the parents. Compared with home-based providers, center-based providers were far more likely to complain about the lack of involvement of parents:

> They just drop their kids off and run. In and out. You don't get a chance to talk to them. If you have something to say, before you can get up, they're gone. So we always have to leave little notes. Those kind of parents you have to remind. It's just—it makes me sad. I think that parents need to get involved.

When I asked Mark, a teacher at Kelly's, to describe the perfect parent, he emphasized communication:

> I guess taking the time out to talk to your teacher. Coming in and asking how the child's day has been, is there any problems we have to work on. But I think you just have these parents—and if we have projects, bring things in, but I think par-

ents just don't have the time any more, and they're just pushing their kid in and leave them, and when they pick them up, there's no time to just sit and talk. They want to be out. The parents are in and out, rush, rush, rush, and it feels like they're just lucky to have a place to take their child. It's a—"I don't care what happens. Just give me the child and leave."

These complaints were far more pronounced at the for-profit center than at the nonprofit centers, possibly due to the higher ratio and the larger number of children in each room.

Although the sample size is too small to be conclusive, the interviews suggest also that those providers in centers working primarily with low-income children see their work more bureaucratically, and emphasize more the role of teaching. For example, one provider in The Caring Place contrasted her work at that center with her earlier work at a larger, for-profit center:

> It was definitely a different type of center from [The Caring Place] to the one out there. I guess I don't want to stereotype, but the parents more than I have here were a lot of single parents, a lot of young parents. A lot of people on welfare. And they tended to have more of an attitude—I think they didn't understand what child care is really about, and what we were providing for their child. . . And it's hard to have relationships with them. You couldn't establish relationships.

This quote suggests that the characteristics of the care recipients affect the definitions of care as well. In both centers serving mostly low-income children, and primarily children on public assistance, the providers focused far more on teaching than caring. A number of factors might explain this. First, the ratios in these centers tend to be larger, thus requiring a greater bureaucratization of care. Second, when providing care for children on public assistance, the centers are contracting with the state as well as the parents. The funding is often sporadic, thus making it difficult for providers to establish relationships with children and their parents. The involvement of the state also further commodifies the labor by establishing a necessary price for the labor and defining more exactly the nature of productive labor. Providers working in a center heavily connected to the state are more bound by the logic of the welfare state in their provision of care than are other providers. This logic is parent rather than child centered, focusing on mothers as potential workers rather than on the needs of the children (Bergmann 1996).

Conclusion

The work of child care resides in a liminal place between the public and private spheres. Depending on their motivations, their training and their background, providers define caring based on models located either in the public or private spheres (Fitz Gibbon 2001). Family child-care workers and "former homemakers" in centers embrace more fully the model of caring reflected in a home setting. This model, however, assumes that the only training providers need is what they have as women and mothers, thus the work is poorly valued and low paid.

Because of this low pay, neither type of provider is able to stay in the profession for very long.

"Teachers in training" briefly exist in this in-between state, but then move quickly to a public venue. Frustrated by the demands of caregiving, they soon seek the higher paying job of teaching in a school system. "Career girls" are truly caught on the threshold, and as with all liminal spaces, it is a dangerous location. Although they see themselves as teachers, they do not have the credentials to be credible in that role; thus, they must emphasize the relational aspects of their jobs. The structure of their work, however, limits the extent to which they can adequately reproduce intensive caring relationships. Family members of teachers in child-care centers pressure them either to stay home and be with their own children or to find a "real" teaching job. The result is an industry with high turnover and staffing difficulties.

Policymakers are beginning to recognize that a strong child-care system is a prerequisite for successful welfare reform and more broadly for a healthy economy. What is less frequently spoken is the reality that "the current child care job market, with few exceptions, itself fuels poverty" (Whitebook and Phillips 1999). Women turn to the work of child care out of love for children, but also because they have few other options. Low wages, no health benefits, and little security increasingly trap those providers who remain. The marginal employment of our child-care workforce limits our ability to provide consistent, reliable, high-quality care. Efforts to increase the education level of providers cannot be successful until the financial benefits are increased and the working conditions improved.

This research demonstrates that the labor market opportunities of the providers and the organizational constraints on their work combine to lead providers to construct a vision of caring that further limits their mobility and life chances. A White middle-class ideology of caring that locates it in the home assumes the existence of a wage-earning spouse who is able to provide benefits and stability. Family child-care providers are often in an economic position to embrace such an ideology.

The definitions of caring employed in center-based work are located more fully in a bureaucratic and professional model of care, thus requiring greater education and training that are often out of reach of low-income women. Caring conducted in a formal facility can be loving and nurturing, if providers are given the autonomy and pay required to maintain high-quality care (Cancian 2000). Until we reward caregivers more fully for their work, simply asking for a higher educational level will not improve the quality of care. A caring environment that does not fragment the work, that values the workers, and that provides opportunities for advancement encourages more fully a complex definition of care that reflects the varied needs of those for whom we care.

Note

1. Nationally, about 30% of children of employed mothers are cared for in child-care centers or preschools, and about 40% of these centers are operated for profit (Hofferth et al. 1991). In 1993, family child-care providers cared for about 17% of the preschool children of employed mothers (Hofferth 1999).

Empowering Forces

Professional Careworkers in the Support Networks of Gay, Lesbian, and Bisexual Youth

Eric R. Wright and Robert E. Connoley

*T*he societal stigma surrounding homosexuality poses special challenges for gay, lesbian, and bisexual (g/l/b) youth (Rotheram-Borus and Fernandez 1995). Researchers have found that "minority stress," or the special psychological and social stress associated with being a member of a stigmatized group, can have serious, negative implications for gay people's mental health and health status (DiPlacido 1998; Meyer 1995). Social support, however, can moderate these negative effects (Vincke and Bolton 1994; 1996), and over the past three decades, various support groups and agencies for youth have emerged specifically to help them cope with the stigma of homosexuality (Herdt and Boxer 1993; Wright et al. 1998). As a result, professional careworkers are playing increasingly important roles in the support networks and socialization of g/l/b youth (Lenihan 1985; Mercier and Berger 1989; Townsend, Wallick, and Cambre 1996).

This chapter explores the roles professional careworkers play in the lives of g/l/b youth. Our analysis is based on a small exploratory study of youths and professionals involved in a well-established program serving this population in Indianapolis. Our aim in this chapter is to raise awareness about and improve our understanding of the roles professional careworkers play in the support networks of g/l/b youth. We describe the range and nature of professional careworkers' interactions with youths and examine the extent that professionals are present in youths' networks.

Minority Stress, Social Support, and Professional Caregiving

Since the 1970s, social scientists have become increasingly interested in the psychosocial impact of the stigmatization and marginalization of g/l/b youth. Numerous studies have documented a strong relationship between minority stress and a variety of negative social and health outcomes (Meyer 1995). DiPlacido (1998) suggested that the minority stress associated with being gay has both external and internal sources. Much of the stress that gay youth and adults experience is the direct result of negative social interactions with prejudiced individuals, ranging from everyday hassles associated with people assuming one is heterosexual to overt harassment (D'Augelli 1998; DiPlacido 1998; Meyer 1995;

Savin-Williams 1994). Internally, minority stress can manifest itself through the internalization of negative societal attitudes, the psychological pressures associated with maintaining a concealed identity, and even internal conflicts resulting from discordant beliefs (i.e., strong religious convictions against homosexuality and a conscious awareness of same-gender sexual attraction) (DiPlacido 1998; Malyon 1982; Shidlo 1994). More important, it is clear that the minority stress associated with homosexuality often takes a significant toll on people's health and mental health status (Grossman and Kerner 1998a; Jordan and Deluty 1998; Meyer 1995; Rosario, Hunter, and Gwadz 1997; Rotheram-Borus, Hunter, and Rosario 1994; Savin-Williams 1994; Vincke and Bolton 1996).

Both researchers and clinicians have theorized that social support is a vital resource for helping g/l/b youths and adults cope with minority stress (DiPlacido 1998). Early theoretical work on the coming-out process specifically identified having networks that are supportive of alternative sexual orientations as being the principal predictor of positive adaptation (Cass 1979; Ryan and Futterman 1998; Troiden 1988). Studies of g/l/b youths' support networks, however, also emphasize that developing and maintaining a network of supportive others is especially difficult in the face of societal homophobia (Ryan and Futterman 1998; Strommen 1993). The supportiveness of these youths' networks is often tied to patterns of disclosure regarding their sexual orientation. Young people are most likely to first come out to close friends and later to family members (Boxer, Cook, and Herdt 1991; Troiden 1988); however, their efforts to seek care and support from these groups are not always successful. Research indicates that adolescents' traditional sources of social support—friends and family—may have difficulty being supportive of openly gay youths (Remafedi 1987; Rotheram-Borus, Hunter, and Rosario 1994; Ryan and Futterman 1998; Strommen 1993). Consequently, traditional avenues of support are often more limited for g/l/b youths than for nongay youths.

Since the 1980s, health professionals and activists have argued that professional careworkers can serve important support functions for g/l/b youth (Gonsiorek 1982; Lenihan 1985; Malyon 1982; Miranda and Storms 1989; Walters and Simoni 1993). Mental health professionals have developed and advocated the use of "gay affirmative psychotherapy" as a tool for helping youths (and adults) develop the psychological and social resources to combat minority stress (Gonsiorek 1982; Lenihan 1985). Simultaneously, activists across the United States began organizing informal and formal support groups for g/l/b youth (Herdt and Boxer 1993; Lenihan 1985; Ryan and Futterman 1998; Wright et al. 1998). These support groups provide safe venues for youth to discuss their emerging sexual identities and expand their social networks to include other gay-identified and/or supportive people. The organization of youth groups, however, varies. Many groups are peer led and run, whereas professionals and/or supportive adults organize other groups. Regardless, the handful of studies of these groups suggest that the networks formed within these groups play important roles in shaping both young people's adaptation to minority stress and their support systems (Herdt and Boxer 1993; Wright et al. 1998). Although there have been several important studies of the support networks of gay men (Berger and Mallon

1993; Vincke and Bolton 1996) and youths (Grossman and Kerner 1998b; Nesmith, Burton, and Cosgrove 1999; Wright et al. 1998), there has been sur- prisingly little attention given to the roles that professionals play as careworkers for these youths. Most studies simply describe the relative involvement of family and nonfamily members (Grossman and Kerner 1998b). Although there are a few studies that address the challenges of professional carework with gay-identified people (Lenihan 1985; Mercier and Berger 1989; Ryan and Futterman 1998), these analyses emphasize formal therapeutic work rather than the professional carework typically available in community-based, youth-serving programs.

This chapter examines the roles professional careworkers play in the lives of g/l/b youth. Specifically, we use qualitative and quantitative data collected from youth and staff involved with a g/l/b youth group in Indianapolis. Because our study examines only one youth group, our research is not representative of all g/l/b youth groups, nor does it characterize the full range of youths in need of help, many of whom are uncomfortable participating in publicly gay-identified programs. In this regard, our study is an exploratory one. Our aim in this chapter is to raise awareness about and improve our understanding of the roles profes- sional careworkers play in the support networks of these youths.

The Study

Our study is based on a qualitative analysis of focus group interviews and a sec- ondary analysis of survey data gathered from youths and staff involved with the Indiana Youth Group, Inc. (IYG). In this section, we provide a brief description of the setting where we conducted the study. We then discuss the qualitative and quantitative components of our study.

The Agency Setting

The IYG is a nationally recognized youth group for g/l/b youths located in Indianapolis, Indiana (Wright et al. 1998). Founded in 1987, IYG is one of the oldest agencies in the country serving this special group of youths. Like other similar agencies, IYG organizes a variety of peer support programs and activities. In contrast to peer-run groups, IYG was founded on the philosophy that support from adults and professionals can complement and augment support from peers. Over the years, IYG has supplemented its peer-support and youth development programming with an array of social and clinical services provided by a paid pro- fessional staff (e.g., mental health counseling, case management services), and evaluations of the IYG programming demonstrate that the overall approach is an effective one (Wright et al. 1998; 1999).

Currently, the IYG staff is composed of a full-time executive director (ED), two full-time program coordinators, and a full-time outreach coordinator. The IYG staff operates as a team, and decisions regarding programming and resources are made as a group. The two program coordinators are social workers by training and share primary responsibility for working with the individual youth and devel- oping and managing the core program activities. The executive director and out- reach coordinator also participate in the youth programming and work with many of the youths on a one-on-one basis. Most of the services are provided at the IYG

Youth Center, an older house located on the near north side of Indianapolis that was converted in 1993 to serve as the headquarters for the agency. In an average month, approximately 150 unique youths participate in various IYG programs, ranging from regular activities like the "Thursday Night Meetings" (which are usually structured discussions or activities) and drop-in center to special events such as the "IYG Prom" or "movie nights." The primary focus of all of the programming is to help youths develop the social skills and psychological resources they need to help themselves. Occasionally, youths come to IYG who have significant mental, physical, or social needs that are beyond the agency's capacity to intervene effectively. In these cases, staff works with the young people to link them with appropriate community services elsewhere in the community through a network of gay-friendly providers (see Wright et al. 1998 for a more detailed description of the program).

Qualitative Focus Group and In-depth Interviews

To explore the nature of the youths' relationships with professional careworkers, we conducted three focus groups with IYG youths and invited them to discuss their relationships with the professional staff. The focus-group interviews were conducted on three separate occasions in January and February 2001. A total of 22 unique youths participated in one of the focus-group discussions. Each group was conducted at the IYG Youth Center and lasted an average of 50 minutes. Sessions were held prior to the regular operating hours to make the meetings more convenient for the youths and to help protect the young people's confidentiality. For the first two groups, an open invitation to participate in a "group discussion" was extended to youths attending various IYG activities. Youths were informed prior to the scheduled meeting that a group discussion would be held to discuss young people's relationships with the professional staff. Participants in the third focus group were selected to include particular groups of youths who were not well represented in the initial discussions (i.e., African-American females). Each focus group was led by the second author and initiated with three questions: (1) "Tell me about how your involvement in IYG began." (2) "how has staff helped you in your coming out process?" (3) "in what other ways has staff helped you or worked with you?" All questions were followed up with targeted probes to concentrate the discussion on roles that staff played in the lives of the youth. The youth discussions were supplemented with in-depth interviews with staff where they were asked to: (1) "Without limiting yourself in any way, define all of the ways in which you work with or help our members." (2) "Define your role with the members."

Field notes from were recorded during all discussions and transcribed after the meetings. The transcripts of the discussions were also presented to the participants for confirmation and accuracy prior to conducting any analysis. Our analysis began with a careful reading of the transcribed notes to familiarize ourselves with the full range of comments. Using grounded theory techniques (Glaser and Strauss 1967), we identified major carework themes present in both the youth and staff comments. Initially, we developed separate typologies for the youths and staff. Although both groups often use different terms to describe their relationships, there is a surprisingly high level of agreement between staff and youths on the basic carework roles. Consequently, our analysis presents the major themes that reflect common views of the professional careworker–youth relationship held by both youths and staff.

Our analysis of the focus groups with youth and in-depth interviews with staff identified five distinct roles for professional careworkers: surrogate parent, mentor/teacher, priest, promoter/advocate, and mediator. Although there were some differences between the youth and staff perspectives, there is remarkable consensus on the overall patterns. Where differences are observed, their comments generally reflected the specific challenges in being on different ends of particular relationships. The typology, presented next, represents a series of five ideal types. The enactment of these role relationships is further complicated by the emotions, attitudes, and relationship history of the specific role-partners involved. Here, we discuss the differences in these ideal roles to highlight the breadth of the functions professional careworkers serve in g/l/b youth's support systems. Throughout, names and identifying information have been changed to protect the confidentiality of the respondents.

Surrogate Parent. IYG staff members are often asked to serve in the role of a surrogate parent because the youths are unable to be completely honest and open with their families of origin. As a result, youths sometimes view staff as constituting a "second family"—people who will help them through personal issues, in a caring way. One example is Jessica's searching for assistance on relationships:

Darlene [staff member] has always been there for me. She lets me ask really stupid questions, and always answers them. I've learned so much from her. I used to be in really bad relationships . . . very abusive. But, Darlene has taught me how to care enough about myself to not get in those relationships. (Jessica, 17, Caucasian)

The staff member, Darlene, elaborated:

Jessica is like so many of our youth. They come to us asking questions that I think should be answered by a parent. But these kids don't have parents that they can talk to. So we do what we can to be the adult in their lives that will be honest and help them with relationships or school or whatever else they may want to talk about. (Darlene, staff, Caucasian)

The surrogate parent role is therefore defined primarily by the nature of the topics addressed. Topics are typically personal in nature and require a staff response that is more than a "clinical" or objective response. Jesse (14, Caucasian) states, "When I go to staff with a problem, I already know what I am supposed to do. I just need someone who will listen and care, and then confirm that I am heading in the right direction."

The second aspect to the surrogate parent role is in the expectations regarding staff responses. With many staff–youth interactions, the assistance will be received with hesitation or trepidation, typical of any adult–youth relationship. But when a young person is the initiator of the request for assistance, and when the assistance is of a personal nature (i.e., dating relationship concerns), then the information is accepted with little or no critique. Much of this trust can be attributed to the fact that g/l/b youths have experienced so much dishonesty or hostility from adults that when there is an adult who accepts them and is willing to help, the assistance is viewed as a gift. Also, as "staff," the professional is given a level of authority greater than that of other adults, because staff members in these types of youth groups are more likely to be viewed as the ultimate authority on g/l/b-related issues.

Amber (17, Caucasian) conveyed her need for an adult parent in her life, "Who am I supposed to ask about dating? I can't ask my mom. I can't ask my friends . . . they're the ones I'm trying to date. (Staff) will tell me their honest opinion." Finally, the surrogate parent role includes the stereotypical relationship between parent and child—nagging:

> [Staff] nags me so much when I'm here. But, I know that when I'm at IYG I have to behave. I know they do it because they care about me. I still don't like it though. (Neil, 15, Hispanic)

This feeling was shared by numerous youths:

> They're worse than my mom. Clean this. Do that. Did you do your homework? I don't mind it. At least they care. (Jesse)
>
> Oh yeh, do they ever get on you around here. It's always like, "did you do your homework?" "Did you turn in that paper?" "Did you remember your girlfriend's birthday?" (Jennifer, 18, African-American)

The staff members acknowledge this part of the relationship as well. Claire (Caucasian) comments, "In a way we are a family around here, so yeh, I do get on them to clean things and do homework." Darlene adds, "Often times we are the only source of discipline in their lives." In fact, several staff members note that the surrogate-family nature of some of their relationships evokes other familial tendencies, most often the desire to take the young people under their wing and protect them. Although the professional staff views this tendency as negative and as being a "mother hen," it does happen on occasion. Darlene describes one such relationship:

> When I first met Craig, I knew he was vulnerable. He had just come out. He was cute, and he was naive. I watched out for him in the meetings and made sure that the more experienced members didn't take him down the wrong paths.

Mentor/Teacher. The mentor/teacher relationship is similar to the surrogate parent relationship, with two subtle differences. First, the topics that define this role are less personal in nature, and tend to be related to being gay, although not always. Subjects may include coming out, navigating relationships with parents, and integration into the g/l/b community, but also include employment and academics. Second, when information is offered, the young person applies a heavier critique than if the information is offered through the surrogate parent role. In the mentor/teacher role, a young person approaches a staff member for guidance on issues where staff members are viewed as "experts." For example, Darlene was approached by Jennifer to assist with the coming-out process:

[Staff] has helped me with so much over the years. They helped with when I first came out. They helped me with relationships issues. They've even helped me with my parents. They've always been willing to give me information that allowed me to make it through tough times, especially when I first came out. (Jennifer)

Through their work together, Darlene was able to provide a framework through which Jennifer could come out to her family.

Every case is different, but our experience has provided some insight into how and when a young person can come out. So, that's what I offered Jennifer. She used some of the information, and some of it she didn't. (Darlene)

Likewise, when Robert needed a summer job, he asked Claire for assistance in getting a job where being gay was not an issue.

I was really struggling to get a job last summer, and when I went to (staff), they helped me with a resumé and interviewing and stuff. I got the job I wanted. (Robert, 18, Caucasian)

The mentor/teacher role is defined also by how much a young person accepts the information offered. As Darlene stated in reference to Jennifer's coming out issues, not all information offered was used. Claire elaborated:

To me it's not an issue of whether they use the information I give them or not. It's more about giving them information, letting them sift through it, and deciding what is best for themselves.

Youths see information offered in the mentor/teacher relationship as being more professional and less personal. Therefore, the level of trust and intimacy is different. Neil explained:

If I go to a staff member for a personal issue, then I'm going to accept what they say without hesitation. But, if I go to them for something like coming out or school, then they aren't me and they can only try and help.

In this regard, staff members see this role as filling a special void because there are few open or socially sanctioned agents of socialization into the gay community. As one staff member put it: "There is no roadmap to being gay. I try to help the members succeed without the pains that I went through." Several staff members explicitly stress the importance of transmitting knowledge of g/l/b culture and history: "By the time they leave our program there are certain things that I feel they should know. That's why I try to teach them gay history and about gay politics. Its important" (Ron, staff, Caucasian). In addition to transmitting lesbian and gay culture, IYG staff also feels it is important to teach the young people basic relationship skills and make sure they understand HIV/AIDS:

I regularly plan learning activities. For example, I wanted to teach basic relationships skills, so we planned activities to support that. Then I follow that information up in my one-on-one interactions. (Claire)

The most important thing to me is that they know all the information about HIV and STDs. If we don't get them that information, then we've failed. (Darlene)

In many cases, without professional careworkers like the IYG staff, youth are often left to "fend for themselves" on the streets or in other places where youth are likely to be victimized or engage in high risk behavior (e.g., using drugs/alcohol, risky sex).

Priest. The priest role is one of immunity. When members are introduced to the IYG program, they are immediately told, "IYG is a safe place." All advertising and marketing mention that the program is a "safe place," and everything that happens is confidential. IYG staff members work hard to create a safe environment because for many youths it may be the only place where they feel that they can be themselves.

As a result, members often perceive staff as a safe ear—as someone that they can tell anything without risk. Jesse stated, "I can tell (staff) things that I can't tell anyone else." And Amber shared, "At IYG, I can tell staff whatever I want. I've never had to worry about that." Often times these "secrets" are relatively benign, but occasionally the information is more serious:

I once told Claire about something I did to my last girlfriend. I was really concerned because she was a member too. But, Claire just supported me and didn't tell anyone. It could have been bad too because if that information got out, she would have made my life very difficult. (Tiffany, 16, Caucasian)

But the role is one of more than a listener; the priest role is one of absolution.

Obviously I'm not going to tell you what I said, but I once told [staff] something that was so bad. I don't know why I did it, but I knew I could trust them. She told me that it was okay. I needed that. (Richard, 17, Caucasian)

It is through this role that youth are able to tell their deepest, darkest secrets, and feel "forgiven" for what they have done. It is then up to the staff to struggle with the issues poured on them.

I don't really want to hear half of the stuff I hear. Some of the stuff really scares me, but I know that no matter what they tell me, it must remain a secret, unless it's about abuse or something like that. (Claire)

Oh man, you have no idea the crazy things I have heard. Don't get me wrong; these are good kids. They've done nothing worse than any other kid, but I'm glad they feel they can come to me and share. It seems like they leave talking to me feeling better about themselves. (Darlene)

This staff as priest role allows youth to work through personal issues in a safe environment. Through the offering of the information, often a sort of absolution is provided that allows the young people to free themselves of their internalized guilt related to what has happened in their lives.

Advocate. The role of the advocate is one in which the young person will use the staff member to promote a specific need or advocate on their behalf. This might come in the more common form of a staff member advocating tolerance in schools or at home, or it might be a more lighthearted role of helping someone get a date.

The role of the advocate distances the staff member from the young person and defines the relationship more as a client–provider one. David, a 19-year-old African American, commented, "I basically look at [staff] as an employee who is supposed to work for me. [Staff] needs to help me survive in school and at home." Eric (16, Caucasian) shares this basic attitude: "I need the staff to keep my school protecting me. If they don't, then who will?" IYG staff members feel similarly about the importance of this role. Claire comments: "When I'm in schools doing a training, I make sure that the audience sees exactly what damage they do with their hatred. Our kids don't deserve the hatred they receive."

In addition, staff members' assistance helps to nurture a sense of empowerment and a belief that it is okay and possible to respond to the negative societal attitudes and behavior regarding homosexuality. Amber explains it this way:

Staff does so much for us. I especially appreciate how they step up to bat for us. You know, they will go into our schools and tell the principal when he's not treating us right. And the cool thing is they don't view us as victims. We can take care of ourselves, but they, being adults, are able to help us in ways that we can't do for ourselves.

Amber's comments indicate that the youths can and do see the more macro-level concerns regarding gay rights and discrimination. Although they see these issues as better addressed by staff, ultimately the young people are both supported and empowered by observing firsthand the professional careworkers' willingness to confront the stigma and engage in advocacy work.

From time to time, young people also rely on the staff members' willingness to help and use the advocate role for more "youthful" aims. For example, members sometimes intentionally disclose information to staff and encourage them to share the information with the larger group:

It's kind of messed up, but I use the staff to help me look good. I'll tell [staff] something, knowing that it will be fed back anonymously to the other members. It's a good way to get dates [laughing]. (Robert)

In this and other instances, staff members often are very aware that this manipulation is occurring and offer no resistance:

> I know they've used me to get dates before, or to make someone jealous. It's all cool. They're kids. They may be gay. They may be abused at home and school. But underneath it all, they're kids. (Claire)

The role of advocate is one in which young people consciously seek the help of staff members to promote a personal need. In this relationship, the personal side of the overall relationship is minimized, while the client–provider dimension of their connection is primary.

Mediator. In the mediator role, the staff bridges the divide between individual members and their schools, their parents, or their peers (including other IYG members). Staff members function as go-betweens for the young people and as a safe source of mediation. Examples of this role in action might be when a young person feels in danger at home emotionally during the coming out process. Staff may be asked to assist the young person by providing information to the parent that gives "professional" support for being gay. Likewise, educators are often unaware of their legal responsibilities in dealing with gay youths, and staff members are asked to work with a specific teacher or school in making the environment safe for a student. Several youth offered examples of this type of support:

> I got thrown out of my house, so I came to the staff and they helped me get back home. They had to talk to my dad for a long time, but things have worked out pretty well since then. (Neil)
>
> I had this one teacher who was always messing with me. [Staff] went to my school and talked to the principal. I don't know what they said, but I haven't had any other troubles. (Amber)

In these ways, staff members' mediation work often extends far beyond individual members and into the community. Staff members, however, also help individuals solve more personal problems. For example, Tiffany recalls an incident: "I was having this huge fight with my girlfriend, and [staff] stepped in and helped us work things out."

The role of mediator portrays staff as having the skills, knowledge, and authority to step in and resolve or facilitate something that is going on in their lives. In many ways, this role reflects the special needs g/l/b youths have for professional help in navigating living in a homophobic society.

Quantitative Youth Social Network Survey

To supplement our qualitative research, we also conducted a secondary analysis of survey data collected as part of an HIV prevention demonstration project evaluation conducted at IYG in the 1990s (Wright et al. 1998; 1999). As part of this evaluation, each young person was invited to participate in a baseline interview within 6 to 8 weeks of entering the program and again at 6-month intervals for the duration of their involvement. The initial participation rate in the survey was 93%, with 58% of those recruited also completing one or more follow-up interviews. Here we examine the 100 young people who completed a baseline interview and a 6- or 12-month follow-up interview. This sample includes 49 young women and 51 young men. The baseline average age of the sample is 17.97 (SD = 1.44) with 47% (*n* = 47) of the sample being between 13 and 17 years of age and 53% being between 18 and 21 years old. Like the surrounding geographic area, the sample is primarily Caucasian (*n* = 86). The largest groups of minority youth are African American (*n* = 6) and Native American (*n* = 5). The majority of the youth surveyed describe their sexual orientation as "gay" or "lesbian" (*n* = 69), with an additional 20% indicating "bisexual" and 11.0% responding "other," "undecided," or "not sure."

As part of this survey, the youths described their personal support networks. Each youth was asked a series of "name generators" designed to elicit the principal confidants and main supporters in a person's life. Specifically, each respondent was asked: (1) "From time to time, most people discuss important matters with other people. Looking back over the last six months, who are the people with whom you discussed matters important to you?" (2) "Who are the people in your life right now who you feel you can depend on for help if you need it?" (3) "Is there anyone who is always talking to you about the important things going on in your life?" A parallel set of name-generating questions were also asked focusing specifically on the people the youths talked to about "emotional or physical health problems" during the same time period. For each unique name mentioned, the interviewer asked a series of descriptive questions about the respondent's relationships with each person nominated. We use these data to describe the extent of professional careworkers' involvement in the youth's networks at baseline and after they have been in the program for 6 months to 1 year. We focus on the total number of network ties mentioned, the number of kin, the number of friends, and the number of general (non-IYG) and IYG professional careworkers named in the youth's networks. We also describe the mean closeness, frequency of interaction, and support separately for the total network, for the general professionals, and for the IYG professionals named. Descriptive statistics for these measures at baseline and follow-up are provided in Table 1. Further details regarding the study are available on request (see also Wright et al. 1998; 1999).

Our quantitative analyses of these survey data provide a different perspective on youth and staff descriptions of their relationships. When asked how many people they can talk to or depend on regarding important matters and health-related concerns, the youths mention an average of six people both at baseline and follow-up (see Table 1). Not surprisingly, the most common groups of people mentioned are friends and family. Both general professionals (e.g., therapists, social workers) and IYG staff are nominated at both time points; however, only about half of the youth mentioned one or more professionals at either wave.

More telling are the findings regarding the qualities of the relationships that the youths report with specific groups of people. Overall, we find that the youths report relatively close, frequent, and supportive relationships with most of their network ties at both waves. However, when the parallel measures for the relationships the young people had with professionals are compared with their over-

TABLE 1

Quantitative Description of the Characteristics of IYG Youth's
Support Networks at Enrollment and Follow-Up, IYG Youth Survey

	Baseline			Follow-Up			
	Mean	SD	Relative Proportion of Total Network	Mean	SD	Relative Proportion of Total Network	t
Network structure and composition							
Total network	6.40	3.11		6.40	3.46		NS
Kin	1.81	1.54	.305	1.92	1.60	.307	NS
Friends	2.67	2.05	.408	2.79	2.41	.446	NS
Professionals (non-IYG)	.62	1.10	.084	.35	.93	.054	2.29*
IYG staff	.41	.90	.060	.47	1.01	.060	NS
Network interactions							
Closeness							
Overall	2.47	.36		2.55	.30		-1.82+
With professionals	1.43	.71		1.28	.62		NS
With IYG professionals	1.25	.56		1.48	.63		-3.44***
Frequency of interaction							
Overall	3.36	.45		3.32	.45		NS
With professionals	1.64	1.05		1.35	.76		2.38*
With IYG professionals	1.46	.90		1.69	.90		-2.21*
Support							
Overall	3.42	.67		3.55	.61		-1.88+
With professionals	1.61	1.24		1.53	1.13		NS
With IYG professionals	1.67	1.24		2.40	1.50		-4.22***

$+ p \leq .10;$ $* p \leq .05;$ $** p \leq .01;$ $*** p \leq .001.$

all networks, we see that their relationships with professional careworkers are more emotionally circumscribed than their connections with their overall personal networks. At the same time, we see an important pattern of change over the course of the young people's involvement in the program. Specifically, the network connections to general professionals appear to decrease slightly. Further, although the absolute number of ties to IYG professionals does not change, all three measures of relationship quality change significantly during the follow-up period. That is, the young people's feelings of closeness, frequency of contact, and perceptions of the supportiveness to IYG professionals all increase significantly, suggesting that youths develop stronger emotional relationships with the openly gay and/or gay-supportive professional careworkers over the course of their involvement in the program.

More telling are the findings regarding the qualities of the relationships that the youths report with specific groups of people. Overall, we find that the youth report relatively close, frequent, and supportive relationships with most of their network ties at both waves. However, when the parallel measures for the relationships the young people had with professionals are compared with their overall networks, we see that their relationships with professional careworkers are more emotionally circumscribed than their connections with their overall personal networks. At the same time, we see an important pattern of change over the course of the young people's involvement in the program. Specifically, the network connections to general professionals appear to decrease slightly. Further, while the absolute number of ties to IYG professionals does not change, all three measures of relationship quality change significantly during the follow-up period. That is, the young people's feelings of closeness, frequency of contact, and perceptions of the supportiveness to IYG professionals all increase significantly, suggesting that youth develop stronger emotional relationships with the openly gay and/or gay-supportive professional careworkers over the course of their involvement in the program.

Discussion and Conclusions

Our study highlights the important roles that professional careworkers play in the support networks of g/l/b youth. The young people's relationships with professionals are complex and multifaceted. In our qualitative data, we identified five ideal typical roles IYG staff serve for the youths, ranging from that of surrogate parent to conflict mediator. These roles are especially interesting because each reflects aspects of these adolescents' lives that can be problematic. In this regard, the role types represent ways that professionals can and do fill the social gaps and fissures resulting from societal homophobia. Our secondary analysis of the social network survey data suggests further that overtime the relative importance of these network connections may increase as they become more involved in youth group activities. Although the absolute number of IYG professional careworkers does not change significant over the first 6 to 12 months of youth involvement with IYG, the social bonds between the youths and the IYG professional careworkers get stronger and more positive.

The central observation that professional careworkers play specialized roles in the socialization of g/l/b youths has important theoretical implications for understanding this population's unique caregiving needs. Heterosexual youths, as they move through the phases of psychosexual development, are generally privileged by virtue of their position in the sexual stratification system. A "heterosexual assumption" pervades our society, and many of the normal social mechanisms that help "straight" youths make sense of and integrate their emerging sexual identities are non-existent for g/l/b youths. In this regard, these youths are systematically disadvantaged and disempowered. IYG and similar youth groups fill these critical social structural voids by providing safe opportunities for these youths to continue their development as adolescents within a gay-friendly/supportive environment.

Professionals, especially gay-identified and/or gay-supportive ones, offer a special social safety net for youth who have difficulty constructing supportive networks of friends and families. The young people's description of the role of surrogate parent, in particular, highlights some of the limits that expectations and experiences of rejection can create for some youth in their ability to rely on parents as supporters during adolescence. When traditional agents of socialization fail, professionals can step in and serve in these capacities.

Professionals, as emphasized by the IYG staff, also help these youth by opening up the g/l/b culture and community. Because of the stigma of homosexuality, accessing information and/or people in the gay community can be a challenge. Much as parents and friends socialize nongay youth to the norms of the heterosexual world, older peers and professionals serve this function with many youth. In our data, both staff and youth commented specifically on the professionals' role in educating them about gay history and politics. In this regard, professional careworkers make the process of integration into the community easier.

The comments of both the youths and staff members we talked with suggest many positive aspects to their relationships. Indeed, the youths and staff members spoke very affectionately about each other. Although the tone was clearly positive, many of their comments given here point to areas where professional careworkers and youths are likely to have relationship difficulties. Both staff members and youths, for example, mentioned the special challenge of establishing a trusting relationship that combined both personal and nonpersonal roles. Staff members, in particular, talked about the delicate balancing act between being a "professional" and being a "friend" and that going too far in either direction could compromise the quality of their working relationship. As noted, youths too were concerned about this line, suggesting that occasionally professional careworkers get too involved "in your business." Occasionally, youths intentionally try to blur this distinction to enlist staff to helping meet more personal needs (e.g., to get a date). In short, both the professional careworkers' and youths' interactions reflect a constant struggle to negotiate the personal and professional boundaries of their relationships. In many ways the language they use and the patterns they describe evoke a sense of "family," yet they also acknowledge that they are not, in fact, biologically or legally family or even true "friends." This tension results from the pressure on professional careworkers to fill critical gaps in the g/l/b-specific socialization process while also needing to maintain a "professional" relationship with the young people.

Although the patterns are clear, our study has two important limitations. First, the data come from an examination of one g/l/b youth program. This raises concerns about possible selection effects and the generalizability of the findings. Clearly, IYG is not representative of all g/l/b youth groups, nor is the IYG staff representative of professional careworkers who work with this population. Youth programs for this population differ in the level and nature of involvement that professionals and/or adult volunteers have, and IYG reflects only one service model. Similarly, the participants we spoke with were all volunteers, and only youth who came to IYG regularly participated. In this regard, the youths in both the qualitative and quantitative components of our study may not be representative of all g/l/b youths, especially those who do not feel comfortable contacting publicly gay-identified agencies. Self-selection into our study may also account for the generally positive descriptions of youth's interactions with the professional careworkers. Second, the qualitative and quantitative data gathered from youth were not collected from the same cohort of youth. Although the patterns and themes evident in both components of this research suggest similar interpretations, the experiences of the youth in the two substudies may, in fact, be different.

In conclusion, professional careworkers appear to fill important social voids in the lives of g/l/b youths—voids generally created by societal homophobia. In many ways, the youths at IYG are truly lucky because it provides opportunities to garner both peer and professional support. Sadly, the current reality is that youth groups like IYG are not widely available, despite their growing popularity and demonstrated effectiveness. IYG and similar agencies get calls and e-mails daily from youth who need help. Youth support groups, though, are not the only potential solution to provide care resources to g/l/b youths. Education-based programs, including gay–straight alliances (GSAs) and teacher/student diversity training programs, and other youth outreach and health care programs also are helping to respond to young g/l/b people's needs, especially those who are not comfortable or capable of reaching out to openly gay agencies. Regardless of the source or location, this study affirms the importance and value of professional carework in empowering g/l/b youths to live in a homophobic society.

Note

This research was supported, in part, by a grant from the Health Resources and Services Administration (HRSA) Special Projects of National Significance (SPNS) Program (BRH9700152) to the Indiana State Department of Health (ISDH), the Indiana Youth Group, Inc. (IYG), and Indiana University. The views and interpretations presented here are solely those of the authors and do not necessarily reflect the opinions of HRSA, ISDH, IYG, or Indiana University. The authors thank the youth and staff at IYG who participated in this research. Direct correspondence to the first author at Indiana University Purdue University Indianapolis, Department of Sociology, 425 University Blvd., CA303, Indianapolis, IN 46202, USA. E-mail: ewright@iupui.edu.

Support Organizations for Parents of Children with Cancer

Local, National, and International Problems and Prospects

Mark Chesler

*T*he diagnosis of childhood cancer is a major shock and stress for the child, parents, and all family members and friends. As parents deal with this chronic and serious illness they become involved in new dilemmas and forms of caregiving. Many of their new tasks require long-term and high-stakes interaction with medical and social service staffs. These sustained, intimate interactions often highlight the tensions between formal and informal care, private and public spheres of caregiving, and the norms governing caring "for" and "about" others (Abel and Nelson 1990; Cancian and Oliker 2000; Stone 2000).

It rapidly becomes clear to most parents that they cannot and need not be alone as they cope with this stress and as they provide care or integrate the provision of care for themselves and their child. Indeed, in addition to working with medical and social service staffs, parents of children with cancer throughout the world are organizing in increasing numbers to create self-help and support groups and organizations. In this effort they are part of the tremendous growth of informal care and voluntary self-help efforts, sometimes called a "revolution" in health care, public service, and community mobilization (Gartner and Reissman 1984). These support groups engage in a wide variety of activities and programs and increasingly exist on a local, national, and even international level.

Local parent groups generally engage in direct service to children and parents, helping family members take care of themselves and in turn helping their children deal with the physical and social–emotional challenges of childhood cancer. They often act as organizational caregivers or service agencies as well as arenas for the mobilization of parent energy to improve or alter medical services. At the national level, organizations of local groups sometimes provide direct services to parents but more often serve local groups' needs, including training leaders, providing communication and coordination across groups, and preparing educational/advocacy materials for wide distribution. They also often engage in public education and advocacy regarding the availability of medical, psychosocial, and social support (including antidiscrimination efforts) to children and families of children with cancer. At the international level a relatively new organization, the International Confederation of Childhood Cancer Parent Organizations

(ICCCPO), provides services primarily to national organizations and has begun to integrate them into a worldwide network of information exchange, resource sharing, and parent–professional cooperation and advocacy.

Sometimes parents form and conduct these groups in the context of harmonious and supportive relationships with local medical clinics, local or national medical associations, and public charities and service organizations. Sometimes these relationships are characterized by conflict and tension. Parents, parent self-help and support groups, and medical staffs and cancer associations all are concerned with the physical and emotional/social health of children with cancer. But their roles and resources in this common concern differ greatly. The differences and potential conflicts parents and parent associations face in these relationships are similar to those reported by other researchers studying processes of formal (professional) and informal (natural—kith and kin) care (Borkman 1990; Powell 1990; Ruddick 1989) or public and private spheres of caregiving (Cancian and Oliker 2000; Stone 2000; Traustadottir 2000). Table 1 summarizes some of these differences encountered as medical and social service professionals and parents try to work together in the care of children with cancer (Chesler and Chesney 1995:206). Stone (2000) provided a similar analysis in what she saw as a series of "tensions" in the shift from private to public forms of caregiving: task (instrumen-

TABLE 1

Major Differences between Parents of Children with Cancer and Professionals Working with These Parents and Children

Difference	Parent	Professional
Function and status	Service recipient	Service provider
	Relatively powerless	Relatively powerful
	Medical visitor	Medical home team/host
Knowledge base	Experiential wisdom	Academic expertise
	Personal	Technical
	Particular	General
	Uncredentialed	Legitimate/credentialed
Interests and accountability	Children	Career or profession
	Particular child	Children/families in general
	Child and family	Medical community
Mind set/emotional state	Emotionally close	Emotionally distant
	Expressive	Detached/cautious
Job and family concerns	Family internal to illness	Family external to illness
	Job external to illness	Job internal to illness

Note: Adapted from Chesler and Chesney (1995:206).

tal care) versus talk (emotional support), detachment versus love, fairness versus specialness, rules versus relationships, schedules versus patience, and work relations versus family relations.

These differences stem from and lead to inequalities in power between formal caregivers and care recipients, power rooted in control of the medical process by physicians. This power difference is escalated by the ways in which social legitimation is provided to some forms of caregiving versus others, in terms of knowledge (technical expertise rather than experiential wisdom), interests (general rather than specific), emotional styles (distant and rational rather than close and expressive), and occupational status (high-status providers rather than lower status recipients). Parent support groups can help recalibrate or equalize this power imbalance by legitimating parental sources of wisdom, articulating common grievances, collectivizing individual resources, and mobilizing and targeting energy.

In this chapter I explore the growing phenomena and implications of caregiving dilemmas associated with childhood cancer parent organizations by: (1) describing what it is that they do to care for and about parents and to help parents take care of their children; (2) describing how these parent groups are organized—locally, nationally, and internationally; (3) highlighting some of the differences between what groups do, and how they do it, in wealthy nations and in less wealthy nations; (4) describing and analyzing how childhood cancer parent groups/organizations relate with medical staffs, public charities, and cancer associations; and (5) suggesting the prospects of cooperation/coalition as ways of working with these interorganizational differences and potential conflicts.

Methods

This report is part of a larger research and action effort focusing on self-help and support groups for parents of children with cancer. Several data sets comprise the source material. In the United States a research staff conducted a series of survey, participant-observation, and intensive interview studies with parents and professionals (medical professionals and cancer association staffs) active in more than 50 local self-help groups for parents of children with cancer (Chesler and Chesney 1995). In addition, I personally engaged in participant observation as a member of the Board and Executive Committee of the U.S. national parents' organization, the Candlelighters Childhood Cancer Foundation, and as a member of several committees and conferences of the U.S. national cancer association, the American Cancer Society. In the international arena I gathered survey, interview, and observational data from childhood cancer parent organizations in 31 different nations and have participated as a member of the Executive Committee of the International Confederation of Childhood Cancer Parent Organizations. The data in this chapter concern primarily the national-level organizations that exist in these nations and their relationships with national-level cancer associations.

What Do Parent Groups/Organizations Do . . . and How Do They Do It?

Childhood cancer is a life-threatening and often chronic illness. Despite substantial medical progress many children die from this disease; many others are compromised physically or emotionally; and all children diagnosed with cancer go through painful and anxiety-producing medical treatments. In the face of this threat to a child's life and future, to parental hopes and dreams, and to family stability, many parents bond together in mutual support and self-help groups. These groups increase parents' abilities to care for their children, and in so doing care for other parents/families who are in the same situation. They often are "caring communities," engaged in what some observers have called "helper-therapy."

At the local level, in specific communities and often linked to specific treatment centers, parent groups generate programs that respond to the major stresses or challenges that children and their families face (Chesler and Chesney 1995; Chesler and Eldridge 2000): informational, practical, social, emotional, and existential. The mix of these stresses, and therefore group programs, differs according to the needs and resources of parents in different locales, but in general groups focus on meeting some or all of the five stresses.

In responding to the *informational stresses* of childhood cancer, groups provide parents with information about the disease and its treatments, about psychosocial issues and coping strategies, about the medical center and staff (e.g., where to find the cafeteria, who to talk with about billing, the styles or characteristics of various physicians and nurses), and about available resources in the community. Group programs directed to the *practical stresses* try to ease parents' burdens of everyday living, including child-care and financial responsibilities. This is done through the provision of financial assistance (to purchase wigs, prostheses, or in-hospital television service for children and to help pay for travel, parking, or extraordinary bills for impoverished families), lodging for parents who must travel long distances (e.g., Ronald MacDonald Houses), respite care, and information about practical issues such as school programs or funeral arrangements and how to manage at-home chemotherapy. Some groups raise funds to contribute to their local hospital—to improve services for families or to support staff research programs. Programs directed at these practical stresses are especially important in the poorer regions and nations of the world, where basic medical treatment (trained expertise, chemotherapy drugs), posttreatment access to clean water and air, and even funds for travel to clinics are either unavailable or prohibitively expensive for all but the very affluent. In responding to the *social or interpersonal stresses* of childhood cancer, local groups often support parents who feel isolated and awkward with their prior families and friends and provide them with alternative social networks through social and recreational events and telephone trees or networks. Some groups also establish summer camping programs for children with cancer, their siblings, and on occasion their entire families, and computer links between hospitalized children and their schoolmates. Groups also help parents deal with the *emotional stress* and personal trauma of a child's life-threatening illness, with potentially intense familial conflict and confusion, and with the ups and downs of hope and fear attendant on treatment. Such programs focus on caring about one another through peer affirmation and cocounseling, emotional "rap sessions," mutual empathy, and conversations or activities that encourage sharing of deeply held feelings (examples of what Hochschild [1983] has referred to as "emotional labor"). In responding to the *existential or spiritual stress* of this illness groups help people make sense of their experience and place it within a framework of spiritual or secular beliefs, including exploring issues of religious faith and challenge. They help create "narrative communities" (Rappaport, 1994) wherein parents discuss their experiences and struggles with God and fate, try to "make sense/meaning" of their new situations, and often create an embracing meta-narrative of stress and struggle in community.

Because the severe and chronic stresses posed by childhood cancer are potentially disempowering, the opportunity to (re)develop a competent and active sense of oneself through mutual sharing, assistance from others in a similar situation, and contributions to others' comfort and growth is vitally important. In addition, however, behaviors rooted in the multifaceted and substantial power differences between professional medical or social service staffs and parents of children with cancer may further disempower parents by eroding their sense of control over their own lives and those of their children. This common theme in caregiving was highlighted by Cancian and Oliker (2000:73), who argued that "Many of the deficiencies in paid caregiving stem from unequal power relations and rigid rules that give too little power to hands-on caregivers and care receivers." In this context, the mobilization of collective energy and engagement with others through group activities can help individual parents (and through them their children) develop a more empowered outlook (Chesler 1991). Such collective action also can help equalize some of the power imbalances inherent in the professional–parent/child caregiving process. Without the possibility of collective action, (re)empowerment is unlikely and people are less likely to receive the care they feel they need.

How Are Parent Groups/Organizations Organized?

At the local level, some parent groups are quite large (30–50 active members and several hundred on a mailing list) whereas others are small (4–6 members). Some create a very formal structure, with bylaws, elected officers, and a not-for-profit tax exemption or charitable license (this is especially necessary for those groups that raise substantial funds), whereas others are quite informal and emphasize intense personal conversations; many groups do both. Some groups are long-lasting (in existence for 20 or more years); others vanish in 2–3 years as leaders burn out or as their children pass beyond this crisis (via either death or cure); still others disappear and rise phoenixlike when newly energized parents emerge and act. Some groups are run by medical staff members (these are not really parent self-help groups, although they may be a useful form of support and counseling), whereas others are governed by parents themselves, perhaps in coalition or collaboration with professionals. As major medical centers and public charities, especially those with large children's cancer programs, expand their interdisciplinary and psychosocial services, they may preempt, duplicate, or even co-opt the possibilities of independent parent involvement and organization. Problems of access, transportation, and networking make it more likely that medical or cancer association staff members and organizations will play these key roles in poorer areas (and in poorer nations).

At the national level, parent organizations generally seek to coordinate and share information and resources (sometimes including money but usually information and advice) among various local groups via meetings, conferences, newsletters, and electronic media. In the United States, the Candlelighters Childhood Cancer Foundation, an educational clearinghouse linked to over 300 parental self-help and support groups, also operates an information hotline for patient/family concerns, an ombudsperson system for second opinions on medical and legal matters, and a leadership training program for current and future leaders of local parent groups. In other countries as well, national-level organizations provide local groups with services that would be difficult and costly to duplicate at each local site (e.g., funds for group activities or to support individual families' needs, national newsletters for parents or young people, camps for patients or survivors or siblings, and resources for group leaders). And most of these national organizations sponsor yearly meetings, either of all parents or of group representatives.

In addition, national groups often have access to influential health-care policy-makers and to the ear of national cancer associations and legislatures concerned with cancer policy, health benefits and insurance availability, discrimination in employment and education, special educational programs for hospitalized or homebound children, funding of childhood cancer research and treatment, environmental regulations that impact cancer, psychosocially sensitive treatment protocols, and more. They often are advocates of change in the delivery of medical and psychosocial care, and thereby represent parent concerns and establish liaison with national organizations of oncologic physicians, nurses, social workers, and psychologists.

There is substantial variety in how and when groups organize nationally. For instance, of the 31 national childhood cancer parent organizations currently represented in ICCCPO, 9 were founded prior to 1985 (8 of these 9 are in the more wealthy nations, while 7 of the 10 founded after 1995 are in the less wealthy nations). Most of these organizations have national boards of trustees or overseers numerically dominated by parents, complemented by professional medical staff members, long-term survivors of childhood cancer, and members of the general public (e.g., public representatives or major donors).

The size of these national organizations also varies considerably. The U.S. parents' organization counts some 300 local groups in its family, Canada 45, and Germany 50; the Japanese organization has only 11 local chapters and Sweden 7. The smallest nations (e.g., Netherlands, Iceland, Israel) often have only one group. Similarly, they vary greatly in the amount of funds they raise: Parent organizations in Japan, and Sweden each raise more than US$500,000 annually (some local groups raise such amounts themselves), whereas associations in many nations, especially those in the less affluent countries, have very minimal funds at best.

In some national organizations there are strong lines of accountability between local groups and the national organization; this is the case in Canada, Germany, and Sweden. In the United States there are only informal linkages among local groups and between local groups and the national organization, with the latter operating primarily as an information agency or educational clearinghouse and network of semi-autonomous grassroots groups. The latter form is also common in the less wealthy nations and in nations where a true national organization has not yet emerged. Part of the difference between national and local forms may be related to the history of parent organizing efforts, and the extent to which national organizations emerged from preexisting local groups (bottom-up) or established themselves first and set out to create local groups (top-down) (Hunter 1993). In a different context, Zald (1970) emphasized the operating differences between the top-down or corporate developmental model where control is centralized and the bottom-up or federation model where the voluntary participation of local units defines the existence or power of the national organization.

At the international level, the International Confederation of Childhood Cancer Parent Organizations (ICCCPO), formed in the mid-1990s, has several core goals:

1. Education—of parents, educators, physicians, nurses, and so on, via parents' special experiential expertise.
2. Public awareness—with regard to childhood cancer, children's and families' needs, the increased likelihood of survival and normality, and the continuing need for medical and psychosocial checkups and support.
3. Mobilization and development—of parents and parent groups at the local and national levels via training parents to act as advocates for medical and psychosocial services, to create and lead their own parent groups and to help strengthen this worldwide movement.
4. Advocacy—of adequate medical and psychosocial treatment, of action against social stigmatization and discrimination, and for advance in medical and psychosocial cure rates throughout the world (especially in the less wealthy nations).

ICCCPO implements this agenda through representation and liaison to national and international cancer associations, physician organizations, and health agencies (e.g., World Health Organization, International Society of Pediatric Oncologists, European School of Oncology), and through newsletters and pamphlets distributed to national parent organizations, meetings at which member organizations share their experiences and suggestions, and a variety of special projects. One of these special projects attempts to promote "twinning" relationships, wherein parent representatives in wealthier nations create personal exchange, training, resource sharing, and ongoing linkages with parent organizations in less wealthy nations.

As Hunter pointed out, such "suprafederations" are increasingly common on the national or international nonprofit or voluntary ("third-sector") organizational scene: They "are in effect defining an organization field or ecological niche populated by organizations of a similar kind" (1993:29). The member organizations of ICCCPO share more than a common interest in the struggle with childhood cancer; they also conduct fairly similar programs, encounter generally similar organizational problems, draw on similar personal and material resource bases, and are located in roughly similar external environs—including their relations with national cancer associations. It is precisely the ICCCPO-sponsored international exchanges of information that led to the realization of both the major gap between organizations in the wealthy and less wealthy nations and the common experience of conflict between local/national childhood cancer parent organizations and local/national cancer associations.

The Gap between Organizations in the Wealthy and the Less Wealthy Nations

In the economically wealthier nations of the world, childhood cancer is increasingly a "curable" disease. Although there are variations by specific diagnosis, more than 70% of the children diagnosed with cancer in these countries (i.e., North America and Western Europe) will survive their illness. These medical successes in no way obviate the threat and stress created by a life-threatening disease and painful treatment. However, compared to the approximately 30% cure rate of the late 1960s and early 1970s (and the truly minimal cure rate of earlier years) this is remarkable progress.

In the less wealthy nations of the world, where the great majority (80%) of childhood cancer diagnoses occur (over 200,000 yearly), overall cure rates approach only 20–30%. A priority on treating other more preventable or communicable childhood diseases, inadequate medical financing, lack of up-to-date physician and nurse training, absent supportive services, and poor public health and nutritional conditions account for this tragedy. As a parent organizer and leader reported from Bangladesh (Mansur 2000:2):

> In this poverty-stricken country of ours recovery rate of this lethal illness is almost nil. Limited treatment facilities, scarcity of medicines, their high cost and long treatment hamper continuous treatment of leukaemic patients. As a result, children with leukaemia have to die. Many parents in Bangladesh are helpless witnesses to the early death of their children suffering from leukaemia. Poor families of leukaemia patients become poorer when they are to bear the high expenses of the treatment.

And a similar scenario is presented by Halmagi, from the Rumanian parent organization (1999:20):

> Pediatric oncology is on a low level because the country is isolated and there is a lack of information and experience and an enormous shortage of medicines and medical equipment. There are no facilities for bone marrow transplants, and there are no instruments for analyses. The hygienic, sanitary and nutritional circumstances are bad and the standard of living is extremely low. Therefore children with cancer in Rumania don't have the same chance for cure as children in better-equipped countries in the West.

Even when facilities are available, the cost of success (or of delaying failure) can contribute to financial ruin for economically vulnerable and marginal families.

But the issues faced by parent groups and organizations in the less wealthy nations are not solely ones of material resources. Different cultural traditions (e.g., about whether a child should be told her or his diagnosis, whether friends and neighbors should know), health care priorities and ideologies, social welfare systems, and even views of appropriate citizen/consumer/patient roles in medical transactions are involved.

Different national traditions of citizen organization and mobilization also affect the development of parent organizations. For instance, the leader of the Bulgarian parent group (Tashkov 2000:10) notes that

> Volunteerism is a hated word in Bulgaria since the time of the previous system, when everything was said to be "voluntary'" but in fact was not at all . . . In the West, there are special programs at Universities such as Johns Hopkins and others where students are being taught to manage NGOs, to fundraise, to work with and motivate volunteers, etc. Such education is not even heard of in Bulgaria. Most people involved in NGOs . . . create their own organization for the purpose of getting funds and not for the goal to help people. And as professional NGO managers are not available, these organizations are active only as long as their projects are funded, and they are not doing anything at all if there is no longer financial support.

These reflections help to explain why parent organizations in the less wealthy nations of the world focus more often on providing financial support to families and helping them access medical treatment and transportation to clinics, and less on social or emotional support or policy advocacy. Unfortunately, as Mansur pointed out (2000:3), sometimes emotional support is all a parent or a parent group can offer:

> Eight year-old Selina had just been awaiting death with a gloomy face at the hospital. CLASS volunteers made her smile again by giving her toys and their company. The volunteers helped Selina smile even thought she was about to die.

In these less wealthy nations, parents' organizing efforts also are focused more often at the local level, and this makes it difficult to build large and effective national-level organizations. The press for adequate treatment and survival for their child, transportation and communication difficulties (including funds for travel to national or international meetings), and lack of organizing skill and resources make it difficult to sustain large, multiunit organizations. In the face of these constraints, the International Confederation seeks to use the skills and resources of organizations in the wealthier nations to build and strengthen local and national groups in the less wealthy nations.

Interorganizational Difference and Conflict

The struggle to provide care and support to children with cancer and their families is made more difficult by the tension, conflict, and lack of sustained cooperation that sometimes exist between childhood cancer parent organizations and medical staffs or public charities like the cancer associations. The history of relationships between these parties has contained substantial conflict and negotiation as well as mutual support and cooperation. In many situations individual medical professionals (including nurses and social workers as well as physicians) and cancer association staffs have been instrumental in initiating and sustaining parent groups and organizations. But all too often these cooperative beginnings have devolved into struggles over fund raising, mission and program priorities, institutional loyalties, and managerial autonomy.

Power inequality and efforts to control a chaotic situation are at the root of many of these struggles. For instance, medical and social service professionals generally act in ways that protect their ability to decide on the physical treatment provided. They also often attempt to influence or control the emotional strategies parents use to cope with the stresses of childhood cancer (Chesler 1990). Many parents who are trying to understand and cope with their situation, inquire about alternative treatments and wonder aloud about the side effects of painful and debilitating chemotherapy and/or radiology. They also may deal with potentially disempowering stress via coping strategies that differ from those preferred by professionals. Whatever the intentions of all involved, and whatever the personal, class, or culture-based reasons for these differences, individual parents may feel confused, trivialized, or intimidated by their disagreements with high-status professionals. In the setting of self-help and support groups, parents can empower themselves by articulating and collectivizing their individual reactions and concerns and generating responsive organizational agendas and programs. However, resultant parental group stances and actions may be challenging to some medical staffs and organizations. At this juncture, organizational conflicts between childhood cancer parent groups and medical staffs or cancer associations may become visible and potent.

In the United States, for instance, a study of 50 local self-help groups of parents of children with cancer indicated that 48% had helpful contact with local offices of the American Cancer Society; 36% had "no contact" or "no helpful contact", and 16% had negative contact (Chesler and Chesney 1995). The reports of negative or nonhelpful contact included unavailability or lack of interest on the part of the American Cancer Society, struggles over the society's local offices' efforts to control or "guide" the content of parent group meetings and newsletters, and attempts to limit independent group fund raising. At the national level, the Candlelighters Childhood Cancer Foundation struggled to balance the important financial support it received from the American Cancer Society with its own need for programmatic independence. This struggle surfaced over issues such as control over the content and style of Candlelighter newsletters and programs, disagreements about either party's relevant expertise, exclusion of American Cancer Society sponsors and funders from Candlelighter plans and programs, exclusion of parent representatives from American Cancer Society sessions focused on childhood cancer, professional criticism of parental expertise, and parental criticism of American Cancer Society priorities and expertise (I emphasize that disagreement and criticism flowed in both directions). In addition, the foundation's programs and parents/families' needs outgrew the level of financial support the American Cancer Society felt able and willing to provide. In the transformation of a 20-year relationship, in 1996–1997, Candlelighters decided to become financially, as well as programmatically and politically, independent of the American Cancer Society.

Several other national-level childhood cancer parent organizations report similar tensions in their relations with national cancer associations. For instance, in 1995, the Childhood Cancer Foundation of Canada severed its financially dependent relationship with the Canadian Cancer Society—for similar reasons and as a result of similar tensions. The German parent organization reports an "ambiguous" relationship with the German Cancer Association, involving a subtle power struggle with "big brother watching every step of the parent groups' movement"; the German Cancer Association appeared quite concerned about the parent organization's effort to fund raise. In Sweden, the parent organization reports "no sustained relationship" with the national cancer association, and a similarly separate and independent relationship is reported by the Italian Federation of Associations of Parents of Children with Onco-Hematologic Diseases.

In some nations a more collaborative, but still cautious, relationship has developed. For instance, in the Netherlands the Dutch Cancer Society and the Dutch Association of Parents, Children, and Cancer do cooperate across clear lines of differentiation. As is the case in many nations, the Dutch Cancer Society focuses primarily on adult cancers, and on fund raising for scientific cancer research, whereas the Dutch Association of Parents, Children, and Cancer focuses solely on children's cancer and deals with many local and personal socioemotional and educational issues of concern to youngsters and their families. Yet there are several indicators of collaboration: The Dutch Cancer Society provides the national parents' organization with a small portion of its yearly budget, it purchases and distributes books and dolls created by the parent organization, leaders of the two associations meet twice a year to share information and program ideas, and the Dutch Organization of Parents, Children, and Cancer is permitted to raise public funds explicitly to meet the psychosocial needs of children and families. Similar patterns of cautious collaboration, with bumps and potholes along the way, exist in many other nations.

The common nature of the struggles, if not the outcomes, makes it clear that these are structural/cultural problems of interorganizational and transnational character. How then can we understand the roots of such conflictual relationships, those that are in open conflict and those that continue in covert conflict while maintaining some degree of collaboration? And how have parent organizations and cancer associations dealt (successfully or unsuccessfully) with them? In the following discussion I focus primarily on these relationships at the national organizational level, although the roots of and responses to these conflicts often are paralleled locally.

In the case of cancer associations and parent groups/organizations, the differences noted previously between parents and medical or social service staff professionals are raised to an organizational level, and take shape in different organizational missions, goals, and operating procedures (see Table 2). Cancer associations are governed and managed by professionals—by medical clinicians and researchers (Epstein 1978) and professional bureaucratic managers—using

TABLE 2
The Potentials for Interorganizational Conflict and Coalition

Dimension	Cancer Associations	Childhood Cancer Parent Organizations
Primary mission foci	Adults	Children/families
	Support for incremental improvement in medical care	Advocacy for change in psychosocial care
	Service to patients/families	Support to/ empowerment of children/families
Management/leadership	Professional control Physicians Organizational managers	Citizen control Parents
	Formal bureaucracy	Informal, grass-roots movement
	Large paid staff	Small paid staff
	Paid staff plus volunteers	Mostly volunteers
Structure	Distinctive roles for "staff"/"client"	Joint roles for "staff"/"client"
	Hierarchy	Loose democracy
	Unit accountability	Unit autonomy
	Permanent, established	Relatively new, evolving
Programs	Fund raising	Fund raising
	Support for research	Little research support
	Support medical staffs	Serve local groups
	Service to individuals— financial, informational	Service to individuals— financial, comradeship, emotional, informational
	Lobbying	Advocacy
	Liaison with other agencies	Liaison with other agencies
Images of clients/ constituents/members	Medical professionals	Parents, youth, families
	Patients	Comrades
	Dependent people	Active and involved people
	Member roles partial, peripheral	Member roles central

typical bureaucratic principles of organizational leadership. Parent organizations are led by parent volunteers, or in some cases professional parent managers, are staffed primarily by volunteers, and are more likely to use grass-roots democratic organizational principles. Especially at the local level and often at the national level, parent organizations are less formally organized than the cancer associations' local/national offices; indeed, in some cases they are barely organized. In sharp contrast to such parental informality and structural variety, the American Cancer Society's local offices are "chartered and incorporated divisions" (Ross 1987), and part of "unitary national organizational entitites with regional and local subdivisions and chapters . . . as single national organizations from the start, and their authority resides in central headquarters" (Young 1989:103–4). Thus, the more formal cancer associations, generally built on the "corporate model" (see the earlier discussion and Young 1989; Zald 1970), often object to the parent organizations' inability or unwillingness to "control" the behavior of local (often "federated model") units or to the problems created by the occasional instability of parent group leadership and decisional processes. The contrast here is between the hierarchical and bureaucratic style typical of large public charities or service organizations and the social movement characteristics of voluntary organizations or alternative human service systems.

In the United States, Germany, and the Netherlands, especially, this difference has been reflected in the cancer associations' discomfort with, and occasional strong objection to, "the nonprofessional" or "nonaccountable" style and quality of parent organizations' management practices and their concern about the (nonprofessionally supervised) educational materials or services created and/or delivered to families. The organizational structure and managerial styles of the cancer associations are typical of the caregiving professional bureaucracies identified by Abel and Nelson (1990), Cancian and Oliker (2000), and Stone (2000). These authors also point to the ways in which the rigid rules or norms and status hierarchies characteristic of professional bureaucracies limit these organizations' abilities to provide emotionally responsive and particularistic care, or even to allow professionals working within them to express their emotionally caring inclinations.

Cancer associations are primarily concerned with adult cancers: Although they operate many excellent research, education and service programs for this large population, childhood cancer issues are a minor concern (Ross's 1987 book, billed as an "official history of the American Cancer Society," contains no mention of childhood cancer issues or services—save one professional conference the American Cancer Society held on that topic—nor of the Candlelighters Childhood Cancer Foundation, which by then had been in a cooperative financial and programmatic relationship with the American Cancer Society for over a decade). One reason is that childhood cancer is a relatively rare disease, accounting for less than 1% of all cancer diagnoses, and thus cannot occupy the major portion of cancer associations' staff members' time and energy. Parents of children with cancer, as leaders or members of self-help groups, are focused solely on childhood cancer, and their organizations run programs just for this specific population. They emphasize that even if childhood cancer is a relatively rare disease, curing a child with cancer results in preserving 60 or more years of productive life and work—an excellent social investment!

Further differences are evident in the relationships members of these organizations have to the job–family balancing act so prevalent in caregiving systems (Stone 2000). Officers and operatives in cancer associations leave their jobs when they leave their offices; cancer is part of their professional employment but not necessarily their total life experience. Parents of children with cancer—in treatment or posttreatment, living or deceased—never leave the cancer experience; when they leave the hospital to go home they continue to focus on the disease and its treatment and effects. In this sense, cancer association personnel are "outside" the experiential reality of childhood cancer, no matter how knowledgeable, caring, and committed they may be. For parents, "inside" this reality, childhood cancer is the major preoccupation of their lives; this escalates for parents who become organizational leaders and focus their energies on assisting others as well as themselves. On occasion, however, this same passionate commitment and the personal crises experienced by these "insiders" may temporarily compromise their ability to function as organizational representatives in the same ways as do the professional staffs of cancer associations; organizational reliability may rise or fall with the quality of their leadership and/or the latest crisis in their child's and family's life

The programs of most cancer associations are directed primarily to fund raising and support of research, although they also generate support programs and services for individual patients and families. Parent organizations are involved in fund raising, but they conduct a much wider variety of social and emotional support, parent/patient empowerment, and social advocacy programs. The goals of most cancer associations also include substantial service and support to the medical profession seeking to control and cure cancer, with an ultimate concern for incremental improvement in the delivery of care to patients. Parent organizations, although they share that overall service mission, more directly support and serve children and families, and in this effort work for more immediate and dramatic change in the delivery of (especially psychosocial) care.

Even when cancer associations and parent organizations appear to have consonant missions and values, their different resource bases and activities mitigate against the development of structural isomorphism, and their different management and governance structures add to the potential for interorganizational conflict. Some cancer associations are likely to see some parent organizations as "fly-by-night affairs," unprofessionally managed and operated; some parent organizations are likely to see cancer associations as authoritarian and hidebound, committed more to their own survival than to service to people in need—especially to children and families. This dynamic reflects, once again, the difficulties of sustaining cooperation between professionals' commitments to universalism or general care and parents' commitments to particularism and unique care.

The organizational differences summarized in Table 2 are not themselves predictive of conflict, just of difference. But several factors ensure the development of organizational competition and conflictual struggles. First, perhaps at an ideological or cultural level, Emerick (1991) and others (see Cancian and Oliker 2000; Chesler 1991; Gartner and Riessman 1994; Powell 1990; Stone 2000) argued that there are core cultural and political tensions between the philosophies of self-help and professional health care, or between formal and informal care, or between public and private spheres of caregiving. The same tensions exist at an organizational level between national self-help or support organizations and national bureaucratic charities or service organizations.

Second, Hasenfeld and Gidron noted (1993) that we can expect conflict or competition whenever organizations operate in the same field of endeavor, with relatively similar missions, and compete for the same or similar resources (e.g., money, people, audience, influence). As Bennett and Di Lorenzo suggested, "The Big Three [referring to the large U.S. health charities—American Cancer Society, American Heart Association, American Lung Association] obviously see new charities as undesirable competition—for donations, government grants, and domination of the disease-research industry" (1994:205). Moreover, in this competition for funds, most cancer associations in most countries use pictures of children in their fund-raising efforts (it is an especially effective and endearing technique), despite the fact that most of their programmatic concern and fund dispersal is focused on adult cancers. This raises the hackles of parent activists who see it as a form of exploitation without adequate recompense (or as intrusion into their "turf" without permission or payoff).

Third, even within a general arena of mission congruence, cancer associations and parent organizations often disagree about the appropriate foci of programs and activities undertaken by parents. Dominated by medical staff members and interlocked with government health agencies (Bennett and Di Lorenzo 1994; Epstein 1978), cancer associations privilege technical and expert medical knowledge over (and sometimes overtly disparage) the commonsense experiential knowledge of parents and children undergoing the cancer experience (Borkman 1990; Ruddick 1990; Wrigley 1990). Parental criticism of medical knowledge and practice is seen as inappropriate, generally cast as uninformed, and occasionally experienced as a threat to the privileged knowledge and position of medical staffs guiding the cancer associations. In turn, parent organizations often object to the elitist assumption that these professional medical or charitable staffs and associations have a monopoly on relevant knowledge and wisdom—especially when it comes to familial, psychosocial, or organizational matters.

These conflicts are most likely to escalate and become overt in the wealthier or more "developed nations," where parent organizations are likely to be more powerful—well-organized, organized on a national level, and with a large resource base. When parent organizations feel strong enough to address ideological differences and resource inequalities, seek autonomy and independence from cancer associations, and pursue goals that may be unique or different, the cancer associations are more likely to feel threatened or challenged—in financial or symbolic terms.

One result of these differences and conflicts is that cancer associations often engage in overt or covert efforts to control parent groups and organizations. They generally are the more powerful party in this relationship, by virtue of their longer history, greater resource base, established medical and governmental links, medical access, and media/public credibility. Thus, they are more likely to vigorously defend their prerogatives, sometimes by attacking parent organizations and sometimes by sitting on their superior resources and "playing a waiting game" for the parent organizations to disappear. Their tactics often take the following forms:

- Prohibition of public-fundraising as a condition for financial support of parent organizations.
- Attempts to edit (and sometimes censor) parent newsletter and pamphlet materials.
- Pressure on parent organizations to cease certain types of programs (e.g., parent-generated research, medical hotlines, medical suggestions).
- Pressure on parent organizations to establish bureaucratic systems of accountability with local support groups.
- Establishment of parallel (but professionally run) parent organizations.

Childhood cancer parent organizations, in turn, are likely to initiate or return fire as follows:

- More or less public challenges to cancer associations' efforts to "use" children to raise money for the fight against adult cancer.
- Development of independent and competitive fund-raising campaigns.
- Creation of coalitions with other child/family focused agencies to lobby for special programs to be provided directly by those servicing children and families.

What Are the Prospects?

Childhood cancer parent organizations are growing in localities and countries throughout the world. In 1997, 24 organizations from 21 countries were affiliated with ICCCPO, but by 2000 the number had grown to 54 organizations from 43 countries (with truly national-level organizations in 31 countries). The issues faced by these parent organizations and the relations between parent organizations and cancer association and medical staffs will continue to be important for the welfare of children with cancer around the globe.

The competition and cooperation between parent organizations and cancer associations reflects a dialectic mandated by their common yet somewhat conflicting goals and struggles for similar resources (York and Zychlinski 1996). If these organizations are to work together successfully, it will have to involve a model of interagency relationships that supports mutual respect for each organization's unique mission, identity and talents. It cannot be on the basis of dominance-dependence ("big brother–little brother") relations, with attendant efforts of cancer associations or medical staffs to control and guide the programs of parent organizations and parent organizations' constant struggles for autonomy. Interestingly, the cancer associations face similar issues with other cancer-related organizations with more specialized and consumer-based interests (e.g., ostomy clubs, breast cancer organizations, prostate cancer groups) or mass patient organizations like the U.S. National Coalition of Cancer Survivors.

The typical power differences between cancer associations and parent organizations are important barriers to new forms of interorganizational cooperation. Because the cancer associations usually have been in existence longer and are more powerful, more established and legitimate, more formally organized, and have a more secure resource base, they are less likely to need or initiate a partner relationship with parent organizations. Moreover, parent organization members, themselves a part of the clientele they feel the cancer associations should be serving, argue that the cancer associations should be reaching out to them and recognizing/using their expertise. In turn, cancer association staffs often feel that the younger, weaker, less professional and more specialized parent organization should make petition to them.

Hasenfeld and Gidron (1993) suggested several options within a more cooperative model of interorganizational relations: referral, coordination, co-optation, and coalition. And Wernet and Jones (1992) discussed the possibility of consolidation, which includes both outright acquisitions (or absorptions of one organization by another) and mergers (or blendings of one organization with another). All these forms have occurred in different locales within specific nations and in different nations. In some cases cancer associations and parent organizations have referred patients and patient families to one another, especially in those cases where the young people involved are at the margins of childhood/adolescence (i.e., in their late teens or early twenties). Active coordination involving the exchange of resources is much less common, although if we consider those cases where cancer associations have helped to provide some funding assistance to parent organizations, have helped to initiate them, or have involved them in educational events and conferences (the initiative and invitation for such events may flow in either direction), that would seem to fit the coordination model. The key here, according to Zald and McCarthy (1987), is exchange relations based on clearly differentiated but interlinked roles and occasional joint projects. The history of these interorganizational relationships also is rife with examples of co-optation, especially when cancer associations have invited parent representatives to attend their meetings as special resources on childhood cancer, but not to participate otherwise. Co-optation also is common in the early stages of development of some parent organizations, when physicians or association staff help to initiate the parent organization and then stay in control. Consolidations occur when the parent organization is so weak that the cancer association can mount a "takeover," either on friendly or unfriendly terms.

The coalition form of interorganizational relationship represents the best common bet for good relationships between local parent groups and medical staffs, as well as for cancer associations and parent groups. Coalitions can occur among organizations and agencies that have some goals in common and some differences and that may compete for some resources (money and recognition) and cooperate on some services (support for families, materials for professionals, lobbying national governments or international agencies for more funds for cancer research and treatment, and joint efforts to create "twinning" relations between centers and groups in wealthier and poorer nations).

The development of effective interorganizational coalitions requires not only recognition of areas of mutual concern and collaboration, but also interdependent relationships between independent organizations. If parent organizations elect or need to be financially dependent on cancer associations, or if cancer associations insist on controlling parent organizations' resources and programs, wars of independence will eventually result. Such coalitions also require mutual respect for acknowledged differences as well as commonalities, and a desire to make use of each entity's unique perspectives, talents, and resources. Above all, they require acknowledgment of past conflict and careful negotiation about current and future turf in pursuit of the best (medical and psychosocial) treatment for all children with cancer and their families/communities. The cancer associations are generally a key source of broadly established legitimacy and resources; the parent organizations are vital links to a narrower but critical patient constituency and a source of unique expertise and energy. They need each other, and children with cancer and their families need them both to work together better.

Note

In preparing this chapter I have appreciated the wise counsel of my colleague Mayer Zald, the generous assistance of many comrades in national cancer associations, parent organizations, the ICCCPO, and the suggestions of several editors connected with this volume.

"Where Teachers Can Make a Livable Wage"

Organizing to Address Gender and Racial Inequalities in Paid Child Care Work

Mary C. Tuominen

*A*fter more than 20 years as a child care teacher, Lauren Tozzi remains enthusiastic about her work. Although she finds great satisfaction in the work of child care, she also speaks of the challenges of the work and of the rewards she experiences through her activism on behalf of child care teachers and providers.[1]

> I love this profession. I love being with kids. I learn from them. And while society says I'm just a baby-sitter, I know in my heart that I've got one of the most important jobs. I'm very serious about my profession. But, I probably could have left [child care employment] a long time ago because of [low] compensation. But, just knowing that I'm part of a movement that's really going to create incredible reform and make incredible changes that will better society . . . Although I love my work, that's probably the driving force [that keeps me in child care]—knowing that I'm part of something that's just big and getting bigger.

The movement of which Lauren speaks is the movement of child care workers and their allies. More than 10 years ago, Lauren became involved in Seattle Worthy Wages, a local chapter of the national Worthy Wages movement, the goal of which is to address the crisis of low wages and high turnover among the early childhood workforce.[2] Organized in 1990, Seattle Worthy Wages identifies itself as a grassroots activist organization of child care teachers, providers, parents, and advocates who seek to better the wages, status, and working conditions of child care teachers and providers. In May 1998 Seattle Worthy Wages joined forces with a labor union, Service Employees International Union/District 925, to undertake a child care labor organizing campaign. Although union organizing campaigns of child care teachers and providers are underway in a small number of cities, namely, Boston, Philadelphia, and Seattle (Grundy, Bell, and Firestein 1999), no published analyses of these campaigns exist. This chapter begins to fill that gap by documenting the necessity of labor organizing among the paid child care workforce, as well as exploring the challenges and opportunities faced by activists in the Seattle child care union organizing campaign.

The Necessity of Organizing: The Gendered and Racial Organization of Paid Child Care Work

In describing the goals of Seattle Worthy Wages, Lauren Tozzi asserted, "We want to create a child care system, a comprehensive child care system where no family or child is denied, but also where teachers can make a livable wage." Lauren's own low wages and lack of employment benefits reflect the need for the living wage of which she speaks. Despite over twenty years of continuous employment as a child care teacher, an associate of arts (AA) degree, additional years of college coursework, and enrollment in (and teaching of) innumerable seminars and workshops in the field of early childhood education, Lauren earns $498 weekly. Although she receives medial insurance (highly unusual among child care teachers and providers), she receives no vision or dental benefits, no retirement benefits, and no unemployment benefits. Because her child care employment occurs under a 9-month annual contract, Lauren often "works odd jobs to earn enough to make ends meet."

The low wages and lack of employment benefits earned by Lauren are common among child care teachers and providers. Over the last decade, wages of child care workers have remained at near-poverty levels. Child care has the highest concentration of poverty-wage workers of any industry (Kasarda 1996). Child care teaching staff are considerably better educated than women in the labor force at large,[3] but they earn less than one-half as much as comparably-educated women (Whitebook, Howes, and Phillips 1998; Whitebook, Phillips, and Howe 1993). In 1998 food servers and service station attendants were among those workers making higher wages than child care teachers and providers (Center for the Child Care Workforce 2000).

Earnings of all child care teachers and providers remain extremely low. However, it is essential to look beyond the "average" wage picture to gain an accurate understanding of the ways in which both race and gender influence wages in child care as well as other forms of paid work.[4] In the U.S. labor force, wages of White women, Black women, and Hispanic women, respectively, represent an increasingly smaller percentage of White men's wages. For every dollar earned by a White man, White women earn 76 cents, Black women earn 65 cents, and Hispanic women earn 54 cents (U.S. Department of Labor, Bureau of Labor Statistics 1999). The gender hierarchy of wages is clearly a racial hierarchy as well.

In addition to receiving low wages, the lack of employment benefits received by Lauren Tozzi is reflective of that of child care teachers and providers nationwide. Fewer than one-third of child care centers provide health insurance to child care employees (Bellm et al. 1997), only 21% of child care centers pay full health care benefits for teaching staff, and fewer than 23% provide health care coverage for dependents of employees (Whitebook et al. 1998). Even fewer centers provide pension or retirement benefits (Bellm et al. 1997).

The low wages and lack of employment benefits in paid child care are reflective of the devaluation of care work (see England and Folbre, this volume), as well as the gendered and racial organization of child care employment (Tuominen 1994). Gender is a primary force that influences who becomes a paid care worker (Cancian and Oliker 2000)—and child care is no exception. Women comprise 42% of the paid work force. In contrast, they comprise 96% of paid child care workers (U.S. Department of Labor, Women's Bureau 1997). Although gender is a primary force influencing the organization and provision of paid child care, race plays an equally central role in organizing the work. Women of color represent 13% of paid workers in the United States (U.S. Department of Labor 1999) but make up one-third of all paid child care workers (Bellm et al. 1997). In addition, poor women and women of color are disproportionately found in entry-level and more poorly paid child care jobs (National Black Child Development Institute 1993; U.S. Bureau of Labor Statistics 1999).

Understanding this gendered and racial organization of child care work enables us to recognize why care workers have not, historically, been a target for labor organizing campaigns—campaigns that seek to improve the wages, working conditions, and status of working people. The definition of *work*, as we know it in the contemporary United States, is associated with activity occurring in the marketplace—activity occurring outside of the world of home and family, activity involving the production of material goods, and activity for which we are paid. In contrast to *work*, our historical conception of *care* is that of an unpaid activity provided by women of color and White women within families and households. Within this bifurcation, *care* is defined as something other than *work* (Daniels 1987; Gordon 1990). This dualistic construction of care versus work leads to the degradation of those who provide care, because when caring "is devalued, invisible, underpaid, and penalized, it is relegated to those who lack economic, political, and social power and status"—disproportionately women, people of color, and immigrants (Nakano Glenn 2000:84). Thus, our historically narrow definition of "work" has led to a narrow definition of "workers" and, subsequently, of labor theorizing and labor organizing. Historical models of both labor theory and labor organizing privilege White male workers in large industrial production facilities—the kinds of work and work sites from which people of color and White women have historically been excluded (Bronfenbrenner et al. 1998).

In the last decade, however, labor theorists and activists have begun reassessing their analyses and strategies regarding labor organizing. This reassessment acknowledges dramatic changes that have taken place in both the workforce and in employment opportunities. Specifically, theorists and activists increasingly recognize the need to respond to a workforce that is disproportionately employed in the service sector (Cobble 1996)—employment that differs dramatically from industrial-sector employment in many ways, not the least of which are the personal and relational aspects of service and care work (Hurd 1993; Uttal and Tuominen 1999). Additionally, the service sector is increasingly populated by married women with young children, workers of diverse racial ethnic identities, and immigrants (Frank 1989; Hallock 1997; Needleman 1993) and is characterized by part-time and high-turnover employment with few employment benefits or promotional opportunities (Frank 1989; Macdonald and Sirianni 1996)—

clearly qualities that characterize paid child care work, as well as other forms of paid care work.

Within the last decade, labor activists have called for new models of organizing intended to meet the needs of this increasingly diverse workforce employed in the service sector (Fletcher and Hurd 1999; Hallock 1997; Hossfeld 1995; Lerner 1991; Nissen 1999; Rathke 1999). In the United States, these new models of organizing have been developed primarily among home health-care workers (Kelleher 1986; Needleman 1998); garment workers (Milkman 1993), and clerical workers (Hurd 1993). Among service sector workers, the most powerful of these labor organizing campaigns are ones in which unions work in concert with existing community organizations—recognizing, learning from, and working with indigenous community leaders (Abrams 1999; Busman 1993; Martens and Mitter 1994).

The Childcare Union Project

Since its inception in 1990, Seattle Worthy Wages members have organized the annual Worthy Wages parade, coordinated leadership retreats, and surveyed child care teaching staff regarding their wages and working conditions. Over this 10-year period Seattle Worthy Wages members facilitated dozens of workshops for child care workers and their advocates to explore strategies for increasing compensation and professional status among child care teaching staff. In these discussions, participants often raised union organizing as one of a number of possible strategies for increasing wages, benefits, and status among members of the child care workforce.

Understanding the well-documented benefits of union membership for women workers (Bronfenbrenner et al. 1998; Pocock 1997), Seattle Worthy Wages members began to seriously consider the possibilities of a union organizing campaign among child care teaching staff. Recognizing their strengths as a social movement organization including their skills in public education and their knowledge of the local child care community, Seattle Worthy Wages members also acknowledged that they had neither the resources nor the experience to mount a major labor organizing campaign on their own. As a result, one of the unions most successful in organizing service sector workers, Service Employees International Union/ District 925 (SEIU/925), caught the attention of Seattle Worthy Wages. In 1996, Seattle Worthy Wages members approached SEIU/925 to explore the possibility of a child care union organizing campaign in Seattle. Prior to committing to the campaign, both organizations engaged in several months of groundwork—identifying leadership within the child care community, conducting research regarding the child care industry in Seattle and King County, and exploring funding for the potential campaign. The work of both organizations bore fruit. On May 1, 1998, Seattle Worthy Wages (the grassroots organization) formally joined forces with SEIU/925 (the union) to organize child care workers under the auspices of a new coalition—the Childcare Union Project (CUP).

Organizers built their campaign around four components: worker education, public education and awareness, public funding for an Early Childhood Education Career Development Ladder (Burbank and Wiefek 2001), and employer organiz-

TABLE 1
Interviewees, Their Organizational Affiliation,
and Racial Ethnic Self-Identification

Name	Organizational Affiliation	Racial Ethnic Self-Identification
Lynne Barbee	SEIU/925 senior organizer	Caucasian
Valerie Brown	Worthy Wages member, CUP organizer-in-training	African-American
Anne Marie Cavanaugh	SEIU/925 organizer	Irish-American
Kim Cook	SEIU/925 regional director	Caucasian
Dorothy Gibson	SEIU/925 organizer/rep	White, Anglo-Saxon, Protestant
Lauren Tozzi	Worthy Wages member	Italian-American
Barb Wiley	Worthy Wages member; CUP organizer-in-training	White

ing. Although the campaign proved successful (the first union contract covering 150 employees in 12 child care centers was signed in December 1999), activists from Seattle Worthy Wages and SEIU/925 faced challenges as they worked together in coalition. Interviews with organizers revealed that although diverse groups working in coalition are touted by many labor scholars and activists as the future of the labor movement, working in coalition to organize diverse workers in diverse neighborhoods is no easy task.

Building on the foundation of standpoint feminism (Hartsock 1983) and diversity feminism (Baca Zinn and Thornton Dill 1996; Naples 1999), I undertook a 3-year field research project, seeking to understand labor organizing through the local knowledge and experiences of organizers participating in the Childcare Union Project coalition. This chapter presents a portion of that field research, drawing extensively on multiple, semistandardized interviews conducted over a three-year period with each of the seven central organizers of the coalition (see Table 1 for an introduction of each of the interviewees, their organizational affiliation, and their racial ethnic self-identification). Organizers generously (and candidly) shared their experiences and analyses, enabling us to understand the challenges, as well as the successes, of activists who seek to organize the diverse and decentralized child care workforce.

Challenges and Opportunities in Organizing the Child Care Workforce

Gender, race, and organizational culture all inform the organization and provision of child care in the contemporary United States. As such, each of these forces is at play when activists seek to organize to address the inequalities evident within and between members of the child care workforce. The Childcare Union Project offers us three important lessons about organizing child care teachers and providers: the need to address and incorporate the relational aspects of care work in organizing efforts; the need for continued attention to address racial diversity, racism, and antiracism work; and the need to recognize and respect diverse organizational cultures.

Addressing Devaluation, Altruism, and Relational Qualities of Child Care Work

The work of care involves attending to the needs of others and facilitating the development of others (Abel and Nelson 1990; Gordon 1996; Waerness 1996). These relational aspects of care work are interwoven with the cultural perception of care as an activity historically provided by women who are motivated by "love" and altruism. These factors work together to complicate the process of organizing child care workers. Nonetheless, the personal relationships between provider and child are central to the work of child care and need to be valued in any campaign seeking to organize child care teachers and providers.

The historical devaluation of care provided by women contributes to a dynamic in which child care workers can internalize the cultural devaluation of care, thus complicating the ability to mobilize members of the child care workforce on their own behalf. Anne Marie Cavanaugh, a former welfare rights organizer and subsequent SEIU/925 organizer assigned to the Childcare Union Project, spoke of the devaluation of women's child care work and its impact on child care teaching staff. Anne Marie recalled, "I could just see it in the eyes of my son's [child care] teachers every day. They weren't recognized at all for the work that they did. It's just like mother's work—so undervalued, so expendable, so unappreciated." SEIU/925 organizer/representative Dorothy Gibson spoke of how this devaluing of care workers contrasts with care workers' affirmation of the needs of care recipients, a practice she has observed in years of organizing women in service sector and care work jobs: "In women's jobs, historically there's the whole women's mentality—taking care of everybody else. You look at the [child care] teachers—at the top of their list of concerns is the kids."

This conflict between caring for others and caring for self is directly related to the relational and emotional commitments that distinguish paid care work from other forms of paid work (Himmelweit 1999; Uttal and Tuominen 1999). Identified as a process that involves both reciprocity and putting others' needs before your own (Tarlow 1996), caring for others can work against the self advocacy needed by members in an organizing campaign. Lynne Barbee served as SEIU/925's senior organizer during the Childcare Union Project campaign and spoke of the altruism of child care workers that complicates the organizing process.

> The most interesting thing about this group of workers is that they're the most unselfish group of people I've ever seen in my life. I mean, they talk again and again about what they're doing for the children. I say, "That's nice, but what about you?" Not that I want them to be selfish, but they have a right to be *more* selfish. I want them to feel like they have that right because there's nothing else that tells them they have the right to be selfish. Everything tells them that they should be sacrificing for the children.

The relational nature of child care work serves to hinder organizing because gendered ideologies surrounding care affirm that a woman's concern for others (the children for whom she cares) take precedence over her concern for self (the need for a living wage for herself and her own family). However, this ideology that valorizes concern for others over concern for self can be reconstructed by workers, such that the relational qualities of care work can also facilitate workers' self advocacy within the organizing process. Lynne Barbee continued:

> There's a point at which the workers say, "I cannot do my job properly if something doesn't change." And so, the frustration that they feel in their inability to provide the kind of service that they want to is what motivates them to say, "Wait a minute. I can't [do this]. It's hurting me because I can't do this." And somehow it starts to affect the way people think about their ability to perform their job. It comes back to people understanding what they have to do for themselves, before they can do the kind of job they want to do.

The transformation of which Lynne spoke is reflective of Carol Gilligan's analysis of the ethic of care (Gilligan 1993 [1982]), in which excluding one's self from care in order to care for others results in a tension between self-sacrifice and care. Gilligan's third stage in the evolving ethic of care is characterized by a differentiation of the self, an acknowledgement of the interconnection between self and others, and a recognition of the choice and responsibility to care. Understanding that ethics of care are socially constructed (Kerber 1993; Puka 1993; Tronto 1993) enables us to more fully understand the ways in which the relational qualities of care enable child care workers to develop the values of self care and self advocacy. As child care teachers and providers negotiate the tensions between caring for the children of others and earning sufficient wages to care for themselves and their own families, they come to legitimate the value of their role in the caring process. Part of their responsibility becomes advocating for the resources that enable them to do their job well. They claim the right to care without putting themselves and their own families at risk (Tuominen 2001). This process is reflective of what social movement theorists term "cognitive liberation" (McAdam 1982)—an essential step in the process toward collective social action.

Recognizing the centrality of relationship in care work, and the relationship between caring for others and caring for one's self, is essential in organizing the child care workforce. Affirming the value placed on caring for others, child care organizers can facilitate an understanding of the resources needed by care workers to provide quality care. In so doing, child care teachers and providers can come to value the wages and working conditions necessary for them to not only provide quality care for the children of others, but to care for themselves and their own families as well.

Defining and Prioritizing Racial Diversity and Antiracism Work

Both Seattle Worthy Wages and SEIU/District 925 are organizations in which historical leadership (respectively unpaid and paid), has been assumed primarily by white women. In the last decade, each organization has begun to address the racial organization of its membership and leadership, albeit in different ways. As Seattle Worthy Wages and SEIU/925 joined forces in the child care organizing campaign, differing organizational understandings of and commitments to addressing racial diversity and institutional racism resulted in tension within the coalition.

In 1997, Seattle Worthy Wages members formally committed to addressing race and racism in the organization of the child care workforce, as well as in their own predominantly White organization. Barb Wiley worked as a child care teacher and as a Worthy Wages activist for several years before assuming the role of organizer-in-training with the Childcare Union Project. Barb spoke of the centrality of antiracism work for Seattle Worthy Wages:

> [To address racism] you really have to put time into creating a coalition. Looking at who's in leadership, the structure of the meetings—all of that has cultural values attached to it. And you have to be really deliberate about building that machine . . . I don't think that real change can happen unless we have a machine that's a social justice machine for child care workers. That is led by child care workers of color and is representative of the Seattle child care work force. And it fights for better child care jobs, but it also fights against racism.

During the last several years SEIU/925, like Seattle Worthy Wages, has begun to address its history as a predominantly White organization. SEIU/925 staff have discussed racial diversity and explored ways of developing leadership among women of color in the rank and file. Thus, when I spoke with Kim Cook, Regional Director of SEIU/925 about the union's commitment to racial and ethnic diversity, Kim asserted:

> I think those of us who are leaders [in the Childcare Union Project] have a real commitment and really want to build a racially diverse union. I mean, we started with a base that was not that [diverse] . . . And so, now we made a commitment. I got to hire two organizers [for the child care campaign] and we made a commitment to hiring a person of color in one of those slots . . . Val Brown is an African-American woman that's a director of a center in the South End [of Seattle]. She's got these incredible connections . . . She's going to be the person to help us figure out what are the needs of the people in that community that we, so far, haven't been successful in reaching out to.

Both Seattle Worthy Wages and SEIU/925 clearly recognized that leadership by women of color who were known within the child care community was central to the goal of organizing a racially and ethnically diverse union. In reflecting on the campaign, Valerie Brown affirmed the importance of her role in organizing but also voiced her concerns about assuming this role in a predominantly White, formal organization. When I asked Valerie, "What has worked well in terms of trying to organize a racially and ethnically diverse union?" she responded:

> They hired me. Hiring a person of color to work with communities of color. That

was something that worked well. I asked a lot of questions before I would go back to my community and talk with them about [the union]. Questions around issues of inclusion and knowing they would have their voices heard at the table . . . And, even though you know you're hired for that, when you're a person of color you struggle. It's like they need somebody to be in the Black community to bring the Blacks in, and I understand that. But it doesn't always feel good. I struggle with that.

Tensions existed between Seattle Worthy Wages and SEIU/925 leadership regarding the perceived degree of commitment to addressing racial inequality. Where SEIU/925 staff spoke of increasing "racial diversity" among members and staff, Seattle Worthy Wages members spoke of a commitment to challenging "institutional racism" within organizational and political structures. For example, Barb Wiley asserted that a commitment to hiring people of color for direct organizing is important, but insufficient in itself as a mechanism to address institutional racism. Barb Wiley and Valerie Brown, both Seattle Worthy Wages members and organizers-in-training, expressed frustration at attempts to engage in antiracism work within Childcare Union Project beyond affirming the importance of leadership of people of color within communities of color. Specifically, these activists spoke of the lack of SEIU/925 staff participation in Undoing Racism training sessions, as well as limited follow up on implementing recommendations of the organizational Change Team that emerged from the antiracism training.

In the coalition work of Seattle Worthy Wages and SEIU/925 we see the contested meanings of racial diversity and racism, and differing commitments to antiracism work. Like other activists, coalition members of the Childcare Union Project "do not create meanings and practices entirely anew, but rather . . . are both constrained and enabled by the cultural and structural resources available to them in a particular historical moment" (Scott 2000:787). The meanings of "diversity" and "racism" and subsequent commitments to address these practices were defined and understood differently by members of the two organizations that formed the Childcare Union Project. As predominantly White organizations seek to diversify, very real challenges exist in addressing racial diversity and racism. Questions arise regarding past and current practices, understandings of racism, and of the need for organizations to adapt and change. If we are to effectively organize across race, careful and continuous attention to the meanings of race, racism, and diversity are essential.

Recognizing and Respecting Diverse Organizational Cultures

In agreeing to work in concert to organize a child care workers' union, Seattle Worthy Wage and SEIU/925 recognized the different strengths that each group brought to the union campaign. SEIU/925 is a large formal organization that exists within a larger national and international labor union and labor movement. As such, SEIU/925 brought resources and contacts (both organizational and financial) that were more expansive than those previously experienced by Seattle Worthy Wages. Seattle Worthy Wages, in contrast, brought extensive knowledge of child care workers and the child care community—their values, needs, and interests—as well as skills in grassroots organizing to generate public aware-ness and support for increased wages and status among child care workers.

SEIU/925 staff recognized that the grassroots organizing and advocacy by Seattle Worthy Wage members were central to the success of early organizing efforts of the Childcare Union Project. SEIU/925 organizer/representative Dorothy Gibson reported, "The unionization of child care centers would not have happened had it not been for Seattle Worthy Wages doing the work they did before." SEIU/925 regional director Kim Cook agreed: "This project is in partnership with Worthy Wages. In fact, the whole organizing developed out of the Worthy Wages organizing model."

Seattle Worthy Wages' members also recognized the mutual benefits of work-ing in coalition with SEIU/925. Barb Wiley reflected:

> One of the main differences [of Seattle Worthy Wages working in coalition with SEIU/925] is the resources. The money, paid staff, the office space. And being hooked into this bigger movement—the labor movement . . . It's just a huge amount of extra power. And we're able to concretely move this group of workers toward the goal—a really concrete goal that we [Seattle Worthy Wages] just couldn't do [alone].

Despite the recognition of mutual benefits to each organization, challenges of working in coalition surfaced early in the campaign. The grassroots organiza-tional culture of Seattle Worthy Wages and the more formal organizational cul-ture of SEIU/925 resulted in differences in communication and organizing style and resulted in conflicts among the two groups. While acknowledging the bene-fits of working in coalition, Barb Wiley voiced the organizational changes expe-rienced by Seattle Worthy Wages as a result of joining forces with SEIU/925.

> I feel the loss of control and autonomy that we had in Worthy Wages. We were sort of a small group making decisions mostly by consensus. We had a lot of space and room to do that. That's different in the Childcare Union Project . . . We hammer out the policies—thinking through every little piece of process that could happen and having a policy for it. We didn't really have that with Worthy Wages. It was more informal. I think that having it for CUP will make us more efficient. It will be great. But, definitely different than Worthy Wages.

The organizational differences between Seattle Worthy Wages and SEIU/925 were also acknowledged by Kim Cook, specifically with regard to the financial resources and responsibilities of managing a large union organization. Kim reflected:

> I'd say the main reason we [SEIU/925] are organizing [child care teachers] in Seattle is because the Worthy Wage group is here. But, the other thing is that we represent a very large group of staff people from the University of Washington. And we have a significant, stable local where we can actually afford to do this kind of expensive, risky organizing.

Kim went on to describe the $234,000 budget for the Childcare Union Project. While the SEIU international provided funding for two organizers-in-training for the campaign, members of the SEIU/925 union local in Seattle funded 85% of the campaign. Kim described her ongoing assessment of the financial and organizational costs of organizing child care workers:

> Frankly, even in our wildest dreams we could maybe end up with a contract for about two hundred workers after a year [of organizing]. That's an incredible amount of work that is not very cost effective for a labor union . . . It's not like our members' dues [the primary source of funding for the child care campaign] are endless.

Thus, the pragmatic and financial concerns of effectively managing a large union contrasted with the historically more informal, grassroots organizing approach of Seattle Worthy Wages. Kim reflected on these challenges of working in coalition.

> Trying to have these two organizations function together, Seattle Worthy Wages and District 925, has been a real interesting challenge. The Worthy Wages folks have been operating for ten years on a much more grassroots, volunteer kind of a basis and they're much, much more into process. And you know, our focus is really product. I mean, we certainly believe in process to the extent that it develops leaders and gives skills to people, but . . . Then there's just the challenge of making sure that Worthy Wages doesn't get lost in all of this, right? They're very aware that they want to keep that identity—that they want to build on the work that they've done over the last decade. So, that's an interesting challenge as well.

As the campaign evolved, both Seattle Worthy Wages and SEIU/925 recognized that conscious attention to distinctive organizational cultures, goals, and structures was essential, and had been insufficiently addressed in the initial formation of the Childcare Union Project coalition. So, several months into the campaign, Seattle Worthy Wages and SEIU/925 entered into a formal partnership agreement. The agreement delineated the roles and responsibilities of each organization within the coalition, and acknowledged that once the child care union was formally established, the Childcare Union Project coalition would disband and the two separate organizations (Seattle Worthy Wages and SEIU/925) would continue to work together on common issues. Lauren Tozzi read from the partnership agreement between Seattle Worthy Wages and SEIU/925:

> And there's a brief description here about what the partnership means: "We recognize that we have different styles and histories and that we have mutual goals and commitments. We hope this document will help clarify a working relationship." We kind of went at it [clarifying roles and responsibilities] in a backward way. But, you know, we learned and we've made mistakes . . . I do wish, though, that we had had a brainstorming [early on] about what partnership meant. Because we all came in with some preconceived notions and assumptions that we all understood one

another—when that discussion didn't take place. I think we could have averted a lot of blood, sweat, and tears.

In coalition work between unions and grassroots community groups, each organization brings differing skills and values to organizing. Unions, for example, bring the financial resources, skills, and contacts needed to negotiate within larger formal organizations and institutions. In contrast,

Women of color and working class women often bring skills that are not so directly tied to the bureaucratic workings, which gives the appearance that these skills are not so essential . . . Culturally, within their own communities, they have been required to develop resources when none seem to exist . . . Yet, the constellation of accepted skills that work within the bureaucracy definitely privilege many white and middle class women. (Albrecht and Brewer 1990:9)

Within the Childcare Union Project, Seattle Worthy Wages activists reported concerns about "lack of recognition for the work that we do." At the same time, as a grassroots group, Seattle Worthy Wages members lacked experience, and therefore knowledge, of the challenges of coordinating and managing a large-scale, "risky and expensive" campaign within a more hierarchical organization. It is essential to remember that working in coalition requires individuals and organizations to move beyond the known boundaries and skills of their own familiar institutional base. Although this movement across boundaries is challenging, it is also necessary if activists are to organize effectively to address the needs of the child care workforce.

Conclusion: Commitment to a Long-Term Process

Organizers of the Childcare Union Project teach us that unions and grassroots child care advocacy organizations have much to offer one another in seeking to better the wages, working conditions, and status of paid child care workers. Each organization brings complementary skills and resources to the work of child care organizing. However, even when activist organizations appear to share common goals, working in coalition is not an easy task. Gender, race, and organizational culture all inform the organization and provision of child care in the contemporary United States, and as such, each of these forces is at play when activists seek to organize members of the child care workforce. The Childcare Union Project teaches us three important lessons about gender, race, and organizational culture in labor organizing among child care workers: first, the need to address gendered ideologies of altruism in care work and to affirm the self-advocacy and resources needed by care workers to do their work well; second, the need for careful attention to the meanings of diversity and racism, especially among organizations that are, historically, predominantly White; and, third, the need to recognize and respect diverse organizational cultures and structures in child care organizing.

More than a decade of community organizing with child care teachers and providers has taught Seattle Worthy Wages member Lauren Tozzi about the complexity and the challenges faced in organizing the child care workforce.

There's so many inequities in this [child care] system. Not just when it comes down to compensation, but with race and gender. I know that we have these great ideals, but it really has to move slow . . . We're still learning about institutional racism . . . I think this whole idea of diversity and multiculturalism—it's very important because we're trying to do it at our work sites and go beyond tolerance, [trying to] do a lot of work as far as what does it mean to be truly inclusive. But, also, be open that people will make mistakes, and I think that that's something we have to work on still.

Experiences of organizers within the Childcare Union Project teach us that although unions and community-based organizations may share long-term goals, they implement those goals within different constraints and values orientations. Grassroots community organizations often value gains in consciousness and the development of emerging indigenous leadership and view these as essential first steps toward politicization and eventual unionization. In contrast, union leaders may argue that if union representation makes the biggest difference in women's economic status, then the goal should be to unionize as quickly as possible (Needleman 1998). Organizer-in-training Valerie Brown recognized these potential conflicts: "To organize child care, you need to take into account the community. And it's not a 'move quick' community, especially with turnover being so high . . . People have to have ownership and ownership doesn't happen overnight."

Although the desirability of a quick and successful union campaign is understandable, activists implementing community-based models of organizing report that building membership, leadership, and commitment in labor organizing campaigns among service-sector workers is an intensive and slow process (Bronfenbrenner et al. 1998; Eisenscher 1999)—but one that is effective in the long run. Among service-sector workers, the most powerful labor organizing campaigns are ones in which unions join forces with existing community organizations and the differing skills and resources of each organization are central in planning and implementing the organizing campaign. To develop such a campaign, however, requires a considerable investment of resources, time, and commitment by existing organizations, be they grass-roots organizations or unions, for both must "rethink their mission, structure and leadership, recasting themselves as flexible and strategic organizations open to new leadership and ideas" (Hallock 1997). To commence such a task among a previously unorganized and diverse workforce, in a devalued occupation, with high turnover is no small undertaking. As successful campaigns among clerical workers (Hurd 1993) and health-care workers (Sullivan 2000) have required several years, we should anticipate no less in campaigns to successfully organize the child care workforce.

The Childcare Union Project teaches us lessons that are valuable to advocates who seek to organize on behalf of care and care workers. The skills, resources, and approaches of union organizers and community organizers are complementary. Unions, including SEIU/925, possess the infrastructure necessary to organize a large, decentralized, and diverse workforce, as well as experience in influencing legislation and public policies regarding employment and workplace reforms.

They have the expertise needed to develop, sign, and monitor the implementation of union contracts. Community-based organizations like Seattle Worthy Wages have knowledge of daily needs of workers, cultural practices within their communities, and indigenous leaders. They have experience in leadership training and education of community members. They can serve and have served as social hubs and bases for social change within communities.

Like other labor unions and child care advocacy organizations, both Seattle Worthy Wages and SEIU/925 endorse the dignity of work, the right of all workers' (including careworkers) to a living wage, and the long-term public benefits (not only to parents, but to all citizens) that derive from affordable, quality child care. When working in concert, grassroots community organizations and unions have much to offer each other, and to careworkers, as we work together to increase the social, political, and economic status of paid care providers.

Notes

The author thanks Valerie Brown and Dorothy Gibson for their comments on an earlier version of this work; Demie Kurz, Andrew London, Naomi Gerstel, and Barb Wiley for their detailed critique of an earlier version; and the Denison University Research Foundation for their financial support of this research. The author assumes sole responsibility for the analysis depicted in this chapter.

1. The term *child care teachers* includes teachers and teaching assistants employed in child care centers. The term *providers* recognizes that a large number of child care workers offer paid group care for children in the homes of providers (e.g., family child care providers) or in the homes of children.

2. For more information about Worthy Wages see http://www.ccw.org.

3. Although less than half of women in the labor force have attended college, more than half of assistant teachers and almost three-quarters of child care teachers report some college background (Whitebook et al. 1993).

4. I recognize the historical use of the term *race* to define groups on the basis of purported biological characteristics. Although I do not endorse this definition or practice, I do believe that the social construction of race has historically shaped the cultural identities and experiences of groups and, as such, race remains a fundamental organizing principle of social relationships in the contemporary United States. In this chapter I use a variety of terms to describe race and racial ethnic identities (e.g., Black, White, African-American, Latina, Hispanic). The terms used reflect the sources from which they are derived (e.g., interviewees, publications).

Activist Mothering and Community Work

Fighting Oppression in Low-income Neighborhoods

Nancy A. Naples

*F*amily, neighborhood institutions, and social networks are key sites for the development and expression of women's political consciousness (see Bookman and Morgen 1988; Gilkes 1988; Naples 1998a; Orleck 1995; Pardo 1995; Sacks 1988a; 1988b). During the mid-1980s, I began a study of community workers living and working in poor neighborhoods in New York City and Philadelphia. I returned to these neighborhoods in the mid-1990s to see how the workers' lives had changed over the intervening years. The goal of this study was to understand the motivations, political analyses, and personal challenges faced by women who devote their lives to the care of their geographic, racial-ethnic, and class-based communities.[1] Analysis of the community workers' political practice reveals how women's performance of apparently traditional female roles can lead them to take revolutionary actions on behalf of their families and communities.[2] As a result of my research on women community workers in poor urban neighborhoods, I developed a complex *intersectional*[3] understanding of their political practice that I term "activist mothering."

I developed the concept of *activist mothering* by examining the everyday practices of the community workers as they articulated them through in-depth interviews. The term highlights the myriad ways these women challenged the academic separation of productive work in the labor force from reproductive work in the family, and from politics. An analysis of activist mothering provides a new conceptualization of the relationship among labor, politics, and mothering—three aspects of social life usually analyzed separately—from the point of view of women whose motherwork historically has been ignored (e.g., Chodorow 1978) or pathologized (Moynihan 1967) in sociological analyses.[4] The notion of activist mothering highlights how political activism formed a central component of the community workers' mother work and community caretaking. It serves to counter traditional constructions of politics as limited to electoral politics or membership in social movement organizations as well as feminist constructions of motherwork and reproductive labor that neglect women's activism on behalf of their families and communities. As a sociological concept, the term captures the ways in which politics, mothering, and labor comprised mutually constitutive spheres of social life for the community workers.

This chapter centers on the experiences of women who lived in low income urban communities when the Community Action Programs were funded through the Economic Opportunity Act (EOA) of 1964, as part of President Lyndon B. Johnson's Great Society programs. The Great Society is a term used to describe antipoverty legislation passed during President Johnson's administration. Johnson's Great Society extended President John F. Kennedy's New Frontier initiatives, which operated under the assumption that by expanding access to health care, education, employment, and training opportunities, the poor could benefit from the then-projected growth of the U.S. economy. Great Society legislation targeted poor communities and individuals living in poverty as well as educational and employment practices. The EOA became one of the most hotly contested legislative innovations of the Great Society. The EOA offered the first government-sponsored attempt to involve the poor directly and formally in decision-making, advocacy, and service provision in their own communities. Early reports on the War on Poverty ignored women's contributions as paid workers, despite the fact that the majority of positions such as community aide, community worker, and parent aide were filled by women. In keeping with the traditional view of women's work as unpaid, the Office of Economic Opportunity (OEO), established by the EOA, defined women's role in the War on Poverty as that of volunteer. Strategies for preventing poverty emphasized expanding employment opportunities for poor men; this marginalized women's employment needs as well as their actual contributions as staff members and administrators of antipoverty programs.[5]

I conducted in-depth interviews with 64 community workers who were hired by the community action agencies funded by the EOA. Forty-two of the women were living in the low-income communities that were the target of the War on Poverty when they were hired by community action agencies and are defined in this study as "resident" community workers; 22 were not residing in these communities and consequently are defined as "nonresident" community workers. Of the 42 "resident" community workers identified for this study, 26 are African American, eleven are Puerto Rican, four are European American, and one is Japanese American. Eighteen of the nonresident community workers are White, three are African American, and one is Puerto Rican. In 1995, I returned to New York and Philadelphia to reinterview 15 of the 64 community workers I originally interviewed in the mid-1980s.[6]

The following discussion illustrates the themes that emerged as aspects of activist mothering in the community work of the women who were living and working in low-income communities in New York City and Philadelphia. I center the experiences of the resident community workers, although many of the nonresident community workers, especially the women of color and White women from working-class backgrounds, also described most of these patterns. I begin by outlining the key dimensions of the community workers' activist mothering and then explore how racism and class oppression contributed to their community work as well as the strategies they developed to fight against discrimination. Next, I describe the activist mothering performed by the community workers' mothers and discuss the tensions between family-based labor and community work. I conclude by demonstrating how the community workers defied dominant definitions of mothering and politics through their activist community care taking.

Conceptualizing Activist Mothering

I did not begin this research with an interest in mothering per se, although I did wish to examine how mothering activities contributed to, or inhibited, political participation. As I reexamined the activists' personal narratives, I recognized how a broadened definition of mothering was woven in and through their paid and unpaid community work which in turn was infused with political activism. The traditional definition of mothering—nurturing work with children who are bio-logically or legally related and cared for within the confines of a bounded family unit—failed to capture the community workers' activities and self-perceptions of their motherwork. The term *activist mothering*, generated through close reading and rereading of the narratives, better expresses the complex ways the resident community workers, especially the African-American and Puerto Rican women, made sense of their own activities.

The community workers lives' were shaped by experiences of racism, sexism, and poverty. They learned to mother as activists fighting in their homes and communities against the debilitating and demoralizing effects of oppression. When we limit our analysis of mothering practices to those activities that occur within the confines of a nuclear family, we miss the material conditions that contribute to differing family forms as well as the social construction of gender and political activism. For example, experiences of racism marked African-American and Puerto Rican community workers' first encounters with injustice in North American society. These experiences informed the antiracist mothering practices they utilized within their own homes and served as a basic target for community work. The conceptualization of activist mothering draws attention to the histor-ically specific context in which many of the women interviewed developed their political analyses and strategies.[7]

Activist mothering not only involves nurturing work for those outside one's kinship group, but also encompasses a broad definition of material and emotional mothering practices. The community workers defined "good mothering" to com-prise all actions, including social activism, that addressed the needs of their chil-dren and community—variously defined as their racial–ethnic group, low-income people, or members of a particular neighborhood. In addition to testifying before public officials, all the resident community workers participated in public protests and demonstrations for improved community services, increased resources, and expansion of community control. Ann Robinson, for example, described her involvement in protests against the city-run hospital in her Manhattan neighbor-hood, for welfare rights, and improved housing, as well as for expanded child-care services and community control of the public schools. Resident community work-ers who did not have children also viewed their relationship to their communities as one of caretaker. Because most of the resident community workers shared the same race and class background and grew up in the same neighborhoods as those on whose behalf they worked, they saw themselves as beneficiaries of their com-munity work efforts as well.

All the resident community workers with children said that, for the most part, a large portion of their community work derived from concern for their children's well-being. The four African-American women and three Puerto Rican women who did not have children traced their motivations for community work to a variety of community-based concerns and viewed their activism as community caretaking more than politics. The term *activist mothering* highlights the community workers' gendered conceptualization of activism on behalf of their communities—often defined beyond the confines of their families, households, and neighborhoods. Central to their constructions of "community" was a convergence of racial-ethnic identification and class affiliation.

Activist mothering includes self-conscious struggles against racism, sexism, and poverty. Racial discrimination was one of the consistent themes expressed by all the African-American and Puerto Rican community workers, and struggles against racism formed a basic undercurrent for most of their community work. Similarity between Puerto Rican and African-American community workers also emanated from their social location in low-income communities. As residents of poor communities, many of the women described how the deteriorating conditions as well as the inadequate education and health services that threatened their children's growth and development fostered an ongoing commitment to community work. Their own mothers helped interpret experiences with racism and classism and instilled in their daughters a belief in their ability to overcome these obstacles. Fathers also contributed to the cross-generational continuity of activist mothering through their community work on behalf of their communities.

Literature discussing women of color's activism further highlights the ways in which racism and a commitment to fight for social justice infuses their political analyses and political practices.[8] Women of color, especially those living in poor neighborhoods, must fight against discrimination and the oppressive institutions that shape their daily lives and, consequently, as mothers and as community activists they model strategies of resistance for children in their own families and communities. For example, African-American women's struggle against racism infuses their mothering practices inside and outside their "homeplace."[9] Lessons carved out of the experiences of "everyday racism" contribute to mothering practices that include "handing down the knowledge of racism from generation to generation."[10] Referring to this practice in her discussion of "homeplace" as "a site of resistance," bell hooks (1990:46) explained, "Working to create a homeplace that affirmed our beings, our blackness, our love for one another was necessary resistance." She argued that "any attempt to critically assess the role of black women in liberation struggle must examine the way political concern about the impact of racism shaped black women's thinking, their sense of home, and their modes of parenting" (p. 46).

Patricia Hill Collins (1990) described the broad-based nature of mothering in the African-American community and highlighted the work of community othermothers who help build community institutions and fight for the welfare of their neighbors. She argued that the activities of othermothers who form part of the extended kinship networks in the African-American community pave the way for the political activism of community othermothers. According to Collins

(1991:129), "A substantial portion of African-American women's status in African-American communities stems not only from their roles as mothers in their own families but from their contributions as community othermothers to black community development as well." Collins and Stanlie James (1993), among others, argued that African and African-American women exemplify this tradition of othermothering and community othermothering that can be found in a variety of places and across time.[11] However, these patterns are not natural or predetermined components of black women's identities. Rather, as analysis of women's community work demonstrates, they are developed in dynamic relationship with particular historic conditions and transmitted through self-conscious socialization practices and political struggles.

Whiteness cushioned the European American resident community workers from facing the dynamics of racial oppression until they became active in community-based struggles. Harriet Towers of Philadelphia did not see racism as a problem in her community work and defined the neighborhood in which she worked as "an integrated one," adding that "I've never been prejudiced myself. I could always work with most everyone." When pressed on this point, she insisted that she always got along with everyone, regardless of race. However, early awareness of class inequality and poverty was central to the narratives of all four White women who were living in low-income neighborhoods when the War on Poverty was declared. Grace Reynolds of Philadelphia described her childhood as one totally defined by struggles for economic survival. Her father was a laborer. Her mother died when she was young and the family was very poor. Her involvement in the antipoverty programs was her first political activity. Brenda Rivers said she first recognized the need to become active at the community level when, as a new mother, she moved from a small rural town to Philadelphia. Brenda, a mother of a biracial child, stressed antiracism campaigns as well as struggles against the causes of symptoms of poverty in her geographic community.

Activist Responses to Discrimination

The African-American and Puerto Rican women interviewed uniformly identified many experiences with racism and sexism as part of their earliest childhood memories. Rita Martinez of East Harlem said she was "guided" into pink collar work, despite the fact that she expressed a desire to pursue a career as a teacher.

> My whole life, since I could remember back, I wanted to be a teacher. And I had mentioned this, and this is very vivid to me, I had mentioned this to an eighth grade teacher . . . and she said, "I don't think you'll make it. You don't have the temperament. You fly too fast." And here's a fourteen year old, and she's saying this. At fourteen, who does not fly off the handle? Think, at fourteen, even at twenty-one you are still sometimes too fast. So that discouraged me. See, the thing that hurt me most was that I cared for that teacher so much. We were very close. And when she said that, I believed her.

Rita was dissatisfied with the training program for beauticians in which she was subsequently enrolled and quit high school at the age of 16. Given this personal history, she was especially excited by the opportunity to fulfill her life-long dream of becoming a teacher through a CAP in East Harlem.

For the four Puerto Rican women who moved to New York City from Puerto Rico or other Spanish-speaking countries, lack of facility with English increased their encounters with racism. Maria Calero was divorced with three children when I met her in 1983. She was working as a program director for a citywide nonprofit agency in New York City. As a teenager, Maria moved to New York City from the Dominican Republic with her family. Her first paid job was as a factory worker. She "hardly spoke the language" and was unprepared for the racism she found. She recalled:

> I remember feeling that I was not a part of the society at all. . . . I had come to this country when I was fifteen so my experience was different from those Hispanic women who were raised and went to school here. I came from a homogeneous society . . . to a society that strongly discriminated.

Maria was also astounded by the racism she encountered within the Hispanic community.

> My father is black Hispanic and my mother is white Hispanic. But my identity was Hispanic, and they were calling me black or nigger. I just got very confused about the racial conflicts within the Hispanic community. But I remember feeling that I was not a part of the society at all, that I was outside of the society.

Maria believed that the contrast between her early childhood experiences in a racially "homogeneous" society and her experiences of racism in this country increased her sensitivity to injustice and discrimination. She was the only community worker to argue that an "outsider" perspective had value for political analysis. However, like other resident community workers, she also valued an "insider" indigenous perspective for its sensitivity to how race, class, and gender dynamics patterned the experiences of poor people of color throughout their daily lives. In fact, Maria's narrative highlighted the interaction of outsider and insider vantage points for shaping personal experiences as well as political analyses.

Although she said she was raised in "a very traditional manner, in a male-dominated family," Maria reported that she was very aware of the broader political environment. She stated:

> Somehow I always had the room to think about issues of social concern. For example, . . . I married very young, but I was concerned in the early sixties about police brutality. I was very much concerned about civil rights issues, and I was very personally aware of discrimination issues.

Maria detailed the problems with police brutality in her Harlem community and also emphasized how "Hispanics had enormous problems getting registered to vote because you had to pass a test" that presumed a certain facility with written English. Her awareness of racism and class discrimination was heightened when she gave birth to her first child and began to investigate the high school dropout rate and how racist teachers had lower expectations for Latino children.

By the time her two daughters were of school age, she had grown increasingly pessimistic about their receiving a decent education in the New York City public schools. She explained:

> I really had to think about what schools my daughters would go to. I wanted them to be educated and I wanted them to go to college, and I wanted them to partici-pate, and I think I had many more dreams for them than I had for myself. But in allowing myself to think a lot about how they were going to be educated and what was going to happen to my daughters, I began to ask questions about the Board of Education, about public schools, about how were Hispanic children being educated in the public schools, and discovering the drop-out rate, the sto-ries from people that were very smart but sent to vocational schools because I began to read studies about teachers' expectations, about how racism got in the way of teaching children. I began to think a lot about education in terms of what was really learning. I wanted them to be educated, but I also wanted my children to be thinkers. And I got very concerned about that.

Her concern for her children's education led to her first leadership experience in a parents' advocacy organization. There she said she deepened her under-standing of the limits of the public education system in New York City, enriched her community work skills, and met many women who modeled for her a kind of political analysis and political practice that drew her further into community activism.

A third of the thirty resident workers with children described their first community work activity as a response to the quality of their children's education. For example, Wilma North traced her career as a community worker to her dis-satisfaction with the educational quality of her children's school. However, her activist mothering led her into other struggles, as she explained, "anything that had to do with the betterment of [my] community and the welfare of those chil-dren going to the elementary school" long after her own children graduated.[12]

Mothers' Activist Mothering

Many of the resident community workers' mothers provided, as one worker stated, a "strong foundation" for their desire to serve their community. A total of seventeen mothers were described by their daughters as informal caretakers in their communities. Five (or 45%) of the Puerto Rican women and twelve (or 46%) of the African American women said their mothers were involved in a variety of helping activities in their neighborhoods. These activities included taking neigh-bors to the hospital, helping care for the elderly, advocating for increased child care programs, fighting school officials to expand educational opportunities for young people, struggling with landlords and police officials to improve the hous-ing and safety conditions in their community, and interpreting for non-English speaking residents.

At the time of the interview, Carmen Hernandez was director of the same education program in East Harlem that had employed her as a bus driver in 1969. Carmen characterized her mother, who was still very active in her neighborhood, as "a frontier community person" who fought for other children's rights as well as her own. Carmen recounted:

> Back in the '50s and early '60s, when it wasn't right for parents to get involved, to be in the classrooms, and to question teachers, she was doing that. She'd ask: "Why?" "How come?" "Give me a reason." "I won't take it just because you said it." "Show it to me." "Let me read it so I can understand what's going on, because verbally that doesn't connect with me." . . . And I used to look at her and she got her point across. And she would fight for different children's rights, and she didn't care whose child it was.

Carmen's description of her mother as an activist and "a frontier community person" mirrors Patricia Hill Collins' (1990) account of how African American women's broad-based mothering practices contribute to their role as community othermothers. Among the many lessons Carmen learned from her mother's activist mothering was the importance of questioning and "dialogue in assessing knowledge claims" as well as the "ethic of caring" (Collins 1990: 212, 215). Mothers also taught their daughters how to create and sustain community ties. These community-building and sustaining skills became one foundation upon which the daughters developed as community workers in their own right.

Josephine Card was in her early fifties and worked in a program for the elderly in her East Harlem community, earning an annual salary of $18,000 in 1985. Josephine learned from her mother's example how important informal networks are to the survival of low-income people like herself. Josephine's mother was a school teacher in Georgia but could not find a job in her field when she moved to New York City in 1929. Her mother had recently died but Josephine continued to feel her mother's spirit with her. She explained:

> There are a lot of things I do, and I get tickled because I think about her and what she would have done, and I know just what she would have done with a lot of stuff. She was a very bright woman. Everybody in the community came to her for anything. If they had problems with bills, if they had problems with burying somebody that lived somewhere else, they'd come to my mother. My mother knew all the funeral directors and she knew all the ministers in the churches and she knew everybody . . . She'd always know who to call. And they'd use her almost like for community consulting. I'm serious! My mother's house was always like a revolving door.

Even after her mother's death, Josephine drew on her mother's teachings to inform her approach to community work, especially the lessons on networking with others to promote community well-being. For example, Josephine decided to accept a paid position for which she at first thought she was unqualified. When during the job interview the members of the board of directors of the new community-based agency told her the names of some of the people with whom she would be in contact through the position, she found that she knew everyone they mentioned. She took the job, and through it she reaffirmed her sense of connection with her community. She remembered: "They wanted a lot. Well, it just so happened that every name they mentioned to me in this community I knew personally. I mean, I really knew them well. So, it was like old home week coming here [to this agency], and I've really enjoyed my work here." The networking skills she learned from her mother helped Josephine in her own community work, enhanced her success as a paid worker, and increased her feelings of personal connection with other members of her community. Josephine's experience further demonstrates the blurring between family-based experiences, paid labor, and social reproductive work.

Negotiating Community Work and Family-based Labor

The above discussion illustrates the broadened definition of mothering that infused the community work of the women in this study. For many, this continued the activist mothering practices they witnessed as children in their parent's home. The fusing of community work and family-based labor frequently meant opening their homes to those in need. Ethel Pearls of Philadelphia described how she invited young people, especially those with children, who had no other place to live or who were having difficulties in their own homes to stay with her and her family. Ethel's children were now grown and out of the house. She continued to offer her home to others even after she was laid off from her paid community work position. The intricate relationship between community work and family-based labor also generated tension between a worker's caretaking responsibilities for her own children and her caretaking work in the community. Some of the women expressed regret that the extensive hours they spent on community work took them away from their own children. Fortunately, the resident community workers were situated within an extensive network of othermothers who assisted them with child care and supported their community work. All of the community workers with children mentioned the importance of other women in their lives who helped them negotiate the competing demands of unpaid and paid community work and parental responsibilities.

Overall, the community workers' activist mothering had contradictory effects on their children's lives. On the one hand, their activism often took them away from their families and many women described the frustration they felt when they did not have enough time to spend with their children. On the other hand, their activism also improved their children's health care and education as well as provided a foundation for upward mobility, paving the way for their college education, among other opportunities. Some children experienced reprisals and other forms of discrimination because of their mothers' activism. Yet, by educating their children on the political organization of their social world and modeling activist mothering, some community workers also contributed to their children's commitment to work on behalf of their defined communities.

Intergenerational Continuity of Community Work

Sabrina Brock's parents played a key role in raising her consciousness about injustice, economic inequality, and racism. She honored the activist mothering she received and credited this early foundation for her endurance as a community worker. In 1995, she discussed how her identity as a community worker was forged out of these early experiences:

> I can't say that I always wake up with unbridled enthusiasm for the day. You get tired. But I think I've been privileged to have my baptism in my values and in my politics early on in my life supported by my family and supported by some watershed experiences. And . . . I got enough support in the small communities and in the small ways that I was organizing to know that that was something that I couldn't turn my back on. That that was who I was. My identity was forged out of those experiences and those values. And that's what kept me young, strong, you know. I guess I'm weary now, but I ain't giving up. I'm going to keep on keepin' on.

Sabrina "keep[s] on keepin' on" despite the difficulties posed by the contemporary political and economic environment because of the firm commitment and political values instilled by her parents as well as an accumulation of personal political experiences that continue to sustain her. However, transmission of political commitment and values from one generation to another is not a simple and unmediated process as Sabrina found when she tried to incorporate her own daughter into her activist work.

Sabrina discovered that there was no legitimate role for her daughter to play in the community actions that drew her time and energies. Although she brought her to demonstrations and other community actions, Sabrina complained that organizers never developed ways to engage younger people in these campaigns and that her daughter, Emma, resented being "forced" to attend her mother's political events. She explained:

> She grew up in that trough, being born in the 1970's. She doesn't come of age until really that land of the 1980's and she didn't become . . . [an] activist but she spent most of her life on picket lines, demonstrations, or whatever. She used to quip: "The only time I've ever seen Washington was to stand in front of the Pentagon or the White House with a barricade, a police barricade, demonstrating. I never saw the Smithsonian museums or why people really go to Washington."

According to Sabrina, the lack of wider context and specific strategies to engage her daughter's political interests and her daughter's resentment that her mother spent so much of her time on political activism, contributed to Emma's "resistance to struggle." She stated:

> It's been a resistance to not having more of my time because I was always at a meeting . . . I always tried to build her into it but we haven't learned as activists that if we're going to take our children with us we have to provide a way for them at their level to participate and feel engaged. We haven't done that well.

Reflecting back over her attempts to incorporate her daughter into her political activities, Sabrina now recognizes the limits of such strategies. Missing from her efforts and those of other activist parents were approaches that would permit their children to engage in their own way and through their own interests and abilities.

Furthermore, many of the community workers complained that their children's needs were sometimes put on hold as the political demands on their time increased. Sabrina defined the needs for nurturing very broadly. Not only did one's children require care, but all those participating in activist struggles need to be nurtured. Sabrina complained: "We don't nurture each other as activists. You know, we just drain each other, requiring more work, more work, more work, more work." She felt that activists were so caught up in the day-to-day struggles that they rarely took time to play or socialize without an activist agenda.

In our discussion of her twenty-two year old daughter Emma's activist orientation, Sabrina at first emphasized Emma's resistance to "struggle." After some reflection she remarked that her daughter has yet to come into her own political personality. However, later in the interview Sabrina noted that Emma was particularly concerned with environmental issues such as protection of dolphins and other sea life—an activist arena in which Sabrina had never been particularly interested. Sabrina commented on her daughter's environmental interests and analyzed the process by which she believes young people develop their own political visions:

> And I think that like the tomato soup commercial . . . of years ago when the two guys are there stirring the thing and one says: "Well, did you put peppers in the sauce?" "It's in there." "And did you put onions?" And he says: "Yeah, it's in there." And he says: "Well did you put the garlic in?" "Yeah, it's in there." "You mean it's all in there?" "It's in." I think my kid is in process and all the values and the experiences are in there and what I want for her is to be able to sort out within a value context where she's going to make her stand. And so if she can commit to dolphins and clean water, ultimately they're mammals and they might translate back to humans.

Sabrina did not view Emma's interest in environmental concerns as a legitimate focus for political activism. For Sabrina, it appeared that environmental activism was acceptable only if it could be shown to benefit human beings directly. In this way, Sabrina would have little interest in building coalitions with groups advocating for environmental issues that could not be directly linked to benefits for humankind. While she was concerned that her daughter would not continue the legacy of activism she bequeathed, Sabrina also narrowly defined what would be acceptable political engagement.

One of the major reasons that people might resist becoming active in social movements on their own behalf, according to Sabrina, is the risk of jail or even death. She discussed these fears in the context of her own political history as well as what her daughter might have internalized. She contrasted the risks of activism with the comforts promised by compromising and living within the consumer culture.

> Because I think some of the legacies of the movements were also, you died. You

were assassinated. They will kill you . . . You know when people realized you go to jail or you died [they became fearful]. And I think this country never faced the hour in that way like they have in other countries. And so when they finally rise up, they're willing to sit in those risks, you know. And I don't think it has to come to that. I just think that's the message . . . You can be happy and have more clothes and more hair and more lipstick and have more boyfriends and money and cars, and housing and marriage and whatever . . . [However] if you choose this way you will go to jail and you will die, you know. And . . . I think those meta messages are always there, as well as the constant devaluation of cooperation, collectivity, [and] community building.

As Sabrina's perspective suggests, rather than understand children's resistance to the struggle for social justice as a consequence of their more politically conservative world view or as individual self-interest, it is also important to examine the extent to which awareness of the physical attacks, arrest, and assassination of progressive community leaders—especially those connected with the Civil Rights Movement—effectively discourages activism among black youth. Those who were brought up in activist households were particularly situated to witness the extent of police harassment and other forms of intimidation against outspoken community leaders like their mothers or fathers. When placed up against the comforts that accrue with a more sedate middle-class life style, the risks of political resistance appear even greater.

Children of activist mothers who witnessed the risks of participation as well as the extensive time commitment required by community work might be discouraged from engaging in community-based struggles for social and economic justice as Sabrina argues. However, even those who wish to continue the legacy face a different political environment that shapes their political perspectives and political strategies in ways that diverge from their parents' approach to politics. Class location further influences the political possibilities for younger activists. As a consequence of their activist mothering on behalf of their children, the community workers were often able to access resources and social networks that contributed to their children's upward mobility. Children of activist mothers who achieved middle-class status and who continued the legacy of community work and political activism did so with a different relationship to their communities and through different political strategies. Loss of advocacy-oriented community action agencies and other community-based programs combined with an increase in poverty within the low-income communities that were the target for the War on Poverty also inhibit the development of younger leaders from these communities who could continue the legacy of community work.

Conclusion

The contradictions that arose from the community workers' negotiation of family-based labor, unpaid community work, and paid work expose how the so-called separate spheres of social life are braided in and through the social relations of community. Most of the resident community workers viewed both their unpaid and paid work as caretaking or nurturing work despite the radical political activities involved. Their involvement in social protests, public speaking, and advocacy as well as grantwriting, budgeting, and other administrative tasks were viewed as a part of a larger struggle—namely, doing "just what needed to be done" to secure economic and social justice for their communities. The dialectical relationship between the dominant discourse on the definition of the political and the community workers' practice of community caretaking contributed to a unique form of community-based political activity that differs profoundly from the civic work of middle- and upper-income men and women who volunteer for not-for-profit associations.[13]

The community workers also challenged traditional notions of gender and mothering in their work and served as models for their children as well as others in their community. All of the women interviewed said they held onto a strong sense of their personal power and, for many, the example given by other activist mothers helped strengthen their belief, already established by their own mothers, in their power to affect change in their communities. As funds were withdrawn from their organizations and problems within their communities increased, many of the resident workers drew comfort from the help they could offer other residents. Shifting focus from processes of collective action to individual service was an effective way for the resident community workers to remain committed to the work under increasingly harsh economic and political conditions, although it also contributed to a process of depoliticization. For many, this shift in emphasis was an adaptive response to the increasingly conservative political environment as well as a result of the control placed on them by government funding agencies.

The community workers' activist mothering and political analyses influenced their children's political commitment to a certain extent (although, of course, the relationship is not determinant; namely, not all of their children became political activists nor shared their mother's political analyses). On one level, class mobility reshaped their children's attachment to a specific low-income or racial-ethnic community. On another level, the shift in the larger political environment during the 1980s and 1990s limited the sites through which the younger generation could find a locus for their political activism or gain leadership training.

Since many of the community workers positioned themselves and their labor within historically specific struggles for community self-determination that was variously defined by the intersection of class, gender, race, ethnicity, and locality, their resistance to the oppressive features of state intervention in their lives was only one manifestation of broader-based struggles for social justice and economic security. While the nature of the struggles changed over time, the community workers expressed continued affinity for the goals of community self-determination and equality. As a result of their unique perspective as workers paid by the state, beneficiaries of social welfare programs, and unpaid caretakers and activists, the resident community workers, in particular, offered an alternative vision of "the just society" that is creatively expressed and passionately lived in their fight against the forces that impoverish their communities.

Notes

1. I have written about this research extenstively, most notably in *Grassroots*

Warriors: Activist Mothering, Community Work, and the War on Poverty (1998b). This chapter contains excerpts from this book as well as other articles in which my research on women community workers appear (see Naples 1991a, 1991b, 1992, 1998d).

2. Maxine Molyneux (1986) differentiated between "practical gender issues" and "strategic gender issues" to capture the way women activists organize around their practical everyday needs for food, shelter, day care, and housing versus organizing around their gender-specific identities. Obviously, this distinction often breaks down in practice, as we see in this analysis of women's community work (also see Kaplan 1997). Although all the women organized around specific survival needs and community-based concerns, many also organized around strategic gender issues.

3. The term *intersectional* refers to analyses that foreground the relationship between gender, race, ethnicity, class, and sexuality, among other dimensions. This approach stands in contrast to other perspectives that concentrate on only one of these dimensions.

4. Also see Glenn, Chang, and Forcey (1994) and James and Busia (1993) for analyses that contest the traditional constructions of mothering based on White, middle-class nuclear family models.

5. EOA's framers and implementers were unprepared for the challenge the Community Action Programs (CAPs) in low-income communities of color posed to the political establishments in different locales. In less than 2 years, political pressures from mayors, other local officials, and traditional social service organizations had already circumscribed the federal government's commitment to maximum feasible participation of the poor. Furthermore, funds available for the War on Poverty quickly subsided as costs for the Vietnam War escalated. The basic assumption of the Great Society, that government must take an active role to reduce poverty, has been replaced by the 1990s assertion that government support for the poor leads to dependency and undermines the work ethic. Whereas the Great Society emphasized the structural roots of poverty, contemporary poverty policy focuses on the individual behaviors and choices of people who are poor.

6. In 1995, I also conducted in-depth interviews with three of their daughters to explore some unintended and rarely acknowledged intergenerational effects of mothers' community work—a theme identified in the initial interviews.

7. My notion of activist mothering differs from maternalist politics used by many middle-class women of the later part of the 1800s and early 1900s to justify their movement into the political or public sphere. Seth Koven and Sonya Michel (1993:4) defined maternalism as "ideologies and discourses that exalted women's capacity to mother and applied to society as a whole the values they attached to the role: care, nurturance, and morality." Maternalist claims were frequently made on the behalf of others—children, working women, immigrants, the poor. Community workers as activist mothers defined themselves as members of the communities they sought to help, thus breaking with the class and racial–ethnic divisions that often limited maternalist politics of earlier eras (see Mink 1995). Yet appeals to their identities as mothers and community caretakers did circumscribe

their self-presentation as political actors, thus limiting their efficacy in the formal political arena.

8. Latinas, Native American women, and Asian-American women have well established traditions of community-based work designed to defend and enhance the quality of life within their communities (see, e.g., Acosta-Belen 1986; Aguilar-San Juan 1994; Allen 1986; 1995; Glenn, Chang, and Forcey 1994; Gluck et al. 1998; Green 1990; Hewitt 1990; Sanchez-Ayendez 1995; Torres 1986).

9. hooks (1990:41). Also see, e.g., Gilkes (1988), Moraga (1981), Rollins (1995), and Scott (1991).

10. Essed (1990:144); also see Carothers (1990).

11. Also see James (1993), Stack (1974), Stack and Burton (1994), and Troester (1984).

12. It is possible to view women's activism on behalf of others in their communities as a form of altruism (Monroe 1996); however, since the resident workers defined themselves as an integral part of these communities, they felt that they directly benefitted from these efforts as well. Rather than view women's community work through the bipolar lens of self-interest versus selflessness or altruism, I explore the workers perception of their relationships with others in their communal network. In this way, it is possible to explore how these ties both motivate and sustain the workers' commitment.

13. See, e.g., Daniels (1988) and Kaminer (1984).

References

Chapter 1

Abel, Emily. 2000. *Hearts of Wisdom: American Women Caring for Kin, 1850–1940.* Cambridge, MA: Harvard University Press.

Abel, Emily and Nancy Reifel. 1996. "Interactions between Public Health Nurses and Clients on American Indian Reservations during the 1930s." *Social History of Medicine* 9:89–108.

Alderson, Nannie T. and Helena Huntington Smith. 1942. *A Bride Goes West.* New York: Farrar and Rinehart.

Boris, Eileen. 1994. *Home to Work: Motherhood and the Politics of Industrial Homework in the United States.* New York: Cambridge University Press.

Boris, Eileen and C. R. Daniels. 1989. *Homework: Historical and Contemporary Perspectives on Paid Labor at Home.* Urbana: University of Illinois Press.

Brookings Institution. 1928. *The Problem of Indian Administration: Report of a Survey.* Baltimore: Johns Hopkins University Press.

Brown, Harriet Connor. 1929. *Grandmother Brown's Hundred Years, 1827–1927.* New York: Blue Ribbon Books.

Cohen, Leah Hagar. 1994. *Train Go Sorry: Inside a Deaf World.* Boston: Houghton-Mifflin.

Cohen, Miriam. 1992. *Workshop to Office: Two Generations of Italian Women in New York City, 1900–1930.* Ithaca, NY: Cornell University Press.

Committee on Neighborhood Health. 1938. "Child Health Services, New York City, A Survey of Child Health Facilities and Recommendations of the Department of Health for the Development of More Adequate Services." New York: Department of Health.

Community Service Society. 1888–1918. "Case Files." New York: Rare Books and Manuscripts, Butler Library, Columbia University.

C.R.S. 1938. Letter to Eleanor Roosevelt, August. Records of the Children's Bureau, record group 102, file 4-9-1-1. Washington, DC: National Archives.

Davis, Michael M., Jr. 1921. *Immigrant Health and the Community.* New York: Harper and Brothers.

Dickson, A. J. 1916. "Social Service in Relation to Contagious Disease Hospitals." *Monthly Bulletin of the Department of Health* 6:19–20.

Donovan, Rebecca. 1989. "'We Care for the Most Important People in Your Life': Home Care Workers in New York City." *Women's Studies Quarterly* 17:56–65.

Ellingwood, Ken. 2000. "L.A. Sinks Into 'Chernobyl of Health Care.'" *Lost Angeles Times* (November 25):A26.

Ellis, Anne. 1929 *The Life of an Ordinary Woman*, ed. Lucy Fitch Perkins. Boston: Houghton Mifflin, Co.

Eulis, Clara. 1907. Letter to Lawrence Flick, Atlantic City, July 4. Papers of Lawrence F. Flick, Archives of the Catholic University of America, Washington, DC.

Farnsworth, Martha Shaw. 1882–1922. Diary. Kansas State Historical Society, Topeka.

Feudtner, Chris. 1995. "The Want of Control: Ideas, Innovations, and Ideals in the Modern Management of Diabetes Mellitus." *Bulletin of the History of Medicine* 69(1) (spring).

F.F. 1939. Letter to Eleanor Roosevelt, November 14. Records of the Children's Bureau, record group 102, file 4-9-1-1. Washington, DC: National Archives.

G.C. 1939. Letter to Eleanor Roosevelt, September 15. Records of the Children's Bureau, record group 102, file 4-9-1-1. Washington, DC: National Archives.

Gillespie, Emily Hawley. 1858–1888. Diary. Iowa City: State Historical Society of Iowa.

Glenn, Evelyn Nakano. 1986. *Issei, Nisei, War Bride: Three Generations of Japanese American Women in Domestic Service*. Philadelphia: Temple University Press.

Glenn, Evelyn Nakano. 1992. "From Servitude to Service Work: Historical Continuities in the Racial Division of Paid Reproductive Labor." *Signs: Journal of Women in Culture and Society* 18:1–43.

Gordon, Donald, ed. 1923. *The Diary of Ellen Birdseye Wheaton*. Boston: privately printed.

Heiser, Alta Harvey. 1941. *Quaker Lady: The Story of Charity Lynch*. Oxford, OH: Mississippi Valley Press.

Heymann, Jody. 2000. *The Widening Gap: Why America's Working Families Are in Jeopardy and What Can be Done About It*. New York: Basic Books.

Hine, Darlene Clark. 1989. *Black Women in White: Racial Conflict and Cooperation in the Nursing Profession, 1890–1950*. Bloomington: Indiana University Press.

Huftalen, Sarah Gillespie. 1873–1952. Diary. Iowa City: State Historical Society of Iowa.

Hunter, Tera W. 1997. *To 'Joy My Freedom: Southern Black Women's Lives and Labors after the Civil War*. Cambridge, MA: Harvard University Press.

J.L. 1939. Letter to Eleanor Roosevelt. July 20. Records of the Children's Bureau, record group 102, file 4-9-1-1. Washington, DC: National Archives.

Jones, Jacqueline 1985. *Labor of Love, Labor of Sorrow: Black Women, Work, and the Family from Slavery to the Present*. New York: Basic Books.

Jones, Jacqueline. 1987. "Black Women, Work, and the Family Under Slavery." Pp. 84–110 in *Families and Work*, edited by Naomi Gerstel and Harriet Engel Gross. Philadelphia: Temple University Press.

Kelman, Mark and Gillian Lester. 1997. *Jumping the Queue: An Inquiry Into the Legal Treatment of Students with Learning Disabilities*. Cambridge, MA: Harvard University Press.

Kessler-Harris, Alice. 1982. *Out to Work: A History of Wage-Earning Women in the United States*. New York: Oxford University Press.

Lord, Margery J. 1940. Letter to G. M. Cooper. February 6. Records of the Children's Bureau, record group 102, file 4-9-l-1. Washington, DC: National Archives.

Mintz, Steven and Susan Kellogg. 1988. *Domestic Revolution: A Social History of American Family Life*. New York: Free Press.

National Recovery Administration. 1934. Hearings on the Pleating, Stitching, and Bonnaz and Embroidery Industry, November 20. Transcript of Hearings, 231-1-06, record group 9. Washington, DC: National Archives.

N.H. 1935. Letter to Franklin D. Roosevelt. February 5. Records of the Children's Bureau, record group 102, file 4-12-1-1. Washington, DC: National Archives.

Osterud, Nancy Grey. 1991. *Bonds of Community: The Lives of Farm Women in Nineteenth-Century New York*. Ithaca, NY: Cornell University Press.

Padden, Carol and Tom Humphries. 1988. *Deaf in America: Voices from a Culture*. Cambridge, MA: Harvard University Press.

Palmer, Phyllis. 1989. *Domesticity and Dirt: Housewives and Domestic Servants in the United States, 1920–1945*. Philadephia: Temple University Press.

Perry, Anna. 1933. "Monthly Report," Lac du Flambeau, Wisconsin, September. Records of the Bureau of Indian Affairs, record group 75, file E779, Washington, DC: National Archives.

Pidgeon, M. E. 1937. "Women in the Economy of the United States of America: A Summary Report." Bulletin of the Women's Bureau no. 155. Washington, DC.

Rawick, George P., ed. 1979. *The American Slave: A Composite Autobiography*, vol. 15, *North Carolina Narratives*. Westport, CT: Greenwood Press.

Reid, Agnes Just. 1923. *Letters of Long Ago*. Caldwell, ID: Caxton Printers.

Report of the Nurses. 1908. "First Report of the Babies' Dispensary and Hospital of Cleveland for the Fifteen Months Ending September 30th, 1907." Cleveland: Hospital of Cleveland.

Reverby, Susan. 1987. *Ordered to Care: The Dilemma of American Nursing, 1850–1945*. New York: Cambridge University Press.

Rosenberg, Charles E. 1987. *The Care of Strangers: The Rise of America's Hospital System*. New York: Basic Books.

Ryan, Mary P. 1981. *Cradle of the Middle Class: The Family in Oneida County, New York, 1790–1865*. Cambridge, UK: Cambridge University Press.

Savitt, Todd. 1978. *Medicine and Slavery: The Diseases and Health Care of Blacks in Antebellum Virginia*. Urbana: University of Illinois Press.

Sims, J. Marion. 1968. *The Story of My Life*. New York: Da Capo.

S.M.B. 1930. Letter to Children's Bureau. May 18. Records of the Children's Bureau, record group 102, file 7-6-1-3. Washington, DC: National Archives.

S.S. 1938. Letter to Franklin Roosevelt. July 3. Records of the Children's Bureau, record group 102, file 4-9-1-1. Washington, DC: National Archives.

Steckel, Richard H. 1996. "Women, Work, and Health under Plantation Slavery in the United States." Pp. 43–60 in *More than Chattel: Black Women and Slavery in the Americas*, edited by David B. Gaspar and Darlene Clark Hine. Bloomington: Indiana University Press.

Stevens, Rosemary. 1989. *In Sickness and in Wealth: American Hospitals in the Twentieth Century*. New York: Basic Books.

Strasser, Susan. 1982. *Never Done: A History of American Housework*. New York: Pantheon.

Technical Committee on Medical Care. 1938. *The Need for a National Health Program*. Washington, DC: Interdepartmental Committee to Coordinate Health and Welfare Activities.

Tileston, Mary Wilder, ed. 1918. *Caleb and Mary Wilder Foote: Reminiscences and Letters*. Boston: Houghton Mifflin.

Trent, James W., Jr. 1994. *Inventing the Feeble Mind: A History of Mental Retardation in the United States*. Berkeley: University of California Press.

Vogel, Morris J. 1980. *The Invention of the Modern Hospital: Boston, 1870–1930*. Chicago: University of Chicago Press.

Women's Bureau. n.d. "Survey material for Bulletins nos. 91 and 92." Records of the Women's Bureau, record group 86. Washington, DC: National Archives.

Yzenbaard, John H. and John Hoffman, ed. 1974. "'Between Hope and Fear': The Life of Lettie Teeple, 1:1829–1850." *Michigan History* 58(2) (Fall).

Z.M. 1940. Letter to Eleanor Roosevelt. August 1. Records of the Children's Bureau, record group 102, file 4-9-1-1. Washington, DC: National Archives.

Chapter 2

Anderson, Elijah. 1999. *Code of the Street: Decency, Violence, and the Moral Life of the Inner City*. New York: W. W. Norton.

Baca Zinn, Maxine and Bonnie Thornton Dill. 1994. "Difference and Domination." Pp. 3–12 in *Women of Color in U.S. Society*, edited by Maxine Baca Zinn and Bonnie Thornton Dill. Philadelphia: Temple University Press.

Brooks-Gunn, Jeanne, Greg J. Duncan, P. K. Klebanov, and N. Sealand. 1993. "Do Neighborhoods Influence Child and Adolescent Development?" *American Journal of Sociology* 99(2):353–95.

Cahn, Naomi. 1996. "Pragmatic Questions About Parental Liability Statutes." *Wisconsin Law Review* 3:399–445.

Carnegie Corporation. 1995. *Great transformations: Preparing youth for a new century*. New York: Carnegie Corporation.

Collins, Patricia Hill. 1991. *Black Feminist Thought: Knowledge, Consciousness, and the Politics of Empowerment*. New York: Routledge.

Dohrn, Bernadine. 2000. "'Look Out Kid It's Something You Did': The Criminalization of Children." Pp. 157–187 in *The Public Assault on America's Children: Poverty, Violence, and Juvenile Injustice*, edited by Valerie Polakow. New York: Teachers College Press.

Dryfoos, J. G. 1990. *Adolescents at Risk: Prevalence and Prevention*. Oxford: Oxford University Press.

Furstenberg, Frank F., Thomas D. Cook, Jacquelynne Eccles, Glenn H. Elder, and Arnold Sameroff. 1999. *Managing to Make It: Urban Families and Adolescent Success*. Chicago: University of Chicago Press.

Garey, Anita and Terry Arendell. 2001. "Children, Work, and Family: Some

Thoughts on 'Mother-Blame.'" Pp. 293–304 in *Working Families: The Transformation of the American Home*, edited by Rosanna Hertz and Nancy Marshall. Berkeley: University of California Press.

Glenn, Evelyn Nakano. 1992. "From Servitude to Service Work: Historical Continuities in the Racial Division of Paid Reproductive Labor." *Signs* 18(1): 1–43.

———. 1994. "Social Constructions of Mothering: A Thematic Overview." Pp. 1–29 in *Mothering: Ideology, Experience, and Agency*, edited by Evelyn Nakano Glenn, Grace Chang, and Linda Rennie Forcie. New York: Routledge.

Hays, Sharon. 1996. *The Cultural Contradictions of Motherhood*. New Haven, CT: Yale University Press.

Kurz, Demie. 1995. *For Richer, For Poorer: Mothers Confront Divorce*. New York: Routledge.

———. 2000. "Work- Family Issues of Mothers of Teenage Children." *Qualitative Sociology* 23(4):435–51.

Lareau, Annette. 1989. *Home Advantage: Social Class and Parental Intervention in Elementary Education*. Lanham, MD: Rowman & Littlefield.

Lareau, Annette and Erin McNamara Horvat. 1999. "Moments of Social Inclusion and Exclusion: Race, Class, and Cultural Capital in Family-School Relationships." *Sociology of Education* 72:37–53.

Larson, R. and M. H. Richards. 1994. *Divergent Realities: The Emotional Lives of Mothers, Fathers, and Adolescents*. New York: Basic Books.

Lerner, R. M., Doris R. Entwisle, and Stuart T. Hauser. 1994. "The Crisis Among Contemporary American Adolescents: A Call for the Integration of Research, Policies, and Programs." *Journal of Early Adolescence* 4(1):14.

Lewin, Tamar. 2001. "Surprising Results in Welfare-to-Work Studies." *New York Times*, July 31, p. 16.

Litt, Jacquelyn. 1999. "Managing the Street, Isolating the Household: African American Mothers Respond to Neighborhood Deterioration." *Race, Gender & Class* 6(3):90–108.

Massey, Douglas S. and Nancy A. Denton. 1993. *American Apartheid: Segregation and the Making of the Underclass*. Cambridge, MA: Harvard University Press.

McDonough, Patricia M. 1997. *Choosing Colleges: How Social Class and Schools Structure Opportunity*. Albany: State University of New York Press.

Moore, D. and S. Davenport. 1990. "School Choice: The New Improved Sorting Machine." Pp. 187–223 in *Choice in Education*, edited by William Boyd and Herbert Walberg. Berkeley, CA: McCutchan.

National Research Council. 1996. *Youth Development and Neighborhood Influences: Challenges and Opportunities*. Washington, DC: National Academy Press.

Neild, Ruth. 1999. "Same Difference: School Choice and Educational Access in an Urban District." Dissertation, University of Pennsylvania.

Newman, Katherine S. 1999. *No Shame in My Game: The Working Poor in the Inner City*. New York: Knopf and the Russell Sage Foundation.

Phoenix, Ann, Anne Woollett, and Eva Lloyd, eds. 1991. *Motherhood: Meanings, Practices and Ideologies*. London: Sage.

Polit, Denise F., Andrew S. London, and John M. Martinez. 2001. *The Health of Poor Urban Women: Findings from the Urban Change Project.* New York: Manpower Demonstration Research Corporation.

Roberts, Dorothy. 1995. "Racism and Patriarchy in the Meaning of Motherhood." Pp. 224–49 in *Mothers in Law: Feminist Theory and the Legal Regulation of Motherhood,* edited by Martha A. Fineman and Isabel Karpin. New York: Columbia University Press.

Scott, Ellen K., Kathryn Edin, Andrew S. London, and Joan Maya Mazelis. 2002. "My Children Come First: Welfare-Reliant Women's Post-TANF Views of Work-Family Trade-Offs and Marriage." *For Better or For Worse: Welfare Reform and the Well-being of Children and Families,* edited by Greg J. Duncan and P. Lindsay Chase-Lansdale. New York: Russell Sage Foundation.

Segura, Denise. 1994. "Working at Motherhood: Chicana and Mexican Immigrant Mothers Employment." Pp. 211–33 in *Mothering: Ideology, Experience, and Agency,* edited by Evelyn Nakano Glenn, Grace Chang, and Linda Rennie Forcie. New York: Routledge.

Simons, Ronald L., Christine Johnson, Rand D. Conger, and Frederich O. Lorenz. 1997. "Linking Community Context to Quality of Parenting: A Study of Rural Families. *Rural Sociology* 62(2):207–30.

Wilson, William Julius. 1991. "Studying Inner-City Dislocations: The Challenge of Public Agenda Research." *American Sociological Review* 56(1):1–14.

Zill, Nicholas and Christine W. Nord. 1994. *Running in Place: How American Families are Faring in a Changing Economy and an Individualistic Society.* Washington, DC: Child Trends.

Chapter 3

Anzaldua, Gloria. 1987. *Borderlands/La Frontera: The New Mestiza.* San Francisco: Spinsters.

Cancian, Francesca M. and Stacey Oliker. 2000. *Caring and Gender.* Thousand Oaks, CA: Pine Forge Press.

Collins, Patricia Hill. 2000. *Black Feminist Thought.* New York: Routledge.

Corvalan, Grazziella. 1977. *Paraguay: Nacion bilingue.* Asuncion: Centro Paraguayo de Estudios Sociologicos.

Dushka, Judith. 1996. "The Mormon Caregiving Network." Pp. 278–305 in *Caregiving: Readings in Knowledge, Practice, Ethics, and Politics* edited by S. Gordon, P. Benner, and N. Noddings. Philadelphia: University of Pennsylvania Press.

Emerson, Robert, Rachel Fretz, and Linda Shaw. 1995. *Writing Ethnographic Field Notes.* Chicago: University of Chicago Press.

Etzioni, Amitai. 1996. "The Responsive Community: A Communitarian Perspective." *American Sociological Review* 61(1):1–11.

Fisher, Berenice and Joan Tronto. 1990. "Toward a feminist theory of caring." Pp. 35–62 in *Circles of Care: Work and Identity in Women's Lives* edited by E. Abel and M. Nelson. Albany, NY: SUNY Press.

Fisher, Jo. 1993. *Out of the Shadows: Women, Resistance, and Politics in South America.* London: Latin American Bureau.

Frankenberg, Ruth. 1993. *White Women, Race Matters: The Social Construction of*

Whiteness. Minneapolis: University of Minnesota Press.

Gil, Rosa and Carmen Inoa Vasquez. 1996. *The Maria Paradox: How Latinas Can Merge Old World Traditions with New World Self-Esteem*. New York: Putnam.

Graham, Hilary. 1991. "The Concept of Caring in Feminist Research: The Case of Domestic Service," *Sociology* 25(1):61–78.

Hay, James Eston. 1993. "Tobatí: Tradition and change in a Paraguayan Town." Ph.D. dissertation. Department of Sociology, University of Florida, Gainesville.

Hooyman, Nancy and Judith Gonyea. 1995. *Feminist Perspectives on Family Care: Policies for Gender Justice*. Thousand Oaks, CA: Sage Publications.

Jelin, Elizabeth. 1990. "Citizenship and Identity: Final Reflections." Pp. 184–207 in *Women and Social Change in Latin America*, edited by Elizabeth Jelin. United Nations Research Institute for Social Development. NJ: Zed Books.

Keefe, Susan, Amado Padilla, and Manuel Carlos. 1979. "The Mexican-American Extended as an Emotional Support System." *Human Organization* 38(2):144–52.

Lopez, Rebecca. 1999. "Las comadres as a Social Support System." *Affilia* 14:24–41.

Messerschmidt, Donald. 1982. "Miteri in Nepal: Fictive Kin Ties That Bind." *Kailash* 9:5–43.

Mintz, Sidney and Eric Wolf. 1950. "An Analysis of Ritual Co-Parenthood (Compadrazgo)." *Southwestern Journal of Anthropology* 6(4):341–68.

Mohanty, Chandra, Ann Russo, and Lourdes Torres. 1991. *Third World Women and the Politics of Feminism*. Indianapolis: Indiana University Press.

Monteith, Richard S., Juan Maria Carron, Charles W. Warren, Maria Mercedes Melian, Dario Castagnino, and Leo Morris. 1988. "Contraceptive Use and Fertility in Paraguay, 1987." *Studies in Family Planning* 19(5):284–91.

Neuhouser, Kevin. 1998. "'If I Had Abandoned My Children': Community Mobilization and Commitment to the Identity of Mother in Northeast Brazil." *Social Forces* 77(1):331–58.

Patrinos, Harry, George Psacharopoulos, and Eduardo Velez. 1995. "Educational Performance and Child Labor in Paraguay." *International Journal of Educational Development* 15(1):47–60.

Potthast-Jutkeit, Barbara. 1991. "The Ass of a Mare and Other Scandals: Marriage and Extramarital Relations in Nineteenth-Century Paraguay." *Journal of Family History* 16(3):215–39.

Potthast-Jutkeit, Barbara. 1997. "The Creation of the 'Mestizo Family Model': The Example of Paraguay." *History of the Family* 2(2):123–39.

Psacharopoulos, George, Eduardo Velez, and Harry Anthony Patrinos. 1994. "Education and Earnings in Paraguay." *Economics of Education Review* 13(4):321–27.

Reinharz, Shulamit. 1992. *Feminist Methods in Social Research*. Oxford: Oxford University Press.

Saffilios-Rothschild, Constantina. 1982. "Female Power, Autonomy, and Demographic Change in the Third World." Pp. 117–32 in *Women's Roles and Population Trends in the Third World*, edited by R. Anker, M. Buvinic, and N. Youssef. London: Croom Helm.

Salgado de Snyder, V. Nelly, and Amada Padilla. 1987. "Social support networks: their availability and effectiveness." Pp. 4–7 in *Health and Behavior: Research for*

Hispanics (Monograph Series No. 1), edited by M. Gaviria and J. Arana. Chicago: Simon Bolivar Hispanic American Psychiatric Research and Training Program.

Selznick, Philip. 1992. *The Moral Commonwealth: Social Theory and the Promise of Community.* Berkeley: University of California Press.

Service, Elman and Helen Service. 1954. *Tobatí: Paraguayan Town.* Chicago: University of Chicago Press.

Stack, Carol. 1975. *All Our Kin: Strategies for Survival in a Black Community.* New York: Harper and Row.

Stevens, Evelyn. 1973. "Machismo and Marianismo." *Society* 10:57–63.

Trujillo, Jaime. 1987. "Sexual Attitudes and Pregnancy in Lower Class Hispanic Women: Psychological Aspects." Pp. 233–38 in *Health and Behavior: Research for Hispanics* (Monograph Series No. 1), edited by M. Gaviria and J. Arana. Chicago: Simon Bolivar Hispanic American Psychiatric Research and Training Program.

Vaughan, Megan. 1983. "Which Family? Problems in the Reconstruction of the History of the Family as an Economic and Cultural Unit." *Journal of African History* 24:275–83.

Vidal, Carlos. 1988. "Godparenting Among Hispanic Americans." *Child Welfare* 67(5):453–59.

Chapter 4

Coontz, Stephanie. 1988. *The Social Origins of Private Life.* London: Verso.

Cowan, Carolyn and Philip Cowane. 1992. *When Partners Become Parents.* New York: Basic Books.

Davidoff, Leonore and Catherine Hall. 1987. *Family Fortunes: Men and Women of the English Middle Class.* Chicago: University of Chicago Press.

Entwisle, Doris and Susan Doering, 1981. *The First Birth: An American Turning Point.* Baltimore: Johns Hopkins University Press.

Fox, Bonnie. 1997. "Reproducing Difference: Changes in the Lives of Couples Becoming Parents." Pp. 142–62 in *Feminism and Families: Critical Policies and Changing Practices*, edited by M. Luxton. Halifax: Fernwood Press.

Fox, Bonnie. 1998. "Motherhood, Changing Relationships and the Reproduction of Gender Inequality." Pp. 159–74 in *Redefining Motherhood: Changing Identities and Patterns*, edited by S. Abbey and A. O'Reilly. Toronto: Second Story Press.

Fox, Bonnie and Diana Worts. 1999. "Revisiting the Critique of Medicalized Childbirth: A Contribution to the Sociology of Birth." *Gender and Society* 13:326–346.

Glenn, Evelyn Nakano. 2000. "Creating a Caring Society." *Contemporary Sociology* 29:84–94.

Goldscheider, Frances and Linda Waite. 1991. *New Families, No Families? The Transformation of the American Home.* Berkeley: University of California Press.

Hays, Sharon. 1996. *The Cultural Contradictions of Motherhood.* New Haven, CT: Yale University Press.

Hochschild, Arlie. 1989. *The Second Shift: Working Parents and the Revolution at Home.* New York: Viking.

LaRossa, Ralph. 1998. "The Culture and Conduct of Fatherhood." Pp. 377–84 in *Families in the United States: Kinship and Domestic Politics*, edited by K. Hansen and A. Garey. Philadelphia: Temple University Press.

Luxton, Meg. 1980. *More Than a Labour of Love: Three Generations of Women's Work in the Home*. Toronto: Women's Press.

Luxton, Meg. 2001. "Family Coping Strategies: Balancing Paid Employment and Domestic Work." Pp. 318–38 in *Family Patterns, Gender Relations*, edited by B. J. Fox. Toronto: Oxford University Press.

MacDermid, Shelley, Ted Huston, and Susan McHale. 1990. "Changes in Marriage Associated with the Transition to Parenthood: Individual Differences as a Function of Sex-role Attitudes and Changes in the Division of Household Labour." *Journal of Marriage and the Family* 52:475–86.

McMahon, Anthony. 1999. *Taking Care of Men: Sexual Politics in the Public Mind*. Cambridge, MA: Harvard University Press.

Perkins, Wesley and Debra DeMeis. 1996. "Gender and Family Effects on 'Second-Shift' Domestic Activity of College-Educated Young Adults." *Gender and Society* 10:78–93.

Rexroat, Cynthia and Constance Shehan. 1987. "The Family Life Cycle and Spouses' Time in Housework." *Journal of Marriage and the Family* 49:737–50.

Rosenberg, Harriet. 1987. "Motherwork, Stress and Depression: The Costs of Privatized Social Reproduction." Pp. 181–96 in *Feminism and Political Economy: Women's Work, Women's Struggles*, edited by H. J. Maroney and M. Luxton. Toronto: Methuen.

Ryan, Mary, 1981. *Cradle of the Middle Class: The Family in Oneida County, 1790–1865*. Cambridge: Cambridge University Press

Taylor, Verta. 1996. *Rock-a-by Baby: Feminism, Self-Help and Postpartum Depression*. New York and London: Routledge.

Walzer, Susan. 1998. *Thinking About the Baby: Gender and Transitions into Parenthood*. Philadelphia: Temple University Press.

Chapter 5

Abel, Emily K. and Margaret K. Nelson, eds. 1990. *Circles of Care*. Albany: State University of New York Press.

Abramovitz, Mimi. 1988. *Regulating the Lives of Women: Social Welfare Policy From Colonial Times to the Present*. Madison: University of Wisconsin Press.

Ahn, Helen Noh. 1994. "Cultural Diversity and the Definition of Child Abuse." Pp. 28–55 in *Child Welfare Research Review, Volume 1*, edited by Richard Barth, Jill Duerr Berrick, and Neil Gilbert. New York: Columbia University Press.

Amato, Paul R. and Joan G. Gilbreth. 1999. "Nonresident Fathers and Children's Well-Being: A Meta-Analysis." *Journal of Marriage and the Family* 61:557–73.

Barth, Richard, Mark Courtney, Jill Duerr Berrick, and Vicky Albert. 1994. *From Child Abuse to Permanency Planning: Child Welfare Services Pathways and Placements*.

Baumrind, Diana. 1967. "Child Care Practices Anteceding 3 Patterns of Preschool Behavior." *Genetic Psychology Monographs* 75:43–88.

———. 1972. "An Exploratory Study of Socialization Effects on Black Children: Some Black-White Comparisons." *Child Development* 43:261–67.

Bellah, Robert, Richard Madsen, William Sullivan, Ann Swidler, and Steven Tipton. 1985. *Habits of the Heart*. Berkeley: University of California Press.

Bowlby, John. 1969. *Attachment and Loss, I*. New York: Basic Books.

Brazelton, T. Berry and Stanley I. Greenspan. 2000. *The Irreducible Needs of Children*. Cambridge, MA: Perseus.

Bronfenbrenner, Urie. 1958. "Socialization and Social Class Through Time and Space." Pp. 400–25 in *Readings in Social Psychology*, edited by Eleanor E. Maccoby, Robert Newcomb, and E. Harley. New York: Holt, Rinehart and Winston.

Brown, Annie Woodley, and Barbara Bailey-Etta. 1997. "An Out-of-Home Care System in Crisis: Implications for African American Children in the Child Welfare System." *Child Welfare* 76:65–83.

Burton, Linda, Donald Hernandez, and Sandra Hofferth. 1998. *Families, Youth, and Children's Well Being*. Washington, DC: American Sociological Association.

Cancian, Francesca M. 1987. *Love in America*. NY: Cambridge University Press.

Cancian, Francesca M. 2000. "Participatory Research. Pp. 1427–32 in *Encyclopedia of Sociology, Volume 3*, edited by Edgar Borgatta and Marie Borgatta. New York: Macmillan.

Cancian, Francesca M. and Stacey J. Oliker. 2000. *Caring and Gender*. Thousand Oaks, CA: Pine Forge Press.

Carrington, Christopher. 1999. *Home: Relationships and Family Life Among Lesbians and Gay Men*. Chicago: University of Chicago Press.

Chao, Ruth K. 1994. "Beyond Parental Control and Authoritarian Parenting Style: Understanding Chinese Parenting Through the Cultural Notion of Training." *Child Development* 65:1111–19.

Courtney, Mark. 1994. "Factors Associated with the Reunification of Foster Children with Their Families." *Social Service Review* 68:81–108.

Dornbusch, Sanford, P.L. Ritter, P. H. Leiderman, D. F. Roberts, and M. J. Fraleigh. 1987. "The Relation of Parenting Style to Adolescent School Performance." *Child Development* 58:1244–57.

Ehrenreich, Barbara and Deirdre English. 1978. *For Her Own Good? Fifty Years of Experts' Advice to Women*. New York: Doubleday.

England, Paula. 1992. *Comparable Worth: Theories and Evidence*. New York: Aldine De Gruyter.

Foner, Nancy. 1994. *The Caregiving Dilemma: Work in the American Nursing Home*. Berkeley: University of California Press.

Furstenberg, Frank F., Jr. 1993. "How Families Manage Risk and Opportunity in Dangerous Neighborhoods." Pp. 231–58 in *Sociology and the Public Agenda*, edited by William J. Wilson. Newbury Park, CA: Sage.

Gauthier, Anne Helene. 1996. *The State and the Family*. New York: Oxford University Press.

Golden, Renny. 1997. *Disposable Children: America's Child Welfare System*. Belmont, CA: Wadsworth.

Gordon, Linda. 1988. *Heroes of Their Own Lives: The Politics and History of Family Violence*. New York: Viking.

Gray, Marjory R. and Laurence Steinberg. 1999. "Unpacking Authoritative

Parenting: Reassessing a Multidimensional Construct." *Journal of Marriage and the Family* 61:574–87.

Hampton, R., and E. Newberger. 1985. "Child Abuse Incidence and Reporting by Hospitals: Significance of Severity, Class, and Race." *American Journal of Public Health* 75:56–60.

Harris, Judith Rich. 1995. "Where Is the Child's Environment? A Group Socialization Theory of Development." *Psychological Review* 102:458–89.

Harwood, Robin L., Axel Schoelmerich, Pamela A. Schulze, and Zenaida Gonzalez. 1999. "Cultural Differences in Maternal Beliefs and Behaviors: A Study of Middle-Class Anglo and Puerto Rican Mother–Infant Pairs in Four Everyday Situations." *Child Development* 70:1005–16.

Hays, Sharon. 1996. *The Cultural Contradictions of Motherhood.* New Haven, CT: Yale University Press.

Kohn, Melvin L. and Carmie Schooler. 1983. *Work and Personality.* Norwood, NJ: Ablex.

Larson, Patricia J. and Marylin J. Dodd. 1991. "The Cancer Treatment Experience: Family Patterns of Caring." Pp. 61–78 in *Caring: The Compassionate Healer,* edited by Delores Gaut and Madeleine M. Leininger. New York: National League for Nursing Press.

Lofland, John and Lyn Lofland. 1995. *Analyzing Social Settings: A Guide to Qualitative Observational Analysis.* Belmont, CA: Wadsworth.

Lubeck, Sally. 1985. *Sandbox Society: Early Education in Black and White America.* London: Falmer.

Maccoby, Eleanor E. and J. A. Martin. 1983. "Socialization in the Context of the Family: Parent–Child Interaction." Pp. 1–101 in *Handbook of Child Psychology,* Vol. 4, edited by Paul H. Mussen. New York: John Wiley.

Margolis, Maxine. 1984. *Mothers and Such: Views of American Women and Why They Changed.* Berkeley: University of California Press.

Marx, Karl. 1972. "The German Ideology." Pp. 110–64 in *The Marx-Engels Reader,* edited by Robert C. Tucker. New York: W. W. Norton.

McLoyd, Vonnie C. 1990. "The Impact of Economic Hardship on Black Families and Children: Psychological Distress, Parenting, and Socioemotional Development." *Child Development* 61:311–46.

Meyer, Madonna Harrington, ed. 2000. *Care Work: Gender, Labor, and Welfare States.* New York: Routledge.

Miller, J. and S. Korenman. 1994. "Poverty and Children's Nutritional Status in the United States." *American Journal of Epidemiology* 140:233–43.

National Academy of Sciences, National Research Council Panel on High-Risk Youth. 1993. *Losing Generations: Adolescents in High-Risk Settings.* Washington, DC: National Academy Press.

Noddings, Nell. 1984. *Caring: A Feminine Approach to Ethics and Moral Education.* Berkeley: University of California Press.

Ogbu, John U. 1981. "Origins of Human Competence: A Cultural-Ecological Perspective." *Child Development* 52:413–29.

Olds, David, John Eckenrode, Charles R. Henderson, Jr., Harriet Kitzman, Jane Powers, Robert Cole, Kim Sidora, P. Morris, Lisa Pettitt, and Dennis Luckey.

1997. "Long-Term Effects of Home Visitation on Maternal Life Course and Child Abuse and Neglect: 15-Year Follow-Up of a Randomized Trial." *Journal of the American Medical Association* 278:637–43.

Parke, Ross D. and Raymond Buriel. 1998. "Socialization in the Family: Ethnic and Ecological Perspectives." Pp. 463–552 in *Handbook of Child Psychology*, 5th edition, vol. 3, edited by Nancy Eisenberg. New York: John Wiley & Sons.

Pyke, Karen. 2000. "The Normal American Family as an Interpretive Structure of Family Life Among Grown Children of Korean and Vietnamese Immigrant." *Journal of Marriage and the Family* 62:240–55.

Ruddick, Sara. 1995. *Maternal Thinking: Towards a Politics of Peace*. Boston: Beacon.

Scheper-Hughes, Nancy. 1992. *Death Without Weeping: The Violence of Everyday Life in Brazil*. Berkeley: University of California Press.

Sherman, Arloc. 1994. *Wasting America's Future: The Children's Defense Fund's Report on the Costs of Child Poverty*. Boston: Beacon.

Silva, Elizabeth Bortolaia, ed. 1996. *Good Enough Mothering? Feminist Perspectives on Lone Motherhood*. New York: Routledge.

Skolnick, Arlene. 1991. *Embattled Paradise: The American Family in an Age of Uncertainty*. New York: Basic Books.

Smith, J., J. Brooks-Gunn, and P. Clebanov. 1997. "Consequences of Growing up Poor for Young Children." Pp. 212–31 in *Consequences of Growing up Poor*. New York: Russell Sage.

Spencer, Margaret Beale. 1990. "Development of Minority Children: An Introduction." *Child Development* 61:267–69.

Stacey, Judith. 1998. "The Right Family Values." Pp. 859–80 in *Families in the U.S*, edited by Karen Hansen and Anita Garey. Philadelphia: Temple University Press.

Steinberg, Laurence, Susie D. Lamborn, Sanford M. Dornbusch, and Nancy Darling. 1992. "Impact of Parenting Practices on Adolescent Achievement: Authoritative Parenting, School Involvement, and Encouragement to Succeed." *Child Development* 63:1266–81.

Suransky, Valerie. 1982. *The Erosion of Childhood*. Chicago: University of Chicago Press.

Thompson, Ross A. 1997. "Early Sociopersonality Development." Pp. 25–104 in *Handbook of Child Psychology*, 5th edition, vol. 3, edited by Nancy Eisenberg. NY: John Wiley.

van den Boom, D. C. 1994. "The Influence of Temperament and Mothering on Attachment and Exploration: An Experimental Manipulation of Sensitive Responsiveness Among Lower-Class Mothers with Irritable Infants." *Child Development* 65:1457–77.

Wendland-Carro, Jacqueline, Cesar Piccinini, and W. Stuart Millar. 1999. "The Role of an Early Intervention on Enhancing the Quality of Mother-Infant Interaction." *Child Development* 70:713–21.

Winnicott, Donald Woods. 1964. *The Child, The Family, and the Outside World*. London: Penguin.

——. 1987. *Babies and Mothers*. Reading, MA: Addison-Wesley.

Chapter 6

Baile, Kathleen A. 1998. "Note: The Other 'Neglected' Parties in Child Protection Proceedings: Parents in Poverty and the Role of the Lawyer Who Represents Them." *Fordham Law Review* 66:2285.

Berrick, Jill Duerr. 1998. "When Children Cannot Remain Home: Foster Care and Kinship Care." Pp. 72–81 in *Protecting Children from Abuse and Neglect*. Vol. 8.1 of *The Future of Children*. Los Altos, CA: David and Lucille Packard Foundation.

Besharov, Douglas. 1998. "Commentary: How Can We Better Protect Children From Abuse and Neglect?" Pp. 120–23 in *Protecting Children from Abuse and Neglect*. Vol. 8.1 of *The Future of Children* 8:1. Los Altos, CA: David and Lucille Packard Foundation.

Cahn, Naomi R. 1997. "Review Essay: The Moral Complexities of Family Law." *Stanford Law Review* 50:225.

Courtney, Mark E. 1998. "The Costs of Child Protection in the Context of Welfare Reform." Pp. 88–103 in *Protecting Children from Abuse and Neglect*. Vol. 8.1 of *The Future of Children*. Los Altos, CA: David and Lucille Packard Foundation.

Czapanskiy, Karen. 1999. "Interdependencies, Families, and Children." *Santa Clara Law Review* 39:957.

Davis, Peggy Cooper. 1997. *Neglected Stories: The Constitution and Family Values*. New York: Hill & Wang.

Dohrn, Bernadine. 2000. "Care and Adoption Reform Legislation: Implementing the Adoption and Safe Families Act of 1997." *St. John's Journal of Legal Commentary* 14:419.

Fineman, Martha A. 1995. *The Neutered Mother, The Sexual Family, and Other Twentieth century Tragedies*. New York: Routledge.

Gelles, Richard. 1996. *The Book of David: How Preserving Families Can Cost Children's Lives*. New York: Basic Books.

Glendon, Mary Ann. 1989. *The Transformation of Family Law: State, Law and Family in Western Europe and The United States*. Chicago: University of Chicago Press.

Gordon, Robert M. 1999. "Drifting Through Byzantium: The Promise and Failure of the Adoption and Safe Families Act of 1997." *Minnesota Law Review* 83:637.

Guggenheim, Martin. 1999. "The Foster Care Dilemma and What To Do About It: Is the Problem That Too Many Children Are Not Being Adopted Out of Foster Care or That Too Many Children Are Entering Foster Care?" *University of Pennsylvania Journal of Constitutional Law* 2:141.

London, Andrew S., Ellen K. Scott, and Vicki Hunter. 2002. "Health-Related Carework for Children in the Context of Welfare Reform." In *Child Care and Inequality: Rethinking Carework for Children and Youth*. New York: Routledge.

Lowery, Marcia Robinson. 1998. "Commentary: How We Can Better Protect Children from Abuse and Neglect." Pp. 123–26 in *Protecting Children from Abuse and Neglect*. Vol. 8.1 of *The Future of Children*. Los Altos, CA: David and Lucille Packard Foundation.

National Commission on Children. 1991. *Beyond Rhetoric: A New American Agenda for Children and Families*. Washington, DC: U.S. Government Printing Office.

National Committee to Prevent Child Abuse. 1996. *Current Trends in Child Abuse Reporting and Fatalities: The Results of the 1995 Fifty State Survey.* Chicago, IL: National Committee to Prevent Child Abuse.

Pagano, Cecile. 1999. "Recent Legislation: Adoption and Foster Care." *Harvard Journal on Legislation* 36:242.

Rimer, Sara. 2001. "Desperate Measures—A Special Report: Embattled Parents Seek Help At Any Cost." *New York Times*, September 10, p. A1.

Roberts, Dorothy E. 1999. "Is There Justice In Children's Rights?: The Critique of Federal Family Preservation Policy." *University of Pennsylvania Journal of Constitutional Law* 2:112.

Schultz, Vicki. 2000. "Life's Work." *Columbia Law Review* 100:1881.

Silver, Judith A., ed. 1999. *Young Children and Foster Care.* Baltimore, MD: Brookes Publishing.

Traub, James. 2001. "Bleak House." *New York Times Book Review*, May 17, p. 24.

Williams, Carol W. 1997. "Personal Reflections on Permanency Planning and Cultural Competency." *Journal of Multicultural Social Work* 5:9.

Woodhouse, Barbara Bennett. 1992. "'Who Owns the Child?' Meyer and Pierce and the Child as Property." *William and Mary Law Review* 33:995.

———, 1996. "'It All Depends On What You Mean By Home?':Towards a Communitarium Theory of the Non-Traditional Family." *Utah Law Review* 1996:569.

———. 1999. "The Constitutionalization of Children's Rights: Incorporating Emerging Human Rights into Constitutional Doctrine." *University of Pennsylvania Journal of Constitutional Law* 2:1.

Cases

Meyer v. Nebraska. 1923. 262 U.S. 390.

Prince v. Massachusetts. 1944. 321 U.S. 158.

Santosky v. Kramer. 1982. 455 U.S. 755.

Stanley v. Illinois. 1972. 405 U.S. 645.

Wisconsin v. Yoder. 1972 406 U.S. 205.

Statutes and Government Documents

Adoption and Safe Families Act. 1997. Pub. L. No. 105-89, 111 Stat (codified as amended in scattered sections of 42 U.S.C.).

Adoption Assistance and Child Welfare Act. 1980. Pub. L. No. 96-262 (codified at 42 U.S.C. §§620 to 629a and 670 to 679a.

Family Preservation and Support Act. 1993. Pub. L. No. 103-66.

Temporary Assistance to Needy Families. 1996. Title III, Public L. No. 104 to 193, Stat. 2105.

U.S. Department of Health and Human Services Administration for Children and Families. 1998. *Final Report of Children Placed in Foster Care with Relatives: A Multi-State Study.* November 19.

42 U.S.C. §671(15).

42 U.S.C. §671(D) to (E).

42 U.S.C. §673.

42 U.S.C. §675(E).

42 U.S.C. §1996b.

143 Cong. Rec. S12210 et seq. 1997.

143 Cong. Rec. S12211. 1997. Statement of Senator Grassley of Iowa (daily ed. November 8).

143 Cong. Rec. S12198. 1997.

143 Cong. Rec. S12671. 1997. Statement of Senator Rockefeller. (daily ed. November 13).

143 Cong. Rec. S12673. 1997. Statement of Senator Craig of Idaho. November 13.

Chapter 7

Abel, Emily K. and Margaret K. Nelson. 1990. "Circles of Care: An Introductory Essay." Pp. 4–34 in *Circles of Care: Work and Identity in Women's Lives*, edited by Emily K. Abel and Margaret K. Nelson. Albany: State University of New York Press.

Aron, Laudan Y., Pamela J. Loprest, and C. Eugene Steuerle. 1996. *Serving Children with Disabilities: A Systematic Look at the Programs*. Washington, DC: Urban Institute Press.

Breslau, Naomi, David Salkever, and Kathleen S. Staruch. 1982. "Women's Labor Force Activity and Responsibilities for Disabled Dependents: A Study of Families with Disabled Children." *Journal of Health and Social Behavior* 23:169–83.

Cancian, Francesca and Stacey J. Oliker. 2000. *Caring and Gender*. Thousand Oaks, CA: Pine Forge Press.

Chavkin, Wendy. 1999. "What's a Mother to Do? Welfare, Work, and Family." *American Journal of Public Health* 89:477–79.

Danziger, Sandra, Mary Corcoran, Sheldon Danziger, Colleen Heflin, Ariel Kalil, Judith Levine, Daniel Rosen, Kristen Seefeldt, Kristine Siefert, and Richard Tolman. 2000. "Barriers to the Employment of Welfare Recipients." Pp. 245–78 in *Prosperity for All? The Economic Boom and African Americans*, edited by R. Cherry and W. M. Rodgers. New York: Russell Sage.

Harrington Meyer, Madonna, ed. 2000. *Care Work: Gender, Labor, and the Welfare State*. New York: Routledge.

Harrington Meyer, Madonna, Pam Herd, and Sonya Michel. 2000. "Introduction: The Right to—or No to—Care." Pp. 1–4 in *Care Work: Gender, Labor, and the Welfare State*, edited by Madonna Harrington Meyer. New York: Routledge.

Harrington Meyer, Madonna, and Michelle Kesterke Storbakken. 2000. "Shifting the Burden Back to Families? How Medicaid Cost-Containment Reshapes Access to Long Term Care in the United States." Pp. 217–28 in *Care Work: Gender, Labor, and the Welfare State*, edited by Madonna Harrington Meyer. New York: Routledge.

Heymann, S. Jody, Alison Earle, and B. Egleston. 1996. "Parental Availability for the Care of Sick Children." *Pediatrics* 98:226–30.

Heymann, S. Jody and Alison Earle. 1999. "The Impact of Welfare Reform on Parents' Ability to Care for Their Children's Health." *American Journal of Public Health* 89:502–5.

Jacobs, Philip and Suzanne McDermott. 1989. "Family Caregiver Costs of Chronically Ill and Handicapped Children: Method and Literature Review." *Public Health Reports* 104:158–63.

Leonard, Barbara, Janny Dwyer Brust, and James J. Sapienza. 1992. "Financial and Time Costs to Parents of Severely Disabled Children." *Public Health Reports* 107:302–12.

Litt, Jacquelyn, Cynthia Needles Fletcher, and Mary Winter. 2001. "Health-Related Carework in Low-Income Households: The Special Case of Children with Disabilities." Paper presented at the Conference on Carework, Inequality, and Advocacy, Irvine, CA, August 17.

London, Andrew S., Ellen K. Scott, Rebecca Joyce, Kathryn Edin, and Vicki Hunter. 2001. *Juggling Low-Wage and Family Life: What Mothers Have to Say About Their Children's Well-Being in the Context of Welfare Reform*. New York: Manpower Demonstration Corporation.

Loprest, Pamela J. and Gregory Acs. 1996. *Profile of Disability Among Families on AFDC*. Washington, DC: Urban Institute.

Lukemeyer, Anna, Marcia K. Meyers, and Timothy Smeeding. 2000. "Expensive Children in Poor Families: Out-of-Pocket Expenditures for the Care of Disabled and Chronically Ill Children in Welfare Families." *Journal of Marriage and the Family* 62:399–415.

McLeod, Jane D. and Michael J. Shanahan. 1996. "Trajectories of Poverty and Children's Mental Health." *Journal of Health and Social Behavior* 37:207–20.

Meyers, Marcia K., Anna Lukemeyer, and Timothy Smeeding. 1996. *Work, Welfare, and the Burden of Disability: Caring for Special Needs of Children in Poor Families*. Syracuse, NY: Center for Policy Research, Maxwell School of Citizenship and Public Affairs, Syracuse University. Income Security Policy Series, Paper No. 12.

Miller, Jane E. 2000. "The Effects of Race/Ethnicity and Income on Early Childhood Asthma Prevalence and Health Care Use." *American Journal of Public Health* 90:428–30.

Montgomery, Laura E., John L. Kiely, and Gregory Pappas. 1996. "The Effects of Poverty, Race, and Family Structure on U.S. Children's Health." *American Journal of Public Health* 86:1401–5.

Newacheck, Paul W. 1994. "Poverty and Childhood Chronic Illness." *Archives of Pediatric and Adolescent Medicine* 148:1143–49.

Neysmith, Sheila M., ed. 2000. *Restructuring Caring Labour: Discourse, State Practice, and Everyday Life*. Toronto: Oxford University Press Canada.

Oliker, Stacey J. 1995a. "The Proximate Contexts of Workfare and Work: A Framework for Studying Poor Women's Economic Choices." *The Sociological Quarterly* 36:251–72.

Oliker, Stacey J. 1995b. "Work Commitment and Constraint Among Mothers on Workfare." *Journal of Contemporary Ethnography* 24:165–94.

Oliker, Stacey J. 2000. "Examining Care at Welfare's End." Pp. 167–85 in *Care Work: Gender, Labor, and the Welfare State*, edited by Madonna Harrington Meyer. New York: Routledge.

Polit, Denise F., Andrew S. London, and John M. Martinez. 2001. *The Health of*

Poor Urban Women: Findings from the Project on Devolution and Urban Change. New York: MDRC.

Quint, Janet, Kathryn Edin, Maria L. Buck, Barbara Fink, Yolanda C. Padilla, Olis Simmons- Hewitt, and Mary E. Valmont. 1999. *Big Cities and Welfare Reform: Early Implementation and Ethnographic Findings From the Project on Devolution and Urban Change*. New York: MDRC.

Rosman, Elisa and Jane Knitzer. 2001. "Welfare Reform: The Special Case of Children with Disabilities and Their Families." *Infants and Young Children* 13:25–35.

Salkever, David S. 1982. "Children's Health Status and Maternal Work Status." *Journal of Human Resources* 17:94–109.

Salkever, David S. 1990. "Children's Health and Other Determinants of Single Mother's Labor Supply and Earnings." *Research on Human Capital Development* 6:147–81.

Scott, Ellen K., Kathryn Edin, Andrew S. London, and Joan Maya Mazelis. 2001. "My Children Come First: Welfare-Reliant Women's Post-TANF Views of Work-Family Trade-Offs and Marriage." Pp. 132–53 in *For Better and For Worse: Welfare Reform and the Well-Being of Children and Families*, edited by Greg J. Duncan and P. Lindsay Chase-Lansdale. New York: Russell Sage Foundation.

Scott, Ellen K., Kathryn Edin, Andrew S. London, and Rebecca Joyce Kissane. 2001. "Unstable Work, Unstable Income: Implications for Family Well-Being in the Era of Time-Limited Welfare." New York: Manpower Demonstration Research Corporation.

Scott, Ellen K., Andrew S. London, and Kathryn Edin. 2000. "Looking to the Future: Welfare-Reliant Women Talk About Their Job Aspirations in the Context of Welfare Reform." *Journal of Social Issues* 56:727–46.

Scott, Ellen K., Andrew S. London, and Nancy Myers. 2002. "Living With Violence: Women's Reliance on Abusive Men in their Transitions from Welfare to Work." Pp. 302–16 in *Families At Work: Expanding the Bounds*, N. Gerstel, D. Clawson, and R. Zussman. Nashville, TN: Vanderbilt University Press.

Seccombe, Karen. 1999. *"So You Think I Drive a Cadillac?": Welfare Recipients' Perspectives on the System and Its Reform*. Boston: Allyn and Bacon.

Stone, Deborah. 2000. "Caring by the Book." Pp. 89–111 in *Care Work: Gender, Labor, and the Welfare State*, edited by Madonna Harrington Meyer. New York: Routledge.

Ungerson, Clare. 2000. "Cash in Care." Pp. 69–88 in *Care Work: Gender, Labor, and the Welfare State* edited by Madonna Harrington Meyer. New York: Routledge.

Williams, David and Chiquita Collins. 1995. "Socioeconomic and Racial Differences in Health." *Annual Review of Sociology* 21:349–86.

Chapter 8

Behrendt, Christina. 2000. "Do Means-Tested Transfers Alleviate Poverty? Evidence on Germany, Sweden and the United Kingdom from the Luxembourg Income Study." *Journal of European Social Policy* 10(1):23–41.

Bergmann, Barbara R. 1996. *Saving Our Children From Poverty: What the United States Can Learn From France*. New York: Russell Sage Foundation.

Cancian, Francesca and Stacey Oliker. 2000. *Caring and Gender.* Thousand Oaks, CA: Pine Forge Press.

Casper, Lynne M., Sara McLanahan, and Irwin Garfinkel. 1994. "The Gender-Poverty Gap: What We Can Learn From Other Countries." *American Sociological Review* 59:594–605.

Christopher, Karen, Paula England, Sara McLanahan, Katherin Ross, and Timothy Smeeding. 2001. "Gender Inequality in Poverty in Affluent Nations: The Role of Single Motherhood and the State." Pp. 199–219 in *Child Well-being, Child Poverty and Child Policy in Modern Nations,* edited by K. Vleminckx and T. Smeeding. Bristol: Policy Press.

Christopher, Karen. "Welfare State Regimes and Mothers' Poverty." Forthcoming in *Social Politics* 9(1).

Esping-Andersen, Gosta. 1990. *The Three Worlds of Welfare Capitalism.* Princeton, NJ: Princeton University Press.

Esping-Andersen, Gosta. 1999. *Social Foundations of Post-Industrial Economies.* Oxford: Oxford University Press.

Glenn, Evelyn Nakano. 2000. "Creating a Caring Society." *Contemporary Sociology* 29(1):84–94.

Gornick, Janet, Marcia K. Meyers, and Katherin E. Ross. 1998. "Public Policies and the Employment of Mothers: A Cross-National Study." *Social Science Quarterly* 79(1):35–54.

Gustafsson, Siv. 1995. "Single Mothers in Sweden: Why is Poverty Less Severe?" Pp. 291–326 in *Poverty, Inequality, and the Future of Social Policy,* edited by K. McFate, R. Lawson, and W. J. Wilson. New York: Russell Sage.

Hernes, Helga. 1987. *Welfare State and Woman Power: Essays in State Feminism.* Oslo: Norwegian University Press.

Hobson, Barbara. 1994. "Solo Mothers, Social Policy Regimes and the Logics of Gender." Pp. 170–87 in *Gendering Welfare States,* edited by D. Sainsbury. London: Sage.

Hochshild, Arlie R. 1995. "The Culture of Politics: Traditional, Postmodern, Cold-modern, and Warm-modern Ideals of Care." *Social Politics* 2(3):331–46.

Kenworthy, Lane. 1999. "Do Social-Welfare Policies Reduce Poverty? A Cross-National Assessment." *Social Forces* 77(3):1119–39.

Knijn, Trudie and Monique Kremer. 1997. "Gender and the Caring Dimension of Welfare States: Toward Inclusive Citizenship." *Social Politics* 4(3):328–61.

Knijn, Trudie and Clare Ungerson. 1997. "Introduction: Care Work and Gender in Welfare Regimes." *Social Politics* 4(3):323–27.

Korpi, Walter. 2000. "Faces of Inequality: Gender, Class, and Patterns of Inequalities in Different Types of Welfare States." *Social Politics* 7(2):127–91.

Leira, Arnlaug. 1998. "Caring as a Social Right: Cash for Childcare and Daddy Leave." *Social Politics* 5(3):362–78.

Lewis, Jane. 1992. "Gender and the Development of Welfare Regimes." *Journal of European Social Policy* 2(3):159–73.

Lewis, Jane and Barbara Hobson. 1997. "Introduction." Pp. 1–20 in *Lone Mothers in European Welfare Regimes,* edited by J. Lewis. London: Jessica Kingsley .

Lister, Ruth. 1995. "Dilemmas in Engendering Citizenship." *Economy and Society* 24(1):1–40.

McFate, Katherine, Timothy Smeeding, and Lee Rainwater. 1995. "Markets and States: Poverty Trends and Transfer System Effectiveness in the 1980s." Pp. 29–66 in *Poverty, Inequality, and the Future of Social Policy*, edited by K. McFate, R. Lawson, and W. J. Wilson. New York: Russell Sage.

O'Connor, Julia. 1993. "Gender, Class and Citizenship in the Comparative Analysis of Welfare State Regimes: Theoretical and Methodological Issues." Pp. 17–31 in *Beyond Equality and Difference: Citizenship, Feminist Politics, and Female Subjectivity*, edited by G. Bock and S. James. New York: Routledge.

O'Connor, Julia S., Ann S. Orloff, and Sheila Shaver. 1999. *States, Markets, Families: Gender, Liberalism, and Social Policy in Australia, Canada, Great Britain, and the U.S.* Cambridge: Cambridge University Press.

Orloff, Anne Shola. 1993. "Gender and the Social Rights of Citizenship." *American Sociological Review* 58:303–28.

Orloff, Ann Shola. 1999. "The Significance of Changing Gender Relations and Family Forms for Systems of Social Protection." A study prepared for the World Labour Report. International Labour Organization.

Sainsbury, Diane. 1994. "Introduction." Pp. 1–7 in *Gendering Welfare States*, edited by D. Sainsbury. London: Sage.

Sainsbury, Diane. 1996. *Gender, Equality, and Welfare States*. Cambridge: Cambridge University Press.

Chapter 9

Abel, Emily K. 2000. "A Historical Perspective on Care." *Care Work: Gender, Labor and the Welfare State*. Edited by Madonna Harrington Meyer. New York: Routledge.

AFSCME. 2001. American Federation of State, County, and Municipal Employees. *Cheating Dignity: The Direct Care Wage Crisis in America*. Available at www.afscme.org/pol-leg/cd01.htm

Becker, Gary S. 1991. *A Treatise on the Family*. Cambridge, MA: Harvard University Press.

———. 1975. *Human Capital*. Chicago: University of Chicago Press.

Budig, Michelle and Paula England. 2001. "The Wage Penalty for Motherhood." *American Sociological Review* 66:204–25.

Burggraf, Shirley P. 1997. *The Feminine Economy and Economic Man*. Reading, MA: Addison-Wesley.

Canter, D., J. Waldfogel, and J. Kerwin, et al., 2001. *Balancing the Needs of Families and Employers: Family and Medical Leave Surveys, 2000 update*. Rockville, MD: Westat.

Currie, Janet. 2001. "Early Childhood Education Programs." *Journal of Economic Perspectives* 15(2):213–38.

Duncan, Greg J., and Jeanne Brooks-Gunn, eds. 1997. *Consequences of Growing Up Poor*. New York: Russell Sage Foundation.

England, Paula. 1992. *Comparable Worth: Theories and Evidence*. Hawthorne, NY: Aldine de Gruyter.

England, Paula. 1993. "The Separative Self: Androcentric Bias in Neoclassical Assumptions." Pp. 37–53 in *Beyond Economic Man*, edited by Marianne Ferber and Julie Nelson, Chicago: University of Chicago Press.

England, Paula and Nancy Folbre. 1999a. "The Cost of Caring." *Annals of the American Academy of Political and Social Sciences* 561:39–51.

England, Paula, and Nancy Folbre. 2002. "Reforming the Social Family Contract" in *For Better or Worse: Welfare Reform and the Well-Being of Children and Families*. Edited by Lindsay Chase-Lansdale and Greg Duncan. New York: Russell Sage.

England, Paula and Barbara Kilbourne. 1990. "Markets, Marriage, and Other Mates: The Problem of Power." Pp. 163–188 in *Beyond the Marketplace: Society and Economy*, edited by Roger Friedland and Sandy Robertson. New York: Aldine.

England, Paula, Michelle Budig, and Nancy Folbre. 2002. "The Wages of Virtue: The Relative Pay of Care Work." Unpublished manuscript, Department of Sociology, Northwestern University.

England, Paula and Nancy Folbre. 1999a. "The Cost of Caring." *Annals of the American Academy of Political and Social Sciences* 561:39–51.

England, Paula and Nancy Folbre. 1999b. "Who Should Pay for the Kids?" *The Annals of the American Academy of Political and Social Sciences* 563 (May):194–209.

England, Paula and Nancy Folbre. Forthcoming. "Contracting for Care." In *Ten Years Beyond Economic Man*, edited by Marianne Ferber and Julie Nelson. Chicago: University of Chicago Press.

England, Paula, Melissa S. Herbert, Barbara Stanek Kilbourne, Lori L. Reid, and Lori McCready Megdal. 1994. "The Gendered Valuation of Occupations and Skills: Earnings in 1980 Census Occupations." *Social Forces*. 73(1):65–99.

England, Paula, Jennifer Thompson, and Carolyn Aman. 2001. "The Sex Gap in Pay and Comparable Worth: An Update." Pp. 551–66 in *Sourcebook on Labor Markets: Evolving Structures and Processes*, edited by Ivar Berg and Arne Kalleberg. New York: Plenum.

Folbre, Nancy. 2001. *The Invisible Heart: Economics and Family Values*. New York: New Press.

Graetz, Michael J. and Jerry L. Mashaw. 1999. *True Security: Rethinking American Social Insurance*. New Haven: Yale University Press.

Harkness, Susan and Jane Waldfogel. 1999. "The Family Gap in Pay: Evidence from Seven Industrialized Countries." CASE paper 30, Centre for Analysis of Social Exclusion, London School of Economics, London, England. Unpublished.

Heimer, Carol and Lisa R. Staffen. 1998. *For the Sake of the Children: The Social Organization of Responsibility in the Hospital and the Home*. Chicago: University of Chicago Press.

Hondagneu-Sotelo, Pierrette. 2000. "The International Division of Caring and Cleaning Work. Transnational Connections or Apartheid Exclusions?" *Care Work: Gender, Labor and the Welfare State*. Edited by Madonna Harrington Meyer. New York: Routledge.

Hondagneu-Sotelo, Pierette. 2001. *Domestica: Immigrant Workers Cleaning and Caring in the Shadows of Affluence*. Berkeley: University of California Press.

Jargowsky, Paul A. 1996. "Take the Money and Run: Economic Segregation in U.S. Metropolitan Areas." *American Sociological Review* 61:984–98.

Joshi, Heather and Marie-Louise Newell. 1989. "Pay Differentials and

Parenthood: Analysis of Men and Women Born in 1946." Coventry, England: University of Warwick Institute for Employment Research.

Kilbourne, Barbara Stanek, Paula England, George Farkas, Kurt Beron, and Dorothea Weir. 1994. "Returns to Skill, Compensating Differentials, and Gender Bias: Effects of Occupational Characteristics on the Wages of White Women and Men." *American Journal of Sociology* 100:689–719.

Lapidus, Gail Warshofsky. 1978. *Women in Soviet Society: Equality, Development, and Social Change.* Berkeley, CA: University of California Press.

Loh, Eng Seng. 1996. "Productivity Differences and the Marriage Wage Premium for White Males." *Journal of Human Resources* 31:566–89.

Lundberg, Shelley and Robert Pollak. 1996. "Bargaining and Distribution in Marriage." *Journal of Economic Perspectives* 10:139–158.

Lundberg, Shelly and Elaina Rose. 2000. "Parenthood and the Earnings of Married Men and Women." *Labour Economics* 7:689–710.

Massey, Douglas S. and Nancy Denton. 1993. *American Apartheid: Segregation and the Making of the Underclass.* Cambridge, MA: Harvard University Press.

McAdoo, Hariette Pipes. 1986. "Strategies Used by Black Single Mothers against Stress." *Slipping through the Cracks.* Edited by Margaret C. Simms and Julianne Malveaux. New Brunswick, NJ: Transaction Books.

Meyer, Madonna Harrington. 2000. *Care Work: Gender, Labor and the Welfare State.* New York: Routledge.

Meyer, Madonna Harrington, and Michelle Kesterke Storbakken. 2000, "Shifting the Burden Back to Families? How Medicaid Cost-Containment Reshapes Access to Long Term Care in the United States," in *Care Work: Gender, Labor and the Welfare State.* Edited by Madonna Harrington Meyer. New York: Routledge.

Mink, Gwendolyn. 1998. *Welfare's End.* Ithaca, New York: Cornell University Press.

Nelson, Julie. 2001. "The Separative Firm." Paper presented at the annual meetings of the International Association of Feminist Economists, Oslo, Norway. July 2001.

Nelson, Robert and William Bridges. 1999. *Legalizing Gender Inequality.* New York: Cambridge University Press.

Neumark, David and Sanders Korenman. 1994. "Sources of Bias in Women's Wage Equations: Results Using Sibling Data." *Journal of Human Resources* 29:379–405.

O'Connor, Julie, Ann Shola Orloff, and Sheila Shaver. 1999. *States, Markets, Families: Gender, Liberalism and Social Policy in Australia, Canada, Great Britain, and the United States.* Cambridge and Melbourne: Cambridge University Press.

Oliker, Stacey J. 2000. "Examining Care at Welfare's End." *Care Work: Gender, Labor and the Welfare State.* Edited by Madonna Harrington Meyer. New York: Routledge.

Preston, Samuel H. 1984. "Children and the Elderly: Divergent Paths for America's Dependents." *Demography* 21:435–58.

Rochelle, Anne R. 1997. *No More Kin: Exploring Race, Class, and Gender in Family Networks.* Thousand Oaks, CA: Sage.

Romero, Mary. 1992. *Maid in the U.S.A.* New York: Routledge.

Shannon, Charles, and Jarrett Barrios. 2001. "What Human Service Workers Need," *Boston Globe,* July 7, 2001, A11.

Sorenson, Elaine. 1989. "The Wage Effects of Occupational Sex Composition: A Review and New Findings." Pp. TK in *Comparable Worth: Analyses and Evidence,* edited by M. A. Hill and M. Killingsworth. Ithaca, NY: ILR Press.

Stack, Carol B. 1974. *All Our Kin.* New York: Harper & Row.

Steinberg, Ronnie J., L. Haignere, C. Possin, C.H. Chertos, and D. Trieman. 1986. *The New York State Pay Equity Study: A Research Report.* Albany, NY: Center for Women in Government, SUNY Press.

Stone, Deborah. 2000a. "Caring by the Book." *Care Work: Gender, Labor and the Welfare State.* Edited by Madonna Harrington Meyer. New York: Routledge.

Stone, Deborah. 2000b. "Why We Need a Care Movement." *The Nation,* March 13, 2000.

Tronto, Joan. 1987. "Beyond Gender Difference to a Theory of Care," *Signs: Journal of Women in Culture and Society* 12, no. 4 (Summer): 644–63.

U.S. Department of Health and Human Services. 1999. *Access to Child Care for Low Income Working Families,* available on line at ww.acf.dhhs.gov/news/press/1999/ccreport.html

Waldfogel, Jane. 1997. "The Effects of Children on Women's Wages." *American Sociological Review* 62:209–17.

Waldfogel, Jane. 1998a. "The Family Gap for Young Women in the United States and Britain: Can Maternity Leave Make a Difference?" *Journal of Labor Economics* 16:505–45.

Waldfogel, Jane. 1998b. "Understanding the 'Family Gap' in Pay for Women with Children." *Journal of Economic Perspectives* 12:137–56.

Whitebook, Marcy. 1999. "Child Care Workers: High Demand, Low Wages." *Annals of the American Academy of Political and Social Science* (May):146–61.

Williams, Joan. 2000. *Unbending Gender. Why Family and Work Conflict and What to Do About It.* New York: Oxford University Press.

Chapter 10

Bergmann, Barbara R. 1996. *Saving Our Children from Poverty: What the United States Can Learn from France.* New York: Russell Sage Foundation.

Cancian, Francesca. 2000. "Paid Emotional Work." Pp. 136–148 in *Care Work: Gender, Labor and The Welfare State,* edited by Madonna Harrington Meyer. New York: Routledge.

Fisher, Bernice and Joan Tronto. 1990. "Toward a Feminist Theory of Caring." Pp. 35–62 in *Circles of Care: Work and Identity in Women's Lives,* edited by Joan Tronto, Emily K. Abel, and Margaret K. Nelson. Albany: State University of New York Press.

Fitz Gibbon, Heather. 2001. "From Babysitters to Child Care Providers: The Development of a Feminist Consciousness in Family Day Care Workers." in *Working Families: The Transformation of the American Home,* edited by Rosanna Hertz and Nancy L. Marshall. Berkeley, CA: University of California Press.

Foner, Nancy. 1994. *The Caregiving Dilemma: Work in the American Nursing Home.* Berkeley, CA: University of California Press.

Fuller, B. and S. L. Kagan. 2000. *Remember the Children: Mothers Balance Work and Child Care Under Welfare Reform (Growing up in Poverty Study, Wave I Findings).* Berkeley, CA: University of California, Berkeley and New Haven, CT: Yale University.

Galinsky, Ellen, Carollee Howes, Susan Kontos, and Marybeth Shinn. 1994. *The Study of Children in Family Child Care and Relative Care: Highlights of Findings.* New York: Families and Work Institute.

Gerstel, Naomi. 2000. "The Third Shift: Gender and Care Work Outside the Home." *Qualitative Sociology* 23(4).

Hays, Sharon. 1996. *Cultural Contradictions of Motherhood.* New Haven, CT: Yale University Press.

Helburn, Suzanne, ed. 1995. "Cost, Quality and Child Outcomes in Child Care Centers." Denver: University of Colorado, Department of Economics, Center for Research in Economic and Social Policy.

Hertz, Rosanna. 1997. "A Typology of Approaches to Child Care: The Centerpiece of Organizing Family Life for Dual-Earner Couples." *Journal of Family Issues* 18(4):355–85.

Hofferth, Sandra. 1999. "Child Care, Maternal Employment, and Public Policy." *Annals of the American Academy of Political and Social Science* 563:20–38.

Hofferth, Sandra, April Brayfield, Sharon Deich, and Pamela Holcomb. 1991. *National Child Care Survey, 1990.* Report 91-5. Washington, DC: Urban Institute.

Macdonald, Cameron Lynn. 1998. "Manufacturing Motherhood: The Shadow Work of Nannies and Au Pairs." *Qualitative Sociology* 21(1):25–53.

Morris, John R. 1999. "Market Constraints on Child Care Quality." *Annals of the American Academy of Political and Social Science* 563:130–45.

Nelson, Margaret K. 1990. *Negotiated Care: The Experience of Family Day Care Providers.* Philadelphia: Temple University Press.

Ritzer, George. 2000. *The McDonaldization of Society,* 3rd edition. Thousand Oaks, CA: Pine Forge Press.

Rutman, Deborah. 1996. "Child Care as Women's Work." *Gender and Society* 10(5):629–49.

Tuominen, Mary. 1998 "Motherhood and the Market: Mothering and Employment Opportunities Among Mexicana, African-American and Euro-American Family Day Care Providers. " *Sociological Focus* 31(1).

Tuominen, Mary. 2000. "The Conflicts of Caring." Pp. 112–35 in *Care Work: Gender, Labor, and the Welfare State,* edited by Madonna Harrington Meyer. New York: Routledge.

Uttal, Lynet and Mary Tuominen. 1999. "Tenuous Relationships: Exploitation, Emotion, and Racial Ethnic Significance in Paid Child Care Work." *Gender and Society* 13(6):758–80.

Whitebook, Marcy. 1999. "Child Care Workers: High Demand, Low Wages." *Annals of the American Academy of Political and Social Science* 563:146–61.

Whitebook, Marcy and Deborah Phillips. 1990. "Who Cares? Child Care

Teachers and the Quality of Care in America. Final Report of the National Child Care Staffing Study." Washington, DC: Center for the Child Care Workforce.

Whitebook, Marcy and Deborah Phillips. 1999. "Child Care Employment: Implications for Women's Self Sufficiency and for Child Development." Working Paper, Washington, DC: Center for the Child Care Workforce.

Chapter 11

Berger, Raymond M. and David Mallon. 1993. "Social Support Networks of Gay Men." *Journal of Sociology and Social Welfare* 20(1):155–74.

Boxer, Andrew M., Judith A. Cook, and Gilbert Herdt. 1991. "Double Jeopardy: Identity Transitions and Parent–Child Relations Among Gay and Lesbian Youth." Pp. 59–92 in *Parent–Child Relations Throughout Life*, edited by K. Pillemer and K. McCartney. Hillsdale, NJ: Lawrence Erlbaum Associates.

Cass, Vivienne C. 1979. "Homosexual Identity Formation: A Theoretical Model." *Journal of Homosexuality* 4(3):219–35.

D'Augelli, Anthony R. 1998. "Developmental Implications of Victimization of Lesbian, Gay, and Bisexual Youth." Pp. 187–210 in *Stigma and Sexual Orientation: Understanding Prejudice Against Lesbians, Gay Men, and Bisexuals*, edited by G. M. Herek. Thousand Oaks, CA: Sage.

DiPlacido, Joanne. 1998. "Minority Stress Among Lesbians, Gay Men, and Bisexuals." Pp. 138–59 in *Stigma and Sexual Orientation: Understanding Prejudice Against Lesbians, Gay Men, and Bisexuals*, edited by G. M. Herek. Thousand Oaks, CA: Sage.

Glaser, Barney G. and Anselm L. Strauss. 1967. *The Discovery of Ground Theory: Strategies for Qualitative Research.* New York: Aldine.

Gonsiorek, John. 1982. "The Use of Diagnostic Concepts in Working with Gay and Lesbian Populations." *Journal of Homosexuality* 7(2/3):9–20.

Grossman, Arnold and Matthew S. Kerner. 1998a. "Self-Esteem and Supportiveness as Predictors of Emotional Distress in Gay Male and Lesbian Youth." *Journal of Homosexuality* 35(2):25–39.

———. 1998b. "Support Networks of Gay Male and Lesbian Youth." *Journal of Gay, Lesbian, and Bisexual Identity* 3(1):27–45.

Herdt, Gilbert and Andrew Boxer. 1993. *Children of Horizons: How Gay and Lesbian Teens Are Leading a New Way Out of the Closet.* Boston: Beacon Press.

Jordan, Karen M. and Robert H. Deluty. 1998. "Coming Out for Lesbian Women: Its Relation to Anxiety, Positive Affectiviity, Self-Esteem, and Social Support." *Journal of Homosexuality* 35(2):41–63.

Lenihan, Genie O. 1985. "The Therapeutic Gay Support Group: A Call for Professional Involvement." *Psychotherapy* 22(4):729–39.

Malyon, Alan K. 1982. "Psychotherapeutic Implications of Internalized Homophobia in Gay Men." *Journal of Homosexuality* 7(2/3):59–69.

Mercier, Lucy R. and Raymond M. Berger. 1989. "Social Service Needs of Lesbian and Gay Adolescents: Telling It Their Way." *Journal of Social Work and Human Sexuality* 8(1):75–95.

Meyer, Ilan H. 1995. "Minority Stress and Mental Health in Gay Men." *Journal of Health and Social Behavior* 36:38–56.

Miranda, Jeanne and Micheal Storms. 1989. "Psychological Adjustment of Lesbians and Gay Men." *Journal of Counseling & Development* 68:41–45.

Nesmith, Andrea, David L. Burton, and T. J. Cosgrove. 1999. "Gay, Lesbian, and Bisexual Youth and Young Adults: Social Support in Their Own Words." *Journal of Homosexuality* 37(1):95–109.

Remafedi, Gary. 1987. "Homosexual Youth: A Challenge to Contemporary Society." *Journal of the American Medical Association* 258:222–25.

Rosario, Margaret, Joyce Hunter, and Marya Gwadz. 1997. "Exploration of Substance Use Among Lesbian, Gay, and Bisexual Youth: Prevalence and Correlates." *Journal of Adolescent Research* 12(4):454–76.

Rotheram-Borus, Mary Jane and M. Isabel Fernandez. 1995. "Sexual Orientation and Developmental Challenges Experienced by Gay and Lesbian Youths." *Suicide and Life-Threatening Behavior* 25(Suppl.):26–34.

Rotheram-Borus, Mary Jane, Joyce Hunter, and Margaret Rosario. 1994. "Suicidal Behavior and Gay-Related Stress Among Gay and Bisexual Males." *Journal of Adolescent Research* 9(4):498–508.

Ryan, Caitlin and Donna Futterman. 1998. *Lesbian and Gay Youth: Care and Counseling*. New York: Columbia University Press.

Savin-Williams, Ritch C. 1994. "Verbal and Physical Abuse as Stressors in the Lives of Lesbian, Gay Male, and Bisexual Youth: Associations with School Problems, Running Away, Substance Abuse, Prostitution, and Suicide." *Journal of Consulting and Clinical Psychology* 62(2):261–69.

Shidlo, Ariel. 1994. "Internalized Homophobia: Conceptual and Empirical Issues in Measurement." Pp. 176–205 in *Psychological Perspectives on Lesbian and Gay Issues: Vol. 1. Lesbian and Gay Psychology: Theory, Research, and Clinical Applications*, edited by B. Greene and G. M. Herek. Thousand Oaks, CA: Sage.

Strommen, Erik F. 1993. "'You're a What?': Family Member Reaction to the Disclosure of Homosexuality." Pp. 248–66 in *Psychological Perspectives on Lesbian and Gay Male Experience*, edited by L. Garnets and D. Kimmel. New York: Columbia University Press.

Townsend, Mark H., Mollie M. Wallick, and Karl M. Cambre. 1996. "Follow-Up Survey of Support Services for Lesbian, Gay, and Bisexual Medical Students." *Academic Medicine* 71(9):1012–14.

Troiden, Richard R. 1988. *Gay and Lesbian Identity: A Sociological Analysis*. Dix Hills, NY: General-Hall.

Vincke, John and Ralph Bolton. 1994. "Social Support, Depression, and Self-Acceptance Among Gay Men." *Human Relations* 47(9):1049–63.

———. 1996. "The Social Support of Flemish Gay Men: An Exploratory Study." *Journal of Homosexuality* 31(4):107–21.

Walters, Karina L. and Jane M. Simoni. 1993. "Lesbian and Gay Male Group Identity Attitudes and Self-Esteem: Implications for Counseling." *Journal of Counseling Psychology* 40(1):94–99.

Wright, Eric R., J. Dale Dye, Michelle E. Jiles, and Melissa K. Marcello. 1999. *Empowering Gay, Lesbian, and Bisexual Youth: Findings from the Indiana Youth Access Project*. Final Evaluation Report. Indianapolis: Indiana University.

Wright, Eric R., Christopher Gonzalez, Jeffrey N. Werner, Steven Thad Laughner, and Michael Wallace. 1998. "The Indiana Youth Access Project

(IYAP): Responding to the HIV Risk of Gay, Lesbian, and Bisexual Youth in the Heartland." *Journal of Adolescent Health* 23(Suppl.):83–95.

Chapter 12

Abel, Emily K. and Margaret K. Nelson. 1990. "Circles of Care: An Introductory Essay." Pp. 4–34 in *Circles of Care*, edited by Emily K. Abel and Margaret K. Nelson. Albany, NY: SUNY Press.

Bennett, James and Thomas Di Lorenzo, T. 1984. *Unhealthy Charities*. New York: Basic Books.

Borkman, Thomasina. 1990. "Experiential, Professional and Lay Frames of Reference." Pp. 3–30 in *Working with Self-Help*, edited by Thomas Powell. Washington, DC: National Association of Social Workers Press.

Cancian, Francesca and Stacey Oliker. 2000. *Caring and Gender*. Walnut Grove, CA: Altimira Press.

Chesler, Mark. 1990. "The 'Dangers' of Self-Help Groups: Understanding and Dealing With Professionals' Views." Pp. 301–24 in *Working With Self Help*, edited by Thomas Powell. Washington, DC: NASW Press.

Chesler, Mark. 1991. "Mobilizing Consumer Activism in Health Care: The Role of Self-Help Groups." *Research in Social Movements, Conflict and Change* 13:275–305.

Chesler, Mark and Barbara Chesney. 1995. *Self-Help and Cancer: Bridging the Troubled Waters of Childhood Cancer*. Madison: University of Wisconsin Press.

Chesler, Mark and Sara Eldridge. 2000. *You Are Not Alone: A Sourcebook for Support Groups for Families of Children with Cancer*. Kensington, MD: Candlelighters Childhood Cancer Foundation.

Emerick, Robert. 1991. "The Politics of Psychiatric Self-Help: Political Factions, Interaction Support, and Group Longevity in a Social Movement." *Social Science and Medicine* 32:1121–28.

Epstein, Samuel. 1978. *The Politics of Cancer*. San Francisco, CA: Sierra Club Books.

Gartner, Alan and Frank Riessman, F. 1984. *The Self-Help Revolution*. New York: Human Sciences Press.

Halmagi, Olga. 1999. "PAVEL: The Parents Association of Rumania." *ICCCPO Newsletter* 6(1):20.

Hasenfeld, Yeheskel and Benny Gidron. 1993. "Self-Help Groups and Human Service Organizations: An Interorganizational Perspective." *Social Science Review* June:217–36.

Hochschild, Arlie. 1983. *The Managed Heart: Commercialization of Human Feelings*. Berkeley: University of California Press.

Hunter, Albert. 1993. "National Federations: The Role of Voluntary Organizations in Linking Macro and Micro Orders in Civil Society." *Non-Profit and Voluntary Sector Quarterly* 22(2):121–36.

Mansur, Osman. 2000. "Suffering and Humiliation." *ICCCPO Newsletter* 7(2):2–3.

Powell, Thomas. 1990. *Working with Self-Help*. Washington, DC: National Association of Social Workers Press.

Rappaport, Julian. 1994. "Narrative Studies, Personal Stories and Identity Transformation in the Mutual-Help Context." Pp. 115–35 in *Understanding the Self-Help Organization*, edited by Thomas Powell. Thousand Oaks, CA: Sage.

Ross, Walter. 1987. *Crusade: The Official History of the American Cancer Society*. New York: Arbor House.

Ruddick, Sarah. 1990. *Maternal Thinking: Toward a Politics of Peace*. Boston: Beacon Press.

Stone, Deborah. 2000. "Caring by the Book." Pp. 89–111 in *Care Work: Gender, Class and the Welfare State*, edited by Madonna Meyer. New York: Routledge.

Tashkov, Dimitri. 2000. "Letters to the Board." *ICCCPO Newsletter* 7(1):10–11.

Traustadottir, Ronnveig. 2000. "Disability Reform and Women's Caring Work." Pp. 249–69 in *Care Work: Gender, Class and the Welfare State*, edited by Madonna Meyer. New York: Routledge.

Wernet, Stephen and Sandra Jones. 1992. "Merger and Acquisition Activity Between Nonprofit Social Service Organizations: A Case Study." *Non-Profit and Voluntary Sector Quarterly* 21(4):367–80.

Wrigley, Julia. 1990. "Children's Caregivers and the Ideology of Parental Inadequacy." Pp. 290–312 in *Circles of Care*, edited by Emily Abel and Margaret Nelson. Albany, NY: SUNY Press.

York, Alan and Esther Zychlinski. 1996. "Competing Nonprofit Organizations Also Collaborate." *Non-Profit and Voluntary Sector Quarterly* 7(1):15–27.

Young, Dennis. 1989. "Local Autonomy in a Franchise Age: Structural Change in National Voluntary Organizations." *Non-Profit and Voluntary Sector Quarterly* 18(2):101–17.

Zald, Mayer. 1970. *Organizational Change*. Chicago: University of Chicago Press.

Zald, Mayer and John McCarthy. 1987. "Social Movement Industries: Competition and Conflict Among Social Movement Organizations." Pp. 161–80 in *Social Movements in an Organizational Society*, edited by Mayer Zald and John McCarthy. New Brunswick, NJ: Transaction Books.

Chapter 13

Abel, Emily K. and Margaret K. Nelson. 1990. *Circles of Care: Work and Identity in Women's Lives*. Albany: State University of New York Press.

Abrams, Kristi. 1999. *Don't Give Up the Fight: The Story of the Fight for Health Insurance for Family Daycare Providers*. Providence, RI: DARE (Direct Action for Rights and Equality).

Albrecht, Lisa and Rose M. Brewer. 1990. "Bridges of Power: Women's Multicultural Alliances for Social Change." Pp. 2–22 in *Bridges of Power: Women's Multicultural Alliances*, edited by Lisa Albrecht and Rose Brewer. Philadelphia: New Society.

Baca Zinn, Maxine and Bonnie Thornton Dill. 1996. "Theorizing Difference from Multiracial Feminism." *Feminist Studies* 22(2):321–31.

Bellm, Dan, A. Burton, R. Shaklee, and M. Whitebook. 1997 *Making Work Pay in the Child Care Industry: Promising Practices of Improved Compensation*. Washington, DC: National Center for the Early Childhood Workforce (Center for the Child Care Workforce).

Bronfenbrenner, Kate, Sheldon Friedman, Richard W. Hurd, Rudolph A. Oswald, and Ronald L. Seeber. 1998. *Organizing to Win: New Research on Union Strategies*. Ithaca, NY: ILR Press.

Burbank, John R. and Nancy Wiefek. 2001. *The Washington State Early Education Career Development Ladder.* Seattle, WA: Economic Opportunity Institute.

Busman, Gloria. 1993. "Comments." Pp. 37–41 in *Women and Unions: Forging a Partnership,* edited by D. Cobble. Ithaca, NY: ILR Press.

Cancian, Francesca and Stacey Oliker. 2000. *Caring and Gender.* Thousand Oaks, CA: Pine Forge Press.

Center for the Child Care Workforce. 2000. *Current Data on Child Care Salaries and Benefits in the United States.* Washington, DC: Center for the Child Care Workforce.

Cobble, Dorothy Sue. 1996. "The Prospects of Unionism in a Service Society." Pp. 333–358 in *Working in the Service Society,* edited by C. Macdonald and C. Sirianni. Philadelphia: Temple University Press.

Daniels, Arlene Kaplan. 1987. "Invisible Work." *Social Problems* 34(5):403–15.

Eisenscher, Michael. 1999. "Critical Juncture: Unionism at the Crossroads." Pp. 217–46 in *"Which Direction for Organized Labor": Essays on Organizing, Outreach, and Internal Transformations,* edited by Bruce Nissen. Detroit, MI: Wayne State University Press.

Fletcher, Bill, Jr., and Richard W. Hurd. 1999. "Political Will, Local Union Transformation, and the Organizing Imperative." Pp. 191–216 in *"Which Direction for Organized Labor": Essays on Organizing, Outreach, and Internal Transformations,* edited by Bruce Nissen. Detroit, MI: Wayne State University Press.

Frank, Dana. 1989. "Labor's Decline." *Monthly Review* 41(5):48–55.

Gilligan, Carol. 1993 (1982). *In a Different Voice: Psychological Theory and Women's Development.* Cambridge, MA: Harvard University Press.

Gordon, Linda, ed. 1990. *Women, the State, and Welfare.* Madison: University of Wisconsin Press.

Gordon, Suzanne. 1996. "Feminism and Caring." Pp. 256–77 in *Caregiving: Readings in Knowledge, Practice, Ethics, and Politics,* edited by S. Gordon, P. Benner, and N. Noddings. Philadelphia: University of Pennsylvania Press.

Grundy, Lea, Lissa Bell, and Netsy Firestein. 1999. *Labor's Role in Addressing the Child Care Crisis.* New York: Foundation for Child Development.

Hallock, Margaret. 1997. "Organizing and Representing Women: Lessons from the United States." Pp. 45–66 in *Strife: Sex and Politics in Labour Unions.* St. Leonards, Australia: Allen & Unwin.

Hartsock, Nancy. 1983. "The Feminist Standpoint: Developing the Ground for a Specifically Feminist Historical Materialism." Pp. 283–310 in *Discovering Reality,* edited by S. Harding and M. Hintikka. Boston: D. Reidel.

Himmelweit, Susan. 1999. "Caring Labor." *The Annals of the American Academy of Political and Social Science* 561:27–38.

Hossfeld, Karen. 1995. "Why Aren't High Tech Workers Organized? Lessons in Gender, Race, and Nationality from Silicon Valley." Pp. 405–32 in *Working People of California,* edited by D. Cornford. Los Angeles: University of California Press.

Hurd, Richard W. 1993. "Organizing and Representing Clerical Workers: The Harvard Model." Pp. 316–36 in *Women and Unions: Forging a Partnership,* edited by D. Cobble. Ithaca, NY: ILR Press.

Kasarda, John, D. 1996. *Family Policy for School Age Children: The Case of Parental Evening Work.* Malcom Weiner Center for Social Policy, John F. Kennedy School of Government at Harvard University, Working Paper Series. Cambridge, MA: Harvard University.

Kellener, Keith. 1986. "Building the Ranks: ACORN Organizing and Chicago Homecare Workers." *Labor Research Review* 8:33–45.

Kerber, Linda. 1993. "Some Cautionary Words for Historians." Pp. 102–7 in *An Ethic of Care: Feminist and Interdisciplinary Perspectives*, edited by M. Larrabee. New York: Routledge,

Lerner, Stephen. 1991. "Let's Get Moving: Labor's Survival Depends on Organizing Industry-Wide for Justice and Power." *Labor Research Review* 18(2):1–16.

Macdonald, Cameron and Carmen Sirianni. 1996. *Working in the Service Society.* Philadelphia: Temple University Press.

Martens, Margaret Hosmer and Swasti Mitter, eds. 1994. *Women in Trade Unions: Organizing the Unorganized.* Geneva: International Labour Office.

McAdam, Doug. 1982. *Political Process and the Development of Black Insurgency, 1930–1970.* Chicago: University of Chicago Press, 1982.

Milkman, Ruth. 1993. "Organizing Immigrant Women in New York's Chinatown: An Interview with Katie Quan." Pp. 281–98 in *Women and Unions: Forging a Partnership*, edited by D. Cobble. Ithaca, NY: ILR Press.

Nakano Glenn, Evelyn. 2000. "Creating a Caring Society": *Contemporary Sociology* 29(1):84–94.

Naples, Nancy. 1999. "Towards Comparative Analyses of Women's Political Praxis: Explicating Multiple Dimensions of Standpoint Epistemology for Feminist Ethnography." *Women & Politics* 20(1):29–57.

National Black Child Development Institute. 1993. *Paths to African American Leadership Positions in Early Childhood Education: Constraints and Opportunities.* Washington, DC: National Black Child Development Institute.

Needleman, Ruth. 1998. "Building Relationships for the Long Haul: Unions and Community-Based Groups Working Together to Organize Low-Wage Workers." Pp. 70–86 in *Organizing to Win*, edited by K. Bronfenbrenner, S. Friedman, R. Hurd, R. Oswald, and R. Seeber. Ithaca, NY: Cornell University Press.

Nissen, Bruce. 1999. *Which Direction for Organized Labor": Essays on Organizing, Outreach, and Internal Transformations.* Detroit: Wayne State University Press.

Pocock, Barbara. 1997. *Strife: Sex and Politics in Labour Unions.* St. Leonards, Australia: Allen & Unwin.

Puka, Bill. 1993. "The Liberation of Caring: A Different Voice for Gilligan's 'Different Voice.'" Pp. 215–39 in *An Ethic of Care: Feminist and Interdisciplinary Perspectives*, edited by M. Larrabee. New York: Routledge.

Rathke, Wade. 1999. "Letting More Flowers Bloom Under the Setting Sun." Pp. 75–91 in *"Which Direction for Organized Labor": Essays on Organizing, Outreach, and Internal Transformations*, edited by B. Nissen. Detroit, MI: Wayne State University Press.

Scott, Ellen. 2000. "Everyone Against Racism: Agency and the Production of

Meaning in the Anti-racism Practices of Two Feminist Organizations." *Theory and Society* 29(6):785–818.

Sullivan, Cathy. 2000. (June 1) *Improving the Quality of Child and Elder Care by Investing in Wage and Career Ladders.* Washington, DC: Center for Policy Alternatives State Issues Forum presentation.

Tarlow, Barbara. 1996. "Caring: A Negotiated Process that Varies." Pp. 56–82 in *Caregiving: Readings in Knowledge, Practice, Ethics, and Politics,* edited by S. Gordon, P. Benner, and N. Noddings. Philadelphia: University of Pennsylvania Press.

Tronto, Joan. 1993. "Beyond Gender Difference to a Theory of Care." Pp. 240–57 in *An Ethic of Care: Feminist and Interdisciplinary Perspectives,* edited by M. Larrabee. New York: Routledge.

Tuominen, Mary. 1994. "The Hidden Organization of Labor: Gender, Race/Ethnicity and Child-Care Work in the Formal and Informal Economy." *Sociological Perspectives* 37(2):229–45.

Tuominen, Mary. 2001. (April 9) *"The Power of Our Voice": Participatory Action Research and the Politicization of Family Child Care Providers.* Berkeley: Center for Working Families, University of California presentation.

U.S. Department of Labor, Bureau of Labor Statistics. 1999. *Highlights of Women's Earnings in 1998,* Report 928. Washington, DC: U.S. Government Printing Office.

U.S. Department of Labor, Women's Bureau. 1997. *Facts on Working Women.* No. 98-01. November. www.dol.gov/dol/wb/public/wb_pubs/childc.htm.

Uttal, Lynet and Mary Tuominen. 1999. "Tenuous Relationships: Exploitation, Emotion, and Racial Ethnic Significance in Paid Childcare Work." *Gender & Society* 13(6):758–80.

Waerness, Kari. 1996. "The Rationality of Caring." Pp. 231–55 in in *Caregiving: Readings in Knowledge, Practice, Ethics, and Politics,* edited by S. Gordon, P. Benner, and N. Noddings. Philadelphia: University of Pennsylvania Press.

Whitebook, Marcy, C. Howes, and D. Phillips. 1998. *Worthy Work, Unlivable Wages: The National Staffing Study, 1998–1997.* Washington, DC: Center for the Child Care Workforce.

Whitebook, Marcy, D. Phillips, and C. Howes. 1993. *National Child Care Staffing Study Revisited: Four Years in the Life of Center-Based Child Care.* Washington, DC: National Center for the Early Childhood Workforce (formerly Child Care Employee Project).

Chapter 14

Acosta-Belen, Edna, ed. 1986. *The Puerto Rican Woman's Perspectives on Culture, History and Society.* Second Edition. New York: Praeger Press.

Aguilar-San Juan, Karin, ed. 1994. *The State of Asian American Activism and Resistance in the 1990s.* Boston: South End Press.

Allen, Paula Gunn. 1986. *The Sacred Hoop: Recovering the Feminism in American Indian Traditions.* Boston: Beacon Press.

Allen, Paula Gunn. 1995. "Angry Women Are Building: Issues and Struggles Facing American Indian Women Today." Pp. 32–36 in *Race, Class, and Gender: An Anthology,* edited by Margaret Andersen and Patricia Hill Collins. Belmont, CA: Wadsworth Publishing Company.

Bookman, Ann and Sandra Morgen, eds. 1988. *Women and the Politics of Empowerment*. Philadelphia: Temple University Press.

Carothers, Suzanne. 1990. "Catching Sense: Learning from Our Mothers to Be Black and Female." Pp. 232–47 in *Uncertain Terms: Negotiating Gender in American Culture*, edited by Faye Ginsburg and Anna Lowenhaupt Tsing. Boston: Beacon Press.

Chodorow, Nancy. 1978. *The Reproduction of Mothering: Psychoanalysis and the Sociology of Gender*. Berkeley: University of California Press.

Collins, Patricia Hill. 1990. *Black Feminist Thought: Knowledge, Consciousness, and the Politics of Empowerment*. Boston: Unwin Hyman.

Collins, Patricia Hill. 1991. "The Meaning of Motherhood in Black Culture." Pp. TK in *The Black Family: Essays and Studies*, edited by R. Staples. Belmont, CA: Wadsworth.

Daniels, Arlene Kaplan. 1988. *Invisible Careers: Women Civic Leaders from the Volunteer World*. Chicago: University of Chicago Press.

Essed, Philomena. 1990. *Everyday Racism: Reports from Women of Two Cultures*. Claremont, CA: Hunter House.

Gilkes, Cheryl Townsend. 1988. "Building in Many Places: Multiple Consciousness and Ideologies in Black Women's Comunity Work." Pp. 53–76 in *Women and the Politics of Empowerment*, edited by Add Bookman and Sandra Morgen. Philadelphia: Temple University Press.

Glenn, Evelyn Nakano, Grace Chang, and Linda Rennie Forcey, eds. 1994. *Mothering: Ideology, Experience, and Agency*. New York: Routledge.

Gluck, Sherna Berger, with Maylei Blackwell, Sharon Cotrell, and Karen Harper. 1998. "Whose Feminism, Whose History? Reflections on Excavating the History of (the) U.S. Women's Movement(s)." Pp. 31–56 in *Community Activism and Feminist Politics Organizing Across Race, Class, and Gender*, edited by Nancy A. Naples. New York: Routledge.

Green, Rayna. 1990. "American Indian Women: Diverse Leadership for Social Change." Pp. 61–73 in *Bridges of Power: Women's Multicultural Alliances*, edited by Lisa Albrecht and Rose M. Brewer. Philadelphia: New Society.

Hewitt, Nancy A. 1990. "Charity or Mutual Aid?: Two Perspectives on Latin Women's Philanthropy in Tampa, Florida." Pp. 55–69 in *Lady Bountiful Revisited: Women, Philanthropy, and Power*, edited by Kathleen D. McCarthy. New Brunswick, NJ: Rutgers University Press.

hooks, bell. 1990. *Yearning: Race, Gender, and Cultural Politics*. Boston: South End Press.

James, Stanlie M. 1993. "Mothering: A Possible Black Feminist Link to Social Transformation?" Pp. 44–54 in *Theorizing Black Feminisms: The Visionary Pragmatism of Black Women*, edited by Stanlie M. James and Abena P. A. Busia. New York: Routledge.

James, Stanlie M., and Abena P. A. Busia, eds. 1993. *Theorizing Black Feminisms: The Visionary Pragmatism of Black Women*. New York: Routledge.

Kaminer, Wendy. 1984. *Women Volunteering: The Pleasure, Pain and Politics of Unpaid Work From 1830 to the Present*. Garden City, NY: Doubleday.

Kaplan, Temma. 1982. "Female Consciousness and Collective Action: The Case of Barcelona, 1910–1918." *Signs: Journal of Women in Culture and Society* 7(3):545–66.

Kaplan, Temma. 1997. *Crazy for Democracy: Women in Grassroots Movements*. New York: Routledge.

Koven, Seth and Sonya Michel, eds. 1993. *Mothers of a New World: Maternalist Politics and the Origins of Welfare States*. New York: Routledge.

Mink, Gwendolyn. 1995. *The Wages of Motherhood: Inequality in the Welfare State, 1917–1942*. Ithaca, NY: Cornell University Press.

Molyneux, Maxine. 1986. "Mobilization Without Emancipation? Women's Interests, State and Revolution in Nicaragua." Pp. 280–302 in *Transition and Development: Problems of Third World Socialism*, edited by Richard R. Fagen, Carmen Diana Deere, and Jose Luis Goraggio. New York: Monthly Review Press and Center for the Study of the Americas.

Monroe, Kristen Renwick. 1996. *The Heart of Altruism: Perceptions of a Common Humanity*. Princeton, NJ: Princeton University Press.

Moraga, Cherríe. 1981. "Preface." Pp. xiii–xix in *This Bridge Called My Back: Writings by Radical Women of Color*, edited by Cherríe Moraga and Gloria Anzaldúa. Watertown, MA: Persephone Press.

Morgen, Sandra and Ann Bookman. 1988. "Rethinking Women and Politics: An Introductory Essay." Pp. 3–29 in *Women and the Politics of Empowerment*, edited by Ann Bookman and Sandra Morgen. Philadelphia: Temple University Press.

Moynihan, Daniel P. 1967. *The Negro Family: The Case for National Action*. Washington, DC: Government Printing Office.

Naples, Nancy A. 1991a. "Contradictions in the Gender Subtext of the War on Poverty: Community Work and Resistance of Women from Low Income Communities." *Social Problems* 38(3):316–32.

Naples, Nancy A. 1991b. "Just What Needed to be Done: The Political Practice of Women Community Workers in Low-income Neighborhoods." *Gender & Society* 5(4):478–94.

Naples, Nancy A. 1992. "Activist Mothering: Cross-Generational Continuity in the Community Work of Women from Low-income Communities." *Gender & Society* 6(3):441–63.

Naples, Nancy A. 1998a. "Women's Community Activism: Exploring the Dynamics of Politicization and Diversity." Pp. 327–49 in *Community Activism and Feminist Politics: Organizing Across Race, Class, and Gender*. New York: Routledge.

Naples, Nancy A. 1998b. *Grassroots Warriors: Activist Mothering, Community Work, and the State*. New York: Routledge.

Naples, Nancy A. 1998c. Review of Temma Kaplan. In *Democracy: Women in Grassroots Movements*, H-Pol, H-Net Reviews, May. http://hnet.msu.edu/reviews/ shorev.cgi?path= 15154895615776.

Naples, Nancy A. 1998d. "The Great Society and the War on Poverty." Pp. 248–50 in *The Reader's Companion to U.S. Women's History*, edited by Wilma Mankiller, Gwendolyn Mink, Marysa Navarro, Barbara Smith, and Gloria Steinem. Boston: Houghton Mifflin Company.

Orleck, Annelise. 1995. "'We Are That Mythical Thing Called the Public': Militant Housewives During the Great Depression." Pp. 189–213 in *U.S. Women in Struggle: A Feminist Studies Anthology*, edited by Heidi Hartmann and Claire Goldberg Moses. Urbana: University of Illinois Press.

Pardo, Mary. 1995. "Doing it for the Kids: Mexican American Community Activists, Border Feminists?" Pp. 356–71 in *Feminist Organizations: Harvest of the New Women's Movement*, edited by Myra Marx Ferree and Patricia Yancey Martin. Philadelphia: Temple University Press.

Rollins, Judith. 1995. *All Is Never Said: The Narrative of Odette Harper Hines.* Philadelphia: Temple University Press.

Sacks, Karen Brodkin. 1988a. *Caring by the Hour: Women, Work, and Organizing at Duke Medical Center.* Urbana: University of Illinois Press.

Sacks, Karen Brodkin. 1988b. "Gender and Grassroots Leadership." Pp. 77–94 in *Women and the Policies of Empowerment*, edited by Ann Bookman and Sandra Morgen. Philadelphia: Temple University Press.

Sanchez-Ayendez, Melba. 1995. "Puerto Rican Elderly Women: Shared Meanings and Informal Supportive Networks." Pp. 172–86 in *All-American Women: Lines That Divide, Ties That Bind*, edited by Johannetta B. Cole. New York: Free Press.

Scott, Kisho Y. 1991. *The Habit of Surviving.* New York: Ballantine.

Stack, Carol B. 1974. *All Our Kin: Strategies for Survival in a Black Community.* New York: Harper and Row.

Stack, Carol and Linda M. Burton. 1994. "Kinscripts: Reflections on Family, Generation, and Culture." Pp. 33–44 in *Mothering: Ideology, Experience, and Agency*, edited by E. Nakano Glenn, G. Chang, and L. Rennie Forcey. New York: Routledge.

Torres, Lourdes. 1986. "The Construction of the Self in U.S. Latina Autobiographies." Pp. 271–87 in *Third World Women and the Politics of Feminism*, edited by Chandra Talpade Mohanty, Ann Russo, and Lourdes Torres. Bloomington: Indiana University Press.

Troester, Rosalie Riegle. 1984. "Turbulence and Tenderness: Mothers, Daughters and 'Othermothers' in Paule Marshall's Brown Girl, Brown-Stones." *Sage: A Scholarly Journal on Black Women* 1(2):13–16.

Contributor Notes

EMILY K. ABEL is Professor of Health Services and Women's Studies at UCLA. She is the author of *Hearts of Wisdom: American Women Caring for Kin* (Harvard University Press, 2000) and *Who Cares for the Elderly? Public Policy and the Experiences of Adult Daughters* (Temple University Press, 1991) and coeditor (with Margaret K. Nelson) of *Circles of Care: Work and Identity in Women's Lives* (SUNY Press, 1990).

FRANCESCA M. CANCIAN is Professor of Sociology at the University of California at Irvine. Her research focuses on carework, gender, family, and sexual assault. Combining research and activism/social change is one of her goals. A current project explores ways of assisting low-income Latina mothers attend college, and studies the impact of family, community, and college programs on success in college. She is the author of *Caring and Gender* with Stacey Oliker (Pine Forge, 2000), and *Love in America: Gender and Self-Development* (Cambridge, 1987). She is past president of the Pacific Sociological Association and of Sociologists for Women in Society.

MARK CHESLER is Professor of Sociology at the University of Michigan, Ann Arbor, MI. He holds a B.A. in Industrial & Labor Relations from Cornell University, an M.A. in Psychology from Hofstra University, and a Ph.D. in Social Psychology from the University of Michigan. His teaching and research focus on the psychosocial aspects of childhood cancer, the organization and mobilization of voluntary and social-change oriented groups, the diagnosis and alteration of organizational racism and sexism, and the use of qualitative and participatory action research methods. He is the author of several books—*Childhood Cancer and the Family, Self-Help and Cancer, You Are Not Alone—An Organizing Manual for Leaders of Childhood Cancer Self-Help Groups*—and over 200 journal articles, book chapters, and technical reports. Mark has extensive experience as a consultant in the area of race and gender diversity and change in organizations, psychosocial programming for survivors of childhood cancer, and the formation and operation of voluntary groups.

KAREN CHRISTOPHER is Assistant Professor of Sociology and teaching faculty in Women's Studies at the University of Pittsburgh. Beginning Fall 2002, she will be Assistant Professor of Women's Studies and Sociology at University of Louisville. Her research consists of feminist analyses of women's paid and unpaid work, including issues of race, class, and gender in labor markets and welfare states; carework; and the feminization of poverty. She has published several articles and chapters on these topics. Her most recent research examines the "pauperization of motherhood" among U.S. women over time.

ROBERT E. CONNOLEY, is Executive Director of Indiana Youth Group, Inc., a social service agency in Indianapolis for gay, lesbian, bisexual, and transgendered youth. Previously he served in various youth development agencies including Boys & Girls Clubs and YMCAs. He earned his doctorate from Purdue University, West Lafayette, in the School of Health, Kinesiology, and Leisure Studies in 1995.

JOANN DEFIORE is the Coordinator of the Sociology and Criminal Justice Program at St. Francis University. JoAnn received her M.A. and Ph.D. in Sociology from the University of Maryland, College Park, where she focused on sociological theory and the intersection of gender, work, and family. She then taught for five years in the Pacific Northwest at the University of Washington, Bothell, campus in the Interdisciplinary Arts and Sciences program. Her teaching interests range from courses on race, class and gender inequality to environmental sociology to community, family, and friendship. Most of her research centers on race and gender inequality, including articles on the gender earnings gap, mothering and women's power in rural Paraguay, and teaching about White privilege, race cognizance, and social action to undergraduates.

PAULA ENGLAND is Professor of Sociology at Northwestern University, where she is also affiliated with the Institute for Policy Research. Her interests are in gender inequality in labor markets and in the family, and on dialogue among sociological, economic, and feminist perspectives. She is the author of *Households, Employment, and Gender* (with George Farkas, 1986, Aldine) and *Comparable Worth: Theories and Evidence* (1992, Aldine), editor of *Theory on Gender/Feminism on Theory* (1993, Aldine), and author of many articles. She has testified as an expert witness in a number of Title VII discrimination cases. In 1999, she was awarded the Jessie Bernard Award by the American Sociological Association for career contributions to scholarship on gender. From 1994 to 1996 she served as the editor of the *American Sociological Review*.

HEATHER M. FITZ GIBBON is an Associate Professor of Sociology at the College of Wooster. Her research areas include the work of family child care providers and the decisions families make in balancing work and family. Her present research involves a comparison of the work of child care providers in child care centers with those that provide care in their homes.

NANCY FOLBRE, Professor of Economics at the University of Massachusetts at Amherst, is also a staff economist with the Center for Popular Economics. Her academic research explores the interface between feminist theory and political economy. In addition to numerous articles published in academic journals, she is the author of *Who Pays for the Kids?: Gender and the Structures of Constraint* (Routledge,

1994) and an associate editor of the journal *Feminist Economics*. Books she has coauthored for a wider audience include *The Ultimate Field Guide to the U.S. Economy* and *The Invisible Heart: Economics and Family Values* (New Press, 2001). She is co-chair of the MacArthur Foundation Research Network on the Family and the Economy and a recent recipient of a five-year fellowship from the Foundation. For more information, see her personal web site at www-unix.oit.umass.edu/~folbre/folbre.

BONNIE FOX is Associate Professor of Sociology at the University of Toronto. Her current research is on the development of gender differences, divisions and inequalities as couples become parents for the first time. Findings from this research appear in "Revisiting the Critique of Medicalized Childbirth" (with Diana Worts) in *Gender & Society* and "The Formative Years" in *Canadian Review of Sociology and Anthropology*. She is the editor of a popular Canadian text, *Family Patterns, Gender Relations*, and is working on a book on the transition to parenthood.

VICKI HUNTER is a Ph.D. candidate in sociology at Kent State University. Her area of specialization is social inequalities. Her research focuses on the use of network-based support among welfare-reliant and working poor families, as well as the utilization of transitional benefits by families leaving welfare. She is currently working on her dissertation, which will draw on longitudinal data from the ethnographic component of Manpower Demonstration Research Corporation Project on Devolution and Urban Change in Cleveland to examine the use of network support among poor urban families who are in the process of leaving or have recently left welfare.

CHRISTA KELLEHER, a Ph.D. candidate in the Department of Sociology at Brandeis University in Waltham, Massachusetts, is completing her dissertation on women's experiences of postpartum care in Canada and in the United States. With a professional background in public policy and politics, her aim is to apply sociological insights to policy development.

DEMIE KURZ, Women's Studies and Sociology, University of Pennsylvania. Kurz's primary research is in the area of gender, the family, and carework. Her current research is on families with teenage children and incorporates the perspectives of both parents and children. This work focuses on age and "generation" as a key aspect of family life and explores how families negotiate children's progression from dependency to autonomy. Her book on divorce, entitled *For Richer, For Poorer: Mothers Confront Divorce* (Routledge 1995), analyzed the social and economic impact of divorce on a diverse group of families. Kurz has also written on the impact of domestic violence on families. She is on the steering committee of the Carework Network, a network of researchers, policymakers, and activists who are concerned with promoting further understanding of carework.

ANDREW S. LONDON is an Associate Professor in the Department of Sociology and the Center for Policy Research at the Maxwell School of Citizenship and Public Affairs at Syracuse University. One major focus of his research is on the organization and provision of informal and formal community-based care to persons living with HIV/AIDS, and the consequences of caring for family caregivers. Recent publications related to these issues include an analysis of the stress-related physical health consequences of informal HIV/AIDS caregiving (LeBlanc, London, and Aneshensel 1997); the integration of informal care, case management, and community-based services as part of a continuum of community-based care for persons with HIV/AIDS (London, LeBlanc, and Aneshensel 1998); the use and integration of paid and unpaid home care by persons living with HIV/AIDS in the United States (London, Fleishman, Goldman, McCaffrey, Bozzette, Shapiro, and Leibowitz 2001); and the influence of integration and conflict on the well-being of "non-kin" HIV/AIDS caregivers (London and Nichols in review). A second major focus of his research is on the effects of welfare reform on family well-being, including the ways that women's efforts to meet the mandates of welfare reform influence their ability to care for their children. Recent publications related to this line of research focus on the work–family trade-offs mothers experience as they move from welfare to work, and how women's welfare-to-work transitions affect their children's well-being (see Scott, Edin, London, and Mazelis 2002; Scott, Edin, London, and Kissane 2001; London, Scott, Edin, and Hunter in review).

NANCY A. NAPLES is author of *Grassroots Warriors: Activist Mothering, Community Work, and the War on Poverty* (Routledge, 1988) which was a finalist for the C. Wright Mills Award of the Society for the Study of Social Problems. She is also editor of *Community Activism and Feminist Politics: Organizing Across Gender, Race, and Class* (Routledge 1998) and coeditor with Manisha Desai of *Women's Activism and Globalization: Linking Local Struggles with Transnational Politics* (Routledge, 2002) and coeditor with Karen Bojar of *Teaching Feminist Activism: Strategies from the Field* (Routledge, 2002). She currently holds a joint appointment in Sociology and Women's Studies at the University of Connecticut. Her main research interests center on exploring the development of women's political consciousness and activism; the role of the state in reproducing or challenging inequality; and how differing community contexts influence women's resistance and political activism.

REBECCA REVIERE is Associate Professor in the Department of Sociology and Anthropology and Director of the Graduate Certificate Program Women's Studies at Howard University. Her research interests include gender differences in morbidity and mortality, race and gender differences in decision making at the end of life, and health care for women in prison. Recent publications include "Meeting the Needs of the New Female Prisoner" in the *Journal of Offender Rehabilitation* (with Young) and "Death and Society: A Feminist Perspective" in *Women's Studies Anthology*, edited by R. Rosenberg (Peter Lang, 2001).

ELLEN K. SCOTT is an Assistant Professor of Sociology at the University of Oregon. With Andrew London of Kent State University, she is a co-principal investigator of the Cleveland ethnographic component of Urban Change, a longitudinal study of the impact of welfare reform conducted by Manpower

Demonstration Research Corporation. Ellen Scott and Andrew London are also co-PIs on another MDRC initiative, the Next Generation Project, investigating the impact of welfare reform on children. From the ethnographic interviews, Ellen Scott, Andrew London, Kathryn Edin (PI of the ethnographic component of Urban Change in Philadelphia), and their graduate students have examined employment aspirations; expectations for, and realities of, the trade-offs single parents face as they juggle the competing demands of parenting and low-wage work; employment transitions and income change as they meet the work mandates of welfare reform; the role of their personal networks in enabling them to make the transition to work; and potential barriers to employment, such as their own health problems, the health problems of their children and other family members, and domestic violence.

MARY C. TUOMINEN is Associate Professor of Sociology at Denison University. Her research addresses the politics and economics of women's carework, social welfare policy, and women's grass-roots political activism. Her most recent publications include "The Conflicts of Caring: Gender, Race Ethnicity, and Individualism in Family Child Care Work" (in M. H. Harrington, ed. *Care Work: Gender, Class and the Welfare State*, Routledge, 2000); "Tenuous Relationships: Exploitation, Emotion, and Racial Ethnic Significance in Paid Childcare Work," (*Gender & Society*, 1999, coauthored with Lynet Uttal); and "Motherhood and the Market: Mothering and Employment Opportunities Among Mexicana, African-American and Euro-American Family Day Care Workers" (*Sociological Focus*, 1998).

BARBARA BENNETT WOODHOUSE holds the David H. Levin Chair in Family Law at the Fredric G.Levin College of Law at the University of Florida, and is the founding director of the Center on Children and the Law. After graduating from Columbia Law School, she clerked for Sandra Day O'Connor at the U.S. Supreme Court. She came to Florida in 2001, from the faculty of University of Pennsylvania Law School, where she was a tenured full professor and founder and co-director of the Center for Children, Policy, Practice, and Research. She has written and spoken extensively, both nationally and internationally, on children's rights in custody, adoption and child protection arenas. She is a member of the Executive Council of the International Society of Family Law and a past Chair of the Association of American Law Schools, Family and Juvenile Law Section.

ERIC R. WRIGHT, is Associate Professor of Sociology at Indiana University Purdue University Indianapolis (IUPUI) and Associate Director of the Indiana Consortium for Mental Health Services Research, a research center at Indiana University. As a medical sociologist, his research focuses on applying social network methods to understand the health and mental health of gay, lesbian, bisexual, and transgendered youth and people living with HIV and serious mental illness.

Index